A

DISTINCT

PEOPLE

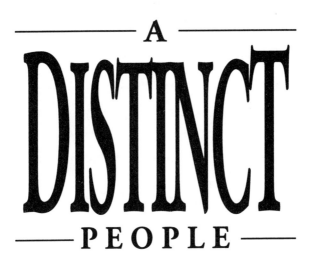

A DISTINCT PEOPLE

A HISTORY OF THE
CHURCHES OF CHRIST
IN THE
20TH CENTURY

DR. ROBERT E. HOOPER

HOWARD
PUBLISHING CO.

3117 North 7th Street
West Monroe, LA 71291

Our purpose at Howard Publishing is:

• **Inspiring** holiness in the lives of believers,

• **Instilling** hope in the hearts of struggling people
  everywhere,

• **Instructing** believers toward a deeper faith in Jesus
  Christ,

Because he's coming again.

A Distinct People: Churches of Christ in the Twentieth Century
© 1993 by Howard Publishing Co., Inc.
All rights reserved.

Published by Howard Publishing Co., Inc.
3117 North 7th Street, West Monroe, LA 71291-2227

Printed in the United States of America

First Printing

Cover Design by Steve Diggs and Friends

ISBN# 1-878990-26-8

A rich heritage for a new generation.

Dedicated to
my grandchildren—
*Clay, Lindsay, Kate, Trey,
and Claire*

TABLE OF CONTENTS

FORWARD

It is a mark of maturity when one decides consciously to examine his heritage. None of us ever appears out of a vacuum. Our human lineage has helped to shape what we are. Countless people have poured their influence into the stream that produced our lives.

Many of us enjoy an annual family reunion. We reminisce aloud. Our children hear tales of their ancestors. These stories are of great importance to us. Our quest for personal identity—our need to find out who we are—includes the memory of what we have been and what our heritage is. Heritage does not play an absolute in who we are; we have the power to select and reject from our background. Yet heritage is significant. I doubt that anyone can adequately know who he is without some effort to trace his roots.

Whenever the subject of the family tree arises, there is the old saw about not looking too far for fear we may find an ancestor hanging from the limbs. Every family I know has some "bad apples" in its background.

Dr. Robert E. Hooper has, in the pages that follow, taken a reflective look at his ancestry. He has sought to uncover and to analyze the forces that have shaped the Restoration Movement in America for almost 200 years. He has found admirable traits and not so admirable characteristics among some of our religious fore-bears. Above all, he points the way to better self-understanding for all of us who make up churches of Christ.

Bob has spent more than half his life studying this movement and these people. This volume is his magnum opus. It is a serious attempt toward an interpretative history of churches of Christ and will fill a distinct need in our ongoing quest to be true to our prim-itivist mission.

Dr. Hooper served as head of our History and Political Science department at Lipscomb for thirty years, stepping aside in 1992 to return full time to the classroom. He has taught Church History, among other subjects, at Lipscomb since 1960. I know him as a friend and as a fine Christian gentleman. I believe you will also be enriched by his scholarly efforts.

Harold Hazelip, President
David Lipscomb University

PREFACE

If history teaches us anything, it shows us that the world has always been in constant flux. It remains so as we move through the last decade of the twentieth century. The past ninety years have seen more change than any comparable period in history. In the scientific and technical world, things not even imagined a hundred years ago are now accepted as everyday necessities. Sending citizens of the planet Earth to the moon and beaming pictures of faraway wars to American homes has changed our entire perspective of the world.

Change, however, has not been limited to science and technology. Ideologically, the world has undergone a major transformation during the twentieth century. Communism and fascism attempted to dominate the first half of the century. With the defeat of the Axis powers in World War II, Soviet communism challenged Western democracies. The conflict, whether in the form of the Cold War or a race for the control of space, came to an end with the destruction of the Iron Curtain and the demise of the Soviet Union. Now, the Third World is on the rise—in no way should we underestimate its role.

Religion has not escaped change. In the first years of the twentieth century, liberal theology challenged fundamentalism. The American religious scene would never be the same again.

Although "church-going" made a comeback in the 1950s, mainline churches, during the 1960s, continued the decline they had experienced in the 1920s and the 1930s. Conservative churches have grown in recent years, although at a slower pace.

In the nineties, religion continues to experience change. What the future holds is difficult to foresee. Whether we are in a post-Christian era or on the verge of another revival, no one knows for sure. One thing we do know: America's churches will continue to change just as society and culture change.

Churches of Christ emerged in the early years of the twentieth century as a product of the cultural and religious changes then engulfing America. Appearing for the first time in the 1906 religious census as a separate religious body, churches of Christ quickly joined the changing religious scene. As a part of the American Restoration Movement, churches of Christ continued the call to return to the New Testament as authority in all religious matters. As was true of many Americans in all areas of life, churches of Christ feared the changes happening around them. There has been a constant struggle within the fellowship between those who opposed change and those who believed that change is inevitable.

Perhaps the song often sung among churches of Christ captures our longing for a constant in the midst of the dizzying twentieth century: "Time is filled with swift transition. . . . Hold to God's unchanging hand." This book is an attempt to show how churches of Christ have responded to change, all the while attempting to hold to the one constant—"God's unchanging hand."

The book you are about to read has consumed fourteen years of my life, yet has never been a burden. By investigating all facets of the American Restoration Movement and then delving into the unassimilated materials of churches of Christ, I have gained a greater insight into my religious heritage. It has made me appreciate even more my place in the religious fabric of America and within the entire scope of the quest for God's purpose for humankind. I have enjoyed discovering how much churches of Christ parallel other quests for New Testament Christianity, whether in the sixteenth, seventeenth, nineteenth, or twentieth centuries.

On the other hand, I have discovered the uniqueness of churches of Christ. This book is not just a narrative of events as they transpired year after year. It is an attempt to discover the ideas behind the events. Often it has required inquiry into the theological background of the Restoration Movement. Beyond theology, it has caused me to search for influences within the cultural milieu—current ideas or events that impacted biblical interpretation. As I studied churches of Christ, I could not escape the influence of strong personalities. The very nature of this study focuses on these individuals. Knowingly or not, they have influenced generations of believers in churches of Christ.

This book would not be possible without the unselfish help of scores of men and women. I am especially grateful to David Howard of the David Lipscomb University library, who, over the years, has discussed his ideas with me and pointed me toward new sources. R. L. Roberts of the Abilene Christian University library shared his knowledge with me on numerous occasions, helping me especially in my understanding of the 1930s.

Many churches, particularly the West End Church of Christ in Nashville, have allowed me to share my understanding of twentieth century churches of Christ with them. I am also thankful for opportunities I have had to present lectures at Abilene Christian University, Harding University, and Pepperdine University. These speaking engagements helped me to gain a better understanding of my intriguing subject.

I am grateful for the input of several men who graciously shared their time with me to make this a much better book. Dr. Douglas Foster, formerly of the history faculty at Lipscomb and now at Abilene Christian University, read some of the earliest drafts of the nineteenth-century material. Without Dr. Timothy Tucker, a former student and valued colleague, numerous interpretations now included in the study would be missing. Another former student of mine, Gregory Tidwell of Columbus, Ohio, has been a constant sounding board for my ideas. He has the ability to conceptualize history, thus giving him a keen insight into the American Restoration Movement. His reading of the manuscript was an invaluable contribution. My son-in-law, Jim Turner, used his newspaper expertise to increase the readability of the book. Two friends, Sam Yinger and Faris Jones, also read the manuscript. Their encouragement is always appreciated. An invaluable reader was Phillip Morrison, former editor of *UpReach* magazine and now managing editor of *Wineskins*. With his ability to turn a phrase, he added much to the readability of the book.

I am also indebted to Denny and Philis Boultinghouse and to John Gibbs. Denny gave me valuable suggestions for improving the book. Philis and John read and edited the manuscript for Howard Publishing Company.

I am not the only one who has lived with the manuscript of this book during the last decade. The former secretary of the Department of History and Political Science at Lipscomb, Mrs. Jo Ann Harwell, typed and printed numerous copies of the manuscript. Our present secretary, Mrs. Jennie Johnson, spent hours compiling the index. My wife, Virginia, has been a constant support in all my writing efforts. She has never resented the time I have spent in the library or at the word processor. She is truly a "helpmeet."

Robert E. Hooper
May 1, 1993

CHAPTER 1

NINETEENTH-CENTURY BACKGROUND FOR CHURCHES OF CHRIST:
A Call to Religious Unity

On the cornerstone of the Southside Church of Christ in Springfield, Missouri, is this inscription: "Church of Christ, Founded in Jerusalem, A.D. 33. This building erected in 1953." This is not an unusual claim; for similar wording can be found on buildings of churches of Christ in many parts of the United States. The Christians who use such cornerstones reason that the church of Jesus Christ began on Pentecost, A.D. 33. Therefore, to be true to the New Testament, the twentieth-century church must trace its origins to the first century.

Churches of Christ, furthermore, disclaim any allegiance to denominationalism. The emphasis is upon the whole church—not a part of it. This being true, churches of Christ have developed an exclusiveness that separates them from other religious groups. Included in their vocabulary are such phrases as "the Lord's church," "the true church," or simply "the church" when referring to churches of Christ.

Accounting for such statements requires a full understanding of churches of Christ—especially the historical roots that produced them as a separate religious movement. The European and American origins of the Restoration Movement—sometimes referred to as the Stone-Campbell movement—are familiar to anyone who has read its history. Out of the early years of the

1

Movement arose multiple strains of religious development. It is possible, from these various strains, to find an understanding of the restoration of first-century Christianity that will lead to an understanding of twentieth-century churches of Christ.

EARLY NINETEENTH-CENTURY BACKGROUND

Even before the nineteenth century, religious change characterized the American scene. The inclusion of the separation of church and state in the First Amendment of the 1787 Constitution guaranteed the voluntary church in the United States. This disestablishment of churches, rather than destroying religion, produced unprecedented growth following 1800. This surge followed a deep religious depression that had resulted from dislocation caused by war and political excitement. During this religious depression, possibly only one person in ten was affiliated with a church.[1] During the years following the American Revolution, political independence, burning deep in America's heart, fired a desire for religious independence. A growing number of persons within the denominations called for a total return to a more biblical understanding of the church.

Looking to the New Testament as their constitution, these people turned their backs on all types of organizations including synods, presbyteries, associations, and sessions. They would not separate the clergy from the laity, nor use the title "reverend" for their preachers, nor accept only seminary preachers. Alexander Campbell stated the position rather succinctly: "We neither advocate Calvinism, Arminianism, Socialism, Arianism, Trinitarianism, Unitarianism, Deism, nor Sectarianism, but *New Testamentism.*"[2]

An early proponent of this restoration principle was Barton Warren Stone. Born in Maryland and educated in North Carolina, he moved to the frontier of Tennessee and Kentucky early in the nineteenth century. He accepted a preaching position for the Concord and Cane Ridge (Kentucky) Presbyterian churches, but soon the revivals flaming across the frontier engulfed him. During August of 1801, he participated in the largest of them all—Cane Ridge. Stone was never the same again. Chastised by his church for participating in the revivals, he and a few friends withdrew from all religious organizations when they presented their "Last

Will and Testament of the Springfield Presbytery" in 1804. Their action gave birth to the American Restoration Movement.

The earliest converts to restoration in the West followed Stone's revivalistic and camp meeting emphasis; but the approach that would eventually encompass most restorers was that of Thomas and Alexander Campbell.

Thomas Campbell came to America in 1807 from Northern Ireland. Unable to find religious peace among his Anti-Burgher Seceder Presbyterian brethren, he led a small group of dissenters in western Pennsylvania toward a new understanding of religious commitment. Seeking to avoid the division he had experienced in his Presbyterian fellowship, he would lead in formulating a statement calling for Christian unity. Meeting with his friends early in 1809, Campbell presented his basis of union: Everything not found in the Bible should be abandoned. The statement climaxed with the rule they would live by: "That rule . . . is this, that where the Scriptures speak, we speak; and where the Scriptures are silent, we are silent."

Campbell wrote a more detailed statement of the idea in his "Declaration and Address." Basic to his newfound conviction was his belief that human opinion must be rejected as authority in the church. He believed that the only way unity could be attained was through a return to and a holding fast "the original standard" (the Bible). Therefore, he wrote thirteen propositions looking toward Christian unity. The first one stated:

> That the Church of Christ upon the earth is essentially, intentionally, and constitutionally one; consisting of all those in every place that profess their faith in Christ and obedience to him in all things according to the Scriptures, and that manifest the same by their tempers and conduct, and none else; as none else can be truly and properly called Christians.

For a motto, Campbell chose "Unity in Truth." "Truth," he believed, "is something certain and definite." [3]

In 1809, Thomas Campbell's family came from North Ireland to join him in America; they quickly shared the excitement of the "Declaration and Address." Alexander, the Campbell's oldest child, was in the midst of his own religious change. He, as had his father in years past, had come into contact with the Independency movement of Robert and James Haldane in Glasgow, Scotland.

Learning of their emphasis on going "back to the Bible," young Campbell refused communion in the Anti-Burgher Seceder Presbyterian church. Likely, his only concern was the reaction his father would have toward his changed views. But in reality, neither father nor son had any reason to fear the reaction of the other.

Young Campbell joined his father and family, along with other members of the Christian Association of Washington, in the Brush Run church. From the first, Thomas chose Alexander to be the spokesman for the new Restoration Movement. Although they associated with the Baptists (they shared in common immersion as baptism), soon Alexander noted a difference in basic theology. To respond to this major point of distinction, young Campbell preached his now famous "Sermon on the Law" in 1816. Christians, said Campbell, are only under the new covenant, the New Testament. Soon, Baptists began to hurl invectives at the young preacher, even accusing him of "heresy." There would remain a tenuous relationship between Baptists and Disciples—as the restorers will be called in this study—for some time. Within a few years the Restoration Movement would separate from Baptists and all other religious organizations.

The Campbell Restoration Movement entered a new phase in 1823 when Alexander began publishing his *Christian Baptist*. Although his debates on baptism gave him a wider audience, the call for restoration had not yet attracted great numbers. In the pages of the new paper, young Campbell developed and explained his understanding of restoring New Testament Christianity. Writing under the heading of "The Ancient Order of Things," Campbell left no doubt about his understanding of the Bible. Following a Baconian inductive method, he proved to the satisfaction of generations to come—especially conservative Disciples— what the Bible states on numerous topics. How did Campbell reason? Following Francis Bacon, who believed that the natural scientist gathers his facts from nature, Campbell concluded that a complete understanding of the Bible can be ascertained from a gathering of facts from the Bible.[4]

Alexander Campbell was a total iconoclast during his *Christian Baptist* days. Any reading of his paper reveals an anti-creedal, anti-clerical, and anti-missionary society position. Why was he so outspoken against generally accepted religious institutions? In his mind, he had the responsibility to undo the immediate past so that the ancient past might be restored. He pursued his goals with a vengeance.[5]

The clergy, claimed Campbell, have always been the perpetrators of extra-biblical religious organizations. All organizations, including missionary societies, eventually become tools of the clergy. Even more alarming to Campbell, however, was the unbiblical nature of the societies. To Robert Semple, the Virginia Baptist, he wrote: "Our objections to the missionary society plan originated from the conviction that it is unauthorized in the New Testament." If they were forbidden in New Testament times, then they are forbidden in all ages.[6]

In 1812, Alexander Campbell submitted to immersion as the only acceptable mode of baptism. In the eyes of many, this made him an exclusivist. While debating William Walker—a Presbyterian—in 1820, he discovered that remission of sins occurs at baptism. When he used this newly-discovered idea in the debate on baptism with the Presbyterian James McCalla in 1823, it was a bombshell dropped among the Baptists. This position, along with his "Sermon on the Law" in 1816, severed all relationships with the Redstone Association of Baptists. Again, this was a position that separated Campbell even more from his religious neighbors.

In 1823, the Campbells, along with Walter Scott, joined themselves to the Mahoning Association of Baptist Churches. Located across northern Ohio in the Western Reserve, the Association was having internal difficulties and was questioning its religious commitments. The yearly meeting of the Association chose Walter Scott as an evangelist to go among the churches. During the years of 1827, 1828, and 1829, Scott led the churches out of the Baptist fold by sharing with them the Restoration plea. As an evangelist, his approach was simple. He used the fingers on one hand to illustrate "the plan of salvation"—faith, repentance, baptism, forgiveness of sins, and the gift of the Holy Spirit. With slight changes, this formula became the basis of five-step, "first-principle" sermons among conservative Disciples and churches of Christ.

INITIAL SUCCESS OF THE RESTORATION MOVEMENT

Why did success attend both the Campbell and the Stone reform movements? The stated goal of the American Restoration

Movement was the unity of all Christians. This was the emphasis of Barton Stone as well as Thomas and Alexander Campbell. In order to gain the unity of all believers, the restorers called everyone to freedom from the tyranny of creeds, confessions, denominations, and the clergy. To embrace freedom meant to return to the Bible in its pristine purity. Thus Alexander Campbell could call for an "up to the Bible" movement. This would bring freedom.

Thomas and Alexander Campbell had direct access to the eighteenth century and the Age of Enlightenment. Having read John Locke and Scottish Common Sense philosophy, based, in part, on Locke's ideas, it became rather simple to accept man's basic goodness and his ability to reason and function by himself. This idea appealed to Americans—especially the common man on his move westward. Again, *freedom* was the byword.

This call to freedom attracted thousands of Americans across the West during the early years of the nineteenth century. It was a simple message, easily acceptable by all. Politically, Americans already knew freedom from tyranny. They had fought and won a revolution against George III—a tyrant in their eyes. In the place of a tyrannical government across the Atlantic Ocean, they accepted first the Articles of Confederation and then the Constitution of 1787. Constitutionalism, properly applied, guarantees freedom from the tyranny of men. Even the First Amendment, separating church and state, was a mighty strike against tyranny.

This is the reason Thomas Jefferson's strict interpretation of the Constitution appealed to the common man. For the first time he felt safe from tyranny. In the same manner, Thomas Campbell called the Bible the Christian's constitution. It was a document that would end religious tyranny and guarantee freedom. If a simple explanation can be given for success during the early years of the Restoration Movement, it must be found in this call to religious freedom for the common man. It was an idea that found ready success in American soil prepared for a broad understanding of freedom—whether political or religious.

CAMPBELL CHANGES DIRECTIONS

The Mahoning Association collapsed in 1830, the same year Campbell issued the *Millennial Harbinger.* Alexander Campbell and Scott were successful in convincing the Baptists of northern

Ohio of the evils of organizations. In turn, they emphasized the need to accept only the New Testament as their religious guide. Campbell, however, was not as pleased with the Association's demise as one might think. Evidently he was having second thoughts about some organizations. Was Campbell in the early stage of changing directions? Or was his opposition merely limited to missionary societies?

In 1834, the year Campbell issued the *Christian Baptist* in one volume, he remarked: "All the principles of the reformation . . . are found in the first volume of [the *Christian Baptist*.]"[7] Yet, only two years later he penned a statement that went counter to the most widely understood meaning of his father's motto, which was "Where the Scriptures speak, we speak; where the Scriptures are silent, we are silent."

> For while nothing can be required for which there is no divine warrant, and nothing will be tolerated which is opposed to the laws and teachings of Christ and the Apostles, the greatest liberty of opinion is permitted as it respects everything which is not revealed. Of this kind are the order of the exercises of public worship, the manner in which the commemorative institutions are to be attended to, the kind of building which the church is to occupy; and in the same class are found the *various ways and means by which the gospel is to spread abroad* (emphasis supplied).[8]

Alexander was now able to accept, in concept, a missionary society to preach the gospel, in addition to other organizations necessary to give some direction to the Restoration Movement.

Campbell had not necessarily changed his mind in all areas. He was still anti-clerical. Now, however, he was afraid of the total freedom engulfing the Disciples. As early as 1832 he took notice of efforts attempting to make worship totally democratic.

> It is not . . . of wisdom which comes from above, nor of even human prudence, to countenance every one who wishes to be heard in the church or in society, or to employ all the members of the community either at one time, or in rotation, to preach, teach, or exhort. We have, indeed, met with some very eager spirits who, as you say, run wholly unsent and uncalled.[9]

W. T. Moore, writing early in the twentieth century, called the era a "chaotic period." He mirrored Campbell's views when he referred to the "anarchial tendencies which characterized the churches." [10]

Campbell concluded the 1830s with concern over the direction of the Restoration Movement. Would extreme positions be its destiny? Was Campbell afraid of losing control of the Restoration Movement? As opposed as he had been to the extreme despotism of the clergy, the 1840s began with Campbell looking equally askance at the extreme of religious democracy, or as he called it "mobocracy." In response, he wrote a series of articles on the "Nature of Christian Organization." From his studies, he now gave all elders in a region, when in special meetings, supervisory positions over all churches. Because of an increasing number of self-appointed preachers within the fellowship, Campbell urged yearly meetings of churches to supervise the ministers. In these meetings the elders would have special directive functions. Alexander Campbell was now a long distance from his positions of early *Christian Baptist* days.[11]

It is this change that would eventually divide the heirs of the Restoration Movement. Churches of Christ, following the lead of Tolbert Fanning, Benjamin Franklin, and David Lipscomb, would be more in tune with the strict Campbell of the 1820s. Disciples of Christ, following the direction of Isaac Errett and James H. Garrison, were to focus more on the inclusive interpretation of the Bible enunciated by Campbell late in the 1830s and in the 1840s.

REAPING THE SEEDS OF DIVISION: ISSUES BEFORE THE CIVIL WAR

Religious societies pervaded the American scene early in the nineteenth century. Whether Bible, tract, or missionary societies, most all denominations had them. Even though the Restoration Movement rooted and grew in the anti-society mold in the West, second-generation Disciples began to clamor for similar organizations. Alexander Campbell's changed views gave credibility to these desires.

Among the second-generation leadership was David S. Burnet. His biographer, Noel L. Keith, is evidently correct when he called Burnet the "father of organized cooperative benevolence, missions and education among Disciples of Christ."[12] He had organized the American Christian Bible Society and the Cincinnati Tract

Society; the structure for the missionary society was already in place.

An 1849 article by Alexander Campbell opened wide the door that allowed him to accept the society. Arguing the exact opposite of his earlier positions in the *Christian Baptist,* he stated: "For my part, I see no necessity for any *positive Divine* statutes in such matters." What Campbell wanted was not an organization specifically for missions, but associations somewhat like those of the Baptists in which "the public press, evangelical missions, domestic and foreign, Bible translations, religious tracts, and moral agencies of every sort . . . might advantageously claim a sort of general superintendency."[13]

Although Campbell accepted the concept of the society, he opposed the proposed Cincinnati meeting. However, contrary to Campbell's wishes, the delegates met in Cincinnati on October 23, 1849 to organize the American Christian Missionary Society. The Sage of Bethany, as Campbell was called in reference to his hometown, remained at home, but his name was central in all the discussions. Led by David Burnet, the society became a reality. The delegates selected Alexander Campbell president. It was not a position he would have advocated in 1823. A divisive factor was now reality among Disciples.

The 1850s saw growing opposition to the American Christian Missionary Society. Among those who stood most strongly against the organization was Tolbert Fanning, a close student of Alexander Campbell's ideas. Residing in Nashville, Tennessee, he founded the *Gospel Advocate* in 1855. The paper's first editorials suggested its direction: It would oppose all innovations that would counter the early direction of the Restoration Movement. Unquestionably, Fanning followed the Campbell of the 1820s.

Conflicts that began in 1849 with the organization of the missionary society culminated in 1857. In that year a series of articles, written by Campbell's associate editor Robert Richardson, appeared in the *Millennial Harbinger.* Titled "Faith versus Philosophy," the articles stirred reaction across the expanse of the Disciples of Christ. The most vocal respondent was Tolbert Fanning, who saw disturbing trends in the articles. In the meantime, Fanning penned several articles on "The Church of Christ." The positions defended were too legalistic for Robert Richardson.

As early as 1842-1843, Richardson had written articles attacking doctrinal orthodoxy and "partyism." Focusing on intolerance, he said of some of his brethren: "They would rather beat about the estuary into which they were first launched, and keep carefully in view of wellknown shores and landmarks." He added: "The Bible is too large and wide a basis for men of little minds."[14]

Many Disciples, especially those of Alexander Campbell's persuasion, preached what some considered cold rationalism. Neither Campbell nor his disciples would give encouragement to the emotionalism prevalent on the frontier. Richardson, however, believed the Restoration Movement had moved to an extreme rationalism to combat emotionalism, "urging in the strongest terms the power and precedency of the word of God." As a result, the Bethany College professor pled for a greater presence of the Spirit in religion.[15]

In the Campbell-Rice debate of 1843, again on the issue of baptism, Campbell emphasized that the Spirit works "only through the word of truth." Several years later, Richardson penned a telling letter to Isaac Errett. Among other things, he wrote:

> The philosophy of [John] Locke with which Bro. Campbell's mind was deeply imbued in youth has insidiously mingled itself with almost all the great points in the reformation and has been all the while like an iceberg in the way—chilling the heart and benumbing the hands, and impeding all progress in the right direction.[16]

Such a position, urged Richardson, leads to a spirit-killing religion. Although later reinstated, Campbell removed Richardson from the editor's chair of the *Millennial Harbinger* as a result of some of his views.

Christians, the professor continued, should never aim at a learned dogmatism. Instead, they should look toward *"a renovation—a regeneration of the soul."* He rejected the word-for-word inspiration of the Bible. "Ideas only, and not the words of scripture, were the dictation of the Spirit." Of the authors of the Bible: "They were not, then, properly inspired *writers,* but inspired *thinkers.*"[17]

Juxtaposed with the ideas of Richardson, Tolbert Fanning represents an emphatic rational approach to the Bible. Fanning had no use for the experiential religion then current on the frontier.

Furthermore, Jesse Ferguson, who espoused spiritualism while preaching for the Nashville church during the 1840s and 1850s, caused Fanning much grief. His travels with Alexander Campbell on two occasions, coupled with the negative influences he had to deal with, helped lead him to his strict interpretation of the Bible.

In the first volume of his *Christian Review* (1844), Fanning stated his own views about the Bible as God's only revelation to man.

> In the nineteenth century there is an all-prevailing delusion, which for grossness far excels all others, and it is to be fondly hoped till the Lord comes it shall have no equal. It is the notion that there is some other agency to communicate to man the truth of God besides the Bible. . . . He who confides in the Bible devotes himself to it for knowledge; but he that looks for light from direct influences, without the dull, slow process of studying, resorts to the secret grove or some other doleful place to converse with an unrevealed mysterious, and unknown God.[18]

From his earliest attempts at preaching, he opposed "mourners' bench" religion. Barton Stone's camp meetings did not appeal to him.

By August 1855, Fanning believed the Ferguson affair in Nashville, higher lawism, and the emotionalism of frontier religion resulted from particular attitudes toward the Bible. Some, he said, maintain that "the Bible is merely a collection of spiritual communications, 'that the book is not an infallible revelation from God;' 'The book,' they say, 'has fulfilled its end, and man soars on.'"[19]

The year 1857 became a time of stormiest conflict. Both Richardson and Fanning penned articles suggesting a deep chasm. Fanning discussed metaphysics, natural theology, transcendentalism, and higher lawism. He named Theodore Parker (a transcendentalist) as the leader in undermining the basic religious views of Americans, and of Disciples in particular. Higher lawism, as defined by Fanning, said: "Whatever a man thinks is right, is right to him. Feeling is thus regarded as the guiding divinity." This sentiment was rampant in every segment of American society.[20]

Richardson's 1857 "Faith versus Philosophy" articles delineated the issues represented in the two directions of the Restoration Movement. Richardson rejected Lockean empiricism.

As Pat Brooks succinctly stated: "Truly a sensitive nerve had been probed." [21] Even more, Richardson accused Fanning of replacing the Bible with Lockean philosophy, based strictly on man's five senses. "It is thus that each sect loves its own philosophical theory of religion better than religion, and labors more earnestly for its diffusion, rejecting from its communion individuals of acknowledged piety because they do not acquiesce in its opinions." Instead, Richardson asserted: "It is CHRIST himself, and not any, nor all of the facts of his history, that is the true and proper object of this faith. . . . The person is forgotten and left out of view." [22]

Probably Fanning's strongest argument was against a speech delivered at Bethany College and included in the *Millennial Harbinger*. Written and presented by W. S. Russell, a young graduate of Bethany, it was endorsed by Campbell. An appalled Fanning saw elements of natural theology in the presentation. Richardson was one of Russell's teachers. He gave his blessings to the speech and placed it in the *Harbinger*. The source of Russell's ideas was clear—at least to Fanning. [23]

Richardson used strong language in describing Fanning. In turn, Fanning labeled "infidel" those who held positions he deemed contrary to the Bible. By the end of the year, Alexander Campbell entered the discussion, accusing Richardson of acting indiscreetly with the issues. Richardson even resigned from the *Millennial Harbinger*. By overtly attacking Fanning was Richardson questioning Campbell's religious and philosophical views?

The lengthy discussions marked the two directions of the Disciples in the years before the Civil War. Although those on either side may not have held such strongly opposing views as Richardson and Fanning, the future was now in focus: these men pointed toward the coming divisions in the Restoration Movement. [24]

Lest the reader conclude that the division was emerging as a North/South confrontation, a brief mention must be made of Benjamin Franklin and Isaac Errett. By the 1850s a cultural shift was under way among northern Disciples. Franklin and Errett, centering their activities in the Midwest, appealed to different constituencies. Disciples were moving away from a rural to a more urban outlook. Benjamin Franklin and his *American Christian*

Review increasingly represented the former. Isaac Errett, with his refinement, appealed to the urban Disciple.

No one owned Benjamin Franklin; he was not easily influenced. While supporting the American Christian Missionary Society—even serving as corresponding secretary in 1857—he always had nagging questions about such organizations. The American Christian Missionary Society was doing good. He supported it because it was expedient, and he urged others to do the same. Nevertheless, toward the end of the 1850s he began a gradual change. As the 1860s progressed, he became adamantly opposed to all societies.

Other changes were evident to Franklin. Churches were demanding a different style of preaching. His biographers noted the change: "Many who, while intelligent in the Bible, were deficient in literary culture, were refused audiences in towns and cities." When the use of choirs and musical instruments in worship became more common after the Civil War, Franklin became concerned. On one occasion during a preaching service, a flute accompanied the singing. After enduring it for two or three evenings, Franklin remarked at the beginning of the service: "Hereafter we will dispense with the whistle." [25]

Of equal concern to Franklin was the call for better literature. He began to receive criticism of the *Review*. The *Millennial Harbinger* no longer had the impact of previous years. As a result, Franklin's paper was the most widely read journal among the Disciples, but the critics wanted "a higher order of literature." They were especially critical of the in-fighting in the fellowship, often reported in the *Review*. Furthermore, the paper was too dogmatic. Its literary quality did not satisfy the more cultured Disciples. Benjamin Franklin, the critics concluded, did not represent the progressive qualities of the Disciples. There was need for change.

Isaac Errett offered the cultural qualities Benjamin Franklin lacked. Although not highly educated in a university, Errett developed speaking and writing styles which appealed to a wide public. His biographer, J. S. Lamar, said of his preaching in Warren, Ohio: "He was easily at the head of his profession in the place, and was regarded by the intelligent public with sincere respect and admiration." General J. D. Cox, former governor of Ohio, wrote of Errett: "His genial cheerfulness was like sunshine wherever he went, and the whole community quickly recognized him as a power for good, and an elevating, purifying, brightening influence in their midst."[26]

Among Errett's earliest writings were his "Walks about Jerusalem." According to Lamar, the articles were attempts to rid the Disciples of an incipient dogmatic spirit. He added: "Its ["Walks about Jerusalem"] educational value was great, as was its strengthening influence upon those who had been longing for a gospel that was indeed *glad* tidings, that was *attractive,* that had more *love* than of *law.*" Evidently, this spirit attracted many Disciples to Errett. In 1859, he accepted the corresponding secretary's position of the American Christian Missionary Society.[27]

In the midst of the Civil War, a small but influential segment of Detroit Disciples asked Errett to organize a second congregation in their city. The attendance at the new congregation grew, and the church prospered under the teaching of Errett. In addition to the separation of the churches along social lines, the new preacher encouraged women to participate in prayer meetings, including reading the Bible, singing, and praying. The Detroit churches were the first in the movement to formally divide. North/South issues were not involved.[28]

Errett and his associates became increasingly critical of Benjamin Franklin and his journal. Said Lamar:

> The editorials [of the *American Christian Review*] . . . were responsive and powerful. Uncircumcised "compromisers" and profane "innovators" were shown no quarter. It was not time for dilly-dallying. The old ship of Zion was in danger. Storms were raging; waves were roaring; timbers were creaking; breakers were ahead; tricky and evil-disposed brethren were concealed in the hold; the prospect was gloomy but *nil desperandum!* The "American Christian Review" was still on board; its sleepless editor was still at the helm; he understood the evil designs of the wicked; and if the *faithful* would only stand up with him, the old ship could be carried safely into port.[29]

The progressive Disciples, sharing Lamar's view of Franklin and his paper, wanted a new journal. The *Gospel Advocate* was neither exempt from their criticism, nor adequate in their view. They described both conservative papers as "being narrow in their views of Scriptural truth, essentially sectarian in spirit, and, in many respects, hurtful rather than helpful to the great cause which they assumed to represent." [30] The result was the formation of the *Christian Standard* in 1866 under the editorship of Isaac Errett. The Disciples were headed toward wider division.

DISCIPLES AND THE CIVIL WAR

The Disciples would have divided had there never been a Civil War. The seeds had already been planted during the 1840s and the 1850s. Nevertheless, the Civil War was an important ingredient in the developing attitudes within the fellowship. Although Tolbert Fanning was a pacifist, he maintained strong southern loyalties throughout the conflict. The same was true of David Lipscomb, Fanning's student at Franklin College. Isaac Errett would have gathered a fighting force for the Union, but a military commission was not forthcoming. His attitudes toward the South were often bitter, as were Fanning's toward the Union. From Hiram College, a Disciple school in Ohio, James A. Garfield recruited students for the Union; students from Franklin College, Fanning's school in Nashville, often accepted officer commissions in the Confederate army.

Conflict centered on the American Christian Missionary Society. When it made a motion—even though in recess—in favor of the Union, Tolbert Fanning became livid. The political tone of the Society also upset Benjamin Franklin. Lipscomb called the hymnal published by the Society "blood bought." The actions of the Society would lead to its early death following the Civil War.

Although Moses E. Lard stated in 1866, "May we boldly say, trusting in God to help us, *we can never divide?*" he was not able to look into the future fifty years.[31] The Disciples survived the Civil War tenuously united; the future would not be so kind.

POST-CIVIL WAR ISSUES

A purpose of the *Christian Standard,* founded in 1866, was to keep the American Christian Missionary Society alive. It was unable to do so. A new organization—usually called the Louisville Plan—emerged from meetings of high-ranking Disciples. Attempting to keep missions closer to home base, the organization could never raise sufficient money to support foreign missions on the national level. In 1874, Disciple women decided to venture into areas where the men had failed by organizing the Christian Woman's Board of Missions. They even began publishing a monthly paper titled *Missionary Tidings.*

Encouraged by the success of their women, Disciple men, led by William T. Moore, presented a plan for foreign missions to the national organization during the convention of 1875. Over the next twenty-five years, the Foreign Christian Missionary Society filled a rather important position among Disciples of Christ.[32]

Benjamin Franklin had supported the Louisville Plan, but he could not endorse the new society. Never again would he support any Disciple organization. For the first time, he called all such organizations unscriptural.

> The conventions themselves are the wrongs, and we cannot cure the evil by attending and trying to mend them. There is but one cure for them and that is to abolish them. The way to do that is not to attend them.[33]

Conservative Disciples—North and South—now opposed all organizations larger than the local church.

During the 1850s and the 1860s, another issue of overriding importance burst onto the scene—the use of a musical instrument in worship. Dr. L. L. Pinkerton, in 1859, placed the first instrument in the Disciples meetinghouse in Midway, Kentucky. Immediately, Benjamin Franklin questioned the propriety of such a move. Pinkerton responded by agreeing to discuss the topic "with any man who can discriminate between railing in bad grammar and Christian argumentation; but I am fully resolved as any man can be to have nothing to do with 'silly clap-trap.' "[34]

St. Louis in the 1860s was the next center of controversy. What should be the attitude within a church when a large segment of the membership opposed the introduction of an instrument? Proponents argued that the Bible does not disallow it. Furthermore, it is only an aid to worship. Isaac Errett used the expediency argument. There is neither authorization nor condemnation in the Scriptures about the instrument in worship. "Our object," said Errett, "is to persuade brethren who favor such use [of the instrument] to hold their preferences in abeyance for the sake of *harmony.*"[35] Opponents to the instrument's introduction in

St. Louis argued that the Bible does not authorize it; therefore, the church should refrain from using it. On this occasion, the St. Louis church decided against the use of the instrument.

The northern Disciple, Benjamin Franklin, was among the most outspoken critics of the instrument's use in worship.

> There is not an excuse in existence for forcing this new element into the worship and imposing it on those who cannot conscientiously worship with it. There is not a man anywhere who claims any authority for the new element, nor one whose conscience demands it. There is not a saint who cannot without any violation of conscience worship without it. . . . We can remain on safe ground, the common ground and the ground on which we have stood in peace and war—on what is *written.* The worship in all its parts—all its elements—is a matter of *revelation—divinely prescribed.* Nothing is acceptable in worship, only that which the Lord ordained.[36]

This position and attitude would give guidance to conservative Disciples in the Midwest.

In 1869, six self-proclaimed moderates in Lexington, Kentucky, began publishing the *Apostolic Times.* The *Gospel Advocate,* the *American Christian Review,* and the *Christian Standard,* they believed, did not fully represent the Disciples. Led by John W. McGarvey and Moses E. Lard, the six editors supported the missionary society but opposed the instrument in worship. McGarvey especially noted the direction of the *Standard:*

> We are moving; we are progressing; at least some among us are advancing. Whether you think the movement is forward or backward depends very much upon the way you are going yourself. Once we had no men among us who were known to tolerate instrumental music in worship. After that there arose some who contended that whether we use it or not is mere matter of expediency. More recently, a few churches have actually used it, and their preachers have approved, but have not often ventured publicly to defend it.[37]

By 1870, Cincinnati had become the acknowledged center of Disciples' activity. It was the home of the *Christian Standard.* The Walnut and Eighth church constructed a new building—including an organ—at a cost of more than $140,000. John McGarvey wondered why W. T. Moore, the preacher, had not opposed the inclusion of the instrument. Robert Richardson, showing concern, shared with Benjamin Franklin his views in opposition to instrumental music in worship. These concerns had little impact. Expediency had become the means of continued progress among Disciples.

Most progressive Disciples placed the instrument in the same category as other expedients—meetinghouses, tuning forks, and songbooks. They argued: Since singing is important, then anything introduced to improve the quality of singing is acceptable in worship. Such an argument, however, did not sway Robert Richardson. He reasoned that a requirement for meeting infers a place of worship. Singing, on the other hand, does not allow anything not directly connected with singing. If the Scriptures mentioned the instrument, then expediency would include such things as what instruments should be used or what the church would desire to pay for a piano or an organ.[38]

An instrument in worship was of less concern among southern Disciples. The cost of such additions was prohibitive to them. Not until 1874 did David Lipscomb discuss the question. He opposed it because of the Bible's silence. Because Lipscomb was tone deaf, he feared that he might make his decision based on his inability to hear the music. In accord with his character, he studied the topic at length. In 1878, he finally confronted the issue. He concluded that tone deafness, instead of a hindrance, was in reality a help in making his final decision—a decision based on the teachings of the Bible. A capella singing, he concluded, is always acceptable to God. Why do something that might be questionable?[39]

DANIEL SOMMER, AUSTIN McGARY, AND DAVID LIPSCOMB: POSITIONS FOR TWENTIETH-CENTURY CHURCHES OF CHRIST

It is impossible to understand churches of Christ in the twentieth century without knowing something of the beliefs of three men—Daniel Sommer, Austin McGary, and David Lipscomb. All three men were to the right of center—conservatives. This does not suggest agreement or collusion. On most issues, Sommer and McGary were more reactionary than Lipscomb. Indeed, it is possible to call Lipscomb a moderate in his relationships with both the ultra-conservatives and the more liberal Disciples represented by the *Christian Standard.*

Daniel Sommer sought the mantle of Benjamin Franklin. He followed Franklin's advice to "keep your eye on living issues."[40] Sommer purchased the *American Christian Review* in 1887, combining it with the *Octograph.* Soon, "Sommerism" became the label associated with his ideas. The editor had a strong cultural bias against cities and large urban churches. He most succinctly presented the views he had held for many years in an 1897 article:

> As time advanced such of those churches as assembled in large towns and cities gradually became proud, or, at least, sufficiently worldly-minded to desire popularity, and in order to attain that unscriptural end they adopted certain popular arrangements such as the hired pastor, the church choir, instrumental music, man-made societies to advance the gospel, and human devices to raise money to support the previously mentioned devices of similar origin. In so doing *they* divided the brotherhood of disciples (emphasis supplied).[41]

By 1889, the Restoration Movement had been drifting in different directions for some years. No one, however, had suggested that real division would occur. On a hot summer day in August 1889, Daniel Sommer participated in a historic gathering at Sand Creek, Illinois. Some 6,000 persons gathered to hear Sommer preach on Sunday morning and then to listen to a prepared statement read by P. P. Warren, an elder of the Sand Creek church. Representatives of area churches had already signed the "Address and Declaration" the previous day. After attacking "innovations in the church," the statement left little doubt where Sommer and his associates stood. The document concluded by appealing to "all such as are guilty of knowingly allowing and practicing the many innovations and corruptions" to reject "such abominations." If the liberal Disciples refuse to do so, "we *cannot* and *will not* regard them as brethren."[42]

Although Lipscomb at first praised the statement, he later criticized it. It was the wrong approach. Sommer was taking a sectarian and legalistic position not found in the Bible.[43] J. C. McQuiddy of the *Gospel Advocate* called the Sand Creek Manifesto "folly."[44] Critical of the *Advocate's* position, Sommer warned: "The Sand Creek Declaration is being adopted, and those who will not do right are purged out as leaven. In course of a few years the Church of Christ will be entirely separated from the Christian Church as any other branch of sectarianism. Hallelujah."[45]

Even including his southern brethren following the formation of the Nashville Bible School in 1891, Sommer spoke harshly of all schools operated by Disciples. These schools "resulted in cursing the brotherhood with a swarm of renovating preachers." These preachers introduced "card-playing, theater-going, pleasure-loving, higher-criticism, church-federations, [and] power-centralizing" into the church.[46] He applied the same criticism to the Nashville Bible School after its founding in 1891 by David Lipscomb and James A. Harding.

Sommer gave a flavor to Midwest Disciples that would have a major impact on churches of Christ throughout the twentieth century.

A second person who influenced a large segment of conservative Disciples, especially in Texas, was Austin McGary. Founding the *Firm Foundation* in 1884, McGary practiced a no-holds-barred frontier journalism. He would fight any innovations threatening to weaken apostolic Christianity. Within the first months of publication, the *Gospel Advocate* and the liberal press, including the *Christian Standard,* came under attack. His first editorial set the tone of the paper:

> The *Firm Foundation* will not attempt to "pipe" the popular airs of the day with pedantic sophomoric swell to get "donors," but will endeavor to sing the "song of Moses and the Lamp," [sic] by the notes of eighteen hundred years ago; notes that unlearned fishermen of Galilee, and one who would not "preach the gospel with wisdom of words, lest the cross of Christ should be made none effect," would recognize as the true ones.[47]

Included in the all-encompassing statement were the issues already facing all Disciples. Add to these the one specifically introduced by Austin McGary: rebaptism.

Rebaptism was the main theme of the first issue of the *Firm Foundation.* McGary attacked David Lipscomb's defense of Baptist baptism, even accusing him of being a "dangerous leader of the blind." McGary believed that "remission of sins" is the reason for baptism and must be so understood by the recipient for baptism to be valid. The Nashville editor's conclusions—baptism is to please God; He is the one who remits sins—were a product of "blindness," "brought on by gradually drifting farther and farther into untenable and unholy attitudes." Why was Lipscomb following such a position? McGary knew: Lipscomb had cut loose from his moorings "to enter the mad race for lucre and the applause of men." Because of their view of baptism, McGary accused Lipscomb and James A. Harding with living in the same liberal camp with W. T. Moore. Its failure to insist on rebaptism made the *Advocate* liberal.

Although Sommer and McGary did not share the same position on rebaptism, they did share similar attitudes toward schools. Schools were the cause of apostasy. These men represent the most extreme right wing of conservative Disciples. As would Sommer, McGary would have a major impact on the twentieth century churches of Christ.

Unquestionably, David Lipscomb was a conservative, a believer in following the Bible as the infallible guide in matters of religion. On the other hand, he urged kindness and gentleness in preaching and writing. He stated in 1914, three years before his death:

> A man who loves to condemn the teachings of others and delights in making "the fur fly" is in temper unfitted for a hearty union of the people of God, and he, in spirit, must work against it. Much of the influence of the plea for the oneness of the people of God was destroyed by the bitter spirit in which it was uttered. . . . There are two sources of danger to the disciples of Christ in this work. One is in a wrong spirit. They will become sectarian in opposing sectarianism. The other is the spirit of compromise. They will leave the truth of God to meet others in a united and similar church. Our rebaptist brethren constitute one such party, the "digressives" [liberal Disciples] constitute the other.[48]

Never was any person so adamant against positions contrary to his understanding of the Bible; yet few exhibited longsuffering and forbearance toward others as did David Lipscomb. His views and attitudes would be followed by most members of churches of Christ in the twentieth century.[49]

In 1909, James A. Allen—emphasizing the task placed upon Alexander Campbell, Walter Scott, and Barton W. Stone to oppose all who tended toward extremes, to "unscriptural and hurtful absurdities"—proclaimed Lipscomb as their direct heir. Listing the Sunday school hobby, opposition to special literature, rebaptism, the laying on of hands, woman's work in the church, and extending the right hand of fellowship as divisive issues, Allen stated: "Brother Lipscomb has stood, like a balance wheel, endeavoring to adhere always to the rational mean."[50]

CONCLUSION

Without understanding the final consequences, Thomas and Alexander Campbell set the stage for the divisions that would splinter the Restoration Movement in the twentieth century. The call for religious reform filled the needs of Americans during the first years of the nineteenth century. It was a time of religious ferment, of Americans accepting religious renewal after witnessing a decline of church membership following the Revolution. The Campbells believed and taught that the way to Christian unity is to teach the Bible—"the truth." *Doctrine,* discovered in the Bible, becomes the key to unity; and *restoration*—the word most often used to describe the Campbell religious ferment—suggests the need to return to the Scriptures. In this manner the church of the first century can be reclaimed.[51]

As the years progressed and second- and third-generation restorers came onto the scene, different interpretations of restoration caused division where unity had been the dream. As later restorers attempted to interpret Alexander Campbell and to search the Scriptures for commands to obey, division became inevitable. It was this heritage that became the lot of churches of Christ in the twentieth century. As a result, Daniel Sommer and Austin McGary represent a very doctrinaire approach to Christianity. Such influences have had a definite impact on churches of Christ.

Not all restorers had the same spirit. Although David Lipscomb was strong in his adherence to the Bible, he never believed he had learned all truth. He was a student of Tolbert Fanning, but he did not accept the overriding role his mentor placed on human effort in salvation. As Gregory Tidwell stated: "While autosoterism [works salvation] leads to intolerance, Lipscomb—having a lower estimate of human nature—could face the possibility of being wrong with equanimity."[52]

Furthermore, he often restudied his positions to see if they were in accord with the Bible, and he exhibited tolerance of opposing views. Lipscomb's pacifist stance and his belief that the Christian should not participate in civil government were not widely accepted; and he would not impose these views on his readers in the *Gospel Advocate,* although he accepted them as truths from the Bible. Furthermore, he hoped others would treat him in the same manner. Even as an old man, he urged the stirring of the pond— the constant search for truth in the Bible.

CHAPTER 2

DIVISION IN 1906:
The Emergence of a
Distinct People

A new century is a time to search for new meaning, or possibly to recover the dream of past years. Both possibilities were alive in the American Restoration Movement. The unity theme that gave birth to the Stone-Campbell movement remained viable, but a different emphasis emerged early in the twentieth century. The changed emphasis divided the fellowship. The differences were clear to most anyone reading the major journals. From St. Louis, James H. Garrison gave leadership to liberal Disciples through the *Christian-Evangelist.* From Cincinnati, the *Christian Standard* followed a more conservative position early in the new century. In Nashville, the *Gospel Advocate,* under David Lipscomb's editorial hand, observed liberal tendencies in both northern journals.

As noted, unity remained a theme during the 1890s. Garrison, however, moved toward ecumenicity. He believed himself to be in the direct stream of the Campbell-Stone movement. Unlike Lipscomb, he did not base his views on a strict return to primitive New Testament Christianity.

Conversely, both the Cincinnati and the Nashville publications held strongly to restoration as the only method of gaining Christian unity. The *Advocate* took a more literal view of the Bible, one that could accept neither the missionary society nor the instrument in worship. These were divisive.

Conflict has been a central theme of the Restoration Movement during the last two decades of the nineteenth century. Nevertheless, a nervous unity remained. Not until the 1890s did David Lipscomb finally recognize that unity could not be maintained. Thus for fourteen years, the division, under way since the 1840s, moved swiftly to fulfillment. It was a time of disillusionment. It was the emergence of a distinct people.

THE BASIS OF UNITY

Defeat in the Civil War caused a prostrate South to reassess its religious posture. Having experienced the crush of a losing conflict, the region turned toward a more biblically-based religion. Nationally, the Disciples most often followed the direction of the nation at large. Expansion and development were key words. The Civil War had only temporarily impeded America's move toward her destiny. Thus northern Disciples more readily accepted a liberal theology based on inevitable progress, characteristic of both industrial expansion and liberal religion. What Lipscomb saw disturbed him deeply.[1]

What he now saw was a pell-mell race toward denominationalism, the thing most opposed by the Restoration Movement at its inception. David Lipscomb, openly shocked and hurt when he heard brethren refer to the church in denominational terms, warned: "All denominations are sinful. God ordained simple churches of Jesus Christ. To convert these into a denomination is to form an institution of man over and above the churches or institutions of God, binding men into one organized party." Furthermore, the movement to restore New Testament Christianity "originated in an effort made by Thomas Campbell and associates to bring about a union among the churches of God by inducing each and all to reject all opinions . . . and . . . inventions of man from the service of God.[2]

Lipscomb, like other editors, recalled, on numerous occasions, the writings of Alexander Campbell, invoking the Sage when denying denominationalism. Often Lipscomb asked his contemporaries: Why form a new party? If societies and organizations are so important, why not simply join forces with Baptists and Methodists? Conversely, he asked those to his right: Why become sectarian by opposing Sunday schools and Bible schools?

Difficulties in the 1890s stemmed from the varying interpretations of Christian unity. As a result, bitter discussion ensued. Lipscomb contended: "When we turn aside to things not taught in the scriptures . . . we divide and engage in strife." On the other hand, James Garrison believed that opposition to anything perceived to be a matter of opinion causes division. Lipscomb continued to call for unity, but saw the Restoration Movement torn by division. While Christian unity was undergoing questioning by various segments of the Restoration Movement in the 1890s, Lipscomb made his position clear:

> There is one great danger in seeking union among men—that is, in uniting with men we may separate from God. Often when we seek to get closer to one body we move away from another. We must be careful not to separate from God, because a union without God is a union in falsehood, a union with death. In any union of Christians, God must be the center and the head. We come into union with God by doing his commandments, by following his directions, and by walking in the light, as he is in the light.[3]

What would it be: Union based on compromise or unity constructed on "the restoration of the ancient order of things?" This most important question drove the Disciples toward division.

HIGHER CRITICISM AS AN ISSUE IN DIVISION

Liberal theology emerged as a major feature of American religion in the 1890s. The Congregationalists were the first to feel the impact of the new thought, followed closely by the Methodists.[4] Soon Baptists, then Disciples, followed the same path. Disciples' involvement became even more pronounced after William Rainey Harper moved to the University of Chicago from Yale in 1891. The Chicago school, through the Disciples' Divinity House at the university, quickly became the focus of liberal thought among Disciples.

Two Disciple journals emerged as leaders in the controversy. The *Christian Standard,* through the pen of John W. McGarvey, focused the attack on liberal theology. For nearly twenty years, beginning in 1892, McGarvey penned an article each week on "Biblical Criticism."

On the other hand, liberal Disciples used the pages of the *Christian-Evangelist* as an outlet. Even though James H. Garrison—the editor—may not have shared many of the views expressed in the articles, he received criticism from across the fellowship. The criticism was justified, if one listens to McGarvey and David Lipscomb. They scolded Garrison for allowing George W. Longan and Alexander Proctor, the Missouri rationalists, space in the *Christian-Evangelist*. When Garrison asked Herbert W. Willett, a Chicago graduate, to write comments on the weekly Sunday school lesson, a storm arose across the brotherhood. The eyes of the storm were focused in Cincinnati and Nashville.

The beginnings of the controversy can be traced to 1872, when Garrison purchased The *Christian* from Longan and Proctor. As early as 1877, Longan, continuing to write in the paper, emphasized the findings of German higher criticism. The Bible must be studied as other works of literature, emphasizing the historical and developmental nature of the Bible. The Bible must fit into a naturalistic world view.[5] In September of the same year he defended those who doubted the authorship of a biblical book:

> Upon whose *ipse dixit* shall such a man be turned over to Satan? I submit, that among just and sensible men, it is enough that some conceited scriblet, whose sense of his own importance is, perhaps, in the inverse ratio of his real merits, has seen fit to pass sentence against him.[6]

Critical of those who accepted inspiration of every detail in the Bible, Longan remarked: "One of these days, we shall learn that the best way to defend the Scriptures is not to put weapons into the hands of the enemy."[7]

John McGarvey could not accept Longan's view of inspiration. Nor could Longan abide McGarvey's views of plenary inspiration. As an example, Longan recalled McGarvey's attempt to rectify the seeming discrepancies between Mark's and Luke's account of blind Bartimeaus. Concerning McGarvey's exegesis, he wrote: "The unsophisticated conscience will say 'what does all this cheap ingenuity signify?' " This theory, Longan added, "makes honest exegesis impossible."

In his characteristic style, McGarvey responded: "It makes me wonder how it has come to pass that honest exegesis and a conscience both honest and unsophisticated are confined to those interpreters who think that the writings of such men as Luke and Mark are merely 'on the whole, valuable and trustworthy digests of gospel history.' "[8] McGarvey's most pointed answer to Longan was a lengthy letter published in The *Christian*.

> The position which you [Longan] take in regard to the inspiration of the New Testament writers is to me a source of real anxiety; for if they were mistaken in regard to any one matter of fact, they may have been in regard to almost any other; and if they contradict one another about matters of which they speak in common, it is hard to believe that contradictions would not have been more numerous had the writers spoken more frequently of the same fact. And if they are mistaken as to plain, simple matters of fact, who can rely on them in regard to matters of doctrine? The acceptance of this theory is a denial of the infallibility of Scriptures. It contains the essence of rationalism, and it is a long stride in the direction of infidelity.[9]

Longan showed his allegiance to the age that spawned higher criticism by responding to his critics: "I can only believe a proposition in the exact ratio of the evidence which supports it, as that evidence is apprehended by my own faculties." Nevertheless, Longan reemphasized his commitment to the Bible as the word of God. However, he remarked: "If my faith in Christ depended upon my ability to satisfy myself that Moses wrote Deuteronomy my life would be ruined. Thank God it does not." [10]

From Nashville, David Lipscomb suggested concern with the direction of the Missouri Disciples. Noting Longan's attraction to the German rationalists, he remarked: "The method of this school is not to denounce any part of the Scripture but to suggest doubts, pick flaws, throw difficulties and offer natural causes in explanation of what the Bible claims as miracles." Lipscomb criticized both Longan and Garrison. Noting specifically Longan's use of Bernhard Weiss as "a strong arm to lean upon," the *Advocate* editor continued: "We too have some of his [Weiss] works in our library. We are glad that it [sic] always puts us to sleep to read them."[11]

Closely associated with Longan on the *Christian* magazine, prior to its purchase by Garrison, was Alexander Proctor. He, too, was a strong proponent of the New Theology. According to David Edwin Harrell, Proctor "preached theistic evolution and condemned the narrow-sectarianism of the Disciples."[12] In 1895, McGarvey and Proctor both appeared on the Missouri Lectures. Following a confrontation between the two men on higher criticism, J. B. Briney wrote McGarvey: "I believe that the tide of the 'higher criticism' craze in Mo. is stayed." Proctor's friends in his home town of Paris, Missouri, "were shocked and grieved by his statements concerning the unreliable character of bible history."[13] McGarvey, not Proctor, represented the views of the "common man."

The discussion intensified as the twentieth century approached. The cause: The Disciples opened the Disciples' Divinity House at the University of Chicago. Following his graduation from the newly-founded University of Chicago, Herbert L. Willett became the director of the Disciples' House. McGarvey asked if Willett opposed President William Harper's liberal theological views? If he did, he was honor-bound to state publicly his positions.[14]

The coeditor of the *Christian-Evangelist* was B. W. Johnson. Much more conservative than James Garrison, the paper—as long as Johnson lived—was not as outspoken in defense of liberal theology and the Disciples' Divinity House. This changed with Johnson's death in 1894. Because Garrison was a member of the Board of Directors of the Divinity House, McGarvey held him accountable for the happenings in Chicago. Said the Lexington, Kentucky, scholar, what "I have read from the pen of Pres. Harper myself, and some from the pens of other professors in his institution, is 'anti-Christian teaching.' If Bro. Garrison does not so regard it, it would be interesting to see him try to defend it."[15]

Why was Willett the focal point of controversy? He did not accept verbal inspiration. Instead, he accepted a progressive, developmental understanding of all human history, including the biblical narrative. Jewish history was only an adolescent stage of the human race. According to William Tucker, Garrison's biographer, Willett's understanding of inspiration was parallel to others who accepted higher criticism. Said Willett: "The Bible was inspired not because of its superhuman accuracy and infallible authority, but because it introduced both the profoundest truths of religion and those personalities in human history who were most worthy of reverence."[16]

Liberal theology, as exhibited in German higher criticism, invaded the Disciples movement in earnest in the 1890s. Both

McGarvey and Lipscomb indicated concern. Even though neither man could look into the future, both saw enough to know that the ideas would eventually divide the Restoration Movement.

LIPSCOMB CONFRONTS THE MISSIONARY SOCIETY IN TENNESSEE

For some years the society had been an issue in the pages of the *Advocate;* not until the late 1880s did Lipscomb become involved in the conflict. The early 1890s saw the topic focused as never before. The reason was obvious: national issues had invaded Nashville during 1887 in the person of A. I. Myhr, who had recently come to Nashville from Missouri. The Missouri background by itself was enough to make Lipscomb suspicious of the new arrival. By 1889, Myhr was advocating a statewide society. Angrily, Lipscomb wanted to know why Myhr would write the following statement: "Many places are waiting anxiously for an evangelist to come and help begin the work." Tennessee, Myhr announced, was a great mission field.

Chattanooga, not Nashville, was the site for the organizational meeting of the Tennessee Christian Missionary Society. Lipscomb, however, raised a question. Why did Tennessee need a missionary society when the Disciples were growing faster in Tennessee than in most areas of the United States? The *Christian-Evangelist* and the *Christian Standard,* quite satisfied, applauded the society's beginning. The *Advocate* equally condemned the society. The conflict was alive in Tennessee.

To make matters worse, the convention chose Nashville for the 1891 state meeting. W. H. Timmons, a fellow elder with David Lipscomb at the South College Street Church, wrote what was likely the sentiment of many: "Brethren, the call has come to us. You must take sides. The cause is ominous. There is no use to cry peace, peace, when there is no peace." When the state meeting concluded, the delegates asked the national meeting to convene in Nashville in 1892. Lipscomb, upset, called the society "the invention of the devil."

The *Christian-Evangelist* issued a strong rebuttal. The *Evangelist* and the *Standard* insinuated that the *Advocate* and its staff were anti-missionary. Again, it aroused strong reaction: Never had *Advocate* writers opposed mission work—only missionary endeavors carried on through a society larger than the church.

Opposition from Nashville in no way deterred the general convention from meeting in the city in October 1892. The meetings did not go unnoticed in the Cumberland River city. Some of Lipscomb's friends called for a counter meeting during the convention. Such a move, Lipscomb responded, would be as wrong as having a missionary society. Why, asked Lipscomb, choose Nashville for the national convention? Was Nashville the logical place for the convention or did the society simply wish to embarrass the nonsociety churches?

Along with the General Christian Missionary Society's session in Nashville, the women's society—the Christian Woman's Board of Missions—also convened in Tennessee's capital city. This organization, begun in 1874, involved Disciple women in mission work. The women conducted their own sessions. Often they spoke to delegates of the larger male-dominated missionary society. This happened on several occasions during the 1892 Nashville convention. The changed attitude toward women's involvement in public forums bothered the more conservative Disciples, especially David Lipscomb. The liberal Disciples, from Lipscomb's perspective, had gone counter to everything the Scriptures teach about women's place in the church.

THE ROLE OF WOMEN BECOMES AN ISSUE

Attitudes among the progressive Disciples had been undergoing change for some years. Isaac Errett, although not favoring the ordination of women, aided the formation of the Christian Woman's Board of Missions. His paper, the *Christian Standard,* opened its pages to those who favored female ministers. Arguments in favor of women filling the preacher's role were many, but the one most often used was culturally based. The *Christian Oracle,* a journal that would be renamed *Christian Century* in 1900, asserted in 1889 that Paul's injunction on woman's silence in the churches was cultural in nature; it must be understood as a local issue: "In this free land [the United States] where customs are so different, women are not 'prohibited from praying, exhorting, and teaching.'" The *Christian Standard* contained an article in 1892 also using the cultural argument. Said the writer: "It may have been wrong for a woman to speak in the churches during Paul's age, but 'in Indiana . . . it is a shame for her not to do so.' "[17]

For conservative Disciples, the ideas favoring wider involvement of women in worship were totally unbiblical. Lipscomb believed these were the result of liberal theology. He stated in 1891: "The habit of women preaching originated in the same [northern] hot bed with divorce, free love, and the repugnance to child bearing." Both J. W. McGarvey and Moses E. Lard adamantly opposed women in the pulpits. "Female agitators [with] idle hands" promoted the idea of women preachers, believed Moses Lard. In his colorful style, Austin McGary left no doubt about his position on the issue: "The way our [liberal] brethren are pushing women to the front, we need not be surprised to soon see [the sisters] pastoring in 'plug-hats and claw-hammer coats'; and playing the theological dude generally."[18]

The Christian Woman's Board of Missions nurtured the increased involvement of women in church activities. Fred Bailey, surveying the issue in his "The Status of Women in the Disciples of Christ Movement, 1865-1900," concluded:

> In the last twenty-five years of the nineteenth century, woman gained a greater voice in the polity of the Christian church. The philosophical theories, which eventually led to ordained women in the 1890s, were closely associated with the growing influence of the Christian Woman's Board of Missions. Ecumenical Disciples looked upon this society as the vehicle by which woman's sensitivity could be harnessed for the church; conservatives considered it a cancer which threatened the stability of both the church and the family.[19]

David Lipscomb had always urged unity in the Restoration Movement. He was never quick to suggest division. The October 1892 conventions in Nashville changed his mind. Lipscomb wrote that the women's society put forth women "to speak, to manage the society, to employ and send out preachers, and to boss their affairs as the men do theirs." He showed his disgust by quoting a brother who had commended the speaking of women because they did "it so deliciously." In subsequent articles, Lipscomb used the "it so deliciously" phrase to punctuate his disgust for women preachers.[20]

The Nashville editor, even with the closing of the convention, would not allow the issue to die. He believed the gatherings had disgraced Disciples in Tennessee. It amazed him that "so little reference was made to the Bible." Lipscomb rejected the speeches that were of the "old Fourth-of-July spread-eagle variety, praising the Anglo-Saxon prowess . . . and glorifying . . . country."

Remembering his own association with the church that evolved into Vine Street, Lipscomb scored the women who preached from the pulpit and the men who listened to them. Listening in the audiences were men of prominence, including C. L. Loos and John W. McGarvey. Referring to the talk of one young woman, Lipscomb remarked: It "could not profit them, and it injured her and lowered the standard of womanly modesty." [21]

David Lipscomb found no virtue in the conventions; James H. Garrison praised the women for their work. Garrison called the attacks by the *Advocate* "inexpressibly unjust, ungalant [sic], and unchristian." Lipscomb responded with a warning to the women that to disobey Paul's command would lead to eternal "death, despite all [of woman's] tender, tearful, heartfelt talks."

The Nashville conventions hurried Lipscomb's changing attitudes toward the Disciples. No longer did he write of the possible reuniting of the Restoration Movement. When in August 1897 he penned three articles indicating his inability to fellowship the larger Disciples of Christ, he spoke what others had been saying for several years. Among the many points made, he especially noted the tendency of the Disciples to run beyond the Bible by building "a foreign society, a home society, a woman's society, a church building society," and many other things not authorized.[22]

Lipscomb believed the missionary society and the introduction of the instrument into worship had liberal and rationalistic tendencies. Even more so, the total abandonment of the Bible to accept new positions for women in the church was theologically liberal to the core. This acceptance of a liberal position convinced him that he could no longer extend fellowship to the Christian church, a term that began to be used exclusively for the more progressive Disciples of Christ.

CONTINUING CONFLICT IN NASHVILLE

During the late 1890s, the Nashville scene became even more explosive. R. Lin Cave had been the pulpit minister of the Nashville Christian Church since the early 1880s. While attending a society meeting in Louisville during the latter part of the same decade, Cave urged the delegates to refrain from sending evangelists to Tennessee. Included in his plea was one important fact: The churches were at peace. Furthermore, churches in Tennessee were doing more in spreading the gospel than churches in other states. The convention, however, did not heed his plea.[23]

Cave was a very popular Nashville preacher for the Vine Street Christian Church, the original Disciples' church in the city. Yet many of his brethren believed him to be indecisive. When T. B. Larimore was unable to fulfill his preaching obligations in North Nashville during 1890, Cave volunteered his services. Talk, it seems, had made the rounds of Nashville that Cave was "soft" on important doctrinal issues. Thus E. G. Sewell, coeditor of the *Advocate,* showed surprise at his preaching: "Some of us had an idea he [Cave] couldn't preach about Pentecost, and the Jailer."[24]

Some years later, Cave's attitude toward the society in Tennessee changed. When it met for its annual state meeting in Nashville in 1891, the convention elected Cave president. Lipscomb, showing his concern, related a conversation with Cave: "Bro. Lipscomb, I would suffer this arm to be cut off before I would do anything in this work [missionary society] that will cause division among the disciples." Henceforth, Lipscomb had little use for Cave's work at what became after 1887 the Vine Street Christian Church.

Furthermore, Cave's biblical usage disturbed Lipscomb. The problem had first surfaced in 1891 when the *Nashville American* asked Lin Cave to write or get someone to write two articles on Tennessee Disciples. Cave gave Lipscomb the historical topic, while he kept the doctrinal one for himself. He failed, however, to write it. He then offered Lipscomb the opportunity to write both articles, a task he readily accepted. As reported by Lipscomb, Cave was uncertain about the relationship of God and Christ. The two men exchanged a series of letters. Lipscomb reported Cave's willingness to accept as saved all men who are honestly seeking to do their best. Cave supposedly told Lipscomb that even Robert Ingersoll could have been saved on this basis.

By 1896, Cave put his doubts about the relationship of God and Christ behind him. Nevertheless, the bitter feelings engendered on both sides would not subside. F. W. Smith, longtime preacher for the church in Franklin, Tennessee, wrote:

> If the brethren of this state refuse to support David Lipscomb in his advocacy of the truth, the time will come when women will occupy your pulpits, and sectarians will have undisputed sway. You may condemn him and turn your back upon him, but for me and my house we will stand by him with our feeble strength.[25]

In 1897, R. Lin Cave left Nashville and the Vine Street church to become president of Kentucky University, now the University of Kentucky. He had preached in Nashville for sixteen years, years in which he was the center of controversy. Was he a victim of the circumstances surrounding the Disciples during those years of growing disenchantment? Or were his teachings foreign to the Bible, as Lipscomb suggested? Whatever the situation, the Vine Street and the Woodland Street churches had accepted both the society and the instrument by the last years of the 1890s. Of Vine Street, Lipscomb remarked:

> The Vine Street church, in Nashville, is a strong church numerically, pecuniarily, socially. It is surpassed by no such church in Nashville of any denomination in social and intellectual and pecuniary ability. It is the weakest church claiming to be Christian in the city. I have known its work for fifty years past. During that time it has not planted a church or sent out a preacher.[26]

The division in Nashville was complete by the early years of the twentieth century. It was only a matter of time until division would be complete both locally and nationally.

LIPSCOMB RESPONDS TO THE CRISIS OF DIVISION

The developing division remained a matter of concern to David Lipscomb. He wrote: "The division . . . going forward in the churches is painful. It wrings the heart with anguish. But God asked: 'Can two walk together, except they be agreed?'"

Continuing, he added: "Division must come until we are all willing to be led by God." Lipscomb, often accused of seeing nothing but the dark side of things, saw a silver lining among the dark clouds of division. Heresies must always come in order to separate the faithful from the digressive. For Lipscomb, there was consolation. More people were faithful to God at the end of the century than had been prior to the beginning of the Nineteenth-Century Reformation.[27]

The year 1899, the fiftieth anniversary of the founding of the American Christian Missionary Society, elicited a sad conclusion from the Nashville editor. Asked to join a celebration of the society's founding, he said he could not—it was an unscriptural organization. His refusal included a reference to Micaiah, in 2 Chronicles 18, who refused to join 400 prophets not faithful to God. Lipscomb placed himself in a similar situation. He, too, must remain faithful to God. Lipscomb then added:

> Nothing in life has given me more pain in heart than the separation from those I have heretofore worked with and loved. The majority seem to be going away and leaving those who stand firm for the old ways. I love to be with the majority, and would certainly go with them, if I were not afraid of offending God in so doing.[28]

Thus by 1899, Lipscomb recognized the inevitability of division.

In no way did this suggest that the Restoration Movement had failed. It had given direction to an entire century. At times, thought Lipscomb, division is a good thing. Wheat must have its chaff purged.

> The darkest hour precedes the rising sun. This means that God purges out, separates the good from the evil, before he blesses; and the days of winnowing and separating the chaff from the wheat are days that seem dark and gloomy to those who undergo the winnowing. Nevertheless, they are days of preparation for greater blessings from on high. They are not days of evil to the faithful children of God. The days of falling away are days of promise to the true Israel.[29]

Furthermore, Lipscomb concluded, reformation movements are happening at closer intervals. As a result, greater numbers will remain faithful to God. Lipscomb encouraged his friends to look at the beginnings of reformation, not at end results. There was a silver lining in the dark cloud.[30]

In the face of division, Christian unity remained a constant theme from Lipscomb's pen. Early in the 1890s, he published a small volume titled: *Christian Unity, How Promoted and How Destroyed.* In the book, Lipscomb emphasized his conclusion that the Bible is the final authority in religion. Across the brotherhood, the book received favorable reviews. Lipscomb, however, was not satisfied. Too many refused to follow the Bible.

As the decade progressed, his expressions of concern became more strident. His emphasis was unity, not union. From his perspective, the more liberal Disciples, by preaching union, had abandoned the restoration positions of the Campbells. Looking toward St. Louis and the *Christian-Evangelist,* Lipscomb scolded editor Garrison for not allowing the pros and cons of the society to be discussed in his paper. True to Lipscomb's understanding of a Christian paper, he believed the scripturalness of the society or any other biblical topic cannot be determined without open discussion. He added:

> The New Testament truths must be taught to successive generations to hold people to the truth of God. Unity in faith and practice is promoted by discussion. Nor should anyone ever think he has learned all truth. Everyone should hold himself open to inquiry on any subject. Without this we can have no intelligent faith.[31]

Toward the end of the 1890s, the inevitable happened. F. D. Srygley, the front-page writer of the *Advocate,* copied an article from the St. Louis *Post-Dispatch* on the possible merger of the Congregational and Christian churches of that city. According to the report, the churches agreed not to compete in the various neighborhoods of the city. Srygley only added a comment or two, but his comments were enough to cause Garrison to respond with vigor. Garrison blamed the *Advocate* for statements that had appeared in the *Firm Foundation.* Garrison, in a personal letter to the editors of the *Advocate,* exploded:

> Editors *Gospel Advocate:* Dear Brethren: What do you think about sowing such seeds as the enclosed broadcast? Is this God's work, or the devil's? I believe it is inspired from beneath, and this particularly mean article from the *Firm*

Foundation gets its cue from the *Gospel Advocate*. Will the *Advocate* make any correction?

> Fraternally yours,
> s/J. H. Garrison
> St. Louis, Apr. 12

Srygley simply reminded Garrison that he had only copied the article from the St. Louis paper. The response did not satisfy Garrison. On May 14 Garrison penned another letter.

> Please do me the favor to strike the *Christian-Evangelist* from your list of exchanges, and do not send your paper to this office any longer, and oblige,
>
> Yours Truly,
> s/ J. H. Garrison

The *Advocate* editors responded by asking where they had misrepresented him. They could not locate a position attributed to Garrison that he had not taken publicly. Concluding their statement to their adversary, they responded:

> The magnitude of our offense is that we do not believe the positions he has taken nor approve the course he is pursuing, and we have given our reasons for the stand we have taken against him in language as clear and as kind as we could command.[32]

The widening breach meant dialogue was now impossible between the two journals. Occasionally a notice appeared in each paper about the activities of the other, but with little comment or controversy. In 1908, Lipscomb remembered the events of 1897 in an article, "The Christian-Evangelist and Christian Unity." Garrison, believed Lipscomb, had gone far toward the positions of Longan and Proctor, the Missouri rationalists. Why such a conclusion? Garrison allegedly had said that he had much more fellowship with Presbyterians and Methodists than with Lipscomb. The division was now an acknowledged fact. Practically, it had existed for a number years.[33]

The event that caused more concern among Disciples than any other was the 1902 annual convention of the missionary society. By the twentieth century the convention was focusing on activities other than missions. Convening in Omaha, James H. Garrison and the *Evangelist* urged the Disciples to cooperate more closely with other religious groups through the National Federation of

Churches and Christian Workers. The convention passed a resolution looking toward such a union.

Nothing had prepared Garrison for the response from the different segments of the Restoration Movement. The *Standard* and John W. McGarvey were livid in their response to such a move. Lipscomb's response was predictable: I told you so. It did not surprise him that Garrison was the leader in the federation movement. Without the missionary society, which helped to destroy unity, the resolution could not have come to the floor. Lipscomb wrote: "There is but one ground for union: Do what God commands, adding nothing thereto, taking nothing therefrom. He is the true friend of God's people who opposes everything in the service of God not required by him." To advance union based on the ideas of man, added Lipscomb, is to promote sectarianism and denominationalism. Continuing, Lipscomb remarked: "Christ came to introduce division as well as to make peace. . . . Union is . . . possible only in Christ. Union out of Christ, is union against Christ."[34]

THE CENSUS REPORT AND FINAL DIVISION

Shortly after the Civil War, Moses E. Lard optimistically pronounced that the civil conflict had not divided the Disciples of Christ. Likely, there were already slight divisive cracks when he made his remark, but the acceptance of division was not officially recognized until the publication of the 1906 census. Even then the chasm might have continued to widen without any internal statement of division had not the Bureau of the Census noticed differences among the Disciples. Its director for the religious section, S. N. D. North, perceived differences within the fellowship after reading various journals among Disciples. North corresponded with Lipscomb to determine if his observations were correct. Lipscomb responded, sadly, that such appeared to be true. In answer to a series of questions posed by the census, Lipscomb gave reasons why the Disciples of Christ and the churches of Christ, the term most widely used to distinguish the conservatives from the larger body of Disciples of Christ, should be listed separately in the religious census.

1. There is a distinct people taking the word of God as their only sufficient rule of faith, calling their churches "churches of

Christ" or "churches of God," distinct and separate in name, work, or rule of faith, from all other bodies or peoples.

2. They are purely congregational and independent in their polity and work, so have no general meetings or organizations of any kind.

3. Their aim is to unite all professed Christians in the sole purpose of promoting simple, evangelical Christianity as God revealed in the Scriptures, free from all human opinions and inventions of men.[35]

Later, North came to Nashville to enlist the help of the *Advocate* and its staff in gathering membership numbers among those known as churches of Christ. Lipscomb had earlier opposed counting membership numbers. Like many others, he recalled God's opposition in the Old Testament to numbering the children of Israel. Nevertheless, in 1906 he was willing to participate. Had not the apostle Paul taught Christians to "obey the powers that be?"[36]

From across the brotherhood came responses to Lipscomb's new course. Some asked: Who gave Lipscomb the right to speak for even a small segment of the Disciples? James H. Garrison voiced surprise that division was happening. Yet, in light of earlier statements of the St. Louis editor, it should not have caught him by surprise. It likely pleased him that finally there was a formal recognition of differences. This move should not have surprised J. A. Lord of the *Christian Standard*. In 1904, Lipscomb had refused to contribute an article to Lord's paper. He could not in clear conscience participate when the special issue would include men, such as Lin Cave, who questioned the inspiration of the Bible.[37]

The entire experience saddened Lipscomb. Most of all, the devotion many were then showing to partyism—both on the right and the left—concerned him. He wrote:

> As impossible as the result seems, all parties, all denominations in religion, must be broken down and swept out of the way before the rule of Jesus can find perfect work on earth. This prospect is discouraging to all who do not believe firmly in God and his word. But the result must come. With this must come a falling away from professed faith in God. Nonetheless, the work must be done. The mission of the word of God is to root up and destroy, as well as to plant and build up. One must precede the other until in the religious world every practice and

party and society and denomination not planted by God shall be rooted up, that the word of God, the seed of the kingdom, may have free course and bear much fruit.[38]

In 1906, Lipscomb suggested what he thought had happened to the Restoration Movement: "The introduction of the societies switched the Disciples off the Bible track and wrecked the movement to return to God's order."

WHY DID DIVISION HAPPEN AMONG DISCIPLES? A RESPONSE FROM ALFRED T. DeGROOT

In looking back before 1906, Alfred T. DeGroot, a Disciples historian and critic of churches of Christ, surveyed the background leading to division among Disciples of Christ. He recognized the causes of eventual division long before it became a reality in 1906. From his perspective, churches of Christ "left" the larger body of Disciples of Christ. This "going out" happened through the efforts of the Census Bureau with the help of churches of Christ and the *Gospel Advocate* in Nashville. DeGroot stated:

> The use of the date 1906 to designate the separation of Disciples of Christ and Churches of Christ is accurate only in that it marks the first publication of a Churches of Christ Preachers List, and also coincides with the year of the United States Census of Religious Bodies which is taken each decade in the year ending with the figure 6. The 1906 event simply recognized a separation which already had taken place, even though, as David Lipscomb said in 1907, "in many places the differences have not yet resulted in separation." A careful examination of the periodical literature of the Restoration Movement during the years 1900-1906 reveals scant references to a separation as taking place at that time. It had already come about.[39]

When did it happen? DeGroot believed the division took place during the 1880s and 1890s. He especially mentioned that conservatives quit attending the conventions. He noted an article from the *Christian Standard* in 1899, the year Lipscomb refused to participate in the fiftieth anniversary of the establishment of the missionary society.

Egotism, intellectual vanity, bigotry, provincial manners, crass and ignorant dogmatism, are natural products of the hermit habit. It is at great intellectual and spirit loss that certain deluded disciples of Christ oppose the assemblages of their brethren in great convocations to worship and counsel together in the name of a common Lord.[40]

DeGroot did not reach the same conclusions as David Lipscomb.

CONCLUSION

There was more to the division of 1906 than simply churches of Christ separating from the Disciples of Christ. Because of the 1902 overtures from the National Federation of Churches and Christian Workers, the *Christian Standard* and conservative Christian churches began to doubt their place within the larger fellowship. In reality, the conservative Christians began to see themselves as separate from both the Disciples of Christ on the left and churches of Christ on the right. The division became a three-pronged split.

For a hundred years the Restoration Movement was tenuously held together by a belief in a plea for Christian unity. When a change developed in the definition of the plea, no longer was it possible for the movement to remain one body. The first group, therefore, that felt it must follow its own course designated themselves as churches of Christ in the census of 1906. The Disciples were digressive. How many members did the census count? There was no way to gain an accurate count given the extreme congregational nature of the movement. The figure of 159,658 was only a small fraction of the nearly 1,000,000 Disciples of Christ.

The decision involved in the census report of 1906 gave recognition to the emergence of a distinct people—churches of Christ.

CHAPTER 3

THE OUTSIDERS:
The Place of Churches of Christ Within Early Twentieth-Century American Religion

In America the twentieth-century has been a time of transition. Rural Americans have moved to cities in increasing numbers. As early as 1930, most of the people of the United States were urban residents. With urbanization, industry replaced agriculture as the major means of livelihood for Americans. Along with the development of cities, secularization increased. Rural mores continued to erode. America changed dramatically as the twentieth-century city completely overtook the rural orientation of the nineteenth century.

American religion did not escape this dramatic change. Some historians, such as Arthur Schlesinger, Sr., attempt to explain all changes in American religion as a rural-urban confrontation, with the more conservative groups defending the dying rural orientation of the previous century. Other historians suggest that the more liberal social gospel emphasis best explains the response of religion to an urban society. Historians of a newer school, however, emphasize that the rural/urban confrontation does not adequately explain American religion. They point to the fundamentalist movement as a northern, urban phenomenon rather than a southern, rural development. Instead of the John Scopes trial of 1925—where Darwinism was contested in Dayton, Tennessee—being the climax of religious conservatism, it was only one small, albeit important, result of American fundamentalism.[1] This event will be discussed more fully in a future chapter

CHURCHES OF CHRIST AND FUNDAMENTALISM

Fundamentalism has become a broad term encompassing all conservative American religious groups. Although most churches of Christ were neither urban nor northern during the nineteenth century, the popular press includes them under the fundamentalist umbrella. Even spokespersons within churches of Christ occasionally use the term *fundamentalist* to describe the fellowship. In evaluating the place churches of Christ hold in this grouping, these questions arise: How can the word *fundamentalist* describe churches of Christ? Where do churches of Christ fit into the mosaic of twentieth-century American religion? Have there been changes in society that, in turn, have caused change within churches of Christ?

If they were not fundamentalists, why were churches of Christ early in the twentieth century somewhat akin to them? The wider religious conflict is an important part of the answer. Fundamentalists began drawing a distinction between the conservatives and the liberals of the late nineteenth and early twentieth centuries. They accepted as true what the liberals denied—the Bible is the divinely inspired word of God.

During the years before the Civil War, those people who became post-Civil War conservatives had been members of the mainline churches. There were few conflicts, as most churches, including the Unitarians, accepted Scottish Common Sense realism. It was the means of dealing rationally with both the supernatural and the natural. Scientifically, the inductive ideas of Francis Bacon and the formulas of Isaac Newton merged perfectly into the philosophical thinking of John Locke's understanding of common sense. With the publishing of Charles Darwin's *Origin of Species* in 1859, much of the scientific community abandoned Bacon and Newton and accepted the new theories associated with Darwin. Shortly, the ideas of Darwin appealed to the liberal bent in many of America's churches and theological seminaries. Combining German higher criticism with the evolutionary vehicle of Darwinism, American religious groups—instead of sharing basic positions—were now on a collision course.

Churches of Christ revolted from the larger body of Disciples of Christ in the same way that the fundamentalists left the ranks of the mainline churches—Methodists, Baptists, and Presbyterians. As discussed in chapter two, churches of Christ appeared for the first time as a separate religious body in the 1906 religion census. For fifty years a breach had been forming within the Restoration movement. The emphasis upon organization, the introduction of instrumental music into worship, the involvement of women in leading public worship, and the acceptance of higher criticism by a large segment of Disciples caused the break. David Lipscomb and those who wrote for the *Gospel Advocate,* along with many others who probably had desired division earlier, declared separation to be a reality. Since many of the same issues impacting the fundamentalists early in the twentieth century also concerned conservative Disciples, the parallel between the movements is noteworthy.

The emphasis is on *parallel.* Indeed, the call for restoration early in the nineteenth century had already directed Disciples along the road that would be, in part, shared by the fundamentalists/evangelicals one hundred years later. Thomas Campbell, in his "Declaration and Address," emphasized the need to return to the Bible as the basis of Christian unity. His son, Alexander, further declared the need for close adherence to the Bible during the early years of the *Christian Baptist.* He called for pure speech, i.e., the very words of the Bible. The early restorers believed the Bible could be understood by all, including the common man. No need existed for creeds, such as the Nicene, or confessions, including the Westminster.

Even though most early nineteenth-century American religious fellowships accepted the Bible as the inspired word of God, none could match the Disciples in emphasizing close adherence to the Scriptures. Asking the religious world to give up their creeds and confessions, the people of the Restoration based their emphasis totally on the Bible. As the century progressed, this conservative thrust became more pronounced among Disciples as more liberal attitudes developed toward the Scriptures. Conservative Disciples, especially those who emerged as churches of Christ, continued the heritage of Campbell's *Christian Baptist* days. When publication of the *Fundamentals,* a series of books written by conservative biblical scholars, began in 1910, many in churches of Christ could share much of what they read in the first and subsequent eleven volumes.

In the same year, the Presbyterian General Assembly issued a statement of "essential" doctrines:

1. The inerrancy of Scripture
2. The virgin birth of Christ
3. His substitutionary atonement
4. His bodily resurrection
5. The authenticity of the miracles

With these statements churches of Christ had little argument. Although premillennialism later replaced the statement on miracles, there remained a general agreement that the liberal thrusts of twentieth-century modernism were dangerous.

With so much in common, it would seem that fellowship should have been pursued between churches of Christ and the fundamentalists. There were, however, at least four areas where churches of Christ were unable to share fellowship. First, since fundamentalism was a marriage of a premillennial-dispensationalist emphasis with the Calvinism of conservative Presbyterianism, any formal fellowship was impossible. The Restoration Movement—from the early days of Stone and then the Campbells—has always been strongly non-Calvinistic. Thus, to openly fellowship fundamentalism would require denial of the belief in man's free will.

Second, premillennialism has never been accepted generally in the Restoration Movement and churches of Christ. One of the bitterest doctrinal battles within churches of Christ was the premillennial conflict that began in 1914 and continued through the 1940s. An important cause for the breakdown in unity talks with Independent Christian churches during the 1930s was the possible leaning of many of the participants toward premillennialism. Congregations that accept premillennialism remain separated from the larger non-premillennial groups among churches of Christ, as they have been since the 1930s.

In the third place, even though the fundamentalists emphasized the inerrancy of Scripture—principally to uphold their prophetic interpretations—they often engaged in Wesleyan pietistic revivalism, as developed by John Wesley in the eighteenth century. Revivalists such as Dwight Moody, Billy Sunday, and Billy Graham have never featured specific doctrinal positions, except the basic five points enunciated by the fundamentalists. Rarely were millennial views expressed. Their sermons emphasized few great doctrines, containing instead lessons on drunkenness, worldly amusements, theater attendance, disrespect for parents, and the need to separate one's self from the world. Moody, in all his revivals, denounced four great temptations: 1) the theater, 2) disregard of the Sabbath, 3) Sunday newspapers, and 4) atheistic teachings, including evolution. Never was there a strong emphasis on the church.

Fourth, the most distinctive characteristic of the Restoration Movement was the call to restore the primitive New Testament church in the nineteenth century. Rather than join in this appeal for the restoration of the first-century church, most mainline religious groups call for a return to the Reformation heritage of Martin Luther, Ulrich Zwingli, and John Calvin. Others within the fundamentalist fellowship, such as those who focus on the Holy Spirit or heightened eschatology, tend to highlight just one such major idea that seemed to be a part of first-century Christianity. Rarely in history has such a large fellowship as the Restoration movement called for a return to the primitive church of the New Testament. Thus within American history the Disciples movement was and is unique.

Because of this call to restore the church in its totality, there was little room to fellowship any group that did not share this emphasis on the doctrines of the New Testament. At times, therefore, churches of Christ have had to face the charge of believing that they alone compose the true church. The real emphasis was always on the call for all churches to abandon their creeds, confessions, and traditions and become simply the church of the New Testament. Alexander Campbell made that plea during the early years of the Restoration Movement. After 1830 he encouraged individuals to leave the fellowship of denominations and become simply New Testament Christians. That same call has remained rather constant among churches of Christ well through the twentieth century.

Alexander Campbell set the stage for this emphasis during the first years of the *Christian Baptist*. In a series of articles titled "The Ancient Order of Things," [2] he introduced a method whereby a person could understand New Testament doctrine, especially as it related to order in the church. Using the Baconian inductive method, he showed that baptism by immersion was the mode practiced in the New Testament. Through the same method he proved to the satisfaction of Disciples in the nineteenth and twentieth centuries the need to observe the Lord's Supper each Lord's Day. Thus using the slogan "Speak where the Scriptures speak; and be silent where the Scriptures are silent," conservative Disciples developed doctrinal positions on the issues of baptism, the Lord's Supper, instrumental music, leadership in the church, the role of women in public worship, and many other issues considered important. If the Bible, they argued, did not specifically command something, that practice should not exist in the church.

The result was that churches of Christ would not base fellowship simply on the five doctrinal positions adopted by conservative Presbyterians or on these positions as they were changed and accepted by the premillennial fundamentalists. Opposition to liberal theology is still shared by churches of Christ and fundamentalists, but a different understanding of doctrine has never allowed fellowship with fundamentalists groups. The two groups simply shared many parallel views in opposition to the increasing influence of liberalism in twentieth-century America.

Post-Civil War religious liberalism was a constant concern of David Lipscomb and other conservatives within the Restoration Movement. The liberalism that would allow the missionary society and the instrument in worship was not the same as the higher criticism of the late nineteenth century, but Lipscomb and his associates believed one easily led to the other. A loose interpretation of Scripture would ultimately undermine a strict acceptance of biblical requirements for the church.

CHURCHES OF CHRIST AND HIGHER CRITICISM

Except for the work done by John W. McGarvey and Hall L. Calhoun, little formal scholarship dealing with higher criticism was available among churches of Christ. Not until 1935 did A. N. Trice and Charles Roberson publish their *Bible vs. Modernism.* They divided their study into two sections: the documentary hypothesis (higher criticism) and Darwinism. Included in the book were discussions of Sigmund Freud and Immanuel Kant, two men the authors believed had undermined belief in the Bible as the inspired word of God. Freud's theory, for instance, is "directly opposed to chastity and virtue and is hostile to the Bible doctrine of temperance and self-control, especially as regards sexual passions, which it claimed should be given free reins and unrestricted license." [3]

Higher criticism thrust its attack at Christianity's very heart, the Bible. In response to the documentary hypothesis, fundamentalists and other Bible-believing groups, including churches of Christ, defended the Bible by declaring its inerrancy. Moreover, Darwinism early became the focus of the controversy because it became the vehicle of higher criticism, especially when the developmental nature of religion was the issue. Average churchgoers did not understand higher criticism or the relationship of the documentary hypothesis and Darwin. They did understand, however, attacks on biblical accounts of creation and man's beginnings.

CHURCHES OF CHRIST AND DARWINISM

By focusing on the Bible, liberal religionists attacked the very core of nineteenth-century religion. For instance, they doubted the biblical account of creation; in its stead they substituted an evolutionary theory. Miracles became myth; the story of Jonah and the great fish was just an allegory. Concern mounted among conservative churches when publishers included Darwinism in college textbooks; concern was even greater when high school science texts introduced evolution to younger children.

As Darwinism became even more intense and widespread, various journals among churches of Christ editorialized against its "infidelity." In Texas, G. H. P. Showalter, editor of the *Firm Foundation,* wrote: "The theory of Mr. Darwin set forth in his 'Origin of Species' and 'Descent of Man' cannot possibly be made to harmonize with the Mosaic account of man's origin as set forth in the book of Genesis." To more fully focus his position, Showalter concluded: "There is no rational stopping place between wholehearted Biblism on the one hand and whole-hearted infidelity on the other."[4] Over the next several years, the *Firm Foundation* published many articles on the issue. In 1922, Showalter took the position that most conservatives occupied: "The Bible does not contradict true science. It is in perfect harmony with it, and every scientific 'discovery' that has yet been made may be shown to be in perfect harmony with the Bible."[5]

Sharing the same position, William B. Riley, a leading fundamentalist and millionaire Minneapolis minister, wrote: "Those of us who represent Christianity have (no) quarrel with science. . . . Christianity like all truth, is not tolerant of error, and it will not harmonize with this pseudo science,—this utterly false philosophy."[6] The same views were held by J. Gresham Machen and William Jennings Bryan, non-premillennialists, but leaders in the fundamentalist movement.

Even before the Scopes' "monkey" trial, William Jennings Bryan was a hero to America's religious conservatives. In 1922, A. B. Lipscomb penned a lengthy article extolling the virtues of Bryan as a defender of the Bible. Especially praised was his refusal to run for the United States Senate in order to give increased time to more important issues such as the passage of legislation to outlaw the teaching of the theory of evolution. Lipscomb concluded the article: "Thank God for Bryan!"[7]

After legislation passed the Oklahoma and Florida assemblies in 1923, the legislatures of Mississippi and Arkansas accepted anti-evolution laws in 1926 and 1927, respectively. The most visible law, however, passed the Tennessee legislature in 1925: "An Act prohibiting the teaching of the evolution theory in all the Universities, Normals, and all other public schools of Tennessee." Some Tennesseans, including a few preachers, opposed the passage of the bill. F. W. Smith of the *Gospel Advocate* applauded the Baptists for urging Governor Austin Peay to sign the new legislation.[8]

John Scopes, a young science teacher at Dayton, Tennessee, challenged Tennessee's anti-evolution law. He stood trial on the charge of violating the law. It was not to be just an ordinary trial in a small rural Tennessee town. Clarence Darrow, the famous trial lawyer, came south to defend Scopes. William Jennings Bryan, the author of Florida's law, former Secretary of State, and former candidate for President of the United States, championed fundamentalism's defense of the Bible against evolution. Covered by newspapers from all over the globe and by the new medium, radio, the trial inspired an unprecedented reaction. Within a few days, two million words were written and spoken in Dayton and were transmitted around the world.[9]

From Nashville, the editor of the *Gospel Advocate,* James A. Allen, covered all the proceedings. Totally involved in Dayton events, he preached each night for the local church. Beginning weeks before the trial, whole pages in the *Advocate* displayed discussions of evolution. Bryan was the subject of several articles, including one by F. W. Smith, who believed Bryan's views on evolution caused his defeat as moderator of the Presbyterian church.[10]

The trial that made Dayton a circus town ended. Even though most media reports indicated that Darrow had bested Bryan, the jury found John Scopes guilty of breaking a state law. William Jennings Bryan, overwhelmed by Dayton's July heat, died suddenly, eclipsing Scopes' conviction. Reporting his death in the *Advocate*, Smith wrote: "I have frequently said publicly and privately that William Jennings Bryan was doing the greatest work against infidelity of any living man."[11] The sarcasm and slurs directed at Bryan by Darrow concerned Smith. He was, indeed, a hero to all believers in an inerrant Bible.

In a private letter to Smith, M. C. Kurfees wrote of Bryan:

> My soul is overwhelmed with grief and sorrow this morning. In my humble judgment, no man could have been taken just now from the public life of the world who would have left a wider or sadder vacancy.

Smith could not refrain from praising Bryan the man and his work in defending Christianity:

> When Clarence Darrow and Dudley Field Malone's names shall have faded from the mein, William Jennings Bryan's name will shine on as a man who dared to stand up before the infidels of the world in defense of the Bible.[12]

Writers and evangelists among churches of Christ agreed with most fundamentalists in their opposition to Darwinism. E. A. Elam, in the introduction to *The Bible Versus Theories of Evolution,* penned a statement familiar to pre-Darwin science based on Bacon's inductive reasoning:

> Science is accepted, systematized, and classified knowledge. With no facts and no knowledge of facts, there can be no science or philosophy. Real science is true. . . .
> There is no conflict between the Bible and science. The theories of men about the teaching of the Bible and their theories about science, differ the width of the heavens. The conflict is

between their theories of the teaching of the Bible and the teaching of science.[13]

The writers included in Elam's book were leaders among churches of Christ in Tennessee and Texas: H. Leo Boles, F. W. Smith, A. N. Trice, A. G. Freed, Batsell Baxter, A. B. Barrett, H. L. Calhoun, C. R. Nichol, Charles P. Poole, and James A. Allen. Two chapters were from David Lipscomb's writings.

Boles' article, "Evolution—What is it?" is representative and shows the close agreement of these writers with the fundamentalists. All commentators in the compilation emphasized the theoretical nature of evolution. A problem arises, declared Boles, when *"mere teachers* of a science" classify evolution as fact. Why do church people, asked Boles, oppose Darwinism?

> In the analysis of this theory we find that it is godless. It originated in heathen philosophy. It began long before Christ made his advent into the world, and is, therefore, Christless. I do not mean to say that all who believe the theory are godless and have no faith in Christ, but certainly, the theory excludes Christianity.[14]

Furthermore, Boles asserted, "when the theory is carried by its advocates and admirers into the realm of morality and spirituality, then it does its worst."

Emphasizing his strong reliance on the Bible as basic to all life, Boles stated the Bible believer's position with boldness:

> Man can only speculate and exercise an uninformed imagination on this point [creation]. Yet the vain imagination of man forms the only basis that man has for the theory of evolution. "God created the heavens and the earth." That settles the matter for all who believe the Bible. He created all things that are upon the earth and gave life unto them. All life came from him. "In him was life." He is the source of all life, as he is the Creator of all things. No theory of man based on human imagination can rob God of the honor of creation; neither can the theory of evolution nullify the simple statements recorded in Genesis. Everything stated in the early part of Genesis expresses and impresses the one grand fact that God is supreme over all; that he is the absolute Architect of the universe; that by the power of his word he created all things and that his wisdom has directed all things. As has been seen, the theory of

evolution deposes Jehovah from his throne and would rob him of infinite plan and purpose. The Bible exalts Jehovah; evolution slanders and debases him.[15]

Agreeing that attacks on biblical Christianity centered in the documentary hypothesis of German higher criticism, and Darwinism, writers among churches of Christ responded with the same basic beliefs and arguments as the mainstream fundamentalists. Not only did Boles quote from many of the current works on evolution, he also made use of *Darwin's Descent of Man,* three of William Jennings Bryan's books—*In His Image, Is the Bible True?* and *The Bible and Its Enemies*—and volumes seven and eight of *The Fundamentals.*

A strong reaction to Darwin and evolution continued to be an important topic of discussion among churches of Christ. A survey of the Abilene Christian University Lectureships, beginning in 1918, shows fellowship-wide concern. Until 1964, more than a dozen lectures dealt with evolution. W. L. Oliphant, in 1926, spoke on the subject, "The Bible and Science."[16] Evolution, he said, is only an attempt to explain origins on naturalistic grounds. Most often, the ACU lecturers shared the fundamentalist argument that evolution is only a theory, not a proven fact. Other lecturers attempted to harmonize the Bible and science. Dewitt Chadwick stated in 1938: "I have no quarrel with science. More power to science!. . . I accept every conclusion scientifically arrived at. I do not accept as truth mere guesses, hypotheses, or theories."[17]

CHURCHES OF CHRIST AND PREMILLENNIALISM

The same wedge, millennial theories, that eventually divided the mainstream fundamentalists became an important theme among churches of Christ during the first half of the twentieth century. Even though premillennialism, a belief in the thousand-year reign of Jesus on the earth, dominated one major thrust of fundamentalism, it was not a significant part of the battle with modernism, a term used interchangeably with liberalism. Modernism was a greater issue than premillennialism.

Fundamentalism was a tenuous movement at best, never sharply defined. The holiness, premillennial, and other conservative religious movements joined forces to do battle with mod-

ernism. The events of Dayton, Tennessee, however, caused fundamentalism to be ridiculed. Such writers as H. L. Mencken continued to direct an acid pen against fundamentalism in general and
William Jennings Bryan in particular, even though he was de-
ceased. The fundamentalists began to disintegrate.
Nonmillennialists held their former friends at arm's length.
Especially was this true of the most outstanding of the conservative Presbyterians, J. Gresham Machen, author of *Christianity and
Liberalism.*

Among churches of Christ, the battle over premillennialism became the dominant theme during the 1920s, 1930s, and into the
1940s. Open premillennial views had never dominated the nineteenth-century Disciples. Alexander Campbell was strong in his
condemnation of William Miller's premillennial views in the
1840s.[18] There were occasional articles in journals of the
Restoration Movement with speculative views on the millennial
dawn or some other aspect of Christ's second coming, but not until
early twentieth century were the ideas held by a definable group.
Robert H. Boll of Louisville, Kentucky, front-page writer of the
Gospel Advocate and a graduate of the Nashville Bible School, introduced the ideas into the *Advocate* as early as 1909.[19] By 1915
he openly stated that Christ's kingdom had not been established
and that the coming of Christ was imminent. Quickly, other
Advocate writers took exception to Boll's positions.

Thus began a controversy that would divide churches of Christ
for thirty years. The premillennial group was never large, but various individuals of the persuasion constantly agitated for debate.
Whether a person or church or school or paper had premillennial
tendencies was a constant concern and even a test of fellowship. A
more detailed discussion of the controversy can be found in the
following chapters.

Growing interest in premillennialism in churches of Christ paralleled the emphasis among fundamentalist groups. Because so
many of the philosophical views critical of the Bible originated in
Germany, some saw World War I as God's means of destroying
Germany and having Christ return to establish his kingdom. Thus,
Boll considered Jesus' statement, "I come quickly," as a recognition of the world conflict to precede the return—a view Boll
shared with all premillennialists. Although the 1920s saw an at-

tempt to maintain fellowship, by 1934 any attempt at rapprochement became suspect by many nonpremillennialists.

Even though churches of Christ shared many of the same interests, even biblical positions of fundamentalists, they were not mainstream fundamentalists. Except for the premillennial group among them, churches of Christ chose to follow a separate road in 1906, isolating themselves from the religious happenings around them. This emphasis or distinction became even more pronounced during the 1920s and the 1930s. The reason was quite simple—at least to churches of Christ. Their plea was a nondenominational call to return to the New Testament idea of the church. They could make no room for emphasis upon union with other religious movements, regardless of common interests.

GROWTH OF CHURCHES OF CHRIST

Though the Bible emphasizes that few will find the narrow way to heaven, American religious groups typically have counted all the people who identify with them. Growth in numbers has always been desirable. Churches of Christ easily adopted this customary practice. The census of 1906, under the leadership of J. W. Shepherd, counted 159,658 members of churches of Christ. The vast majority were in the southern states, from Tennessee west to Texas. By 1916, the figure grew to 317,937, and to 433,714 in 1926. During the same time period, the number of congregations increased from 2,649 to 6,226. Churches of Christ, from every indication, steadily gained strength in numbers during the first third of the twentieth century.

Growth among conservative Disciples throughout the nineteenth century was strongest in rural areas. David Lipscomb urged a strong emphasis on rural churches because, as he recognized, country dwellers would eventually move to the county seats and then on to the growing towns and cities, taking their religion with them. Thus, the twentieth century has been characterized by growing urban churches and the decline of rural churches, many of them killed by the lure of the cities and employment. The changing character of churches only mirrored the demographic changes happening throughout the southern states. Cities such as Atlanta, Memphis, Louisville, Dallas, Houston, and Nashville were passing the 100,000 population figure by the early twentieth century. With the movement of people from the hinterland to the cities, it was only natural that urban churches would participate in the growth. The urban church became a reality among churches of Christ.

In most southern cities, the oldest and largest Disciple churches usually followed the more liberal developments. As an example, the two largest churches of the Restoration Movement in Nashville, Vine Street and Woodland Street, followed the progressive pattern of churches in other cities even before the turn of the century. The Christian Church in Memphis was the first in Tennessee to accept the organ as a part of worship.[20] The development of urban churches of Christ came much later. Most of the growth of conservative Disciples resulted from the rural to urban movement of members who did not engage in the liberal/conservative conflicts of the 1890s.

In Nashville, a strong evangelistic outreach began in the 1880s. Through the preaching of James A. Harding and a host of lesser-known men who often worked at secular jobs during the day and preached in the evenings, congregations flourished in various parts of Tennessee's capital city. Beginning with the College Street church in South Nashville, members "swarmed" throughout the city. By 1900, eighteen congregations, with 4,500 members, existed in Nashville.[21] By 1939, when the *Gospel Advocate* devoted a special issue to the church in Nashville, the count had reached sixty-five congregations in Davidson County.[22] The growth in Nashville can be attributed first to the work of David Lipscomb and his associates as they preached throughout the city; second, the impact of the Nashville Bible School, founded in 1891; and third, the Hardeman Tabernacle Sermons, the first series preached in 1922.

What happened in conservative congregations in Nashville happened much more slowly in other cities. Memphis churches trace their beginnings to the early twentieth century and the Halbert Avenue church. The O. D. Bearden family moved from Nashville to Atlanta in 1902 to establish the first congregation following the division among the Disciples. Although Birmingham is not typical of older southern cities, the major thrust of churches of Christ in that city can be traced to the influence of John T. Lewis. He moved to Birmingham shortly after graduating from the Nashville Bible School. A congregation had formed by late nineteenth century in Chattanooga, after the missionary society organized in that city during 1890.

Throughout Texas, churches of Christ were stronger in the rural areas than in the developing cities. The Disciples of Christ were more numerous in the urban areas. On the other hand, in counties without large towns, churches of Christ dominated.[23]

Writing in 1920, G. H. P. Showalter, editor of the *Firm Foundation,* recalled the lack of strength of urban churches in 1902. He told of one weak church in Fort Worth, one in Dallas, a small group meeting in San Antonio, and a small church in Austin, the home of the *Firm Foundation.* Houston and Galveston did not have congregations. In 1920 he reported seven churches in Fort Worth with 2,000 members, five congregations in Dallas, four in Houston, two in San Antonio, and a large church in Austin.[24] By 1940 there were sixty-five churches in these same cities.[25]

Though evangelism dominated churches in these cities, the typical growth pattern of southern urban churches, as earlier suggested, was a rural-to-urban movement. Many of the city churches kept much of their rural orientation. One change, however, emerged: There was greater demand for full-time preachers—in all cities except Nashville. In 1919, Showalter reported that all four churches in Houston had full-time preachers—G. A. Dunn at Central, Oscar Smith at Houston Heights, Early Arceneaux at Spring Street, and W. C. Wilson at Magnolia Park. Seeing preachers as keys to evangelizing the cities, the *Firm Foundation* editor called for more full-time preachers.[26]

In 1922, an event mentioned earlier gave tremendous impetus to churches of Christ in Nashville and throughout the South. The Nashville churches, working in concert, sponsored N. B. Hardeman of Henderson, Tennessee, in a series of city-wide meetings. Overflow crowds jammed Ryman Auditorium at noon and in the evenings to hear Hardeman. Never had anything focused on the plea of churches of Christ to return to the New Testament pattern of worship and Christian unity as did these meetings. Texas brethren, impressed by the results, began calling for similar meetings in their cities.

By 1920, interest began developing in cities outside the southern region of the United States. The only city in the North with a sizable membership in churches of Christ previous to 1920 was Indianapolis, Indiana. Overall, the work in the Midwest, led by Daniel Sommer, remained overwhelmingly rural. Showalter described the work in St. Louis as "a few brethren struggling against great odds."[27] In 1921 a small group began meeting in New York City.[28] At the same time, both the *Gospel Advocate* and the *Firm Foundation* were urging brethren to support the building program of the small church in Washington, D. C.[29] The church in Chicago was meeting on the eighteenth floor of an office building.

Urban development was a new concern among churches of Christ. During the years between the Civil War and 1900, David Lipscomb had urged young men to remain on the farm. Jobs were not readily available in Nashville and temptation was much more prevalent in the city. But in 1904, Lipscomb emphasized what the urban church should do to reach the unchurched, especially among the poorer classes. He observed:

> He [the teacher] will find the poorer and humbler classes of the community more approachable and more open to receive his teaching than what are regarded as higher classes. They are the better class to begin with, too. They more readily act. Then, it makes a good impression on other classes to see one interested in helping and saving the lost and the outcasts. It is much easier to burn a pile of logs by kindling the fire at the bottom than at the top. So communities can be leavened and molded better and more effectually by beginning at the bottom and working upward.[30]

He added: "If persons will go to our cities in this earnest spirit, follow up the ways suggested, be earnest in seeking the salvation of all, almost anyone can succeed among the people." His suggestions worked. Churches of Christ grew more rapidly in Nashville than in any other city of the United States, mainly because they met the needs of people. Even as late as 1945, this growth occurred despite few full-time preachers filling the pulpits of Nashville churches.

CHURCHES OF CHRIST AND BENEVOLENCE

Because of, or concurrent with, the development of the urban church, churches of Christ began reaching into several areas of concern. The 1910s and the 1920s saw the establishing of homes for orphans and, in Nashville, a home for the aged. Nowhere did city churches become as involved with the physical needs of its citizens as did two churches in Nashville. The impact of two men—A. M. Burton and J. C. McQuiddy—can be seen in the work of the Central church in downtown Nashville and the Russell Street church in East Nashville.[31]

An associate of David Lipscomb since the 1880s when he joined the *Advocate* as business manager, McQuiddy led Russell Street in an outreach program. Noticing the suffering in Europe at the outbreak of World War I, McQuiddy stated: "The need and suffering in Europe are no doubt appalling. There are thousands of people who need help in our own country. We should spend what we can, and also to teach our children to do likewise, to clothe the naked and feed the hungry."[32] A. M. Burton, a businessman and the major force behind the establishment of the Central church in 1925, voiced the same concern.

Russell Street continued McQuiddy's emphasis on helping the poor and the hungry. Nashville, like the rest of the nation in 1918, faced difficult times when struck by the influenza epidemic. The hospitals filled to overflowing. The Russell Street church made its building into a makeshift hospital "for the relief of the poor and friendless sufferers in Nashville." [33] One physician gave his services, and the church furnished a nurse for the duration of the epidemic. Yet not until 1926 did the Russell Street church become totally involved in its outreach program. Especially concerned about proper care for expectant mothers and their children, the church established a day-care center. A sick ward for the poor was added. Milk was available through the Russell Street church clinic for undernourished children of the community. Doctors and dentists gave their services to staff the clinic. S. H. Hall, the preacher for the church, wrote: "We want the hospital to meet every need here, and especially of the poor in all East Nashville or the nearby sections of the county.[34]

The Central church began for the specific purpose of serving both the spiritual and physical needs of Nashville's citizens. Even before the congregation organized, the leaders purchased property for outreach—evidently through the urging and generosity of A. M. Burton. Burton stated the philosophy behind the program at Central:

> True religion and practical Christianity is a matter of faith and works, of profession and performance, of theory and practice.

It ministers to the body, mind, and spirit. True religion is a religion of faith, hope, and love; the religion of holiness and righteousness; the religion that prays for and works for the doing of the will of God on earth, here and now, as it is done in heaven.[35]

Burton told of the involvement of the Central members in the program that functioned seven days each week. Included was a day-care center for the children of working mothers, medical and dental care for the needy, food for the hungry, a nurse for every emergency. The church furnished lodging for those who could not provide for themselves. Such elementary needs as a drinking fountain, showers, and lavatories were provided for the guests of the church. Those with special clothing needs had access to a clothing room. The church helped the unemployed to find work. The entire community had an invitation to attend a noon worship each day. Those who could not attend in person could listen by radio, first over WDAD and then WLAC, a station connected with Burton's Life and Casualty Insurance Company of Tennessee.

The secular press joined the church leaders in telling the entire nation of Central's program. Reporting the sordid surroundings of the area around Central's building, the St. Louis *Post-Dispatch* recorded: "Then came this congregation of good people. They believed that the church should be where the multitudes are, and are going to do their best to make the actual spirit of the Man of Galilee a living thing in their community."[36] Ira A. Douthitt, a preacher, stated: "I sat daily . . . and saw carried out, not in theory, but in practice, New Testament Christianity. . . . I have never seen anything quite so much like the Jerusalem church in reality as is the work of this congregation."[37] J. D. Tant, a rough, Texas, frontier-type preacher, criticized churches of Christ for not reaching out in the manner of the Salvation Army. He then added: "I am glad that Brother A. M. Burton . . . sees the necessity of a daily church and is working toward that line. I am glad that Brother Burton is not a preacher, else I fear he would be dropped from the preacher ring for suggesting such a change in our practice."[38]

CONCLUSION

By the middle of the 1930s, churches of Christ had become a fellowship that attracted great attention in various parts of the

United States. Of course, the greatest membership remained in the historically predominant areas—Tennessee, Arkansas, North Alabama, Southern Kentucky, Oklahoma, and Texas. Besides these areas, conservative influences remained significant in the Midwest, where the ideas of Daniel Sommer and the *American Christian Review* dominated. During the late nineteenth century, James A. Harding preached in the Detroit area, establishing a strong conservative base. Early in the century, graduates of the Nashville Bible School planted the seed for future growth in the Los Angeles area.

Churches of Christ cannot be fully understood by simply comparing them with conservative churches on one hand and contrasting them with liberal denominations on the other. To know the churches of Christ more completely requires an in-depth study of the ideas, attitudes, conflicts, and men who shaped the movement.

CHAPTER 4

A SEARCH FOR DIRECTION—1906-1930:
N. B. Hardeman and Sarah Andrews

The natural flow of history from ancient times to the present has always been change—sometimes dramatic, sometimes ordinary—from one century to the next. Historians search for these changes, which often involve conflict. Within these changes and conflicts, the search for direction takes place. Notice, for instance, the impact the Greek victory over the Persians had on subsequent Greek history. Likewise, note how Luther's nailing of the Ninety-five Theses on the Wittenburg church door influenced Western civilization. The Industrial Revolution was also characterized by tremendous change. It fostered political and philosophical changes that continue to influence the twentieth century.

The era of the late nineteenth and early twentieth century was one of those important periods of change. The United States became one of the world's three major industrial nations. For the first time, she could not remain aloof from the concerns of Europe and the world. Even though he campaigned on the theme "He kept you out of the war," Woodrow Wilson in 1917 declared war on Germany and the Central Powers. It was a new direction for the United States.

Religion, as noted in previous chapters, did not escape change. In fact, American religion changed more explosively than other areas of life. With the rise of liberalism late in the 1800s, the nation watched as religious wars raged through the first quarter of the twentieth century. Fundamentalism suffered an overwhelming defeat at the Scopes' trial in 1925, but liberalism was empty—it offered nothing of substance to the people. It succumbed to a new theological direction labeled *neoorthodoxy.* American religion was not well; it needed direction.

What happened in religion nationally was reflected on a much smaller scale within the Disciples of Christ. Even though many, including David Lipscomb, could not see clearly all the directions the Disciples were taking, by 1900 there were at least three major thrusts within the larger movement. In 1906, churches of Christ, through Lipscomb, declared themselves to be a different group from the larger body of Disciples. Yet, within that larger group, a cauldron boiled, leading to an open break in 1927. Indeed, within all segments of the Restoration Movement, there was a search for direction.

Traveling by oneself can be lonely, and directions are not as easily found if other seekers are not along for comparison. This is not to suggest that churches of Christ became lost in the loneliness of their conviction. But since they no longer considered the liberal Disciples a part of the same movement and because concern with the religious left continued, for the most part, churches of Christ were alone in many of their convictions. Thus, they launched out into an open sea, neither as a part of the fundamentalist movement nor as proponents of liberal theology.

The time frame of this chapter, 1906-1930, was characterized by a major search for direction among churches of Christ. Many who had been leaders in the long struggle against liberalism within the Restoration movement would die during this period. The greatest loss was David Lipscomb, whose death occurred on November 11, 1917. For many years the question had loomed: Who would inherit David Lipscomb's mantle? A host of men were available, but none had been through the half-century of change involving every facet of American life. Besides Lipscomb, death took J. C. McQuiddy, James A. Harding, E. A. Elam, E. G. Sewell, T. B. Larimore, and Lipscomb's Texas counterpoint, Austin McGary.

But every generation provides representatives to walk in the shoes of those departed. Along with those already mentioned in previous chapters must be added H. Leo Boles, president of David Lipscomb College on two different occasions; R. H. Boll, the leader in the premillennial movement within churches of Christ; G. H. P. Showalter, editor of the *Firm Foundation* and a great advocate of evangelical outreach; and Hall Calhoun, who left the Disciples in 1925 to follow more comfortably the directions plotted by churches of Christ. The black church had one of the outstanding evangelists of all time, Marshall Keeble.

In order to develop clearly the directions explored by churches of Christ from 1906 to 1930, two individuals—N. B. Hardeman and Sarah Andrews—illustrate major thrusts of the era.

N. B. Hardeman represents two important developments. First, his work as an educator shows the importance of schools to churches of Christ. Second, the Hardeman Tabernacle Sermons, beginning in 1922, focused on the outreach of the church in Nashville. Like nothing before, these meetings gave direction to churches of Christ.

Representative of those who carried the gospel to foreign countries during this era is Sarah Andrews. Miss Andrews literally spent her entire adult life in Japan, remaining even during the years of World War II. Since the Great Commission required each generation to share the gospel with the world, evangelization at home and abroad was extremely important to churches of Christ. Having opposed the missionary society movement, it became imperative for churches of Christ to develop their own methods for supporting missionaries. They were determined to accept the biblical imperative for evangelism without abandoning biblical methodology.

FURTHER DIVISION AMONG DISCIPLES

Acquaintances long cherished are not easily abandoned. Scribes within churches of Christ could not turn their backs totally on the Disciples, whether they were readers of the more liberal *Christian-Evangelist* or the moderate *Christian Standard,* which had now become involved in the issues. As 1909 approached, many among the Disciples wished to celebrate the centennial of Thomas Campbell's "Declaration and Address." Pittsburgh, Pennsylvania, was the site for the mass gathering. But as soon as the centennial was announced and committees formed to plan the program, a major controversy erupted. The General Centennial Committee selected forty speakers for the convention. One speaker, Herbert L.

Willett, became the focus of controversy. A longtime writer for the *Christian-Evangelist,* he was proposed and backed by the liberal element among Disciples. The conservatives opposed him adamantly.

In Nashville, the *Advocate* watched the argument with interest. Having opposed Willett from his first association with the University of Chicago, David Lipscomb felt much closer to the *Christian Standard* in this particular argument. In November 1908, one year before the centennial, Lipscomb copied two long columns of comments by *Standard* readers applauding the stance of the Cincinnati-based paper. Since the 1902 convention, when the federation issue was uppermost in the minds of the Disciples, the *Standard* had questioned the concept of the missionary society. Now, in 1908, Lipscomb could say:

> A truism we must learn is that service in all human organizations must lead away from God; service in divine institutions must lead closer to God. All service in human societies will lead away from God; all service in the true church of God will lead us closer to God.[1]

Shortly before the centennial convention began, Lipscomb penned a short article summarizing his understanding of the basis of Christian unity:

> A man in spiritual and eternal matters ought to stand on safe and solid ground. He ought in religion, above all else, to seek solid ground on which he will stand. A person can do this without doubt or uncertainty.

He then illustrated his positions with a number of current issues: (1) Faith saves. Lipscomb responded: "If faith will save a man, a faith that works through love and leads one to show his faith in Christ by being baptized into Christ will not destroy his salvation." (2) The Lord's Supper—"No one believes partaking of the Supper will injure or interfere with the salvation of others. All may safely partake of the Supper every 'Lord's day.'" (3) Instrumental music—"All may worship without the organ. This is safe ground." (4) The annual missionary society meeting that would take place during the following month in Cincinnati—"No one doubts we may all work through the church. This is safe ground on which all may stand." [2]

Following the centennial celebration, M. C. Kurfees titled an article "Professor Willett and His Sympathizers Triumphant." He criticized the *Christian Standard* for even attending the celebration. Already, the *Standard* believed the convention's actions directly and openly endorsed Willett's heresy. He scolded:

> Cannot our brethren of the *Christian Standard* see the wrong in all of this? They loudly protested against the federation movement, but the *Christian-Evangelist* and the *Christian Century* side in the contest carried the day. In the recent fight against the Willett sympathizers they made an equally loud protest, backed by a multitude of supporters; but in the final issue the *Standard* had nothing to do but take off its hat, bow to the victors, and go to the Centennial with Mr. Willett on the programme. "What shall the harvest be?"[3]

A second division within the Disciples now appeared inevitable.

Less than ten years later, the issue surfaced at the College of the Bible in Lexington, Kentucky. By 1917, only six years after J. W. McGarvey's death, a struggle arose as to who would control the school. From every indication, McGarvey had picked Hall L. Calhoun to succeed him as president of the College of the Bible. But by 1917, the liberal element of the Disciples had gained control. M. C. Kurfees, a former McGarvey student and a graduate of the College of the Bible, noticed the controversy in the *Gospel Advocate*. Calhoun had voiced his positions through the *Christian Standard*. His major contention was that the professors at the college were teaching higher criticism. Of the situation, Kurfees wrote:

> It is almost inconceivable that such a situation should arise at the very seat of learning so recently occupied by that brilliant and lovable trio—Graham, Grubbs, and McGarvey, the last named of whom chose, as his specialty, the higher criticism of the Bible, and devoted the last twenty years of his life to an unceasing and telling battle against destructive criticism.[4]

With no place to turn, Calhoun resigned from the College of the Bible and accepted a position on the faculty of Bethany College. Evidently, he planned to spend the remainder of his life at Campbell's school. His conscience, however, would not allow him to remain within the ranks of the Disciples of Christ. Thus, in 1925, he announced his decision to turn from the divisive issues of the society and instrumental music and join ranks with churches of Christ. He accepted a position with N. B. Hardeman at Freed-Hardeman College in Henderson, Tennessee. After one year at Henderson, he moved to Nashville where he filled the pulpit for a number of churches, including Belmont and Central. He died in 1935.

Similarly, F. W. Smith noticed through the *Advocate* in late 1927 that the conservative Christian churches had met in a separate conference in Indianapolis. During the Memphis convention in 1926, a rather large delegation had decided they could no longer associate with the United Christian Missionary Society. Noticing what had been written in the *Christian Standard* as the reason for the Indianapolis convention—"to take care of what the brethren term 'our plea' "—Smith could not comprehend what had really been accomplished by the separate convention. Critical of the convention, Smith wrote: "This business of 'our plea' was born of the denominational idea, and it is nothing more than a denominational slogan. What all should desire . . . is the New Testament plea *stripped of every semblance of denominationalism.*"[5]

N. B. HARDEMAN'S PLACE AMONG CHURCHES OF CHRIST

For fifty-two years the name David Lipscomb had been synonymous with the conservative Restoration plea. When Lipscomb died at age eighty-six, his death marked the end of an era. A number of his younger associates would continue his emphasis for several years, but other men of a new generation began to exert their influence within the fellowship of churches of Christ.

For instance, in Texas, G. H. P. Showalter edited the *Firm Foundation*. Graduates of the Nashville Bible School, such as C. R. Nichol and R. L. Whiteside, had gone to Texas where they carried on important evangelistic work. In Nashville, H. Leo Boles was president of the Nashville Bible School, renamed David Lipscomb College in 1918.

In West Tennessee, two men were gaining prominence as a result of their preaching, debating, and school work. Located in Henderson, A. G. Freed and N. B. Hardeman were destined to have a tremendous impact upon churches of Christ, especially in the search for direction following 1906. Particularly was this true of Nicholas Brodie Hardeman, whose work in education, preaching, and debating was unmatched during the 1920s and 1930s.

On May 18, 1959, almost 800 persons gathered at Memphis's Peabody Hotel to honor N. B. Hardeman on his eighty-fifth birthday.[6] As the various speakers recalled the events of his life, the story of one of the most influential men within churches of Christ for over fifty years unfolded. From across America came leaders of the nation, the state of Tennessee, and churches of Christ. Senator Lyndon B. Johnson of Texas stated: "Dr. Hardeman has spent his life sowing seeds among the souls of men and nurturing the minds of the young." Marshall Keeble, the black evangelist, telegraphed a message: "Congratulations for your long and devoted service in the kingdom of Christ. I count it one of the blessings of my life to have been for many years a fellow laborer in His vineyard."

Nicholas Brodie Hardeman was born on May 18, 1874, at Milledgeville in West Tennessee. The Hardeman family came in contact with the Restoration plea in 1890 when J. A. Minton of Alabama held a meeting in their community. Impressed with the sermons, Dr. and Mrs. John B. Hardeman were soon baptized. In the same year, young Brodie went to Henderson to attend West Tennessee Christian College. Here Brodie was baptized by R. P. Meeks, the brother-in-law of T. B. Larimore.

Henderson became the Hardeman home in 1893. Two years later, A. G. Freed, who would have a tremendous influence on N. B. Hardeman over the next thirty-five years, became president of West Tennessee Christian College. Under Freed's tutelage, Hardeman received his B.A. and M.A. degrees, the latter from Georgia Robertson Christian College, the name given to the school in 1897. From his earliest years, Brodie Hardeman was involved in his lifelong pursuits—preaching and teaching. He delivered his first sermon on April 8, 1897, at Enville, Tennessee. Two years previously he had begun teaching at a community school in Kenton, Tennessee.

Because of the inroads of the missionary society and other innovations into Georgia Robertson College, Freed and Hardeman withdrew from teaching and administrative positions at the school. In 1907, the two men decided to begin a new school in Henderson. They opened the National Teachers' Normal and Business College in 1908. This school continued as a private institution of Freed and

Hardeman until 1919, when a board of trustees renamed the school Freed-Hardeman College. The two men continued as president and vice-president until both left the school in 1923, with Freed accepting a position with David Lipscomb College in Nashville and Hardeman entering full-time evangelism. In 1925, Hardeman would return to the school as its chief executive.

HIGHER EDUCATION AMONG CHURCHES OF CHRIST

In the meantime, Hardeman had made an indelible mark in giving direction to churches of Christ. By this early association with schools, he demonstrated the importance of education for churches of Christ. Schools were needed for the education of preachers and leaders who would serve churches across America and around the world. By 1925 schools had been established in a number of places. In Spencer, Tennessee, Burritt College had operated since 1849. But the most enduring educational institution was the Nashville Bible School. Established in 1891, the school received direction from such men as Lipscomb, James A. Harding, William Anderson, J. S. Ward, E. A. Elam, and H. Leo Boles. The school produced leadership for churches of Christ from its first year of operation.

Except for Freed-Hardeman College, education among churches of Christ can be traced directly to the ideas of David Lipscomb. By the early twentieth century, schools were being established in Kentucky (Potter Bible School) and Texas (Abilene Christian College), patterned after the Nashville school. In each instance, graduates or administrators of the Nashville Bible School were leaders in the new schools. James A. Harding moved from Nashville to establish Potter in 1901. His son-in-law, J. N. Armstrong, involved himself in a series of schools, culminating in Harding College, Searcy, Arkansas, in the 1930s. Armstrong graduated from the Nashville Bible School.

In west Texas, other graduates of the Nashville Bible School dreamed of a school. A. B. Barrett supplied the energy for the first effort to establish a school in Abilene. With a gift from Colonel W. J. Childers, the school opened in the fall of 1906. Over the next several years a number of men shared leadership positions, including R. L. Whiteside and James F. Cox. In 1912, Jesse P. Sewell accepted the presidency of the school, which proved to be a fortunate decision. Sewell, a Nashville Bible School graduate, made a lasting impression on Abilene Christian College and churches of Christ in Texas and across the United States.[7]

Among the innovative contributions of Abilene has been the annual Bible lectureship. Begun in 1918, the lectureship was the idea of A. R. Holton, a young member of the faculty. From the first, the lectures drew brethren in churches of Christ from across Texas, reaching far into other states and foreign countries. In a sense, the lectures have become a "clearinghouse" for ideas within the fellowship, while fostering goodwill and the exchange of ideas from a broad range of brethren. The lectures have continued each February.[8] Other schools, including David Lipscomb College and Freed-Hardeman, borrowed the concept of the lectureship. Abilene and Freed-Hardeman, however, have been the most successful in staging brotherhood-wide gatherings. In recent years, Pepperdine University has attracted large crowds to its spring lectureship.

OPPOSITION TO HIGHER EDUCATION

Not everyone in churches of Christ shared this emphasis on education. From the time of Alexander Campbell, there had been among Disciples strong feelings against a professional education for preachers. As mentioned in chapter one, Daniel Sommer and Austin McGary were the most vocally opposed to a college educated ministry. They continued their opposition into the twentieth century.

After initially venting his views, Sommer wrote little on education until Lipscomb and Harding established the Nashville Bible School in 1891. Following Harding's departure for Bowling Green, Kentucky, in 1901, Sommer opened a full-scale war against colleges or, as he called them, "religio-secular schools." He opposed the use of the Lord's money to found schools and then, in turn, giving them divine names, i.e., Christian. Furthermore, the colleges caused a sense of pride among preachers, even a "clergy" attitude. He argued that colleges tend to foster the idea that a person cannot preach without a college education.

Sommer believed he had "saved" the land north of the Ohio River from the "college craze." It had cost him five or ten years' writing time, but he believed it was worthwhile. So important was the issue to him that, in 1907, he took time out from other work to debate B. F. Rhodes on the college issue. The following year Sommer and J. N. Armstrong engaged in a written debate on the same subject. As a result of his continuing attacks on schools, Sommer alienated himself from many members of churches of Christ, especially in the South. On the other hand, Sommer had a special antipathy toward Southerners and southern churches. After 1900 Lipscomb warned E. A. Elam that if he differed with Sommer, he would be "abused roughly." During 1913 Elam and Sommer carried on a lengthy written discussion about Bible schools.

In the South and Southwest, Austin McGary and J. D. Tant shared many of the same concerns voiced by Sommer. Usually supportive of schools, Tant voiced his concerns in the *Firm Foundation* in 1922. He opposed such terms as "our schools," emphasizing his own views by asking his brethren, Why not a Christian farm? He added:

> Paul says it pleased God by the foolishness of preaching to save them that believe, but it seems many Texas preachers think God is better pleased with our Christian colleges. . . . But to call them "our Bible schools," or "our Christian schools" is not only misleading, but it gives you power over the church by calling them church institutions, and calling on the church to support them.

Specifically, he criticized Abilene Christian College for asking members of churches of Christ to contribute $250,000 to help the school. Such a sum would support a preacher for 250 years, he calculated. If 200 people were converted each year, it would mean 50,000 saved persons. He added his typical conclusion: "Brethren, we are drifting and eternity alone can tell the end."

Running counter to much written in the papers, Tant did not believe Christian schools aided the moral and spiritual upbuilding of the church. Very likely representing his own background, the Texas frontier preacher warned: "The churches have gone to the extreme for big and educated preachers, and are demanding college preachers."[9] J. W. Chism, recognizing the permanency of colleges, could not refrain from warning churches not to become too impressed with college degrees.[10] Sharing a view eventually accepted by Daniel Sommer, Foy E. Wallace, Jr., said that "individuals, not churches should support them [colleges]." He added: "Keep the school out of the church, in the realm of secular institutions, where it belongs."[11]

But often on the same pages were glowing reports of the schools or desperate pleas for help, whether the schools were in Tennessee, Texas, or Arkansas. C. R. Nichol summed up the attitude of most writers in the *Gospel Advocate* and the *Firm Foundation:* "The church of Christ is sadly in need of many men of broad and liberal education from a school which is careful to inculcate the fundamentals of the Christianity we read about in the New Testament."[12]

THE HARDEMAN TABERNACLE SERMONS

At various times throughout the twentieth century, Nashville has been referred to as "Jerusalem" by some within churches of Christ. Despite their usually humorous and sometimes cynical nature, such references suggest the importance of Nashville throughout the years to the conservative Restoration plea. By 1920, the membership of churches of Christ in Nashville surpassed that in other cities in America. In fact, the membership exceeded that of the Christian churches of the city. Only Baptists and Methodists counted more members in the city on the Cumberland River. Because of this unprecedented success, others looked toward Nashville for direction.

For a number of years there were informal discussions about how churches of Christ might share the Restoration plea with the people of Nashville. In the fall of 1921, a formal meeting convened, to which men from congregations throughout Nashville came to discuss a citywide evangelistic campaign. The Charlotte Avenue church accepted the responsibility of selecting men from other congregations to serve as a steering committee. Later, others were appointed to head various working committees, looking toward a major series of meetings during the spring of 1922. In the "History and Description of the Meeting" section of the *Hardeman Tabernacle Sermons,* the compilers wrote:

> Everything seemed to be right for such a meeting. The time was ripe. It was ripe from the standpoint of a strong force of loyal adherents to the cause to back the movement—a harvest of three-quarters of a century of labor of stalwart and loyal la-

borers in the Master's vineyard in planting the cause in Nashville. It was ripe, too, from the standpoint of a general awakening of religious interests dominating the city at the very time and season of the year at which the meetings were held.[13]

After much deliberation, the committee selected N. B. Hardeman as the preacher and C. M. Pullias as the song director. Following the distribution of thousands of ink blotters and leaflets, the preferred method of advertising at the time, the meeting began on March 28 and continued through April 16, 1922. Never had churches of Christ sponsored such a meeting in Nashville or any other American city. Each sermon appeared in full in either the *Nashville Tennessean* or the *Nashville Banner*. The response from the city was tremendous. Huge audiences gathered for noon and evening services. Crowds estimated at 6,000 to 8,000 attended many of the services, with others unable to find a place in the auditorium. Some two hundred baptisms resulted from the meeting.

The first Hardeman Tabernacle Meeting was a success; another was scheduled for 1923. In 1928, Hardeman returned for his third meeting. Ten years later, he came back to the city to discuss in detail the question of premillennialism. The fifth and last of the series was in 1942. Altogether, Hardeman preached 127 sermons in the five meetings. He dealt with the church, the Bible, conversion, Christian unity, and premillennialism. Never had any one thing done so much to give churches of Christ direction as the Tabernacle Sermons. Of Hardeman's place, William Woodson stated:

> In the years of the Tabernacle Sermons he [Hardeman] occupied a unique place among churches of Christ in Tennessee. In his work the threads of thought from early leaders in the movement, writers and teachers he had, and his own studies were gathered together. In his work, therefore, the movement reached a high water mark in its consciousness of its identity. . . . Consequently, one may regard the main thoughts of the movement known as churches of Christ as having been gathered, clarified and explained in the work of this man.[14]

INSTRUMENTAL MUSIC IN WORSHIP

The plea for restoration sounded with clarity through the voice of N. B. Hardeman. But many issues within the movement remained unsettled. Since 1859, the question of instrumental music had disturbed the Disciples of Christ. Signifying the importance of the music question to the church in the twentieth century, Clark Braden (pro-instrument) debated Joe S. Warlick in Dallas, Texas, in 1898. Two years later the new century would see the issue escalate in importance. Hall L. Calhoun defended instrumental music in a series of articles. M. C. Kurfees responded to Calhoun. Basically, the issue centered on whether the instrument is a part of worship or only an accompaniment. Kurfees suggested that he had no objections to the instrument in the place of worship if it were only seen like a bouquet of flowers. The discussion aborted when Calhoun failed to send additional articles.

Henderson, Tennessee, became the center of conflict during 1903, when those opposed to both the instrument and the missionary society challenged the pro-instrument and missionary society brethren. As a part of the controversy, J. Carroll Stark of McMinnville, Tennessee, met Joe S. Warlick of Dallas in debate. This particular confrontation centered on the Greek word *psallo,* i.e., whether or not the word signified an instrument of music. Stark, of course, suggested that it did; Warlick denied such a meaning, asserting that the term signified the heart as the instrument.[15]

In 1908, J. B. Briney and W. W. Otey met in Louisville, Kentucky, to discuss the instrument-in-worship. Briney defended the right to use the instrument, while Otey argued against the use of the piano or organ in worship. Why was there such a strong emphasis on instrumental music during the first quarter of the twentieth century? Why would men such as Otey and Briney spend days arguing the pros and cons of the instrument as a part of worship? Professor Woodson emphasizes the importance of the issue in his *Standing For Their Faith:*

> The significance of the issue of instrumental music in worship for churches of Christ . . . had become such that they felt if they were able to sustain their argument on this issue they were also able to sustain their whole position as a unique religious body.[16]

To have failed to defend their position on music in worship, churches of Christ would have overthrown their entire rationale for their movement.

Among churches of Christ, M. C. Kurfees of Louisville, Kentucky, produced the most thorough study of music in worship. After investigating the subject with a group of young men in Louisville, Kurfees compiled a book titled *Instrumental Music in Worship.* The statement in favor of singing and in opposition to the instrument in worship was so complete that J. B. Briney recognized the book as "the most elaborate and plausible argument . . . that has ever been published in opposition to instrumental music in worship, and may be regarded as the final word on that side of the question."[17]

There were those, however, who responded to Kurfees, possibly because the book demanded a response if the use of the instrument were to remain a viable alternative. Even though Briney believed Kurfees' arguments were the best available in defense of singing in worship, in 1914 he felt it necessary to respond. The most outstanding attempt at answering Kurfees was a book by O. E. Payne titled *Instrumental Music is Scriptural.* Published by the Standard Publishing Company of Cincinnati, the gist of Payne's argument was that instrumental music is included in the Greek word *psallo* as baptism by immersion is included in the Greek word *baptizo.* For the first time, the advocates of instrumental music made the instrument mandatory in worship. The *Christian Standard,* in reviewing Payne's book, stated:

> O. E. Payne . . . has . . . rendered a valuable service to all who need posting on this subject—and it is our conviction that all of us, especially all the ministers, should be prepared, at a moment's notice, to answer this question and to answer it in a forceful way.[18]

In 1923, Nashville became the center of the controversy. A group styling itself the Commission on Unity, headed by John Cowden of Nashville, finally agreed to a debate. Ira Boswell of Kentucky defended the use of the instrument; N. B. Hardeman opposed. The widespread feeling then and continuing throughout the years is that the Hardeman-Boswell debate was a landmark event for churches of Christ. Held before overflow crowds in Ryman

Auditorium, this event also gave direction and stabilization to churches of Christ in Tennessee and beyond.

Reports of the debate among churches of Christ were overwhelmingly favorable toward Hardeman. A. B. Barrett wrote glowing reports for the *Firm Foundation.* The crowd, estimated at 6,000, caused him to suggest that the throng was larger than the crowds who had heard Sam Jones, the well-known southern evangelist for whom the Ryman Tabernacle was constructed in 1891. Catching the importance of the encounter, Barrett stated: "This affair will soon become history, and, I predict, a historic event withal, for never has there been a more important thing undertaken among us in the South."[19]

John Cowden's report in the *Christian Standard* was slanted in Boswell's favor. The *Standard* voiced the general attitude of those among the instrument-using Disciples when it called churches of Christ "non-progressive brethren."[20] The *Christian-Evangelist* took notice of the instrument controversy by dismissing it as an issue fought many years before. Of churches of Christ, the editor wrote: "These good brethren meant well, as did the persecutors of Christ, but they were legalists and seemed never to have caught a glimpse of the 'liberty wherewith he has made us free.' "[21]

ORPHAN HOMES AND HOMES FOR THE AGED

Although not quite in the same category as schools, the establishing of orphan homes and homes for the elderly during the 1920s also suggests a maturing of churches of Christ. David Lipscomb had taken the lead in establishing the Fanning Orphan School during 1883 in response to the wishes of Tolbert and Charlotte Fanning. The school continued until the early 1940s, when the property became the location of Nashville's airport.

During the second decade of the twentieth century, J. C. McQuiddy led in organizing the Tennessee Orphans' Home in Columbia, his hometown. The home moved later to Spring Hill. In Texas, a number of homes were proposed and put into operation, including the Boles' Home and the Belle Haven Orphan Home. The Boles' Home, established in 1923, is the only surviving Texas facility begun during this period. Still another home was proposed for Canadian, Texas. But this work was transferred to the Tipton (Oklahoma) Orphans' Home.

Help for the elderly was much slower in developing. In Texas, the *Firm Foundation* included long discussions as to whether homes for the aged should be constructed. When a letter writer suggested that each congregation should care for its elderly, editor Showalter answered that Christians who lack a home need places to live. On through 1922 the discussion continued, with J. B. Nelson of Dallas defending the right of individuals to establish such organizations. Evidently, the home Nelson sought was never established, as Steve Eckstein gives 1947 as the founding date for the first home for the aged in Texas.[22]

In Tennessee, the initial effort to establish a home for the elderly came in 1926, when the Chapel Avenue church opened its facility. One of the last gifts made by Mrs. David Lipscomb, Sr., was a one thousand dollar donation to the home. A sense of urgency arose when someone discovered that the Little Sisters of the Poor (a Catholic order) were caring for twelve elderly members of churches of Christ. The desire to help orphans and the elderly aroused little opposition during the 1920s.

ASSESSMENT OF N. B. HARDEMAN

With the 1922 and 1923 Tabernacle Sermons and the Boswell debate in 1923, N. B. Hardeman reached a position of leadership among churches of Christ at an early age. It would be a mistake to suppose that he had reached a high plateau and that his place would begin to recede. Indeed, over the next several years the Hardeman name would be a household word among the churches. Called back to Nashville on many occasions, he drew huge crowds wherever he spoke. When the Central church opened its building in downtown Nashville on December 25, 1925, Hardeman gave the first sermon. Returning to Henderson after his Nashville triumphs, he made Freed-Hardeman College into a school recognized for its "soundness" and as a producer of preachers for churches of Christ.

Hardeman continued with the school until 1950. Even though seventy-six at the time, he continued to preach regularly across the breadth of the United States. He held 108 meetings in fourteen states from 1950 to 1965. From that first sermon at Enville when he substituted for A. G. Freed, he spent sixty years doing what he most enjoyed, preaching the gospel of Christ.

At the age of ninety-one, Nicholas Brodie Hardeman died on November 25, 1965, in Memphis, Tennessee. On the campus where he had served for so many years, the school conducted a memorial service in his honor. One of his former students and associates, W. A. Bradfield, said of him:

> As an educator and evangelist, N. B. Hardeman was unquestionably one of the greatest influences in the church of Christ in the first half of the twentieth century. May God bless his memory now and forever more.[23]

SARAH ANDREWS: MISSIONARY TO JAPAN

In accordance with the Great Commission given by Jesus—"Go into all the world and preach the gospel"—the Restoration Movement emphasized from the earliest years of the nineteenth century the responsibility of evangelizing the United States and the world. From those earliest times, the evangelist did the vast majority of his preaching in the local community. But as the years passed, the emphasis began to change. Calls came from distant states and even foreign countries. In 1849, the Disciples decided that the best method of accomplishing the evangelistic mandate was through the formation of the American Christian Missionary Society.

Scant mission work was done by conservative Disciples prior to 1906. The one exception was in Japan. The island nation held a certain aura for the readers of journals among churches of Christ. The *Gospel Advocate* and the *Firm Foundation* chronicled the work of J. M. McCaleb, who went to Japan in 1891. He was followed by E. Snodgrass and William J. Bishop. McCaleb began his work in the Orient shortly after his graduation from the College of the Bible in Lexington, Kentucky. Snodgrass was at first supported by the Foreign Missionary Society, but ceased working with it in 1892. Bishop was the last of these three to go to Japan. The death of his wife shortly after their arrival in the islands interrupted his work.

Within a few years, young people began thinking about the possibilities of entering mission work, especially in Japan. Among these was Sarah Andrews of Dickson, Tennessee.[24]

Miss Andrews, born the year J. M. McCaleb and his wife entered Japan, was the daughter of Mr. and Mrs. Will Andrews. Her mother had long entertained an interest in Japan, even desiring to serve as a missionary in that far country. Sarah prepared herself for foreign work in Japan by attending Normal College in Dickson and, later, David Lipscomb College and the state college in Memphis. From the first, her support came from the church in Dickson, with I. B. Bradley serving as treasurer of her fund.

Arriving in Japan in 1916, Sarah Andrews worked with McCaleb in Tokyo for a number of years while learning the language. During this training period, Sarah met a young Japanese girl, Oiki San, and her mother. Miss Andrews converted both women. Oiki San became a lifelong companion of Miss Andrews. Completing her education, Miss Andrews and her companions moved south of Tokyo to Okitsu, where the young missionary opened a kindergarten. Through her efforts, a large Bible school developed among the women and children. At opportune times, they called a preacher who would baptize the new converts. By this method Miss Andrews established a number of congregations. Her initial work finished, she and her companions would move on to establish other churches. By World War II, congregations existed in Okitsu, Shizuoka, Shemedza, and Mumadzu.

Deeply committed to her mission, Sarah Andrews literally worked herself into illness. On several occasions she had to return to the United States to regain her health. In 1923, I. B. Bradley, Robert S. King, and Mrs. David Lipscomb, Sr., urged churches and individuals to provide funds to purchase a prefabricated house to be transported to Japan. In all, they raised $6,000 for the purpose. Miss Andrews lived in this house for the remainder of her life.[25]

At Okitsu, Miss Andrews wanted the Christians to have a place of worship. She encouraged Americans to give money toward the construction of the building. Once it was finished, she recognized it as a major work encouraged by Mrs. David (Aunt Mag) Lipscomb. As Sarah prepared to leave for a furlough in 1927, the congregation gathered in front of the church building for a picture with their friend. Said Miss Andrews: "Some folks may think and talk of being in Japan as a sacrifice, but to me leaving is the supreme sacrifice."[26]

In 1941 the war, long feared, erupted between Japan and the United States. Not willing to relinquish the church's property to the government, Miss Andrews refused to leave Japan. Interned in a camp, then in her own house, Sarah Andrews faced starvation. Only by selling her furniture piece by piece was she able to sustain her life. Finding her barely alive at the end of the war, the American government had to nourish her back to partial health and strength before she could travel to the United States. Traveling to America in 1945, she determined to return to her adopted country because the Christians there needed her: "That is my work and my people. I can do more there on a cot than here on my feet." [27] On April 30, 1949, Miss Sarah Andrews sailed from her home country back to her adopted homeland, Japan. At age fifty-seven she could say: "I am indeed happy and thankful to be at my post of duty here again. . . . I tremble as I face the vast opportunities here, and shall trust God at all times for guidance and help." [28] She continued teaching at Numadzu until felled by a stroke. A second stroke took her life on September 17, 1961. She had requested burial in Japan, among her people, a request gladly granted.[29]

What did the Japanese think of her? When she returned in 1949, several newspapers told of her coming back to Japan. Bradley quoted from a letter he received from a Japanese Christian, who extolled the virtue of Sarah Andrews.

> Sister Andrews is the most efficient worker among all those in this field. She has gained the good will and confidence of all those who know her and her work. She has done the most substantial work here.[30]

THE 1920S: A DECADE OF MISSIONS

Sarah Andrews was not alone in Japan. Within two years after her initial work, the O. D. Bixler family sailed for Japan. They were followed by the E. A. Rhodeses, Harry R. Fox, Sr., and his family, and Herman Fox and family. In 1925, Barney Morehead and his wife, Nellie, joined the Japanese work.[31] In 1928, the Carl Etter family arrived in the islands.[32] Besides these families, three other single women made their marks as missionaries to the Japanese—Lillie Cypert, Hettie Lee Ewing, and Clara Kennedy.

Miss Ewing entered the Japanese work because of an encouraging letter from Miss Cypert.[33]

The 1920s witnessed the greatest push by churches of Christ since 1906 to locate men and women in overseas countries. Besides the interest in Japan, other missionaries located in China, India, the Philippines, Brazil, and the continent of Africa. While Japan was the destination for the largest contingent of missionaries, China beckoned George and Sallie Benson. They were joined by Miss Ethel Mattley, the E. L. Broaddus family, and the Oldhams.[34] To India went the George K. Desha family in an attempt to salvage earlier mission work.[35] Orla and Ethel Boyer and Virgil and Ramona Smith were supported in Brazil by churches of Christ in the United States.[36] Even though Hawaii was an American possession, still the Max Langpaaps were considered foreign missionaries there.[37]

Next to Japan, the most impressive mission effort by churches of Christ was in Africa. In 1896, John Sherriff, a native of New Zealand, organized the first of the missions. Centered in Rhodesia, the Ray Lawyers and the George Scotts manned the Sinde mission. Dow and Alice Merritt, along with Will and Adelia Short, were responsible for the Kabanga mission. Following the tragic death of Lawyer in 1927, Sherriff asked when churches of Christ would send doctors and nurses to the mission.[38]

Interest in missions rose to its highest pitch toward the end of the 1920s. George Pepperdine sponsored George Benson in a series of meetings in the Philippines.[39] Pepperdine also made a trip to the Orient where he viewed the mission effort. He urged the 500,000 members of churches of Christ to give one penny each day for mission work.[40] In this way, a thousand missionaries could be sent and supported in Japan. In Nashville, a mission emphasis meeting convened at the Central church in 1928 when the Moreheads were preparing to return to Japan. They had also persuaded Miss Edith Langford to go with them. Also at the meeting was Herman Fox, on leave from his mission in Japan. So interested were Nashvillians in the effort that Robert S. King, a strong advocate of missions, reported in the *Advocate:*

> The farewell meeting for our missionaries at Central church in Nashville was the greatest meeting of its kind in the South. Hundreds were not able to get a seat and stood around the walls

and in the aisles during the entire two-hour program and many lingered another hour talking to the missionaries and bidding them Godspeed.[41]

G. H. P. Showalter, editor of the *Firm Foundation* and a great supporter of foreign and home missions, said: "The churches of Christ are probably more keenly aroused at the present than during recent years in gospel missions."[42]

Even though the number of missionaries totaled fewer than sixty-five in 1928 and the support was meager, still the effort was pointing in the direction churches of Christ knew they must go. The search for direction had found expression in the men and women who were willing to leave home and family for foreign countries because they believed and accepted the challenge of the Great Commission. Those at home heeded Mrs. Lipscomb's urging: "Every Christian is a missionary, and must either go, give, or pray."[43]

CONCLUSION

N. B. Hardeman and Sarah Andrews were featured in this chapter as examples of their era. But a great host of others contributed mightily in giving direction to churches of Christ. During this period, churches of Christ looked inward to discover their identity and then outward to tell others who they were and to plead with all to join them in restoring New Testament Christianity.

CHAPTER 5

INTERNAL ISSUES—
1906-1930:
R. H. Boll, H. Leo Boles, and T. B. Larimore

The previous chapter dealt with positive emphases and the discussions concerning schools and the instrument that gave direction to churches of Christ after 1906. Despite this cohesive search for direction, internal difficulties continued to frustrate that search. James A. Allen, in the middle of the 1920s, emphasized the crisis he believed churches of Christ were facing:

> Indications point to the approach of a great crisis in the struggle for a restoration of the Apostolic order of Christian work and worship. All of God's people should stand perfectly united for the contest. The various factions created by the anti-Sunday school hobbyists, the rebaptism devotees, and by the anti-Bible school schismatics are lending support to the enemy and are weakening the Cause. Speculative theories of the millennium and unfulfilled prophecy are doing their detrimental work. Our transgressive brethren [Christian church], while loudly protesting their identity with those struggling for Restoration, have gone entirely over to its opponents.[1]

Internally, it was a time for searching.

By early 1909, the struggle for internal direction was well under way. Two men represent the major thrust of the search in churches of Christ. Robert H. Boll, early in the twentieth century, introduced the study of prophecy, leading within a few years to an

87

open avowal of premillennialism. In 1927, H. Leo Boles accepted the task of debating millennial ideas with Boll through the pages of the *Gospel Advocate*. The issues were similar to those debated on the national scene: the time of the establishment of the kingdom, the Jews' return to Israel, and the return of Christ to rule for a thousand years on David's throne. For the first time, readers of the *Advocate* and members of churches of Christ could read and understand the issues. It was a time of learning.

Toward the end of the 1920s, the nature of the church became the center of attention. The nineteenth century Restoration Movement called for everyone to abandon denominationalism and become Christians only. In the twentieth century, many began to associate in a much more narrow sense "the church" with "the Church of Christ." Building on the ideas of Alexander Campbell, Barton Stone, Tolbert Fanning, and David Lipscomb, elder statesmen of churches of Christ fought this narrowed understanding of the church. This was second only to premillennialism as an issue of great concern.

The desire to keep the church doctrinally pure required a constant encounter of ideas. Some have the ability, however, to hold themselves above the scarring battles while pursuing their evangelistic work. T. B. Larimore stood tall throughout his life, giving stability during the conflict of ideas.

ROBERT H. BOLL AND PREMILLENNIALISM

Premillennialism, as an issue, impacted churches of Christ for thirty years. Most likely the issue would have surfaced without the advocacy of Robert H. Boll. Through him, however, it became a dominant theme. For fifty years he led the premillennial movement from his home base in Louisville, Kentucky.

Robert Henry Boll was born on June 7, 1875, in Badenweiler, Germany. His early education pointed him toward the priesthood of the Roman Catholic Church. Unable to live peaceably with his stepfather, young Robert moved with an aunt to the United States in 1890. He first lived in Zanesville, Ohio. He then moved on to Tennessee, where he came under the influence of professor T. E. Allen of Lavergne, Tennessee. From Allen he learned about the individual's responsibility toward God. Dr. J. M. Gooch challenged Robert's Catholic background. As a result of these influences, on

Sunday, April 14, 1895, Robert H. Boll was baptized by Sam Harris in a pond on the Columbus Brittain farm near Nashville.

In the fall of 1895, Robert walked twenty miles to enroll in the Nashville Bible School. Since Boll was unable to pay his way, James A. Harding provided work for the young man. He delivered his first sermon at the Nashville jail. During the summer of 1896, his friend Bob McMahon arranged a three-week meeting in the small community of Accident. It was almost a disaster. The crowds, beginning small, dwindled over the next two or three nights. By Boll's own admission, the sermons were poor. But by Saturday the crowds increased, the sermons improved, and R. H. Boll finished his first meeting with seven baptisms. His life's work was before him.[2]

He graduated from the Nashville Bible School in 1900. From the Bible School, Boll moved to Texas where he preached and helped Joe Warlick edit the *Gospel Guide.* The young editor discovered a latent talent for writing. In 1903, he moved to Louisville, Kentucky, and the Portland Avenue church. He continued in Louisville for the remainder of his life, with the exception of one year in Lawrenceburg, Tennessee.

An event of 1908 may have had a deep impact on Robert Boll's religious ideas. F. L. Rowe sought the advice of M. C. Kurfees and Boll as to who should debate Charles T. Russell, a leader of the Jehovah's Witness movement. They recommended L. S. White of Denton, Texas. Boll attended the debate in Cincinnati. According to Robert Welch, "Boll came away enamored of Russell's style and ready to proclaim boldly the doctrine of premillennialism."[3]

Whatever the case, Boll shortly became the front-page writer for the *Gospel Advocate.* Soon, articles began appearing on biblical prophecy. Thus he introduced the topic that would challenge churches of Christ for thirty years—premillennialism. But not until 1915 would the issue be openly taught in the *Advocate,* again on the front page by R. H. Boll. In response, F. B. Srygley noted that for the first time *Gospel Advocate* subscribers were reading that the kingdom had not been established. Soon the publishers decided that the ideas were not only divisive, but wrong. F. W. Smith, a columnist for the *Advocate,* accepted the assignment to respond to Boll.

In order to gain support, Boll and his associates involved David Lipscomb in the controversy as an advocate of the premillennial theory. In response, the editors inserted an article by Lipscomb. He shared with *Advocate* readers the same ideas he had held for many years: he did not understand the book of Revelation, and anyone who spent undue time on prophecy was forgetting the most important ingredients of Christianity. Showing his understanding of the history of premillennialism in American history, he recalled the William Miller episode of the 1840s and the attendant problems. He concluded: "The older of this generation, having seen the result of these mistaken interpretations, are not so ready to accept the present war [World War I] as a pointer to the near approach of the end as are the younger and more sanguine." Showing the concerns of an old man, he added: "While I am not sure as to the time of his coming, I am anxious for that appearing."[4]

Attempting to maintain unity and fellowship, the editors published another Lipscomb article titled "Has the Kingdom Been Established?" They then asked Boll if he agreed with Lipscomb. He answered "yes," with the exception of one minor point. Then, using Lipscomb's name, the editors asked Boll not to raise nonessentials to the same level of importance as essentials. They further asked: "Will Brother Boll declare a belief of these things essential to salvation? If not, then why continue to agitate them?"[5]

The publishers removed Boll from his position on the *Advocate*. By the end of 1915, however, they reinstated him with an announcement that "all differences between Brother Boll and the editors and publishers have been amicably and satisfactorily adjusted."[6] By December 15 of the same year, it became clear that Boll would not abide by the directive banning speculative ideas from his articles. The attempt at continued fellowship faded. The issue shifted to a broader emphasis.

Louisville, Kentucky, became the center of the premillennial movement. In that city the conflict focused on the Highland church where E. L. Jorgenson served as preacher. Two other men important to the premillennial controversy were members of the congregation—Robert Boll and Don Carlos Janes. Two prominent leaders of the church, R. O. Rubel and C. A. Taylor, opposed the introduction of the premillennial views into the church. Subsequently, the church withdrew from Rubel and Taylor. Some forty members of Highland sided with Rubel and Taylor and formed the Bardstown Road church.[7]

In the meantime, the work of Boll and friends was progressing. They moved the magazine, *Word and Work,* from New Orleans, where Stanford Chambers had introduced premillennialism. Now the speculative views of Boll and Jorgenson had a voice from Louisville. No longer would they suppress their views as private opinions. Consequently a number of churches, in addition to Highland, divided over premillennialism.

A side issue involved the relationship of various missionaries with the premillennial issue. As early as 1920, missionaries to China had defected to the Seventh Day Adventists, evidently as a result of premillennialism. Because J. M. McCaleb, a missionary to Japan, continued close relationships with both Jorgenson and the Highland church, F. B. Srygley wondered about McCaleb's relationship with premillennialism.[8] In fact, for several years McCaleb's articles did not appear in the *Advocate.* To know of McCaleb's work in Japan, most members of churches of Christ had to turn to the *Firm Foundation.* Furthermore, Showalter published Don Carlos Janes' missionary articles. The *Firm Foundation* carried an entire series relating Janes' visits to mission points around the world. In 1925, McCaleb articles reappeared in the *Advocate.*[9]

Premillennialism would not go away. As early as 1918, the *Gospel Advocate* announced its decision to not publish anything written by Boll. M. C. Kurfees, an editor of the *Advocate* and preacher for the Campbell Street/Haldeman Avenue church in Louisville, concluded:

> When men thus persist in teaching and spreading divisive opinions—things which God does not require, and from teaching which they could properly refrain—there is but one proper thing to do, and that is to oppose them with all our might with the word of God. Let them be faithfully pointed out and marked as false teachers and schismatics.

Far removed from Louisville, the *Firm Foundation* did not comment on premillennialism in depth until 1925. In that year, J. B. Nelson penned several articles on "The Kingdom and the Second Coming of Christ." At about the same time, C. R. Nichol and R. L. Whiteside published a small book in response to Boll's speculations. G. C. Brewer, who was then preaching in Sherman, Texas, suggested that Nichol, Whiteside, or Nelson should agree

on a proposition with Robert Boll and "discuss them to the finish
. . . and let the rest of us keep out of the fight." He concluded:
"Frankly, I do not believe the issues are worth discussion . . . but
they are being discussed, then why not treat them as we do other
issues—fight them out with their strongest opponent."[10] In 1927,
editor Showalter quoted two debate topics Boll had signed: (1)
"Resolved, that Daniel 2:35-44 was fulfilled on Pentecost. I
deny."[11] (2) "Resolved, that Christ is now sitting on David's
throne. I deny." At least, Showalter concluded, these give something of Boll's positions. He assigned Early Arceneaux the responsibility for writing a number of articles on the troublesome issue.

H. LEO BOLES: IN OPPOSITION TO PREMILLENNIALISM

There are eras in history electric with excitement; there are
other times best suited for contemplation and rest. Some men and
women seem to exist for those times of confrontation; others are
horrified—even afraid—when called to conflict. Had H. Leo Boles
selected a time to be born, likely he would have chosen just those
years in which he lived and worked.

Henry Leo Boles' life spanned nearly three-quarters of a century when change was the order of the day. Within the smaller
confines of the Restoration Movement, Boles witnessed the major
changes taking place as churches of Christ separated from the
more liberal Disciples of Christ. Moreover, he witnessed the internal difficulties surfacing during the early years of the twentieth
century among his own brethren. He watched with eagerness the
Hardeman Tabernacle meetings. He edited the *Advocate* during the
first of these meetings in 1922. As an educational leader, he served
as president of David Lipscomb College on two different occasions—1913-1920 and 1923-1932. Always in demand as a
preacher, Boles had a full and eventful life at the very center of activity among churches of Christ.[12]

Born on February 22, 1874, on Flynn's Creek in Jackson
County, Tennessee, H. Leo Boles came from a distinguished fam-
ily of the Restoration Movement. He was the great-grandson of
"Raccoon" John Smith, a nineteenth-century leader in the
Restoration Movement. Henry Leo's father was Jefferson Boles, a

farmer-preacher in the Upper Cumberland area. His father married three times, the first two wives dying and leaving children to be reared. In all, there were seventeen children in the Boles household.

Schooling for the children would not be easy. But young Henry Leo determined to get an education: His total education to this point would not add up to one complete year. In 1892, Leo Boles and his brother, Smith, entered Center College in Cannon County. Here they studied the basic courses—spelling, geography, reading, composition, and history—both American and Tennessee. Because of their father's illness, they soon left school.

At age nineteen, even with limited educational experience, Leo began his teaching career. In that first year he fell in love with one of his students, Cynthia Cantrell, leading to marriage in 1894. The birth of Cleo Cantrell Boles blessed the home on July 14, 1895, but three days later, Cynthia died from uremic poisoning. Leo took young Cleo to his father's home; he took this time to pursue more education.

He attended Dibrell College for nearly two years, then transferred to Burritt College at Spencer, Tennessee. Boles, having no money, supported himself while in school, completing his work in 1900. Moving to Texas, he taught school for two years, searching for direction in his life. Returning home, he traveled on the meeting circuit with his father during the summer of 1903. This may have been a turning point in Leo Boles' life, for he determined to spend his life preaching the gospel of Christ.

The price of a train ticket determined where H. Leo Boles, at the age of twenty-nine years, would continue his education. It cost only three dollars to travel to Nashville, while the charge to Bowling Green and James A. Harding's school was $5.73. In 1903, he enrolled in the Nashville Bible School, where he studied for seven years, much of the time under the direct tutelage of David Lipscomb. Nashville remained home for H. Leo Boles for the remainder of his life.

Following graduation, Boles continued at the Bible School as a member of the faculty. When E. A. Elam resigned the presidency in 1913, David Lipscomb personally recommended Boles for the position. Boles continued as president until 1920, leading in the change of the school's name to David Lipscomb College. Throughout this period and continuing through 1929 (the scope of this chapter), Boles involved himself deeply in his school work and writing. Unquestionably, he exerted as much influence upon churches of Christ during this era as any person.

Therefore, it came as no surprise that Boles in 1927 inherited the task of debating R. H. Boll on the various aspects of premillennialism.[13] Boles was an intense student of the Bible. He would never go into any responsibility unprepared. The same was true of R. H. Boll. From May to November they filled pages of the *Advocate* with arguments for and against a number of basic issues. These included, first, a discussion of the restoration of Israel. The two debaters then argued whether or not the kingdom of Christ had been established. The third issue discussed was: Does Christ now reign or will he reign over the earth for a thousand years? Then, turning the arguments around, Boles responded that Christ is now on David's throne, a position Boll denied. The final topic dealt directly with the premillennial return of Christ. Boles pushed Boll hard to answer what he meant by the "imminent" return of Christ. Boll refused to name a date, but he did suggest the events that would happen prior to Christ's return could happen at any time— the return of the Roman Empire and the return of the Jews to the Holy Land.

The debate ended on an amiable note. Even though the disputants remained convinced of their positions, both men believed good had been accomplished. Possibly, they believed, everyone better understood the issues. Boles, in fact, believed enough agreement existed between the two men that they could "fellowship each other as brethren in the Lord." The first major hurdle of the 1920s had been met and fellowship remained. In the 1930s, the same topic would be discussed at greater length, but feelings of mutual accord would not exist.

BIBLICAL NAMES FOR THE CHURCH

What would proponents of restoration call themselves? Even though they urged undenominational Christianity, they realized that those who accepted the plea of restoration would have to be distinguished in some manner. Alexander Campbell favored the phrase "disciple of Christ." Barton Stone, from the first, used the term "Christian." What would they call themselves collectively? There was no major problem among most when they simply referred to themselves as "the church." The phrase "Disciples of Christ" has been used to describe the broad spectrum of the Restoration Movement since the early days. From the initial years, the two names most often placed on the meetinghouses of the churches were Church of Christ and Christian Church.

Considering the problems faced in the 1830s, it was inevitable that a discussion would follow in later years concerning the name of the church and who were Christians. The question surfaced with the rebaptism issue. David Lipscomb followed the view held by most restorers: when one is baptized to please God, it is God who adds that person to the church. It is possible, then, for Christians to be in denominations if they were baptized for the correct reason— to obey God. As noted in chapter one, Austin McGary of the *Firm Foundation* advanced the position that one must be baptized "for the remission of sins." Instead of being a promise, remission of sins became a part of the command. Christians, McGary stated, could not be in denominations, a position shared by many of his associates. In 1898, Lipscomb, seemingly tired of the discussion, penned a lengthy paragraph on baptism. He especially wanted to show what baptism accomplishes.

> The office of baptism is to introduce him who believes in God through Christ and repents of his sins into Christ Jesus, into his spiritual body; by which he becomes a member of the body of Christ. In this act of entrance into Christ he puts on Christ; his sins are forgiven; he is consecrated to the service of God; he is born of water and the spirit; he fulfills the righteousness of God for justifying man; he finds the answer of a good conscience; is saved from his sins; is translated into the Kingdom of God's dear Son. The same act that introduced him into Christ secures to him all these blessings and privileges and others not here enumerated.[14]

With the separation of 1906, the issue would become even more pronounced.

The *Gospel Advocate* provided the forum, with the older members of the staff following the positions enunciated by David Lipscomb. Early in the 1920s, M. C. Kurfees penned a series of articles titled "Bible Things by Bible Names."[15] Many, he believed, were using the phrase "church of Christ" in a sectarian sense. "Unless our present day use of the term 'church' includes all the

children of God in the territory to which it is applied, we are
plainly and unquestionably using it in a sectarian sense, and hence
are not, in such instances, calling Bible things by Bible names." To
further clarify himself, Kurfees continued:

> No one can properly claim that persons are in the church of
> God unless they have complied with the terms which God him-
> self stipulated for that purpose, and not merely a substitute for
> them.

More specifically, he said: "The name or designation, 'church
of Christ,' is coming to be used, in some sections of the country, to
the exclusion of every other New Testament designation of the
church." As a result, the use of church of Christ to distinguish a
group from the Methodist church, Baptist church, or Presbyterian
church is to use a sectarian term.

> To say the "Christian Church" and mean nothing more than the
> people constituting the movement inaugurated by the
> Campbells, or to say "the church of Christ" and mean nothing
> more than those of that movement who do not use organs, soci-
> eties, and other innovations, is as sectarian as it is to call a part
> of the church "the Baptist Church," "the Methodist Church,"
> "the Episcopal Church," or by any other denominational name.

As expected, Kurfees received many questions and several criticisms. A. M. George, writing in the *Firm Foundation,* disagreed
with Kurfees: "No man can be a Christian and a Babylonian [a
member of a denomination] at the same time." When Kurfees
stated that all the reformers of the nineteenth century—the
Campbells, Stone, Scott, Franklin, Lipscomb, McGarvey, and all
others—accepted the same position he held, George answered that
he did not care what the Franklins and the Lipscombs believed: "I
shall undertake to prove [my position] by scriptures, not by the
great preachers. The great preachers are to blame for all the
Babylonish rubbish with which the church is littered today."[16]

In Texas and through the pages of the *Firm Foundation,* John
E. Dunn espoused Kurfees position. Dunn suggested: "If we speak
of the College Street congregation as being the church of Christ
(the body of Christ is the church) in Waxahachie, we use a sectarian expression, because it leaves out some of God's children in
Waxahachie. To speak scripturally, the body of Christ in

Waxahachie must include every one who have [sic] been born of water and the spirit." He then added: "Those who worship at College Street do not claim to be the only Christians in Waxahachie, but we do claim to be Christians only."[17]

J. D. Tant responded: "I fear Brother Dunn, in trying to get the Digressives in as a part of the church of Christ at Waxahachie, is going to pull the gate a little too high, and let many of us who are only sects be lost."[18] The contest between the various groups of Texas Disciples over the instrument and missionary societies had been so bitter that it became much easier to draw the line somewhat tighter than in Tennessee and Kentucky. Thus A. M. George could answer Kurfees' statement, "we should 'indorse all the truth taught by the denominations and condemn all the error.' To do this, I think I will have to condemn the whole business."[19]

In 1928, N. B. Hardeman preached his third series of sermons in Nashville's Ryman Auditorium. Where the first two series had dealt with doctrinal issues, especially those things usually referred to as "first principles," Hardeman concentrated on the church in 1928. Basing many of his first sermons on history, he traced the church's victories, sufferings, and failures through the events of 1900 years. In the middle of his twenty-one sermon series, Hardeman introduced the restoration principle, tracing the idea from the Independency movement of James and Robert Haldane in Scotland through the questioning of religious practices of James O'Kelly and Abner Jones. He introduced Barton W. Stone, Thomas and Alexander Campbell, and a host of associates to illustrate the plea for restoring the church of the New Testament. His special emphasis was upon Alexander Campbell's relationship to churches of Christ. Did he found a church? Hardeman answered, "No." "The one thing he tried to impress was that churches founded by men were unscriptural, and were responsible for a divided state of affairs."[20]

He followed this sermon with three speeches on Christian unity. His thrust was the divisiveness of denominationalism and the need to reject all sectarian positions and be "Christians only." He urged: "Let us tear down our denominational fences, get rid of those things that pen us off into parties, and stand once more as a unit."

Fearful those listening might mistake his plea, Hardeman emphasized his lack of interest in converting anyone to another denomination. He called all to be Christian.

> I have never been so egotistic to say that my brethren with
> whom I commune on the first day of the week are the *only*
> Christians on this earth. I never said that in my life. I do make
> the claim that we are Christians *only*. But there is a vast differ-
> ence between that expression and the one formerly made.[21]

As to those who would be included in the church in Nashville if
Paul were to address a letter to the church in the city as he did at
Corinth, Hardeman stated: "Every Christian in this city would be
included and thus addressed." Continuing, he remarked: "Every
child of God in this city is a part of the church, and, therefore, the
obligation to lay aside everything tending toward a partisan spirit,
rests upon him the more heavily."[22]

In 1929, F. W. Smith, a regular columnist for the *Advocate* and
the preacher for the church in Franklin, Tennessee, wrote the com-
mentary for the *Young People's Quarterly,* a Sunday school book-
let published by the Gospel Advocate company. On the first day of
the year, he received a letter from a brother in Union City,
Tennessee, critical of the use of the phrase "The Christian Church"
as the topic of a lesson. Besides condemning the use of "Christian"
for the church—"the church does not belong to Christians but to
Christ"—the correspondent disagreed with Smith's statement that
the church includes all the saved on the earth: "I believe every denomination is a synagogue of Satan and a promoter of division
which is in open rebellion against God. They all together consti-
tute spiritual Babylon and are harlot daughters."

In response, Smith reprinted the introduction to the *Quarterly*
lesson. Concluding, Smith wrote: "In seeking to escape sectarianism, we should avoid referring to the church of the New Testament
in a sectarian manner by making it contain less than what the Bible
means by 'the church of God' or 'the church of Christ.'" Relative
to the use of the term "Christian church," Smith believed the
phrase simply means "a church made up of Christians." He then
added: "For it to express *ownership* it would have to be written,
'the Christian's church.'"

Indicating his former identification with those termed
"Christian church," Smith related how many older members of the
church referred to and still refer to the "Christian church." But, he
added, the term is often used today to identify the digressive
brethren. Smith bemoaned the situation: "I have long since learned

that a majority of the preachers and other members of the church have a sectarian idea in their minds when they speak of the church of Christ." A part of the cause, Smith suggested, is to fail to recognize others as holding to some truth. Furthermore, he added: "To speak of them [denominations] in the way our brother does renders his efforts to enlighten them useless, because they will turn a deaf ear to his message. When you accuse people of being dishonest in their religion, styling them 'the synagogue of Satan,' etc., you drive them from you."[23]

F. W. Smith did not defend his views alone. Within a month, a G. C. Brewer letter appeared commending the article. Brewer, too, was misunderstood and accused of accepting unscriptural positions. This he emphatically denied. "My position is exactly the same position that Brother Smith had taken in the editorials. . . . It is the same position that was held by Brethren Lipscomb, Sewell, McQuiddy, and F. D. Srygley; the same position that Brethren Elam, Kurfees, Smith, and all others who have a nonsectarian view of the church [hold]." Furthermore, the narrow sectarian spirit held by some "is far greater transgression from New Testament Christianity than the use of instrumental music."[24]

Both Brewer and Smith continued receiving critical comments from across the country, including letters from J. Petty Ezell, John T. Lewis, and Cecil B. Douthitt. In response to Douthitt, Brewer related an incident in the 1908 W. W. Otey–J. B. Briney debate on instrumental music. Otey used a chart telling "what the church of Christ" believed and what "the Christian church" believed. Briney, responding to the chart, said he belonged to both. A number of amens were heard, many from those classified as "loyal" brethren in churches of Christ. Then Brewer wrote:

> Our older brethren did not make the distinctions that we make. They had a much better grasp upon the idea of a nonsectarian church than most of us have. We are far more sectarian than they were. (I am prepared to prove this any day.) The plain fact is that they were better educated, better informed, better balanced, as a rule, than we are today. . . . The cause of this is easily seen. We have ceased to emphasize broad culture and profound Bible knowledge and have exalted men into the position of "big preachers" simply because they can preach a few first-principle sermons and "skin" the sects, when they are wholly deficient in many other respects.[25]

Some could not accept the term "Christian" to designate the church. Early in the twentieth century, the usage became totally dependent upon the separation of the society/instrument group from the nonsociety/noninstrument group. In response to Foy E. Wallace, Jr., Smith said he could not find in the New Testament the term "church of Christ" used in reference to the entire church. Therefore, if brother Wallace wanted to use a biblical term, then he must abandon "church of Christ" for some other term. Churches of Christ in Romans 16:16 refers to individual congregations, not the whole number of congregations worldwide.

In response to John T. Lewis, a former student at the Nashville Bible School, M. C. Kurfees used David Lipscomb's emphasis on the church. First, he quoted Lipscomb as writing: "I do not think any name was given as a distinctive name. They are oftener than otherwise called simply 'churches' without any modifying word." Again he used Lipscomb to indicate how some use the name in a sectarian sense.

> There are some in sectarian churches who obey God and follow him in spite of the sectarianism of the churches in which they find themselves. As examples, there are persons in the Baptist, Methodist, and Presbyterian churches who are baptized to obey God rather than to please the sects. In this they arise above the sectarian spirit despite the parties in which they find themselves. They ought to get out of the sectarian churches, but they see so much sectarianism in the nonsectarian churches that they think they are all alike.[26]

Would churches of Christ, pleading for undenominational Christianity, escape the pitfalls of sectarianism while they continued to call for a return to the New Testament for their authority?

T. B. LARIMORE: A STABILIZING INFLUENCE

Undenominational Christianity is difficult to plead without developing a sectarian stance. The very nature of any restoration movement tends toward a partisan spirit. Having "a thus saith the Lord" and the techniques of confrontation causes an issue-oriented fellowship. The constant search for truth, Lipscomb averred, requires the occasional stirring of the stagnant pond. As recently as 1920, M. C. Kurfees urged: "Let no Christian man or woman oppose controversy. As long as truth has to clash with error, controversy will be inevitable." [27]

On the other hand, there have always been those who will not engage in the "clash of ideas." In fact, the great majority of men and women who have pled for the restoration of New Testament Christianity have never been involved in public confrontation. This has been that silent stream—that stabilizing influence—keeping the plea for undenominational Christianity alive throughout two centuries. A representative of such an influence is a man who preached throughout the last third of the nineteenth century and well into the twentieth. While the controversy concerning the church raged in 1929, T. B. Larimore died in California. Larimore had lived his life as a Christian, a faithful member of the church, but he never became embroiled in the myriad controversies among his brethren. Instead, he was a stabilizer. At his death the papers, the *Gospel Advocate,* the *Firm Foundation,* and the *Christian Standard,* hailed him as a great Christian man.

The emphasis of the Restoration Movement from the times of Barton Stone and the Campbells was to seek the biblical truth and to follow it. Within a short while, however, charges and counter-charges were hurled between various factions. The Stone disciples were displeased with the direction of the Campbell movement. Because of several doctrinal conflicts, including those surrounding the atonement and the Holy Spirit, the Campbells questioned the Stone movement. In 1857, controversy divided Tolbert Fanning and Robert Richardson, with their friends lining up on either side. This type of partisan spirit has engulfed the Restoration Movement in every era.

For this reason David Lipscomb called his generation to center on the truths of the Bible, not on a party spirit. Thus in 1907, Lipscomb wrote: "A sectarian is one who defends everything his party holds or that will help his party, and opposes all that his party does not hold or that will injure the strength and popularity of his party. . . . Hence the party lines define his faith and teaching." On the other hand, the truth seeker will discover truth wherever he finds it. Lipscomb added: "A true lover of truth seeks out and appropriates as his own every truth he finds, no matter who holds it or teaches it. All truth is the heritage of the truth lover and the truth seeker." [28]

Lipscomb's statement identifies Theophilus Brown Larimore.[29] A short study of his life shows a different spirit from those who were issue oriented. Larimore was born on July 10, 1843, in East Tennessee; little is known of his youth. His father, evidently from a rather prominent family, was never a part of the home. Larimore, however, enjoyed a very close relationship with his mother. Prior to his teenage years, young Larimore gladly helped her earn the family living.

Even though his mother needed Larimore to help support the family, she knew his need for education. Therefore, she sent him across the mountains in 1859 to Mossey Creek Baptist Academy (presently Carson-Newman College). Here he became interested in religion but failed to experience salvation.

> They tell me that those who surrender entirely to Jesus, and seek religion with all their hearts, shall find it. I have not found it, and I can not find it. Either the doctrine is wrong, or I have not sought with all my heart. Surely I can not be mistaken as to my own purposes. They may defend the doctrine by impugning my motives and denying my sincerity; but I know I have been honest with myself, and have sought with all my heart.[30]

Although he did not "get religion" while at Mossey Creek Baptist Academy, he did receive a diploma from the school.

The Civil War provided an interesting insight on T. B. Larimore. He was a member of the Confederate army, serving in a number of battles, the Logan Cross Road skirmish and Shiloh being the most important. At Logan Cross Roads, General Felix K. Zollicoffer was mortally wounded. Young Larimore, under a flag of truce, accompanied General Simon B. Buckner to retrieve their fallen leader. At Shiloh, Larimore watched for the Federal gunboats, even writing the dispatch to General Albert S. Johnson when he sighted the enemy. He did not, however, as a participant, see the end of the conflict. He was captured while scouting in his own Sequatchie Valley. Given the choice of an army detention camp or becoming a noncombatant, he chose the latter. His war was over. Years later, during special celebrations of former Confederate soldiers, Larimore participated fully, even donning his old uniform.

Because of living difficulties in the midst of war in Tennessee, Larimore removed his family to Kentucky. At Hopkinsville, he was baptized on his twenty-first birthday. Two years later he preached his first sermon. While in Kentucky, he supported his family by hauling wood and teaching school. In the fall of 1866, Larimore traveled to Nashville to continue his education at Franklin College. From his own pen he told how he thought he was already an educated person, one who should be teaching instead of being taught. He indicated, however, that the testing by the faculty quickly identified his weaknesses—he could memorize, but he could neither think nor reason.

It was, nevertheless, a good year for him. He had the opportunity to study under Tolbert and A. J. Fanning, although it was not the same Franklin College in existence prior to the war. The original college buildings burned shortly after the civil conflict. Completing a year, maybe somewhat more, he decided to move to Alabama, where he contracted to teach at Mountain Home. On leaving Franklin College, Tolbert Fanning said to Larimore: "I have never failed to correctly read a man, when I had a good chance. You may never accumulate a fortune, but *you'll never depart from the faith or bring reproach upon the cause of Christ.*"[31] Fanning read his man properly!

Alabama would be his place of work for most of the next several years. The school at Mountain Home did not succeed, so he preached and taught school in West Tennessee for a few months before returning to Florence, Alabama. In the meantime, he married Miss Esther Gresham of Florence. On the small Gresham farm Larimore decided to establish a school—Mars Hill Academy. Larimore, however, did not have sufficient funds to build a school. Being a determined man, he borrowed enough money to construct a classroom building. For the next seventeen years, he involved himself in one of the greatest works of his life.

Beginning each morning at four o'clock with chapel, study filled the student's day, including daily instruction in the Bible. Always interested in the preaching of the gospel, Larimore met daily with the young men who planned to preach. Among his students at Mars Hill were J. C. McQuiddy, F. D. and F. B. Srygley, F. C. Sowell, E. A. Elam, Lee Jackson, and J. H. Halbrook. Many of these young men eventually found their way to Nashville and worked with David Lipscomb on the *Gospel Advocate*. Was the school a success? Based on the quality of its graduates, it certainly was.

From across the country, urgent calls came for him to preach. Even more, deep in his own heart Larimore wanted to give additional time to proclaiming the gospel. Therefore, the school closed in 1887. For the remainder of his life, Larimore spent his time preaching, giving most of his efforts to special evangelistic work. Only on rare occasions did he attempt to "settle down" at one locality to preach for a single congregation. These attempts were never satisfactory.

Why was T. B. Larimore so successful as an evangelist? He had qualities of voice, personality, and a command of the English language that made him an exceptional public speaker. M. C. Kurfees said of him: "He was one of the best educated men of his day in the English language, and one of the most polished and accurate in the use of it whom it was ever my pleasure and privilege to hear."[32]

Larimore did not possess some qualities most thought necessary to be a successful preacher. He was not a debater. He could not and would not become embroiled in controversy: it was totally against his nature. F. D. Srygley described him:

> There is a gentleness in his nature that impresses itself upon the churches he builds up, the pupils he teaches and the converts he makes. . . . Wherever he labors, he not only instructs people in the doctrine of Christ, but teaches and shows them how to receive, retain and cultivate the *Spirit* of Christ as well.[33]

Those who might question his methods never questioned Larimore's loyalty to the Bible.

How did he see himself? Why did he take the direction he did? In a private letter to F. D. Srygley, Larimore said:

> I do not pitch into my brethren who do not do exactly as I do, or understand every thing just as I do, for two reasons: 1. I can understand how it is possible for them to act correctly and still not always do as I do. 2. I love my brethren, and, long, long ago solemnly resolved to never go to war with them, or, rather, *against* them. It seems to suit some good brethren to dispute with each other; but it does not suit me.[34]

In reference to the church, and especially the divisions surfacing within the church during his lifetime, Larimore described himself:

If I know what and where I am, I belong to the church of Christ; not a branch or wing of it, or a party in it; but to the church itself. I propose to never stand identified with one special wing, branch, or party of the church. My aim is to preach the gospel, do the work of an evangelist, teach God's children how to live, and, as long as I do live, to live as nearly an absolutely perfect life as possible. To this end, I am ready to go wherever and when ever duty calls, always using myself and all that I possess in the cause of Christ in the way that I think will accomplish most good.[35]

If any person ever accomplished what he set out to do, Larimore did. It is estimated that many more than 10,000 people were baptized under his preaching. During one six-month meeting at Sherman, Texas, 254 accepted baptism. At the newly established South Nashville church, the home congregation of David Lipscomb, 121 were immersed during a six-week meeting. With such success he became a living legend.[36]

During the last years of his life, readers of the *Gospel Advocate* looked forward each week to his articles, "Word from Washington," and then to his "Greetings from the Golden Gate," when he made his final home in California. These articles—many of which were also included in the *Firm Foundation*—continued well into 1929, the year of his death.

F. L. Rowe, of the *Christian Leader,* wrote G. C. Brewer that T. B. Larimore "was the nearest approach to Christ that he had ever seen among men." Agreeing with the assessment, Brewer related a conversation with a number of preacher friends about his remedy for doubt and fear:

When I become gloomy and doubts trouble me, and when my faith in humanity begins to waver, I go and get one of Brother Larimore's books and read some of his sermons and letters, and the world gets brighter, human souls seem more precious, my heart becomes tender, and God is nearer and heaven a reality.[37]

The impact of Theophilus Brown Larimore continued through his "boys" of Mars Hill days. Others caught the spirit of this man and have carried it to the present day. Because of his kind, the Restoration Movement, as seen in churches of Christ, has found stability in each generation. Without Larimore and his spiritual children, the dream of the Restoration Movement would be beyond reach.

CONCLUSION

A turbulent decade came to an end on December 31, 1929. America and the world were now facing a financial depression that would last through much of the 1930s. It had been a decade of important events, while churches of Christ searched for direction. By 1930, many of the directions had been determined. But what lay ahead would be carried on by younger men. Those who had been involved in the conflict of ideas culminating in the separation of churches of Christ from the Disciples of Christ in 1906 were either dead or beyond the ability to give leadership. The period from 1906 to 1930 saw the deaths of David Lipscomb, James A. Harding, G. Dallas Smith, J. C. McQuiddy, Austin McGary, E. G. Sewell, E. A. Elam, and T. B. Larimore. In 1931, M. C. Kurfees joined his fellow laborers in death, followed shortly by F. W. Smith.

What of the future? Would others come forward to give leadership to a new generation? Would they have the same spirit and concern of earlier leaders? One thing was certain: the next generation would find someone to walk in the shoes of those departed.

CHAPTER 6

FROM OUTSIDERS TO TENTATIVE INSIDERS: War and Peace Among Churches of Christ

As discussed in previous chapters, churches of Christ were searching for direction following the recognized division in 1906. It is simple enough to say that churches of Christ continued on the same path blazed by Barton W. Stone and the Campbells early in the nineteenth century. On the other hand, the hundred years between the beginnings of the American Restoration Movement and the separation of churches of Christ from the larger Disciples of Christ was a period of developing differences. These differences emerge, in part, in the makeup of American culture. However much a people might try, it is difficult to escape history and the culture in which they find themselves. Religious groups, including churches of Christ, are not immune to the prevailing culture.

Some religious fellowships have attempted to withdraw from the larger culture. Most Americans know the quaint ways of Mennonite and Amish communities. Yet even these have not been able totally to escape the world. Churches of Christ have never deliberately withdrawn into secluded communities, but there has always been a definite emphasis on separation. Historically, churches of Christ have followed certain ideas that make them exclusivists in the eyes of historians. This exclusivism is often traced to Campbell's early emphasis on immersion as the only mode of baptism. As the years passed, opposition to the missionary society

and the instrument in worship, followed by the refusal to fellowship the Federation of Churches and Christians Workers caused the
exclusivist label to adhere even more tightly.

These developments, plus the acceptance of liberal theology by
the left-wing Disciples, caused the separation of churches of Christ
from the Disciples of Christ. In many ways, it was a rejection of
the prevailing religion of the early twentieth century. In fact,
churches of Christ chose to remain outside the mainstream of
American religious life.

As the years passed, moving on toward World War II and beyond to the years of their greatest growth during the late 1940s and
the 1950s, churches of Christ, not unlike their religious neighbors,
became more wedded to the culture around them. But the difficulty of tracing the matter is bound up in cultural, and even moral,
issues that changed over the years: attitudes toward movies, dancing, mixed (male and female) swimming, playing cards, and a
dozen other things emphasized in the preaching of the 1930s and
1940s.

Even though there has been an occasional suggestion that baptism should be reopened as an issue or that fellowship should be
broadened, the major doctrinal characteristics have not changed
since 1906. Internal issues have appeared and have resulted in
some division, but not sufficient to cause the loss of identity. War
and peace is one issue, however, that shows a definite change from
an almost "outsider" position to one that has brought churches of
Christ much closer to national norms.

Never had there been a consistent position taken by nineteeth-
century Disciples toward war and peace. Therefore, this chapter
will focus on the different positions held within churches of Christ
concerning war and peace, with a quick review of the ideas of
Tolbert Fanning and David Lipscomb.

THE PACIFIST POSITION

Tolbert Fanning was a strong proponent of the Christian remaining aloof from political involvement, including war. As early
as the Mexican War, he openly published his opposition to
Christians participating in the conflict. He stated his opposition to
political involvement: "Christians are commanded to abstain from
all appearance of evil, and participation in political companies as

officers or members is wrong, and members of the church should be sharply reproved for so acting."[1] As the Civil War approached, he urged Christians to refrain from the conflict. It was not the Christian's battle.

David Lipscomb, on the other hand, was staunchly patriotic during his Franklin College days and throughout the first years of his public work. Democracy, he said, was "the first fruit of Christianity." The ballot box was sacred. As the years passed into Civil War, his views dramatically changed. Now he could not participate in any government. Like the Anabaptists of the sixteenth century, he believed government existed for those who refuse the rule of God. Therefore, war was not the obligation of the Christian. God's people must give allegiance only to him. Lipscomb often quoted Jesus: "If my kingdom were of this world, then would my disciples fight."

Lipscomb's in-depth study of the Christian and government during the Civil War became lead articles in the reissued *Gospel Advocate* in 1866. Several years later the articles appeared in book form under the title, *Civil Government*. Great numbers of Disciples, especially in the South, accepted his ideas. Others, including John W. McGarvey, thought his views quaint. Daniel Sommer totally and completely opposed them. Isaac Errett concluded that Lipscomb only mirrored the views of the defeated South. Nonetheless, Lipscomb continued sharing his conclusions through the pages of the *Gospel Advocate*. He was often challenged, but not deterred. Thus, many in churches of Christ, especially the graduates of the Nashville Bible School, taught these ideas across the wide expanse of the United States.[2]

There was no uniform, stated political position among churches of Christ. When World War I approached, most possible positions appeared in the various journals of the fellowship. Lipscomb's views received wide acceptance, but any reading of the *Gospel Advocate* and *Firm Foundation* shows a weakening of the position. Those who desired to apply for conscientious objector status were urged to read Lipscomb's *Civil Government*. A. J. Jernigan, writing in the *Firm Foundation,* drafted a letter to President Woodrow Wilson stating that churches of Christ were "truly thankful for the liberty we have under [the flag] in being permitted to worship God." Nevertheless, Jernigan stated, we "cannot conscientiously take up arms to kill." He then added:

> We, therefore, most earnestly petition and pray that every member of the church of Christ be exempted from compulsory military service in the army or navy of the United States, and that we be permitted to continue to worship God in the way we believe to be right.[3]

WORLD WAR I: A CLASH OF IDEAS

Positioned at the other extreme among churches of Christ was Daniel Sommer, editor of the *Apostolic Review.* Defending America's involvement in World War I, Sommer noted that God forbids murder. Therefore he "commands someone *kill the murderer.*" He was ashamed of his German ancestry when he saw how the Kaiser disregarded treaties signed with other nations. At the time Germany declared war on the United States, Sommer called Wilhelm II "an international outlaw."[4] Debating J. N. Cowan in 1926, Sommer urged Christians to treat the government as we would want the government to treat Christians. Therefore, when the government drafts Christians to defend their country, "we undoubtedly have a scriptural right to do so [participate in the conflict]." As a Christian would protect his home against the ruffian, so should he protect his country from an aggressive nation.[5]

A. B. Lipscomb, front-page writer for the *Gospel Advocate,* represented pacifism among churches of Christ. On March 8, 1917, before the declaration of war, Lipscomb responded under the title, "Why I Am a Pacifist."

> With a kind of sneer in his voice, a man asked me the other day if I were a pacifist. When I replied in the affirmative, his next question was: "Why?" "Because Jesus was," is the best answer I have to give. "When he was reviled," he "reviled not again;" "when he suffered," he "threatened not," but "committed himself to him that judgeth righteously."[6]

Quoting William Lyons Phelps at length, Lipscomb agreed with the writer in the *North American Review:* "Would it not be well to give Christianity a chance?"

The pacifist's position was difficult during World War I. The war's purpose, to "make the world safe for democracy," was noble in the eyes of most Americans. Thus critics called the pacifist "slacker," "mollycoddle," and "milksop." In response to such thrusts, Lipscomb urged: "Dare to be called a coward for Jesus' sake!" But Lipscomb did not oppose noncombatant service. "It is a safe rule to say that a Christian can do consistently for humanity in this crisis what he might do consistently in time of peace. For that matter, there is no reason why Christians, along with others, should not enlist in the regular army and navy to render humanitarian service under military discipline."[7]

J. C. McQuiddy, editor and publisher of the *Advocate,* while upholding the rights of the conscientious objector to nonparticipation in war, had only scorn for one who would use conscience to escape combat, when his beliefs and actions did not reflect this position. "Men should not be shirkers now," said McQuiddy.

> If they claim exemption when they really have no right to such claim, it will only make it harder for the really conscientious objector to war to secure exemption. Men who vote and take part in our government and who favor Christians doing this cannot consistently plead exemption on the ground of religious convictions against war.[8]

In Texas, G. H. P. Showalter, editor of the *Firm Foundation,* permitted in-depth discussion of the war issue. One writer in 1914 encouraged Christians to be peaceful like Christ, while another scribe early in 1915 urged helping Europeans already involved in the war. As the war progressed, A. M. George, a regular contributor to the *Firm Foundation,* asked: "How can there be compatibility between God's kingdom and citizenship in civil government?"[9] Under the heading "Can a Christian Go To War?" W. W. Carter argued that since Christ would not allow his subjects to fight for the establishment of his kingdom, how then could they fight for the governments of this world or help the war effort in any way?

John T. Hinds, front-page writer for the Texas paper, urged churches to remain aloof from the business of warfare.[10] Because of these and other anti-war and anti-government statements, A. W. Young suggested, in response to the Espionage Act of June 15, 1917, "Our beliefs and opinions against war could be considered treasonable."[11]

After allowing all sides a hearing, Showalter made his position clear in June 1918. Suggesting that a Christian's relationship to government did not change when peace becomes war, Showalter wrote: "Where did the apostle make any distinction in supporting the government in war, and supporting the government in times of peace?" He added:

> The apostle requires it [support of the government], and especially at a time when so much is involved—when the rights, liberties, and happiness of so many millions of humanity are being tried in the balance—does it to me appear of the greatest solemnity and of the highest importance. For my part, I think that every Christian should the more carefully discharge his duty as a citizen now.[12]

Sharing the belief that Christians may oppose combatant service, he could not understand the Mennonite position of total and complete conscientious objection. Clearly, the editor believed that democracy was threatened, for he urged Christians to support their government in "suppressing this outlaw nation [Germany]."

Even though editors among churches of Christ took a more tolerant position toward participating in the military efforts in Europe, still the pacifist position remained an alternative. Many desired continued discussion of the topic in the *Gospel Advocate,* but such conflict was muted. Years later, G. C. Brewer stated that he could not get permission, because of government regulations, to write in behalf of the conscientious objector.

In the face of almost total involvement in the war hysteria, some 64,693 American citizens asked for noncombatant status. When these reported for induction, however, only 4,000 finally applied for some phase of noncombatant service. Of these, only 1,060 were total objectors to war—the Mennonites, Quakers, and Brethren furnished the overwhelming numbers—634. Churches of Christ had thirty-one, while the Jehovah's Witnesses, or Russellites, had sixty.[13] When one considers that churches of Christ had some 200,000 members in 1917, ranking sixth in the list of conscientious objectors is rather revealing. The Lipscomb's pacifist view remained strong in the brotherhood.

Young men facing military service in 1917 were not alone in making Christian decisions. The noninvolvement of churches of Christ in any organization larger than the local congregation caused problems for individual Christians and churches during World War I. The United States government recognized the need for spiritual help for the military. Therefore, the government designated the YMCA to oversee the placement of Protestant preachers in military camps. The Knights of Columbus served the same purpose for Catholics.

Working through the YMCA concerned many in churches of Christ. Thus, J. C. McQuiddy and others of his staff found it necessary to explain the "Y's" function. The YMCA cannot "interfere with the religious belief and teaching of any faithful minister of the gospel." McQuiddy further stated:

> There is no reason for discussing the propriety or scripturalness of entering this open door and taking advantage of this opportunity to preach the gospel to our sons who have been conscripted by the government for its service. . . . People on the outside have no right to assume superior goodness over those who are on the inside. . . . While it should be freely conceded, and is freely conceded, that these men [conscientious objectors] rank high in point of character, yet we dare not say they rank any higher than the many thousands upon thousands of young men who have felt impelled by their conscience to stand back of the government and to defend the country that they love.[14]

Officially, the *Gospel Advocate* opposed the war, but McQuiddy had a special reason to feel the way he did. He had one son in the army, another in the navy.

The *Advocate* also urged churches of Christ to help the sick and suffering in Europe. Under the leadership of A. B. Lipscomb, the editor solicited funds for the Armenian and Syrian Fund and the Poland Fund. The solicitation raised over $16,000 from individuals and congregations.[15] E. A. Elam became interested in working through the Red Cross to help the wounded in France. Guy E. Snavely, an official of the American Red Cross, suggested how a church might support a hospital bed for a year. Responding to the opportunity, the Bethlehem church—Elam's congregation in Wilson County, Tennessee—contributed $700 to endow a bed.

The Antioch church (now Schochoh) near Franklin, Kentucky, followed Bethlehem's example.[16] W. T. Kidwell in the *Firm Foundation* wrote: "The Red Cross people are simply acting the part of the Good Samaritan and this they can do only as the people furnish the money. There is certainly a difference in the specifically appointed things to be done by the church, and the general good we may do along life's way as opportunity is presented."[17]

Most who held a strong pacifist position were graduates of the Nashville Bible School. As a result, it is not surprising that H. Leo Boles and J. N. Armstrong, president of what is now Harding University, were strong proponents of pacifism. During the war students and teachers at the Bible School signed a petition addressed to the government asking to be exempted from military service. Abilene Christian College, however, gave evidence that pacifism was no longer a major direction of churches of Christ. The school participated in the Students' Army Training Corps. Young men who participated gained their education at government expense and earned a commission in the army. A spokesman for the school commented: "Our school is for genuine ministerial students, not for slackers."[18]

THE LEAGUE OF NATIONS

Following the war, Woodrow Wilson's call for the United States to enter the League of Nations received overwhelming support in the nation's churches. What was true nationally was especially true in the pages of the *Gospel Advocate*. The League did not receive as much coverage in the *Firm Foundation*. John Hinds favored the League, but his reason for urging peace was the enormous cost of war: "There is no use to bankrupt the world as well as kill off its citizens. It is to be desired that real world peace will come."[19] A. M. George was pessimistic when he asked, "Will the nations ever beat their swords into plow-shares?" Peace movements, he believed, were built on a false premise; therefore the League of Nations would not work.[20]

Two *Advocate* writers openly favored the League of Nations. Interestingly, both J. C. McQuiddy and M. C. Kurfees often indicated their nonpolitical stance. Nevertheless, since Jesus encouraged peace and taught his followers to be peacemakers, then all Christians should favor any attempt to bring peace to the world. Commenting on the peace conference at Versailles in 1919, Kurfees remarked: "Let us hope and pray that it will put an end to war, if not forever, at least for a long time."[21] Fearful that criticism and even opposition to the League of Nations might destroy the experiment in peace keeping, McQuiddy responded emphatically: "Christians should rejoice that the sentiment of our nation and government is such that it favors peace. This sentiment is due to the Bible and its influence. Christians, therefore, should do nothing that will discourage peace among the nations of the earth." He concluded:

> Let me encourage all of our readers to be constructionists and not destructionists. We all know that peace is a good thing, and a thing to be much desired; and while we may not agree with all of the plans that are made to bring it about, let us not be among the "knockers," but let us work as God directs us to in order to help and bless the world.[22]

Kurfees was more specific, noting in irony that "some preachers in Kentucky" criticized the government for going to war and then criticized the government for getting involved in proposing the League of Nations.

But the Senate of the United States rejected the League. Wilson could not carry the nation into the peacekeeping organization. A last ditch effort to save the League included a poll of preachers sponsored by the National Committee on the Churches and the Moral Aims of the War. McQuiddy noted that 17,000 preachers favored the League of Nations, while 805 opposed it. He was aghast that such a number would be opposed "to a righteous peace among the nations of the earth." [23]

In 1920 Kurfees deplored—even criticized—those who opposed the League of Nations for selfish or party reasons.

> It is most deplorable, indeed, that a great issue of worldwide interest with possibilities of incalculable good to all mankind should be clouded by partyism or selfishness in either church or state. If the demon of party politics can be relegated to the rear, and Christians themselves will consent, for the time being, to suspend controversy over their differences about Christians and war, here is a common ground where all parties and all creeds in both the civil and the religious realm can stand shoulder to shoulder and push together for the common weal of mankind.[24]

Commenting on Kurfees' article, McQuiddy remarked: "It is antichristian to discourage peace. No Christian will knowingly do anything that will in any way destroy peace and bring strife and bloodshed." [25] The wrangling between Republicans and Wilson, and concerning sectionalism, isolationism, and disillusionment all led, finally, to the refusal of the United States to become a part of the League. It met defeat on March 19, 1920, when the needed two-thirds majority could not be mustered in the Senate.

PACIFISM EMPHASIZED AFTER THE WAR

War and military preparedness remained a constant theme of journals among churches of Christ. E. A. Elam, the strongest of the pacifists on the *Advocate* staff, quickly became active again after the war. It concerned him that imprisoned conscientious objectors had been forgotten. He could not abide the comparison of soldiers dying on the battlefield with Jesus dying on the cross. Calling for a recognition of individual convictions, Elam wrote:

> The government which respects the religious convictions of a religious sect, as the Quakers, cannot do otherwise than respect the conscientious convictions of the individual. This must be done or there can be no religious liberty.

Recalling David Lipscomb's strong positions on civil government and his influence throughout the fellowship, it appalled Elam that a "service flag" hung in the building of the South College church in Nashville where Lipscomb had served as an elder. Even Christians had become "dancing mad" in support of the World War.[26] Elam evidently recognized that patriotism and nationalism had made great inroads into churches of Christ.

Receiving a letter from H. L. Meeks commending Elam's articles, J. C. McQuiddy responded:

> The men who stand firm for their convictions of right certainly are to be commended for the course they have taken, and it is very probable that if the attention of the government is called to the fact that these men [conscientious objectors] are being held in prison, something will be done for their relief.[27]

Nor could A. B. Lipscomb allow the praise of Sergeant Alvin York, the outstanding Tennessean and World War I hero, to go unchallenged:

> I dare say that the general public is misled in proclaiming York as the greatest hero—that is, if we are to see the matter as God sees it. There were hundreds of boys who refused to take up arms because they could not go contrary to the teachings of the meek and lowly Nazarene. They were not slackers, for they did what they could do conscientiously, performing the most menial tasks with uniform obedience and cheerfulness. But despite his humility and cheerfulness, the sure-enough conscientious objector was misunderstood and in many instances he was mistreated.[28]

"Perhaps," said Lipscomb, "after all has been said and God's inventory is taken, we will find our greatest hero, like Joseph of old, languishing in jail."

THE NEED FOR PEACE

Even though the United States did not participate in the League of Nations, a nagging feeling remained: Something had to bring about disarmament. During 1921-1922, the Washington Disarmament Conference met specifically to deal with worldwide naval power. The religious press, including the *Gospel Advocate,* watched with interest. Under the heading "Battleships or Bread," A. B. Lipscomb stated:

> The United States, England, and Japan seem to be vying with each other as to which can build the largest and most powerful navy. It does seem that the nations should have learned by this time that preparedness does not prevent war.

He then added: "How much better to preach to them the gospel of peace instead of compelling boys and young men to study and learn militarism!" [29] Lipscomb, agreeing with other religious leaders, believed disarmament must be encouraged during times of peace.

Lipscomb believed the Washington Conference had accomplished much good, even if it was only that men of different nationalities could discuss rationally their differences and attempt to find solutions. Sharing Lipscomb's emphasis on disarmament, K. C. Moser, a well-known evangelist in the southwest, believed Germany would not have tried war had she not been fully armed.

Moser pleaded: "Even if disarmament of the nations would not prevent wars, it would at least postpone them, and thereby give time for serious thought which might lead to arbitration." Noting the growing costs of arming nations, Moser urged:

> Let disarmament be talked about in the home, taught in the schools, proclaimed from the pulpit, and championed by the press, "till nations shall beat their swords into the plow- shares, and their spears into pruning hooks," and learn war no more.[30]

Most Americans welcomed the opportunity to fight in defense of their nation and democracy during World War I. Even though there were numerous slackers and 4,000 conscientious objectors, those numbers were small compared with the 2,810,296 men in- ducted into the military. Nevertheless, the suggestion that America needed a peacetime draft fell on deaf ears. A strong response came from all sections of the public. John Dunn was among the first to push the alarm. He had served for nearly two years in the army under the auspices of the National War Work Council. He shared camps, troop trains, ocean transports, and marches with the sol- diers. He remarked: "I had every opportunity by bitter experience to know the life of the soldier and the effects of such a life upon his character." Why did he oppose universal military training? The American soldiers made up the superior army in the European war, even though they were not brought up under military training. Furthermore, the soldiers themselves opposed universal training. Pleading, Dunn wrote:

> I should like to see a crusade waged all over America to crystalize public opinion against making every citizen a sol- dier. Training to fight breeds war. I believe the very day our country adopts such a policy, she starts on the downward path to ruin.[31]

Sharing many views with Dunn, E. A. Elam allowed his frustra- tions of three years to spill onto the pages of the *Advocate*. With a pointed thrust, Elam stated: "I have as much right to express my judgment on so great and grave an international political issue [League of Nations] as any man." Not being allowed to voice his real views during World War I, Elam asked: "For what are our sons but *slaves,* when forced to train for war and forced into war."

Elam and G. C. Brewer were both critical of the *Advocate* for not allowing them the right to present their pacifist views during the war. Very likely the editors warned against a strong pacifist thrust in the paper because of the Espionage Act of June 1917 and its revision in May 1918, sometimes called the Sedition Act. Almost anyone who criticized the government, its leaders, the nation's flag, or the Constitution, or made pacifist statements was subject to severe penalties.

Knowing that the League might not be accepted by the United States, Elam asked what preachers should do if such were the case?

> Preachers of the gospel and the church of God do not stand for and preach peace because it happens to be a law of nations, but because it is a law of God. They stand for and preach it when nations are at war in order to influence them to obey God and cease to shed blood.

With special reference to the universal training of American young men, Elam stated that the president could not be consistent by advocating a League of Nations while pushing for a huge system of militarism. Furthermore, Elam deplored political leaders, older men, passing laws that sent young men without the vote to war.

> One of the most unrighteous, unjust, and horribly cruel things is for rulers or lawmakers to vote or declare war, exempt themselves, and to force helpless and tender boys, who know nothing of its causes and who had nothing to do with bringing it about, to fight.[32]

Congress vindicated the concerns of Dunn and Elam on June 4, 1920, when it passed the National Defense Act. Instead of an army drafted from civilians, the Congress allowed a standing army of only 280,000 men, compared with the 500,000 men asked for by the military. The bulk of the military would be National Guard and Organized Reserve.[33]

PACIFISM IN A DILEMMA

Strong advocates of an anti-war position were denied space in the religious press during World War I. Therefore, the views of E. A. Elam and H. Leo Boles had to await the end of the conflict to be heard. Of all scribes among churches of Christ, none was as vocally opposed to war as Boles, twice president of David Lipscomb College. In 1923, Boles penned eleven articles under the overall title of *The New Testament Teaching On War.* First published in the *Advocate* and then gathered into a pamphlet, Boles announced that war is anti-Christian and opposed to the principles of Christianity. In the author's view, there was no possible way for Christians to be involved in war.[34]

During the early 1930s, as the threats of war drifted toward America from far away Asia and from across the Atlantic in Europe, G. C. Brewer answered a querist concerning the Christian's relationship to government and involvement in war. After stating a position much in line with that of David Lipscomb, Brewer responded to those who would accept noncombatant service:

> But, granting that all who ask for noncombatant service receive it, there is still the question of whether or not the noncombatant part of an army, which is essential in all armies and in all wars, is not as much a part of the war machine as the combatant forces. And those who stay at home and buy war stamps, war bonds, and in other ways contribute to the funds, are also participants in the slaughter.[35]

Knowing that the rumblings in Europe meant war for the United States at some future time, Brewer suggested a question Christians should ask themselves:

> What is our attitude toward politics and war? . . . [A]nd while we are trying to decide, we should remember that the old Book says: "Thou shalt not kill," "Resist evil," "Pray for your enemies," "The weapons of our warfare are not carnal," etc.

Pacifists among churches of Christ were caught in a dilemma. While anti-war views historically had a Christian base, during the 1920s and 1930s pacifism became more secular. In 1936, Brewer discovered this dilemma. Recognizing the accord struck between liberal religion in America and socialist/communist sympathizers, Brewer drew a distinction between political pacifists and Christians who desire peace or who oppose participation in war. Seeing communism as a cause of unrest in America, Brewer stated:

> They declaim loudly against "imperialistic war," and disguise their vengeful and bloody purpose with the garments of peace and fare forth as professional *pacifists*. They want to disarm, debilitate, and Chinafy other nations while red Russia becomes an armed camp—a military nation, militant, mobilized, and marching toward the overthrow of civilization. They train and arm their revolutionaries who are in our nation posing as citizens and running for office![36]

Even though Brewer adamantly opposed all totalitarian systems, including communism, Nazism, and fascism, he still could not bring himself to advocate military action as a Christian method for defeating such ungodly systems. In 1939, with war raging in Europe, Brewer again asked the question:

> What shall Christians do under present conditions? What can Christians do? The answer to these questions must be determined by where Christians are. *It must be understood that Christians cannot engage in carnal warfare. A Christian cannot slaughter his fellow men, regardless of what they do to him or even to his religion.* If Christians, therefore, are in Poland or Germany at this time, there is probably nothing that they can do except to die. Christians in France and England may be spared with their lives, but they will probably have to support the war in one way or another. In the United States, Christians are especially blessed, as they have always been. They may even get their passions aroused here and be guilty of unChristian feelings.[37]

Why was the world on the brink of total war? Once-civilized nations were turning from God to false philosophies, said Brewer. "All the nations have to a degree forgotten God, and either at the present or in the future they are going into hell." Furthermore, the same tendencies noted elsewhere in the world were at work in the

United States in 1939. "We see strong tendencies toward a dictatorship in our own country. We see much evidence that people disregard God, and that some of them have eliminated him from their thinking."[38]

H. Leo Boles, as mentioned earlier, was the strongest proponent of Christians remaining aloof from war. Buttressed by his writing, the *Advocate* remained the leading journal among churches of Christ to take a pacifist and noncombatant position toward World War II.

> It is a trite saying to call war sinful; however, it is true. No Christian can encourage, engage in, or knowingly and willingly profit from armed conflict in war at home or abroad. No Christian can maintain his Christian loyalty to God, Christ, and peace and accept military service or support military machinery of war. The whole spirit of war is against everything for which Jesus stands.[39]

In response to those who defended participation in war by saying: "I have no part in the making of the laws, and, therefore, I am not responsible for what I do as a soldier," Boles said that a Christian can never lose his individual responsibility. Nor can he shift that responsibility to an army or its leadership. How can one practice evil during war and be declared righteous, while in peacetime the same person would receive punishment? Boles carried on an unrelenting campaign against Christian participation throughout the duration of World War II.

From every indication, however, the majority among churches of Christ did not share the attitudes presented through the *Advocate*. A son of B. C. Goodpasture, the *Advocate's* editor, served in the armed forces of the United States. Evidently he made his own decision, as Goodpasture never attempted to force a noncombatant position on his children. Even an *Advocate* writer, R. L. Whiteside, made no distinction between the noncombatant and the soldier with a gun. "It is my firm conviction that a vote pledges the voter to sustain the government in any work necessary to its existence."[40]

Tracing his views back to World War I, Showalter of the *Firm Foundation* continued his combatant views throughout World War II. In fact, the pages of the Texas paper were much more open to advocates of Christian participation than to those who were pacifists and noncombatants. Besides the views expressed in the *Firm Foundation,* the most strident pro-war views appeared in the *Bible Banner,* edited by a former editor of the *Gospel Advocate,* Foy E. Wallace, Jr.

During 1939 and 1940, most articles in the *Firm Foundation* were rather general. Leslie G. Thomas suggested that each Christian had to determine the position he would take on the issue of combatant service, since there was not a consensus among churches of Christ. L. R. Wilson was thankful that the United States made provisions for preachers and preacher students. Furthermore, 50 percent of the positions in the military were of a noncombatant nature, Wilson noticed with pleasure. Nevertheless, the decision, he believed, remained a personal one.[41]

Where preachers worked directly through the YMCA during World War I, the new world conflict called for an alternate plan. The United States established a chaplaincy corps, where men who wished to serve had to meet specified qualifications. A number of men among churches of Christ applied for and received commissions, including Fred W. McClung and Frank Traylor. Edwin W. Hampton, former member at Winfield, Kansas, met death in action on December 18, 1943, while serving as a chaplain in Belgium.[42] Each of these men urged others to volunteer as chaplains. But Carl Spain asked a series of questions indicating his opposition to such service: "Is a chaplain responsible to the elders of a church? Is a chaplain supported by the church, or is he hired by the government?"[43] Answering his own questions, Spain noted that a chaplain is commissioned as a first lieutenant, paid by the government, and is responsible to the government. R. O. Kenley, defending conscientious objection to war in the *Firm Foundation* questioned whether a Christian could be a chaplain. He stated: "If a chaplain preached to soldiers the truth he would be tried and shot as a saboteur."[44] Even though the papers' positions were in conflict, both the *Firm Foundation* and the *Gospel Advocate* carried reports from the chaplains.

WORLD WAR II: CHANGING VIEWS

Two weeks following the bombing of Pearl Harbor on December 7, 1941, G. H. P. Showalter laid the foundation for many in churches of Christ to take an active part in the recently declared war.

> But what brought on the present horrible and disastrous war? It was because bad men secured and exercised control of the government of the aggressor nations. Faithless men! Haters of God and despisers of good men led the unhappy people into the tragedies and unutterable horrors of modern wars.[45]

It was an opinion not far different from G. C. Brewer's, but Showalter followed his reasoning to make World War II a just war. On the other hand, Brewer did not see any war in which the Christian may fight.

Since Japan attacked the United States, M. C. Franklin defended overt action by all citizens, including Christians. Never has God disallowed his people to fight in self-defense. Furthermore, God in times past aided his people in destroying the enemy. "There are gangster nations, as well as gangster individuals, to which honor is an unknown quality, and they must be dealt with as gangster individuals."[46] Those opposed to Christians serving in the military often used such arguments as to suggest that Christians might be killing a brother in Christ or, even worse, by bombing Tokyo, Christians might become baby killers. Showing a strong prejudice against both Germany and Japan, T. B. Wilkinson said that "no one wants to bomb babies except the Germans and Japs, no American soldier does." Furthermore, the Germans killed babies as fixed policy.

On the other hand, Wilkinson contended, Americans bombed cities to shorten the war, even though babies might have been killed. Others possibly were killed in the combat zone because the Germans used babies as shields. Wilkinson continued:

> Just as long as such criminals are allowed to go scot free and made national heroes of, like old Hindenburg at the close of the other war, we will have wars, and bigger wars. No nation has any more right to wage war upon another nation than one individual has to make war upon another.[47]

Such ideas caused deep concern among a dwindling number of pacifist spokesmen within churches of Christ. As had been true for several generations, the most adamant opposition to the Christian participating in combat came from Nashville through the pages of the *Gospel Advocate*. Led by H. Leo Boles and J. N. Armstrong before and during World War II, the publication made a strong plea for the conscientious objector. Therefore, when a special need arose to care for young men who declared themselves conscientious objectors, B. C. Goodpasture and his associates on the *Advocate* responded—Goodpasture editorially and Boles with numerous articles.

A point of conflict among churches of Christ was whether or not to support those men who had been placed in Civilian Public Service Camps. These camps were authorized by the government, but the support and operation was under the auspices of the historic peace churches—Quakers, Mennonites, and United Brethren. If the individual could not provide support for himself or if his family could not or would not support him, the sponsoring churches were asked to provide the support. B. C. Goodpasture responded to the need:

> These members of the church in camps for conscientious objectors should support themselves, if they are able. But if they cannot, and their relatives cannot or will not support them, then the congregations of which they are members should come to their aid. They should be dealt with as any other worthy member of the church in need. It is generous of the United Brethren to support our boys, but we should not let them do it. It is our responsibility.[48]

H. Leo Boles was more strident in his urging. Calling them "heroes in the service of God," Boles reprimanded those who referred to the COs as cowards, a term reportedly used by an elder of the church.

> These young men are worthy of better treatment from Christians. Such elders (?) are cowards. They fear public sentiment and the unpopularity of the world. They think that it is an expression of patriotism and loyalty to the government to persecute Christians who are suffering because of their convictions.[49]

In March 1943, Goodpasture received a letter from James P. Miller of Philadelphia, Pennsylvania, explaining in greater detail the situation confronting young Christians in the camps. According to Leroy Dakin, field secretary of the three peace churches sponsoring the camps, seventy-three young men from churches of Christ were in the camps as of October 1942. Recalling his conversation with Dakin, Miller wrote:

> These seventy-three boys from the church of Christ were not taught to be conscientious objectors by the Brethren, Friends, or Mennonites, but in their own Bible schools and by their own teachers and preachers. It is only fair, therefore, that you help us in a financial way that we may be able to carry the burden of their maintenance.

In a letter from Dakin, the secretary indicated that each young man costs the camp $35 per month. As of October 31, 1943, the total cost had reached $11,509.11. Reminding Miller that the government did not provide any funds, Dakin described the conviction of the men as

> a symbol of that freedom of conscience which is basic to every freedom for which we say we are fighting this second World War. They constitute a tiny minority in the life of our churches, but their presence tests our fidelity as Christians. If we do not deal as Christians should with this minority in the membership of our churches, how can we hope that God will use us to teach and lead our nation to deal wisely with minorities in our national life?[50]

By June 1943, organized response to the needs of the conscientious objectors began. I. B. Bradley of Dickson, Tennessee, agreed to forward funds to the various camps. The *Firm Foundation* received some money, which quickly went to the proper places. Californians formed an ad hoc committee known as the Service Committee for Conscientious Objectors to serve as an information point and also to receive funds for the support of the young men. Included on the committee were J. M. McCaleb, T. H. Bumstead, R. N. Squire, Wade Ruby, Boyd Field, and James L. Lovell. An early meeting in the Los Angeles area raised in pledges $300 per month for the work.[51]

At the end of World War II, 199 men of churches of Christ had been serviced in sixty-seven Civilian Public Service Camps around the United States. This was out of a total of nearly 12,000 American conscientious objectors. Considering the enormous number of draftees in the military during the war effort, the percentage is minuscule. There were many others—the number will never be known as records were not kept—who chose to accept noncombatant service instead of fighting. With the addition of these, the vast majority of Americans—and members of churches of Christ—chose to participate fully in the military.[52]

Not every one supported the conscientious objectors. Some, in fact, harshly criticized anyone who held the position and equally those who both defended them and asked for help. Writing in the *Bible Banner,* Foy E. Wallace, Jr., could not support those who would not defend their country. In answer to the call to pay the costs of upkeep of the conscientious objectors, W. W. Otey, writing in the *Firm Foundation,* penned the harshest statement against the COs. It was not a reflection on the church when support was not forthcoming, but on that small number of men who taught these men to follow their conscience instead of right judgment. Suggesting these men to be "slackers," Otey urged that money be raised to heal the wounds of those who were willing to give their lives so the hundred might "live in safety and ease." He concluded: "Suppose that all our boys were conscientious objectors like these few, how long would it be till the Japs and Germans would be here murdering, robbing, raping women and girls and binding all in barbaric slavery."[53]

FOY E. WALLACE, JR.'S, INFLUENCE ON THE ISSUES

For a hundred years, southern Disciples learned—first from Tolbert Fanning and then from David Lipscomb—not to participate in war or even in government. At various times those ideas came under attack, but never so strongly as at the outbreak of World War II. Some suggested Lipscomb formed his views as a result of the Civil War, a situation entirely different from that of the early 1940s.

As an argument against Lipscomb's *Civil Government,* the suggestion that the Civil War changed him was mild compared with O. C. Lambert's analysis. Better known for his anti-Catholic publications, Lambert believed Lipscomb's views of government were basically the same as espoused by most premillennialists, especially Jehovah's Witnesses.

Since premillennialism was a live issue among churches of Christ late in the 1930s and early in the 1940s, Lambert's attacks undermined the Christian pacifism of Lipscomb. Foy E. Wallace, Jr., published Lambert's analysis in the *Bible Banner* with his own comments. "In looking back over the years in which this book [*Civil Government*] and others like it were circulated among the brethren, it is not hard to see how the theories of Premillennialism found soil in which to grow among churches of Christ." To avoid questioning as to where his ideas would lead, Wallace quickly added: "It is not charged that David Lipscomb was a premillennialist (he was not) but his book, beyond the possibility of reasonable denial, contains the seeds of that system." [54] Since Wallace was so anti-premillennial and also a strong advocate of Christian participation in World War II, the two positions together made premillennialism the vehicle of the anti-war sentiment among churches of Christ. In the minds of some, premillennialism and pacifism were companion errors.

Wallace attacked both the conscientious objectors within churches of Christ who took a completely pacifist position and those who accepted noncombatant roles. He had earlier (1936) taken a noncombatant position toward war, but by 1942 he was among the leading proponents of total involvement in the worldwide conflict. In response to the noncombatant, Wallace stated:

> Since it is admitted that a member of the church can scripturally engage in non-combatant service, and still be a Christian, it follows, in their way of thinking, that a member of the church can make the ammunition and make the guns that shoot it, and still be a Christian. But the member of the church who takes up right where the other left off, cannot be a Christian. The first member is *not responsible* they tell us, but the second member is responsible. It looks to me like it is the fellow who gets himself into that way of thinking *who is not responsible.*[55]

Wallace further emphasized the idea that says the non-Christian can be a soldier to protect the Christian, who will not go to war, "is about the most conveniently selfish and cowardly convenient doctrine ever pronounced by good men."

Not all shared Wallace's view. After a harsh exchange in their respective papers, B. C. Goodpasture concluded an article by suggesting:

> This editor teaches Christians to be in subjection to the powers that be in everything that is in harmony with God's revealed will. If it comes to a clash between the powers that be and God's will, we ought to harken to God rather than men. The editor is willing to suffer whatever consequences this course may bring. He will not retract and join the popular side when the going becomes hard.[56]

Whether one agrees with Wallace or Goodpasture, the fact remains that the majority of young men in churches of Christ accepted the military as their duty during World War II. Whether in Europe or in the Pacific, thousands of young men served with distinction. Many gave their lives for their country.

In August 1945, the war concluded with the surrender of Japan following the dropping of atomic bombs on the Japanese mainland. It was now a world looking toward peace. How would this peace be secured? Already the machinery was in place leading toward the United Nations. After the first World War, the dominant editorial comment in the *Gospel Advocate* favored the League of Nations. It disappointed the editors when the Senate of the United States refused the League. But after World War II, little comment appeared either for or against the United Nations in any of the papers published within churches of Christ. Whether this was a general sign of acceptance or that the editors were not as political after World War II is difficult to determine.

The only negative statement concerning the United Nations came from H. Leo Boles' pen. Following the San Francisco conference in April 1945 and the acceptance the United Nations Charter, Boles could not understand why prayer had not been a part of the agenda. He wondered: "Who believes that man is capable, without the help of God, to draw up terms of peace for the nations of the earth?"[57] It was a new world, unlike the one Boles knew in his native middle Tennessee.

CONCLUSION

By its very nature, the Restoration Movement promotes a withdrawal from the general culture. With emphasis upon a return to the church of the New Testament as the basis of Christian unity, becoming a part of the larger religious community is not possible. For this and other reasons, churches of Christ could not continue fellowship with the Disciples of Christ after 1906. Nevertheless, it was impossible for churches of Christ to escape the larger culture of which they were a small part. What would cause members of churches of Christ to more and more accept a patriot position in reference to war would also, as time passed, cause erosion in other areas. Possibly J. D. Tant's statement, often made, best states what happened in every area: "Brethren, we are drifting."

CHAPTER 7

A PEOPLE TO BE CONSIDERED—1930-1939:
Foy E. Wallace, Jr., and G. C. Brewer

Decades have a way of defining themselves. The 1920s, often referred to as "the Roaring Twenties," ended on a somber note of economic depression. It was a legacy left to the 1930s that would alter forever the direction of the United States.

The event that defined the 1930s was the Great Depression, stretching throughout the decade until interrupted by World War II. It was a time unlike any in American history. American lives changed: for the first time, America's people looked toward Washington begging for help.

As has been true of every era in American history, religion played a major role during the 1930s. H. L. Mencken had led the assault on conservative religion, especially the southern variety. Observers pronounced it dead. It was, however, a premature obituary. Liberalism, on the other hand, expired, having no substance to sustain itself or the people it wished to attract. In its place came neoorthodoxy, a hybrid of old liberalism and biblicalism. Conversely, conservative religion in America attracted increasing numbers of Americans who needed help to find direction for their lives. Conservative churches were not touched by the religious depression that many historians described.

What was true across the broad spectrum of conservative religious groups was, for the most part, true of churches of Christ dur-

ing the 1930s. There existed a strong aversion to religious liberalism of all kinds and, conversely, an equally strong emphasis on the
Bible. As noted in chapter three, the relationship of churches of
Christ to other conservative churches was almost nonexistent. In
fact, the debating of various religious topics with other conservative groups, especially Baptists, remained characteristic of
churches of Christ.

What happened to churches of Christ during the Great
Depression? Did they decline, as suggested by the religious census
of 1936, or did they grow as did other conservative churches?
How did churches of Christ compare with fundamentalist and
evangelical churches? To answer these questions, comparisons
will be made in church growth, radio evangelism, education, and
evangelistic outreach.

Churches of Christ could not escape controversy within the fellowship. Often it became much more than a search for truth. The
social and economic unrest became the stage for conflict. During
the 1930s, the paramount issue was premillennialism. The central
figure in this conflict was Foy E. Wallace, Jr. Indeed, no other person was as important to this decade as was Wallace. G. C. Brewer
was also prominent in the events of the 1930s. More often than
not, Wallace and Brewer were on opposite sides on the major issues.

GROWTH OF CHURCHES OF CHRIST DURING THE 1930s

What was the status of churches of Christ during the 1930s?
The previous ten years had seen a growing evangelistic outreach to
foreign countries and into areas of the United States never before
reached. The census report of 1926 showed a marked increase
over 1916. Thus it surprised and disappointed leaders among
churches of Christ when the 1936 census suggested a substantial
decline in both members and churches.

These figures cause some to believe that churches of Christ followed the national decline of mainline churches. Figures involving
mission work, total membership, and support of various church activities showed a national decline in the mainline American
churches between 1925 and the early 1940s.

Conservative churches were not in a depression during the years 1929-1942. True, the conservatives lost the leadership of the mainline churches during the first third of the twentieth century, but conservatism staged a major comeback during the last years of the 1920s and during the 1930s. This renewed strength enabled fundamentalist churches to project conservatism into the leadership of American religion. This thrust carried over into the post-World War II years when evangelicalism became the dominant wave of American religion.[1]

If the 1936 census accurately reported the facts, truly a depression existed among churches of Christ. Listing 309,551 members, the census reported the loss of 2,411 churches during a ten-year period. On the other hand, William Woodson's count of baptisms reported in the *Gospel Advocate* for the 1930s paralleled the large number of baptisms reported in the *Firm Foundation.*[2] Reports in the *Firm Foundation,* for the most part, came from west of the Mississippi. During 1931, 1932, and 1933, the total baptisms reported in the *Firm Foundation* were 13,715, 14,329, and 13,370, respectively. In the same years, the reports enumerated new churches established as ninety-two, sixty-three, and sixty-eight.[3] Similar totals appear for later years. Even with the possibility that 25 percent of the combined totals of the *Firm Foundation* and the *Advocate* may have been duplicates, the results remain impressive.

W. E. Brightwell, news editor of the *Advocate,* added up the baptisms of June and July for 1934, 1935, and 1936. It worried him that the total 1936 June and July baptisms was only 1,815, a decrease of 26 percent from the previous year.[4] A correspondent, A. G. Hobbs, Jr., also voiced concern because fewer baptisms were reported than in previous years: "I believe that our 'letdown' or 'letup' in a strong doctrinal preaching is the cause of the whole trouble. . . . Is our lack of growth due to our lack of distinction?"[5] Even though these writers expressed concern, every indicator suggests growth throughout the decade. In December 1938, Brightwell counted 17,945 baptisms reported through the *Advocate.* Possibly, he suggested, this was the greatest number ever reported for any one year. The increase probably represented only half of those baptized during the previous twelve months.[6]

When John Allen Hudson received a copy of the 1936 census, the depressed numbers for both members and congregation appalled him. This total, he quickly added, was smaller than the numbers for 1916. "This report," he said, "cannot be right." Why was the 1936 report wrong? Probably, he answered, "we" failed to respond to the census bureau's requests for information. As an addendum to Hudson's article, the *Advocate's* editor noted the census listed only twenty-six churches in Alabama towns beginning with *A.* The *Advocate's* subscription records showed fifty-two towns beginning with that letter.[7]

Whether or not the total membership reached 500,000 or possibly 600,000 as Hudson suggested, evidence from all quarters indicates that the decade from 1926 to 1936 was a growth period. What was happening in other conservative churches was also true in churches of Christ.

THE 1930S: A TIME FOR EVANGELISM

The key to continued growth within any religious fellowship is evangelism. And evangelism characterized churches of Christ in the 1930s. Both the *Gospel Advocate* and the *Firm Foundation* gave significant space throughout the 1930s to mission efforts at home and abroad. For instance, F. B. Shepherd called for the establishment of 125 new congregations and 15,000 baptisms during 1931.[8] His call for baptisms was rather low considering the *Firm Foundation* reported nearly 14,000 for that year.

Evangelism among churches of Christ remained strongest in the regions of earliest strength—the South and Southwest. Continuing the emphasis of the previous decade, however, other regions—far removed from the South—received attention. The papers constantly reported on Don Hockaday's work in Montana. Lloyd Smith was located in Tacoma, Washington, while Emmett Wainwright began preaching for a small church in Seattle. Later in the decade, Otis Gatewood began working in Salt Lake City, Utah.

Naturally, the *Firm Foundation*—located in Texas—emphasized the West. Throughout the 1930s, a constant stream of editorials and reports filled the paper telling of the work and needs of the western states. Arizona, Colorado, Nevada, Idaho, and Oregon were added to the earlier reports. On the other hand, Arthur Graham offered a lengthy report from the Northeast in 1939. This report painted a bleak picture of past efforts, and the prospects for the future in the most heavily populated section of the United States were not much better. Within the area included, reaching into eastern Pennsylvania and New Jersey, Graham reported only 23 congregations with a total of 760 members. Fewer than half the churches had their own meetinghouses. Only six of those churches were in New England, the same number counted in New York state. P. D. Wilmeth—supported by Nashville's Hillsboro church—had recently gone to New York City to work with the small congregation in Manhattan.[9]

The papers carried many articles urging workers to go among minority groups. In 1931, F. B. Shepherd asked white churches to support black preachers among their people.[10] At least two Indian men—James White, a graduate of Freed-Hardeman College, and Scott Sherdee, a graduate of Abilene Christian—returned to their people, the Sioux, to preach the gospel. White gave some time to the Oneida in Wisconsin, his wife's tribe.[11] Rather early in the century, a Japanese congregation began meeting in Los Angeles. It continued to flourish in the 1930s. As the decade progressed, urban churches of Christ in Texas heard the call of Mexican-Americans.

The early 1930s saw the number of foreign missionaries grow to fifty-seven adults and fifty-two children.[12] Realizing the small number of missionaries relative to the population of the world, Harry R. Fox, Sr., called for a hundred foreign missionaries by the end of the 1930s. Even though some missionaries continued to go to various places around the world, the total did not increase as Fox desired. Continuing his interest begun in the 1920s, George Pepperdine prepared long articles for the *Firm Foundation* urging more concern for Far East missions.[13]

Late in the decade, the world situation, especially in the Far East, interfered with mission efforts. By 1938, all missionaries in China had fled to Hong Kong. Even though J. M. McCaleb reported that forty-two missionaries had served in Japan since 1892, only seven remained in 1939 to care for nineteen churches. Other missionary efforts planned for late in the 1930s were postponed due to growing world tensions.

By the end of the decade, churches of Christ seemed poised to push quickly into all sections of the United States and into foreign countries. But World War II stifled overseas missions, except for work done by American soldiers in foreign countries. In America, however, the war aided the establishment of churches in many areas where none had been before. The movement of people from the South and Southwest, encouraged by the military and defense work, led to the formation of new congregations. The Dupont Company, with a large facility in Old Hickory, Tennessee, a suburb of Nashville, transferred men across the United States to plants operated for the Government's war effort. One congregation resulting from transfers was the Richland, Washington, church where the majority of the initial group meeting in 1944 were men from Old Hickory.[14] This story could be told many times over in all regions of the United States.

THE USE OF RADIO IN EVANGELISM

Pulpit evangelism, even though dominant, was not the only method used during the 1930s. Sharing the same emphasis as other conservative religious fellowships, churches of Christ began extensive use of radio. The first radio preaching took place in Nashville when the Central church began broadcasting over WDAD in 1925.[15] With the formation of WLAC, Central enlarged its radio ministry to several hours each week. N. B. Hardeman preached in a special effort during the holiday period at the end of 1926. All sermons were beamed over a large region; the church received a thousand responses from the broadcasts.[16] Even with the limited number of radio receivers, the church estimated an audience of 50,000 to 100,000 for the sermons. So extensive were the broadcasts over WLAC, owned by A. M. Burton's Life and Casualty Insurance Company, that many people began referring to the call letters as **We Love All Campbellites.**

In Dallas, the Pearl and Bryan church led the way in Texas broadcasting. Beginning January 1926, the church broadcast over station WRR on each first Sunday evening and through the facilities of WFAA every fifth Sunday evening.[17] J. B. Nelson urged sister congregations to install radios so the broadcast might be heard by a larger audience.[18]

Other cities began radio ministries. Before long a call came for a national radio hookup. Endorsed by Showalter of the *Firm Foundation,* the possibility met a cool reception from the *Gospel Advocate.* Noting the reluctance of the networks to sell time to churches and prohibitive costs of $150,000 per year for a thirty-minute broadcast each week, *Advocate* editor John T. Hinds suggested the money might be better spent in sending preachers and singers to various places across the country.[19] Even though the national programming would not begin until the 1950s, a number of churches tried the next best thing. They purchased time in 1939 for two fifteen-minute programs over the Mexican station XERA in Del Rio, Texas, the world's most powerful radio station.[20]

Radio became such an important medium of evangelism that the *Gospel Advocate* and the *Firm Foundation* began listing radio broadcasts. By the end of the decade, the *Advocate* listed more than one hundred separate programs. Radio had been discovered by the church.

HIGHER EDUCATION DURING THE 1930S

A fourth area, education, received increased emphasis by conservative churches during the 1930s. Liberals had "captured" most denominational institutions during the early years of the twentieth century. Fundamentalist groups turned to Bible institutes and summer camps for the educational experiences needed to carry on through the 1930s, with only a few liberal arts schools, such as Wheaton College, offering degrees. All fundamentalist educational endeavors, including the liberal arts schools, enrolled record numbers during the depression decade. Such educational enterprises provided a springboard for the fundamentalist/evangelical efforts in the post-World War II era. [21]

The four schools operated by members of churches of Christ suffered financially as a result of the depression. Abilene Christian College, Harding College, David Lipscomb College, and Freed-Hardeman College had large deficits which almost closed their doors, but by the end of the decade, all had cleared their debts.

Surprisingly, all four schools had record enrollments during the decade. In 1939, ACC reported five enrollment records in nine years. During 1938-1939, Harding enrolled the largest student body in its history with a record thirty-seven graduates. Freed-Hardeman College reported, in October 1938, that residence halls were "running over." Lipscomb in the same year reported a record enrollment, with more than 200 freshmen. Besides these schools, George Pepperdine, in 1937, endowed a new school in California. Batsell Baxter, Pepperdine president, reported in 1938 an enrollment of 241 students when the school had facilities for only 200.[22]

Why such an upsurge in college enrollment? Perhaps fewer work opportunities in a depressed economy made it an excellent time to pursue an education. There were other reasons. Evidently strong feelings existed that faithfulness to religious convictions could best be served by an educational experience in a Christian environment. Editor Showalter emphasized this point in 1934: "We can never maintain ourselves as a strong body of people if, [sic] we turn over the matter of child training to the denominations and the state." [23]

This positive emphasis was not always shared by others. J. D. Tant urged the establishment of Bible chairs at the state universities instead of supporting Christian schools. He had a strong aversion toward college-trained preachers.[24]

It pleased college administrators to count missionaries as their graduates. Harding College and its predecessors, Cordell and Harper Colleges, were early known for the training of missionaries. Soon the leading preachers within the brotherhood were graduates of the Christian colleges. The schools provided a distinct service for churches of Christ in training preachers and missionaries.

THE *GOSPEL ADVOCATE* AND THE *FIRM FOUNDATION:* RIVALS

If the ends and the beginnings of eras can be located, then one era came to an end in 1929 and a new one began in 1930 for churches of Christ. As noted in chapter five, many who had been leaders in years past, including David Lipscomb and James A. Harding, died during the previous two decades. So complete was the disappearance of recognized leaders that an entirely new leadership arose. Already G. H. P. Showalter had made a place for himself as editor of the *Firm Foundation*—so much so, in fact, that the *Gospel Advocate's* Texas subscription list dwindled to the point that the *Firm Foundation* was claiming the leadership in subscribers as early as 1930.[25]

Accompanying Showalter on the *Firm Foundation* staff was the cream of Texas preachers: C. R. Nichol, R. L. Whiteside, Early Arceneaux, W. L. Oliphant, W. D. Bills, T. H. Ethridge, and Horace W. Busby. Possibly in an attempt to reverse this loss of readership west of the Mississippi River, the *Gospel Advocate* reached into Texas for its new editor, Foy E. Wallace, Jr. A new era began for churches of Christ in 1930 when Wallace accepted the editor's chair of the *Advocate.* Three years later, J. D. Tant commented on Wallace's move to Nashville.

> I feared when he went to Nashville that he was wandering from his earlier training. But Foy tells me he still holds the Bible ground he always has held. . . . Since C. R. Nichol, R. L. Whiteside, and John T. Lewis have been added to the staff— men who have always stood firm against sect baptism—it may be they will yet bring the *Advocate* out on Bible ground along all lines. [26]

Whatever the publishers had in mind by bringing Wallace to Nashville, the direction of churches of Christ was set for the next two decades.

If a difference could be noted between the two leading papers, it would be in their different emphases. Under Wallace's editorship, the *Advocate* became the outspoken leader in opposition to premillennialism. On the other hand, the *Firm Foundation* developed a strong emphasis on evangelism, both domestic and foreign. Along with this emphasis, W. D. Bills edited a column on congregational expansion during much of the decade, giving examples of growing churches from throughout the readership area—Texas, Oklahoma, Arkansas, and California. Jesse P. Sewell submitted articles dealing with the educational program of the local church.

Was there a rivalry between the East and West, divided by the Mississippi River? "Theophilus" may have expressed a common feeling in the *Firm Foundation,* contending that Tennessee preachers thought they were the only ones who could really preach.[27] Three years later (1933), William T. Owen of Alhambra, California, wrote to the *Firm Foundation:*

> The *Advocate* has been ruling the church of Christ with a high hand, and if you can break this ecclesiastical body in the church, that alone, I think, will have been one of the outstanding accomplishments of this generation.[28]

Considering also their long-standing differences on rebaptism and Christians in the sects, it is clear to see that two strong segments existed within churches of Christ.

FOY E. WALLACE, JR., AND G. C. BREWER:
ANTAGONISTS

Foy E. Wallace, Jr., was a Texan with family roots in Alabama.[29] His father, Foy E. Wallace, Sr., was one of the better-known preachers in Texas. Therefore, preaching was an important part of the Wallace family. Young Foy was born on September 30, 1896, in Montague County, Texas. At age thirteen he was baptized at Sherman. Only three years later, in 1912, he preached his first sermon at Hillsboro, Texas. No one doubted what he would do with his life, as preaching had been his interest since earliest remembrances.

To better prepare himself for preaching, Wallace attended Southwestern Christian College and Thorp Springs Christian College. At these two schools he studied under F. W. Smith, A. G. Freed, F. L. Young, C. R. Nichol, R. L. Whiteside, and A. R. Holton. Everyone who knew him at the time said that Foy Wallace possessed a brilliant mind and spent long hours in study. Even though he attended two Christian schools, he always questioned the support and even the place of educational institutions among churches of Christ.

As a preacher, his earlier years were his most successful. Using a textual (chapter and verse) emphasis in preaching, he baptized thousands during the 1920s and 1930s. He possessed charisma, always using his smile to great advantage. Even though his humor was calculated, it was an effective tool in the pulpit. As the years passed, Wallace became a preacher's preacher. He continued in great demand, his sermons becoming increasingly instructive on issues facing the church. They also increased in length, often extending to two hours or more.

Not only did Wallace change the *Advocate* in 1930, he also underwent a personal change. With a new platform, he became issue conscious. With his first articles in the *Advocate,* Wallace attacked majority rule in the churches, a growing concern in the 1930s. In the early months of his editorship, he emphasized his position on the support of Christian schools, which was, the individual can—but the church cannot—support schools. On this point Wallace and G. C. Brewer had their first disagreement. Brewer believed individual churches could support schools if the elders choose to do so. More will be said later on this issue.

Premillennialism had been a live topic among churches of Christ since 1915. After 1930, it emerged as the most important doctrinal concern in the pages of the *Gospel Advocate*. Wallace and Brewer both opposed the doctrine, but they disagreed as to their methods of opposition. As a result of their contrary approaches, a breach formed between the two men that would never fully heal. In fact, two streams within churches of Christ emerged, one represented by Wallace and the other by Brewer.

Before continuing the story of the 1930s, the background of Grover Cleveland Brewer must be sketched.[30] Brewer was born on Christmas Day, 1884, in Giles County, Tennessee. The Brewer family knew hardship firsthand. They had lost their land before Hiram Brewer, husband and father, died at age forty-seven.

Cleveland Brewer heard and responded to the gospel in 1899 or 1900. His mother, Virginia Maxey Brewer, was baptized earlier by T. B. Larimore. Therefore, the Larimore name was well known to young Brewer from early childhood. When only a teenager, Brewer walked several miles to hear the famous preacher. By his own admission, his life was never the same again. Possibly because of this encounter, Brewer committed himself to preaching. Larimore encouraged him to attend the Nashville Bible School, but because Ashley Johnson offered employment opportunities, he decided to attend Johnson's school at Kimberlin Heights, near Knoxville, Tennessee. The next year Brewer transferred to the Nashville Bible School where he studied part-time for six years.

Early in life he came under the influence of a number of men who helped mold his thought for the remainder of his days. By adding to Larimore, Lipscomb, and Harding the names of M. C. Kurfees, E. G. Sewell, A. G. Freed, and E. A. Elam, the list of people shaping the direction of Brewer's life is expanded.

Brewer's located work carried him to Chattanooga, Columbia, Winchester, and Memphis, Tennessee. In Texas, he served churches in Cleburne, Sherman, and Lubbock. Brewer, however, was never satisfied when involved exclusively in local work. Several weeks each year were spent in evangelistic meetings.

G. C. Brewer exerted a tremendous influence among churches of Christ through his meetings and his weekly articles in the *Gospel Advocate*. With the death of most of the staff writers of the *Advocate* within five or six years of each other in the 1920s and

1930s, Brewer was left alone to continue the thrust of Lipscomb, McQuiddy, Harding, Sewell, Smith, Elam, and Kurfees.

Besides his preaching and writing, he also engaged in a number of debates with a variety of opponents. His best-known opponent was Judge Ben B. Lindsey of Denver, Colorado, who upheld "companionate marriage." On April 2, 1928, before 1,600 people in Memphis, Brewer angered and defeated (according to a count of hands) his opponent. Besides Lindsey, Brewer debated advocates of evolution and atheism. Within more familiar religious circles, he met Baptists in thirty-five debates while staging fifteen with Seventh-Day Adventists and conducting a number of others with Universalists, Mormons, and Pentecostals.

With the conflicts and challenges of the 1930s, two men emerged as leaders among churches of Christ. The leadership roles of Wallace and Brewer were clearly seen for the next three decades in their preaching, debating, and writing. Both men were leaders. Each man enjoyed his position.

Foy E. Wallace, Jr., and Premillennialism

There are individuals who thrive on controversy. Foy E. Wallace, Jr., was such a man. Serving as editor of the *Gospel Advocate* gave him a forum few among churches of Christ enjoyed. The issue, surfacing in the early 1930s, was a renewed emphasis on premillennialism. This time it would not be simply a difference of opinion; it would be an issue that would disturb and destroy fellowship. On July 21, 1932, Wallace noticed premillennialism under the title "Teaching Things Essential."

> They admit their prophesyings to be "not strictly essential," but they think that brethren who do not speculate themselves should in docility tolerate and forbear while they do. Indeed, these brethren seem to think that Christian liberty is a license to speculate when they please without regard for the unity of the brotherhood. They use more paper and ink teaching these things which they admit are not essential then they do teaching things that are essential—strictly essential.[31]

It was the beginning of a fight that would continue for many years and that would involve the entire fellowship of churches of Christ.

As 1932 passed, the articles became more focused. Noting that Robert Boll and his Louisville associates used Christian liberty to defend their right to teach prophecy, Wallace answered: "The man who pleads for his Christian liberty versus Christian unity thinks more of himself than he does of Christ." In the same article, Wallace wrote:

> The plea we have to offer the unsaved world is too great to allow dreamy brethren to dwindle it down to phases of Adventism, Russellism, and a lot of stray guesses under the guise of prophesies. . . . Let churches of Christ and gospel preachers stand united on the gospel of Christ—the world's only hope in this crucial hour. [32]

On October 20, 1932, Wallace printed a challenge from Charles Neal. Neal, of Winchester, Kentucky, signed the affirmative of the following statement: "The Bible clearly teaches that, after the second coming of Christ and before the final resurrection and judgment, there will be an age, or dispensation, of one thousand years in duration." Neal then challenged: "Who will deny, who will sign on the dotted line?" Wallace responded: "We think he should be accommodated, so his challenge has been accepted." [33]

In some respects, the Wallace-Neal debate had as great an impact within churches of Christ as the Hardeman-Boswell debate of ten years previous, which discussed the music question. Where the 1923 debate had been between men of two dividing fellowships, Wallace and Neal were of the same brotherhood. For five days, January 2-6, 1933, the debate continued. Even though the contestants at times became caustic, still Wallace was not yet telling people they could not believe premillennialism as a private judgment. He extended his hand to Charles Neal and said: "Here is my hand Brother Neal. . . . Here is my hand, Brother Boll. We will not tell you to quit *believing* them [speculative views of prophecy]. We only ask you to quit pushing them on us. Will you do it?" [34] Only later would Wallace call in question those who remained noncommittal. Following the discussion, Wallace's stature increased. He reached the pinnacle of his influence, and set the issue of premillenialism in place to dominate the fellowship for the next several years.

OPPOSITION TO WALLACE'S APPROACH

Some, however, questioned Wallace's approach. F. L. Rowe of the *Christian Leader* wished that some Bible house would publish a Bible without including the book of Revelation.[35] During Abilene Christian College's 1934 lectureship, G. C. Brewer had a featured position. In a time slot Foy Wallace had been assigned but could not fill, Brewer criticized Wallace's strong stance against premillennialism. He did not believe the issue sufficiently important to divide churches of Christ. In fact, Brewer had even advised Wallace against debating Neal.

Even though the published lectures did not specifically mention Wallace, Brewer's remarks definitely included the *Advocate's* editor.

> Sometimes in our zeal for the truth we lose our love for souls. . . . This is the rankest sort of sectarianism. . . . If our manner of contending for the truth keeps people from believing the truth, or drives them away from the truth, then we are ourselves enemies of the truth instead of its friends even though we believe it sincerely.

More pointed to the issues, Brewer continued:

> If we love souls of men to the extent that we are willing to preach to, pray for, and labor to save a vile reprobate (and we should do this), why will we then destroy a man who is clean in life, earnest in heart and faithful to God in everything except some minor point? This point may have to do with the state of the dead, or the question of what will become of the heathen or the millennium or some other fanciful, far-fetched or untaught question. . . . It is because some men cannot see things in a sober, calm, considerate, judicial manner that we have hobbyists and fanatics.

Such men, said Brewer, will "press [a single issue], emphasize it and almost idealize it."

Toward the end of his lecture "A Plea for Unity," Brewer stated: "A radical never converted anybody. A ranting partisan never reflected honor upon any cause. A bitter, bickering, contentious man is not welcome in any company of sane souls." He then added:

Littleness, captiousness, Phariseeism dwarfs the soul, paralyzes the heart and vitiates sympathy and love and all other noble impulses at their very sources. Such a spirit stabs spiritual religion dead at your feet, and turns you into a rabid, ranting, rag-chewing, hair-splitting hypocrite, as self-deceived, self-righteous and self-assured of your own "loyalty" and "soundness" as the ancient Pharisees who were your exact prototype.[36]

Brewer's position offended Wallace. They may have once been friends, but the Abilene speech ended whatever feelings of cordiality Wallace had toward Brewer. Wallace responded:

The injury to the cause of truth could not have been greater had R. H. Boll appeared on the program in person instead of being represented by Brother Brewer. . . .The Abilene speech is the most unfortunate, ill-timed deliverance that has been made by an influential gospel preacher in a decade. It can be construed only as an effort to break the influence of the *Gospel Advocate's* opposition to this party. It means that Brother Brewer cannot be relied on to protect the church from speculation and opinionism.[37]

Brewer now became a "Bollite," not a premillennialist, but one who would not condemn the doctrine. From Wallace's perspective, the prophecy question was equal to the society issue and the music controversy that led to the 1906 division. There was no place for compromise.

R. H. Boll in his *Word and Work* made the issue more controversial when he used the term "creed maker" [38] in reference to those who would not allow Revelation chapter 20 to be taught as written. Wallace could not allow Boll's allegation to go unanswered. The Boll movement, stated Wallace, was sectarian because it (1) fraternized with the Christian church, (2) borrowed the prognostications of the Seventh-Day Adventists and the Russellites concerning the "signs of the times," and (3) accepted the operation of the Holy Spirit in a person's conversion as only a theory.[39] It was no longer a discussion involving matters of opinion; it was now a doctrinal conflict threatening the fellowship of churches of Christ.

Shortly thereafter in 1934, L. L. Brigance of Freed-Hardeman College promised Wallace that all Bible teachers at the college stood as one against "Bollshevism." In the same paragraph he called the movement "Boll Evil." Editorially in the *Advocate,* F. B. Srygley asked where the other schools stood on premillennialism.[40] Quickly, E.H. Ijams of Lipscomb and Frank L. Cox of Abilene endorsed Brigance's positions on all speculative questions.[41] For several weeks J. N. Armstrong of Harding College remained silent. Early in 1935, however, Armstrong announced that he too opposed speculative teaching. But he denied any responsibility to report to anyone. Furthermore, he thought premillennialism was too much an issue. Continued discussion, he suggested, would cause strife, and finally, the conflicts would bring division among churches of Christ.[42] Srygley thought Armstrong's opposition to Boll was too compromising.[43] Thus, within two years the issue threatened the fellowship.

FOY E. WALLACE, JR., AND J. FRANK NORRIS ON PREMILLENNIALISM

In the meantime, on November 5-7, 1934, premillennialism was the issue debated by Foy E. Wallace, Jr., and J. Frank Norris, a fundamentalist-Baptist, of Fort Worth, Texas. Huge crowds, estimated at between six and seven thousand, attended all sessions of their debate. As many as 800 preachers from churches of Christ were present. Both sides claimed victory.[44]

Both men wanted the debate published, but they could not agree to all the particulars. Finally, Norris published only his speeches, stating on the title page: "Read the debate that so thoroughly annihilated the opponent that he refused to have his side published."[45] In 1944, Wallace published an entire issue of the *Bible Banner* (which he began in 1938) filled with the exchange of letters and telegrams concerning the debate's publication. Even ten years later, Wallace wanted his readers to know that he was not satisfied with the way Norris handled the book in 1934. Therefore, he refused to have his speeches included.[46]

Characteristic of one-issue movements, premillennialists among churches of Christ tended to fellowship horizontally those of like convictions in other religious organizations. In fact, during the Norris-Wallace debate, Norris on several occasions invited premillennial members of churches of Christ to the podium. Included were Dr. Eugene V. Woods of Dallas and Frank M. Mullins, preacher for the Mount Auburn Church of Christ, also in Dallas.

Norris even called Mullins to speak in defense of premillennialism.[47] Because of this strong emphasis by the premillennialists, few were surprised that the issue became extremely volatile during the last years of the 1930s and the early 1940s.

WALLACE CONDEMNS NEUTRALS

Some three months following the Norris debate, Wallace made his strongest statements concerning those neutral toward premillennialism. He especially directed his barbs at J. N. Armstrong. Noticing an article by the Harding president, Wallace stated: "The article is lacking in a forthright stand for the truth on a vital issue." He then added:

> When the line has become so radically drawn that college presidents and prominent preachers will have to "go on record" definitely one way or the other, instead of trying to hide as neutrals in no man's land, they shall then deserve no credit and should receive no respect for taking a stand after the battle is over.[48]

Wallace included G. C. Brewer in his assessment. He mentioned specifically that Brewer had only read half of the Wallace-Neal debate. Implying that others were not, Wallace wrote: "We are set for the defense of the truth." Later in the same year, Wallace emphasized: "It is imperative that a firm policy of dealing with this premillennial movement be maintained."[49]

J. D. Tant stood foursquare in strong denunciation of those who would not take an adamant stance against premillennialism. Applauding Wallace's demand of Armstrong, Tant stated: "It is a general impression among the churches where I go that the Harding College as well as the Central church in Nashville with few exceptions is in full sympathy with the Boll foolishness."[50] Because G. C. Brewer held a meeting for churches of Christ in Fort Worth using J. Frank Norris' tabernacle, Brewer was suspect and the Fort Worth churches were included in the Norris faction. Some two years later Tant stated in the *Gospel Advocate:* "If we blot out the past and ignore their [Boll followers] departures, I will yet live to see R. H. Boll editor of the *Gospel Advocate* or president of Harding College."

WALLACE FOCUSES THE ISSUES IN THE *GOSPEL GUARDIAN* AND THE *BIBLE BANNER*

In 1934, the publisher released Wallace from the editorship of the *Advocate*. Without the editor's chair, he no longer had a public forum. Therefore, in October of 1935 he issued the *Gospel Guardian*. It was his paper. He knew what he wanted to write. Error could now be attacked with ungloved hands. Neutrals, or "Bollites," would not escape his pen: "We shall attend to apologists and neutrals who carry water on both shoulders and as often as they appear we aim to see to it that they either take one bucket off or spill them both." [51]

A number of other brethren also raised the banner that was waved so furiously by Foy Wallace. H. Leo Boles indicated changed times since his debate with Boll in 1927. Of Boll and his friends, Boles stated: "They have gone beyond the boundary not only of truth, but of reason and brotherly love." [52] Fanning Yater Tant, warning against being infected with the spirit of the age, stated: "We must keep the church militant." [53]

In January 1936, the *Guardian* came forth in a red cover. The entire issue dealt with premillennialism in general and R. H. Boll in particular. Now Wallace called Boll and his friends "wolves in sheep clothing." [54] In response to Wallace's harshness, Ira C. Moore, editor of the *Christian Leader* and an opponent of premillennialism, titled an editorial "Ouch" when he received his personal copy of the red-cover *Guardian*. He added: "It might be well to keep this magazine out of the hands of the young people or those easily impressed, or whose sympathies are easily aroused. They might think it persecution." Closing the special, Wallace included a one-page criticism of G. C. Brewer: "Brother Brewer has not done one thing to strengthen the defense of the truth on these issues but has said and has done many things, both publicly and privately, to weaken it."

Before the *Guardian* ceased publication in 1936, Wallace included a number of men in a special group.

> All the neutrals in the church are Bollites—that class of members among us led by J. N. Armstrong, G. C. Brewer, Claude F. Witty, Flavil Hall, et al., who say that they do not believe the doctrine and whose sympathies seem to lie wholly on that side. [55]

Wallace wrote for the *Firm Foundation* between the time the *Guardian* ceased until he began the *Bible Banner* in 1938. Showalter had taken over the subscription list of the failed paper. Among the articles penned by Wallace was one that condemned the use of *Great Songs of the Church,* edited by E. L. Jorgenson, an associate of R. H. Boll. Said Wallace: "He [Jorgenson] has given his book free to our colleges and to some of the influential churches such as Central Church of Christ, Nashville, Tennessee, in order to boast that his song book was being used by them."[56] Any association, even the use of a hymnal, made churches and schools suspect and even Bollite.

From 1938 until 1949, Wallace published the *Bible Banner.* The issues and attitudes that would involve the fellowship for years to come were formulated early in the journal. William Wallace, Foy Wallace's son, stated: "The *Bible Banner* helped shape attitudes and form loyalties destined to crystalize into a movement of dissent in the 1950s."[57]

Always dominant in the *Bible Banner* was Wallace's relentless attack on premillennialism and Bollites. But this was not the only concern. In the first issue, Wallace noted:

> The present generation has not enjoyed the thorough indoctrination accorded former generations under the giants of early restoration days. There must now be a general return to militant preaching, the old type of preaching—and the old type of journalism—plain first principle preaching and teaching and writing that defends the truth against all errors, teachers of error and institutions of error by name, make, model, and number.[58]

Only in this way, he continued, can the church be salvaged from another digression. For the remainder of this chapter, however, the premillennial issue will be the only topic discussed.

In the same year Wallace began his new paper, the focus on premillennialism again centered in Nashville. It had been ten years since the third Hardeman Tabernacle meeting. Could N. B. Hardeman again fill the Ryman Auditorium? The crowds came. The meetings were successful; Hardeman's theme was premillennialism. F. B. Srygley stated: "[Hardeman] thinks that premillennialism is connected with the taproot of all of our differences and troubles at the present time." The ultimate purpose of the meeting was unity, stated Srygley; he believed it accomplished its goal. He then added: "Many have learned the truth who never knew it before, and we are more nearly solidified in our opposition to premillennialism." The Central church did not support the meeting. This added fuel to the allegation that Central was at least Bollite.[59]

An important theme of the Lipscomb Winter Lectures in 1939 was "isms." G. C. Brewer spoke on the closing night. His theme: Premillennialism. From the perspective of Foy Wallace, Brewer was "soft" on the issue. The answers given in this lecture and other sermons and articles would not and did not satisfy Brewer's detractors. Brewer would not venture a theory on Revelation 20. Nevertheless, he did not expect "millennial conditions," ever to prevail "in the present age." [60] In 1941, at the publication of his *Contending for the Faith,* Brewer evidently felt it necessary to include an article on premillennialism. As to the premillennialist, Brewer stated: "He is exceedingly visionary and impractical. He has no hope for the world; no confidence in the success of any of our efforts and no interest in any subject that does not in some way relate to his *imminent rapture* and *his thousand years' reign* with Christ on earth." But even here he could not refrain from making a thrust at the militant anti-premillennialists—they were "hobbyists."[61]

Foy E. Wallace's barrage swept wider in 1939. In response to Brewer, he called attention to articles in the *Gospel Advocate* where Brewer expressed his opinion that premillennialism had been stopped. Wallace responded:

> So reporter-like he [Brewer] gives the public "observations" on what has been going on in the front line and trenches! great is the courage! mighty is the valor! marvelous is the loyalty! that dares to release such "observations" during such a fight! All the neutrals are now assured as to who has won the fight, and can get on the winning side![62]

Filling numerous pages during 1939, Wallace drew attention to premillennialism as he believed it existed in one form or another at Harding College, David Lipscomb College, and Abilene Christian College.

WALLACE RETURNS TRIUMPHANT TO NASHVILLE

In April and May of 1939, Foy E. Wallace, Jr., made his triumphant reentry into Nashville. This was only his second time in the city since his release from the editorship of the *Gospel Advocate* in 1934. Some twenty congregations held simultaneous meetings covering two weeks in April and May. Wallace came at the invitation of the Chapel Avenue church. All in all, it was a successful effort, with 172 baptisms reported from the twenty churches. But the highlights of the two weeks were the special lectures Wallace gave on Sunday afternoons. The first Sunday sermon drew an estimated crowd of three thousand to Dixie Tabernacle, where Wallace discussed "What the Church in Nashville Must Do to be Saved." The *Advocate* reported that Wallace

> condemned institutionalism, modern Judaism, and a compromising attitude toward truth. He stressed the necessity of keeping the church evangelistic, rather than missionary. He condemned one-man missionary societies, and said the name "missionary" was "borrowed from the denominational garbage can." [63]

The *Advocate* concluded its report with the statement: "It was a very strong sermon, well received, which at times caused his audience to sway in astonishment."

On the second Sunday, Wallace spoke on "Premillennialism." The Tabernacle filled to overflowing, many standing for the two-hour sermon. In addition to the stated subject, Wallace

> cited instances of calling on sectarians to lead prayer, affiliation with ministerial alliances, and similar evidences of a softening attitude toward error. Among his suggestions for remedying the situation were these: The elimination of soft preaching from the pulpit, distinctive preaching on the radio, purging the schools of sympathizers with premillennialists, and a sturdier type of religious journalism. [64]

The *Advocate* closed the review by stating: "The lectures the last two Sundays were probably plainer than any preaching done in Nashville for several decades."

How did Wallace react to his Nashville venture? It was, he said, "the greatest meeting I have ever held in Nashville."

Nashville and churches of Christ had changed since 1934. He
noted especially the failure of the Central church to support the
1938 Hardeman meetings, even refusing to announce them over
their radio programs. Yet, said Wallace, they had announced meetings by premillennialists.

> Back of all this is the blight of Bollism. It is in the Central
> church. It is in the College [Lipscomb]. It is in some of the
> other churches. . . . Nashville has both premillennialists and
> Bollites. The church suffers most from the latter—for they are
> the traitors in our ranks. They are modern digressives. They
> hold the exact attitudes the digressives held fifty years ago, to a
> tee.[65]

In his *Bible Banner* article, Wallace did not mention his financial problems among the reasons for leaving the city and the
Advocate in 1934. The reason he gave in 1939 was the lack of support from his associates. He remembered that he had trusted his
fellow editors, relied on them "in the crisis." "In this I was mis-
taken; they could not be relied on; I was painfully disillusioned."

He returned to Nashville a conquering hero who had not been
heard in 1934. The *Gospel Advocate,* with its new editor, B. G.
Goodpasture, represented the softness toward the issues facing the
church; David Lipscomb College harbored Bollism.[66]
Furthermore, Clinton Davidson, a successful New York businessman and a former student at Potter Bible School, was traveling the
country urging the formation of a new "non-fighting" journal.
Because of Davidson's association with Abilene and Harding,
Wallace condemned the leaders of these schools. Davidson was
not a faithful Christian while in New York, said Wallace, but now
he wants to determine the direction of churches of Christ.

Instead of creating a new paper, Cincinnati's *Christian Leader*
was purchased and headquartered in Nashville. Its mailing address
was the same as that of the Central church. With Davidson sponsoring the paper, it was easy for Wallace to brand the journal as
neutral, even Bollite. Noting that he had reliable information that
Davidson had worshiped with a "digressive" church in New York
and had taught a Sunday school class for them, he quickly added:

> Shall we stand by, brethren, bowing to a false idea of "ethical
> journalism" and see a digressive leader arise, take over a large
> paper, and promote digression through compromise in our very

ranks? If the brethren all over the country knew the actual facts, these movements among us that have the circulation, and could furnish the facts, have apparently got *scared and squatted.* So the fight must be waged by some of us at the disadvantage of personal handicaps and limited means. We may lose the fight, we may be slandered, sued, and prosecuted, but we shall not surrender. To the last man our password will be: THEY SHALL NOT PASS.[67]

The new *Christian Leader* did not last. Its battle for survival was too intense. The colleges became even more the focus of the conflict. Continued thrusts were made at J. N. Armstrong at Harding. Charles H. Roberson of Abilene was accused of teaching premillennialism—a position he denied. David Lipscomb College found it necessary to answer its critics, issuing a bulletin to counter what it called rumors. The school placed an advertisement in the *Firm Foundation* to take the edge off allegations that Lipscomb taught premillennialism. Stated the advertisement: "Not one member of the Lipscomb faculty believes or teaches any of the various forms of 'premillennialism.' Not one of the graduates, including all the young preachers, who have left Lipscomb in all the years of the present administration, believe or teach any form of 'premillennialism.'"[68]

As late as 1942, Wallace continued attacking Harding and Abilene, and Brewer's "softness." But the last major conflict came in 1943 when E. H. Ijams resigned as president of David Lipscomb College and a number of Lipscomb faculty were questioned as to their beliefs about premillennialism. Even though the Ijams departure was ostensibly caused by the premillennial conflict, it was rarely mentioned in the papers. Bitterness divided the school's supporters, but Batsell Baxter returned to the campus as president. Many have wondered since that fall day whether premillennialism or personalities were the real issue.

By the middle of the 1940s, the intense fighting over premillennialism subsided. Wallace had done his work well. Churches of Christ would not follow Robert Boll and his Louisville brethren into the sectarian camp of premillennialism. Only a few outside the Louisville area openly advocated the doctrine. But many began to hold Wallace at arm's length. He was not the champion the majority wanted to follow. The *Gospel Advocate,* according to Wallace, became soft when it hired B. C. Goodpasture as editor.

Goodpasture stated in his first editorial the policies of the *Advocate:*

> The discussing of issues must be dignified and edifying. It will not let its columns be filled with wrangling and disputing about questions of no profit. Bitter and offensive personalities are not to be found in its columns.[69]

The *Firm Foundation* no longer affirmed its loyalty to Foy E. Wallace, Jr.

THE IMPACT OF FOY E. WALLACE, JR.

The Wallace mentality, however, became rather widespread during the last years of the 1930s. Because many of the papers would not publish scathing and denunciatory articles, a number of men resorted to printed and mimeographed articles, often unsigned, sent through the mails. Among this number was Price Billingsley. One lengthy open letter to Horace Busby attacked him because of his "softness." Wrote Billingsley:

> Brother Busby, ask yourself if you preach after the pattern of inspired men. . . . Many of our sorriest examples of church conduct are loudest in your praise, and those who least insist on strict adherence to the word and those who hate plain preaching are your most ardent admirers.[70]

Following Foy Wallace's Nashville triumph, Billingsley penned an open letter to Leon B. McQuiddy, the owner and publisher of the *Gospel Advocate*. Recalling the memory of McQuiddy's father, Billingsley remembered: "There were giants in those days! In titantic struggles with evil forces of the world, they stood not on the order of politeness. . . . Alas, those battlescarred veterans are gone from the earth forever!" His second paragraph deplored the conditions of the late 1930s. It was a time when the church was filled with persons ignorant of "the gospel cardinals in contrast with sectarian error." "The colleges," stated the writer, were turning out "sectarian-like little pastors." If this were not bad enough, "the disease of Bollism" was increasing. Clinton Davidson, the "big digressive from the east," was welcomed by the "high priests of sweetness and compromise, A. M. Burton and E. H. Ijams" to

Nashville. He called E. W. McMillan, the preacher for the Central church, "the hand picked softie" of Davidson.

Turning to McQuiddy, Billingsley asked: "What have YOU done to meet this awful threat to the church?" Recalling the pioneers, he urged McQuiddy to follow their path. "These were bred to fight, born in a storm, as it were, and their spirits leap [sic] to meet the challenge of any who would pervert the gospel." Billingsley warned: "And to your teeth, Leon, I tell you that whoever in high place would for sheckles or fair name with the world betray such as these [the pioneers] shall have poured upon him their measureless scorn." If the friends of the pioneers, said Billingsley, begin to feel that the *Advocate* is weak, "they will turn from you forever. Thus the *Advocate* will fail, . . . and you with it." [71]

What was the impact of the intense infighting among editors, preachers, and college administrators? Could the issue of premillennialism have been settled in any other way? The answer to the second question can never be fully known. But William Wallace, Foy Wallace's son, wrote of the first question:

> The victory was not without tragic implications for the brethren who were active in the opposition to millennial theories. Attitudes, alienations, resentments, methods, policies and procedures growing out of the thirties lingered to plague discussions of other issues in the 1940s. [72]

On the other hand, many within churches of Christ shared F. L. Rowe's position. In response to a letter from J. Edward Meixner of Pittsburgh, Pennsylvania, Rowe wrote:

> I am glad to have you express yourself regarding the tactics of Brother Wallace. I don't know what in the world he hopes to accomplish by circulating such stuff among the brethren. It only serves to embitter good brethren instead of trying to bring them together. One of their group of writers held a meeting in my home church. He preached four very forceful sermons, largely pugnacious, and I asked him at the supper table to preach a sermon on the Prodigal Son. He hesitated a minute and then said, "Brother Rowe, I cannot do it. I never have studied that subject." From my way of thinking, we need a little more of the love of God among our brethren and a little more

of the spirit of the publican in humility, and then perhaps we
can have a united church and renew our plea for unity.[73]

CONCLUSION

Churches of Christ shared the patterns of other conservative
American churches during the 1930s. The 1936 census to the contrary, the fellowship increased in numbers. Interest in the new
medium—radio—grew. Higher education, even in the face of depression, prospered, at least in new students. The evangelistic
spirit remained among churches of Christ.

On the other hand, there were strains within the fellowship. The
divisive spirit within churches of Christ during the 1930s was a
natural outcome of a people overcome by the Great Depression. It
was not a spirit unique to churches of Christ; according to Wilbur
J. Cash, it was a southern phenomenon.[74] He described it as the
"steel ideal" inherited from the Reconstruction era of the South
following the Civil War. Defensively, the South developed an intolerance of new ideas or even ideas that differed from the established norm of the region. It was easy for some to transfer this
same intolerance to religion. The 1930s, a time of economic and
social uprootedness in the South, easily fostered an intolerance of
opposing views, whether from within churches of Christ or not.
Foy E. Wallace, Jr., a charismatic leader, built an intolerance in
people by his strident positions on most issues. By sharing a position with Wallace, who was sure of his position, his hearers gained
a sense of self-worth.

The sharply drawn opinions and the intolerance inherent in
these ideas did not perish with the new decade. The major issue—
premillennialism—would not remain the chief concern. Other
questions and other men would take center stage. This spirit of intolerance, often cloaked in a defense of the gospel, would further
divide churches of Christ in coming decades.

CHAPTER 8

Issues of Consequence— 1930-1950:
Foy E. Wallace, Jr., G. C. Brewer, and Batsell Baxter

Churches of Christ were given to extremes during the 1930s and 1940s. Evolving from fellowship lines tightly drawn over millennial doctrines, similar views on other issues became matters of consequence.

Although churches of Christ call for a return to the New Testament as authority in all things religious, invariably, differing interpretations of the teachings of the Bible arise on many issues. Therefore, this chapter deals with the unity discussions with the conservative Christian churches and the conflict over colleges and their support by churches (especially as this issue influenced other discussions of institutionalism among churches of Christ).

One major issue developed from a positive emphasis toward evangelism following World War II. American soldiers and sailors returned from the wars of Europe and the Pacific, determined to return as missionaries. Opposition to mission methods introduced after the war arose from some who were educated on ideas developed during the 1930s. It was an issue that would have far-ranging consequences.

Some men and women are naturally resistant to controversy. While Foy Wallace, Jr., and G. C. Brewer, along with their associates, dealt polemically with various issues, others attempted to remain aloof while the conflicts swirled around them. Many among

157

churches of Christ refused to "line up" for or against the issues debated in the papers and urged from the pulpits. Among these was Batsell Baxter, a determined man of peace who often provided stability in unstable situations. He, along with others, gave continuity and stability to churches of Christ through the turbulent decades of the 1930s and the 1940s.

EMPHASIS ON UNITY IN THE 1930S

The Restoration Movement, with an emphasis on unity, has paradoxically known its share of division. In 1832, the Stone and Campbell movements made a concerted effort to join themselves into one united force. From 1832 to 1849, the Restoration Movement remained basically united. But with the introduction of the missionary society, the Restoration Movement began to divide. By 1906, with the chasm widening, churches of Christ could remain no longer united with the Disciples of Christ. Moreover, the rift within the larger Disciples movement widened until 1926, when two separate conventions met. Thus by 1927, three branches of the Restoration tree existed.

Lurking under the surface has always been a desire to reclaim all branches of the movement into a single body. An unlikely attempt developed from the friendship of Daniel Sommer, editor of the *American Christian Review,* and Frederick D. Kershner, the dean of Butler University (a Disciple school) in Sommer's hometown of Indianapolis, Indiana. In the midst of an exchange of ideas, Kershner in 1930 invited Sommer to speak during Butler University's Midsummer Institute. Kershner had a desire to rekindle the original oneness of the Restoration Movement. Evidently Sommer shared this emphasis as he corresponded with Edwin Errett, the editor of the *Christian Standard*—a Christian church publication—about "the oneness of the disciple brotherhood."

In addition to accepting an invitation to speak on the 1931 Midsummer Institute program on "the causes and curses of the dissensions among the disciples," Sommer also made a trip to Baltimore to discuss differences with Peter Ainslie, an ultra-progressive Disciple. Following these events, Sommer published *An Appeal for Unity.* Sommer seemed ready to redirect his efforts toward unity. But this new emphasis would not last.

Even though Sommer's interest in unity was not as pronounced among his southern brethren, he decided to travel to the "Southland," as he called it, to visit among churches of Christ. Likely his rapprochement discussions with Kershner had aroused his desire to visit his brethren in the South. In 1933, therefore, he traveled throughout the South and Southwest visiting a number of schools, including David Lipscomb, Freed-Hardeman, and Abilene Christian colleges. Relations improved somewhat because of this visit.[1]

In 1938, James DeForest Murch, a staff writer for the *Christian Standard,* reviewed a number of steps leading toward a series of yearly conferences between members of churches of Christ and Christian churches. Noting the divisions of the nineteenth century, Murch wrote: "Now, seventy years afterward, the first serious effort is being made to bring about a better understanding and restore the lost unity of a people that should never have been divided."[2]

As early as October 1935, Murch had suggested the possibility of unity in a Christian Action conference in Toronto, Canada. Several responded favorably to the overture. On October 10, 1936, Murch proposed a national fellowship meeting of conservatives and progressives. One respondent was Claud Witty of the West Side Central Church of Christ in Detroit. Sharing the same dream, Murch and Witty began corresponding with other interested persons. The strongest response came from the Central states and Southern California.

Cincinnati, Ohio, served as host for the first effort. Twelve men met, equally divided between Christian churches and churches of Christ. A "portentous gathering" was the observation of the *Christian Leader.* Murch and Witty shared with those in attendance their "Approach to Unity":

> 1. *Prayer.* Definite private and congregational prayer for unity, seeking the leadership of Christ.
> 2. *Survey.* Seeking to determine how much we have in common in faith and practice.
> 3. *Friendliness.* Establishing individual friendly relations by exchange of fraternal courtesies and through fellowship meetings.
> 4. *Co-operation.* Joint activity in enterprises which will not do violence to personal or group convictions.

5. *Study and Discussion.* Open-minded study and humble discussion of the things which at present divide us, in order to discover the way to complete and permanent unity.

Secondly, they proposed a series of national meetings whose theme would be Christian unity.

Other "conversations" were held at Indianapolis and Columbus, Indiana; and Los Angeles and Ontario, California. Besides Claud Witty, those from churches of Christ attending one or more meetings included A. R. Holton, George W. Hardin, E. L. Jorgenson, Allen Killom, George Pepperdine, Don Carlos Janes, W. Sommer, T. W. Phillips II, Samuel E. Witty, and Batsell Baxter. On the Pacific Coast, Ernest Beam circularized ministers of churches of Christ favoring the "effort toward unity."

Even though Witty and Murch circulated 10,000 copies of "A Plea for Unity Among Churches of Christ," they recognized that the vast majority on either side were "either indifferent to what was being done or openly opposed." Indifference and opposition did not deter the calling of the first national meeting for Detroit on May 3 and 4, 1938. The sessions were scheduled at the West Side Central Church of Christ. Concerning the nature of the meeting, Murch stated: "It will have no official character, no advisory character, no representative character."

Before the Detroit meeting, Claud Witty pled for the unity that was the theme of the early restorers.[3] He urged all to

> go back to the divinely given pattern and study it, pray over it, and even shed tears over it, till we can once more follow its divine guidance and go among the churches and restore the sweet fellowship that was on two former occasions the heritage of God's people—once during the apostolic period and once in the early days of the Restoration Movement.

With this introduction, the Detroit meeting opened on a note of fellowship. From churches of Christ, Don Carlos Janes organized a season of prayer, E. L. Jorgenson led the singing (the instrument was not used in any of the sessions), and George Benson spoke on missions, followed by addresses from J. N. Armstrong and H. H. Adamson. Murch believed the effort a success, although the response from journals among churches of Christ was not entirely favorable.[4]

Both the *Gospel Advocate* and the *Firm Foundation* noted the sessions, but did not unconditionally welcome the efforts. The *Advocate's* interest in the rapprochement began in September 1937.[5] In December, Witty responded to objections voiced by F. B. Srygley, who noted more emphasis on union than unity. Unity, he urged, can only be accomplished when the New Testament becomes the basis of accord. Witty, however, took exception to Srygley's conclusions. "Certain editors and preachers have passed the word along that nothing good will ever come of the effort. Somehow they seem to know, or think they know, that we are trying to sell the churches of Christ down the river." He added:

> If those brethren who seem to boast that they have the truth—the whole truth, and nothing but the truth—will now start moving toward the place where they can truly worship the Father in spirit as well as in truth, I feel certain that thousands of our liberal brethren will be there before them, ready to worship the same Father both in spirit and in truth.[6]

F. B. Srygley introduced another reason for opposing the unity meetings. As he read Murch's *Christian Action,* he became convinced of Murch's premillennialism. Furthermore, Srygley knew Jorgenson and Janes, avowed premillennialists, who participated in the various organizational meetings. Instead of gathering in great meetings with those who hold different views on a number of issues, Srygley concluded: "I am more interested in teaching people to walk with Christ and the apostles than I am in getting up something that will not bring unity."[7]

Other staff writers on the *Advocate* expressed similar views. H. Leo Boles, arguing from the autonomous nature of churches of Christ, opposed the discussions because of the ecclesiastical nature of the Christian church. The Christian church, he said, is a denomination.[8] G. C. Brewer could not attend the Detroit meeting, he said, because he was not and could not be a spokesman for churches of Christ. He was not opposed to the principle, neither was he afraid of being asked to compromise his views, nor was he fearful of criticism from his brethren. He added, however:

> It will do no good for men from the two sides to meet before a common wailing wall and weep together over the departed glory of our ancient Zion, and then do nothing to rebuild the city and to restore it to its pristine glory. There is repairing,

restoring and rebuilding to do. But first, to carry out the figure, for the exiles now in Babylon there is some *returning* to do.

Brewer continued:

> We cannot unite by agreeing to forget our differences. . . . *These issues touch our practice,* and one side or the other will of necessity have to undergo a complete change of front before we can be together. *There is no third side to which we could go. . . . There is no compromise position—no neutral ground.*[9]

On the other hand, J. N. Armstrong of Harding College favored the discussions. To those critical of Claud Witty, Armstrong stated: "I do not see how Witty could have turned a deaf ear to such an opportunity." Of his involvement, he remarked: "If any brethren feel inclined to criticize me for contributing my bit to the effort, let them forbear till they hear my speech, and then they are welcome to wade into it."[10]

G. H. P. Showalter devoted an entire issue of the *Firm Foundation* to the unity theme. The paper opposed any movement calling for compromise. Predictably, the editor saw the unity meetings as futile unless the Christian church abandoned the instrument.

> The one and only possible, practical, feasible, basis for the union of all God's people that is acceptable to God is a complete return to the Bible. All of us can accept the one Christ, the one church and the one law of God, the New Testament, the new covenant.[11]

He showed no interest in participating in any unity meeting at any time or at any place.

Where Srygley focused on Murch and premillennialism, Cled Wallace viewed the entire Detroit meeting as a gathering of premillennialists. Noting the "love" radiating at Detroit from Murch toward Jorgenson and Janes, Wallace stated: "He has not wasted either ink or breath in telling how much he loves Foy Wallace, Walter Brightwell, F. B. Srygley, R. L. Whiteside, or N. B. Hardeman."[12] Similarly, Srygley criticized E. E. Wallace of the *Christian Leader,* who seemed to overreact in favor of the unity emphasis.[13]

From Cincinnati, the *Christian Standard* observed the reaction across the entire spectrum of churches of Christ and Christian churches. Most statements from periodicals among churches of Christ, they noted, were adverse, although "the *Christian Leader* has been notably fair in its treatment." Also, the *Apostolic Review,* Daniel Sommer's paper was, according to the *Standard,* in full sympathy, as was *Word and Work,* R. H. Boll's journal. Witty and Murch indicated that both the *Christian Standard* and the *Christian-Evangelist* "have been quite cordial."[14]

Without delay, preparations began for the 1939 unity meeting in Indianapolis. The focus of the 1939 meeting was the paper read by H. Leo Boles of Nashville and the *Gospel Advocate.* Boles mentioned that his great-grandfather, "Raccoon" John Smith, participated in the 1832 unity meeting at Lexington, Kentucky. The results, however, of the twentieth-century meeting would not be the same as those of its predecessor.

Boles quickly established his position. He was not representing churches of Christ; he spoke only for himself. The paper shocked many in attendance. From a remark made to Edwin Errett somewhat later, Boles had understood that his was to be a position paper, a statement as to how unity might be established. Whatever his understanding, the paper had a major impact. All opinions, he stated, must be kept private, and that all "opinions, ways, inventions, devices, practices, organizations, creeds, confessions, names, manner of work, except those plainly presented and clearly required in the New Testament" must be put aside. He then delivered his emphasis:

> Brethren, this is where the churches of Christ stand today; it is where unity may be found now; it is where you left the New Testament; it is where you left the churches of Christ, and it is where you can find them when you come back. On this ground and teaching, and only on this, can scriptural unity be had now; on these basic principles of the New Testament Christian unity may always be had.[15]

Boles' friends applauded his speech. W. L. Totty stated: "He told them in no uncertain terms what had caused the division and what it would take to bring about unity." The *Advocate's* new editor, B. C. Goodpasture, remarked that Boles had presented "the only safe and acceptable grounds of unity."[16] A former member of the Christian church, E. C. Kiltenbah, believed that the only way to gain unity is to respect the silence of the Scriptures.[17]

Edwin Errett reacted to Boles' conclusions. Boles did not fully understand the people who were extending the hand of fellowship. Said Errett:

> This [Boles' emphasis on the missionary society and Everett Gates' understanding of the Restoration movement] is not a true statement of the matter, and, to speak quite frankly, Brother Boles had abundant reason to know that it does not constitute a fair statement. We have no thought of unity with the group that disowns Bible authority upon the basis of its unique inspiration, and Brother Boles should know the fact.[18]

Errett refused to allow Boles to label the Christian church a denomination, especially by using the United States government as a source. The difference between the two men was their understanding of Christian liberty. For Errett, it would allow the instrument in worship. For Boles, the silence of the Bible would not allow things not commanded. On this point the two groups failed to find accord in 1939. Errett stated:

> Boles disclaims any intention to say that others must come to the anti-instrument brethren. He states as his only objective that all must come to the New Testament. And that is my objective, we are not so far apart.[19]

Even though proponents held other annual meetings, the 1939 session ended any major move toward accord. The 1941 meeting was not as well attended as previous sessions. Possibly, the issues within churches of Christ, especially premillennialism, would not allow further discussion. Or maybe the deaths of recognized leaders, such as Daniel Sommer, who became ill on leaving the 1939 meetings, discouraged others in the discussion of unity.[20] Whatever the other causes, World War II accelerated the cancelation of the 1942 meetings.

BATSELL BAXTER: LEADER IN HIGHER EDUCATION

Fifteen years prior to 1906, the date when churches of Christ were recognized separately from the Disciples of Christ, education was becoming important among southern conservatives. Beginning with the Nashville Bible School in 1891, the establishing of schools among churches of Christ continued into the 1980s.

In 1992, the total included seventeen junior and senior colleges—seven with graduate programs—and 150 elementary and secondary schools. The vast majority of the latter group have been established since 1970.

Organizing and sustaining the colleges were men who gave their lives to the schools. The names of David Lipscomb, James A. Harding, H. Leo Boles, Jesse P. Sewell, N. B. Hardeman, and J. N. Armstrong are synonymous with education among churches of Christ. One person who must always be included in the list is Batsell Baxter. In all, Baxter taught in six schools operated by members of churches of Christ. When special needs or difficulties arose, the schools called Baxter. He had the perfect spirit of T. B. Larimore. He was a stabilizer.

Baptized by Larimore in 1895, Baxter's entire life exhibited the qualities of the Alabama preacher. Born November 17, 1886, in Sherman, Texas, Baxter entered the Nashville Bible School, where he studied under David Lipscomb. He preached his first sermon in 1908. Baxter, however, was never a "full-time" preacher, giving his major efforts instead to teaching in and administering colleges. In addition to his training at the Bible School, he received his B.A. degree from Texas Christian University and his M.A. from Baylor University.[21]

Batsell Baxter married Francis Fay Scott on July 12, 1911. They had one son, Batsell Barrett Baxter, a major influence among churches of Christ beginning with the 1950s. In many ways the spirit that lived in the father became the spirit of the son.

At his death, his longtime associates remembered those characteristics that made the elder Baxter attractive to the various schools and to the larger fellowship of churches of Christ. A. R. Holton recalled him as a coworker at Thorp Springs College:

> His work as a teacher was outstanding in its influence on students. He gave the impression as being deeply interested in truth for its own sake and what it could do in liberating the personality of the student. One seemed to have no fear or other complexes by being under his instruction. All felt free to ask questions and make comments.

Commenting on his death and his Bible teaching at David Lipscomb College, Holton stated: "His going away was as he had wished. He taught the Bible the last day he lived." [22]

Others who worked with him at Abilene Christian and at Lipscomb mentioned qualities that made him in demand by all schools. Dr. Frank Pack, a student and then an instructor under his direction at Lipscomb, remembered:

> In his quiet, yet powerful way, he impressed our lives with the principles of New Testament Christianity. His quick humor, his facile comment, his humility, his devotion to truth, his ability to unmask error and evil and show up their true character, his consecrated home life, his deep personal faith—these are qualities I especially remember about Brother Baxter.[23]

A Baxter appointee as the head of the Bible faculty at Abilene Christian College, E. W. McMillan, stated emphatically:

> Batsell Baxter could see the furthest into the future, see through the guile of others best, and make the clearest observations under crucial circumstances of all the persons I have known. He could live around people, work with them, get along with them, and see through them as clearly as the sunlight without being unfair to them or trying to harm them.[24]

With such qualities, he used his life in service to others.

After teaching at Thorp Springs and Cordell (Oklahoma) Christian College, Baxter accepted in 1919 a social science teaching position at Abilene. He continued in this position until he was elected president of the school in 1924, a post he held until 1932. During this era the Christian school had few critics. Some, however, began questioning the methods of support—especially the appeals to churches. When Baxter became Lipscomb's president in the fall of 1932, little did he know that Daniel Sommer, the perennial antagonist of Christian schools, would visit the campus in 1933. While there, Sommer spoke in chapel on three occasions. His attitudes toward schools began to change. Sommer then traveled west to Abilene. Following his Abilene visit, he announced that he had been wrong about the schools—they were not claiming to be church schools to escape taxes. Sommer now shared the position espoused by a growing number: the schools could be supported by individual Christians, but not by churches from their treasuries.[25]

Already Foy E. Wallace, Jr., had enunciated a similar position. As early as 1931, Wallace voiced the view that Christians have the right to conduct schools on the same basis as they can operate any other business.[26] C. R. Nichol and John T. Hinds shared Wallace's position.[27] F. B. Srygley, even though he had other problems with Daniel Sommer, agreed with Sommer's conclusions—as did most *Gospel Advocate* staff writers. "I do not believe that contributions should be made to these schools or any other secular business from the public treasury of the church." [28]

THE COLLEGES FACE THE DEPRESSION

Of course schools had their advocates for support from churches. But even the schools could not allocate very much time to the discussion of support. They were faced with a depression that threatened their very existence. David Lipscomb College lost both residence halls by fire within a few months in 1929 and 1930.[29] Even with major gifts from A. M. Burton and Mrs. Helena Johnson, both of whom were connected with Life and Casualty Insurance Company, the school's debt grew to $350,000 by 1935.[30] Not until 1941 was the debt finally retired.

Abilene Christian College struggled under a financial crisis with the failure of Nashville's Caldwell & Company.[31] The school owned valuable property, but administrators had needed liquid assets to pay for new construction. Therefore, they had borrowed money from the Nashville firm, using the property as collateral. When the loan was called, G. C. Brewer urged brethren everywhere to come to Abilene's rescue.[32] Abilene stood to loose property worth $1,000,000 if help were not forthcoming.

In the meantime, Harding College moved from Morrilton to Searcy, both in Arkansas. Faced with dire financial difficulties, J. N. Armstrong called for the "brotherhood" to come to the school's aid. Through special arrangements, Harding weathered the depression and emerged a much stronger school on the Searcy campus.[33]

At Freed-Hardeman College, the problems were not as public. Administrators and teachers mortgaged their homes, shared their preaching income, and used other means of livelihood so the college could exist through the depths of the depression. All schools approached the decade of the 1940s with much more financial stability than they had had early in the 1930s.

CHURCH SUPPORT OF COLLEGES

Where Showalter and others could not determine completely how they felt about colleges, G. C. Brewer recognized the possibility that harm could come from such discussions about the schools. In 1932, responding to Daniel Sommer, Brewer urged: "Brethren, let us not cause division over every difference of opinion." [34] Yet the mentality of the 1930s led to division. Showalter questioned athletics, especially football at Abilene Christian College. Based on what he called reliable information, Showalter contended that Abilene spent more money on "football than on religion and the Bible." [35] So strong were his strictures on athletics that one writer praised the *Firm Foundation* for its stand and wanted to know where the *Gospel Advocate* and *Christian Leader* stood on athletics.[36]

In the face of this uncertainty by some and open opposition by many, three men defended an individual church's right to control its own disbursement of funds. Before Batsell Baxter accepted the presidency of David Lipscomb college in 1932, he defended the right of churches to contribute to schools. Baxter agreed to the principle of individual giving, but he suggested that individuals, on their own initiative, also give into a collective treasury of Christians for disbursement to good works. He even asked: "Where is there any New Testament authority for a Christian to give to any good work in any way than as an individual through the church?" He concluded:

> If you give the money through the church and in the name of Christ, the church gains respect and the name of Christ is glorified. If you give it without any relation to Christ and the church, you get the praise, and Christ and the church are left out.[37]

Possibly the most outspoken defender of churches contributing to colleges and other benevolent organizations was G. C. Brewer. He asked Daniel Sommer whether schools are good and whether it is right for Christians to support them. Sommer responded in the affirmative. Then Brewer answered: "If they [schools] are right—if they are doing a good work—any church of Christ, as a free and independent congregation, could contribute to schools whenever it felt disposed to do so." [38] Along with Brewer, H. Leo Boles—

twice president of David Lipscomb College—reminded his brethren that churches are independent and autonomous and therefore are free to support schools if the elders choose to do so.[39]

These ideas arose during an era of growing concern for institutionalism—colleges, orphan homes, and cooperative methods of supporting missionaries. Arguing that "we are institutionalized already," Foy E. Wallace, Jr. wrote:

> Institutions are inclined to assume power as they grow and, consciously or unconsciously, to control preachers and churches. From the schools into the churches young people go as potential leaders and it is easy to see how churches in the future may become what the schools have in their power to make them.

He noticed especially Harding College conferring honorary "Doctor's Degrees" on select preachers, including George Benson for his work as a missionary in China. In the *Bible Banner,* Wallace ridiculed the granting of an honorary degree on "Dr. G. C. Brewer, L.L.D." As an added warning, Wallace reminded: "Remember that it was the colleges, not the societies, that swept the church into digression."[40]

"THE CRISIS WE ARE FACING":
EMERGING ISSUES IN CHURCHES OF CHRIST

Having been involved with the college issue, some saw an approaching crisis. Focusing on what he called "The Crisis We Are Facing," W. E. Brightwell authored four, long articles in the *Gospel Advocate* during 1936. Though scattered articles appeared voicing the same concerns in the various papers before 1936,[41] these were the first to draw attention to many of the issues that would face churches of Christ for the next several decades.

Brightwell asked John T. Hinds to pinpoint the reason for the problems facing churches of Christ. Hinds responded: "Big business!" Agreeing, Brightwell stated: "From business, from government, from the religious world we have absorbed the ambition to do big things in a big way. Hence, we cannot afford to offend anybody." Looking at three areas, Brightwell concluded that churches of Christ had reached a place in 1936 where respect and recognition were more important than holding the ancient landmarks. As a result, the fellowship declined to a level of soft leadership. No longer were men of David Lipscomb's caliber giving direction to the churches. He added: "We reached maturity without adequate leadership and in the midst of a worldwide economic, political, moral, and spiritual depression."[42] From another perspective, G. C. Brewer remarked in 1938: "Our big men are dead."[43]

Brightwell recalled the rugged individualism of rural America of earlier years, adding that by 1936, with the move to the city, this ruggedness disappeared. He suggested that the premillennial movement was a reaction to "the rugged viewpoint of the Restoration movement, of which they have grown tired!"[44] Therefore, churches of Christ turned to less rugged means of accomplishing their goals. Desiring respectability, churches began hiring "pastors" and constructing huge expensive buildings. Thus the professional preachers and fine buildings are closely related: "These leaders [elders] are careful to select the right man [preacher] and coach him to not discuss anything that might offend. They must hold all the paying members together, regardless of discipline or doctrinal purity, until the church debt is paid."[45]

Add to these the growing emphasis in 1936 on radio preaching and schools, and it is possible to see Brightwell's concern for the church. As to the radio, he wrote: "There is a strong temptation to play safe and build up a clientele of regular listeners."[46] The writer would not place strong blame on the schools for the plight of the churches, but he remarked:

> You see the weakness of the church and how it is drifting. Are you satisfied with the position of the teachers in our Bible colleges upon the specific issues involved in this situation? Is leadership coming from the schools to combat these influences and save the day?[47]

With such an array of concerns in 1936, Brightwell's prediction in 1934 seemed much closer to becoming reality: "The next religious war will be fought around the issue of institutionalism. . . . We [churches of Christ] were late in starting [institutions]. But give us time for we are headed right smack in the same direction. Church debts, institutions, and cooperative enterprises will assuredly enslave and destroy us as it has enslaved and destroyed others."[48]

With the first issue of the *Bible Banner* in July 1938, Foy Wallace quickly voiced his concerns, especially about the influence generated by the colleges. Said Wallace: "When it comes to pass that 'Our Alma Mater which art in Abilene' can command the loyalty and devotion from an alumni equal to the homage due 'Our Father which are in heaven'—that is college domination plus."[49]

The issues Wallace raised in 1938 carried into the next decade after World War II. All the colleges engaged in expansion plans. For instance, Abilene quickly announced a $3,000,000 campaign. David Lipscomb College wished to raise $1,000,000 for new buildings on the Nashville campus. Opposing ACC's plea for church support, Roy E. Cogdill wrote: "If they [schools] can be defended as a church-supported work, we should apologize to the digressives for being wrong in our contention against their benevolent and missionary societies." Noting that "'liberals' among us have felt for some time that church support for such institutions as Abilene College is all right," Cogdill quickly challenged G. C. Brewer's advocacy of churches contributing to colleges.[50]

The school most often recognized for soundness, Freed-Hardeman College, became involved in the issue when N. B. Hardeman called for church support of the colleges. Wallace and Hardeman had always been allies in their basic positions, but with Hardeman's advocacy of church support, he found himself aligned with Brewer opposite Wallace, his brother Cled Wallace, and Roy Cogdill. Church support of colleges will be a topic of a future chapter.

BATSELL BAXTER: A STABILIZER

In the meantime, the schools used Batsell Baxter in a variety of ways. In each case he was a stabilizing influence. When the special needs of Lipscomb developed during the depression, Baxter heeded the call of his alma mater. G. H. P. Showalter, on a visit to Tennessee in 1934, called attention to the quality that made Baxter always in demand. "I have always regarded Batsell Baxter as one of the sanest and safest Bible teachers. He is careful, conscientious and conservative."[51] Baxter never served any of the schools long-term. He introduced stability, then stepped aside for others to lead. Thus, in 1934 Baxter returned to Abilene as a teacher of Bible, while E. H. Ijams, who had come from Los Angeles as dean in 1932, became Lipscomb's new president.

Baxter's work, however, was not finished. He again moved to Nashville in 1936 as vice president of Lipscomb, a capacity he filled until called in 1937 to be president of a new school in California. George Pepperdine, influenced by G. C. Brewer, decided to endow a school bearing his name in Los Angeles. Again, Baxter remained only two years, resigning because of the poor health of both himself and his wife. Following a year's rest and travel, he accepted a position on Harding's Bible faculty. Again, he was a stabilizer. Critics felt Harding had too much premillennial influence. During his first year at Harding, Batsell Baxter's wife died suddenly while he was hospitalized in an adjoining room. Instead of this tragic event curtailing his involvement in yet another crisis, he accepted in 1943 the presidency of David Lipscomb College. Ijams had resigned under pressure involving alleged teaching of premillennialism at the school, leaving a wide fissure in Lipscomb's faculty. Baxter was needed to close the rupture. He continued in this capacity until 1946 when Athens Clay Pullias became president.[52]

This time, however, Baxter did not leave. Remaining at Lipscomb as president emeritus and as head of the Bible department, he continued in this role until his death in 1956. Characteristically, he taught his Bible classes on the day of his death. He had spent his life in a capacity rather different from the majority of leaders among churches of Christ. He preached, but was not a regular minister. He contributed regularly to the papers, writing a regular article titled "This and That" in the *Gospel Advocate,* but he never edited a paper. He was, however, president of three Christian colleges and taught Bible at six schools. He made a difference during the turbulent years of the 1930s.

PLANNING FOR THE POST-WAR YEARS

The Christian's relationship to war was a major subject among churches of Christ during the last years of the 1930s. What should the Christian young man do? What should be the attitude of the church toward war? These questions became even more important on December 7, 1941, when Japan bombed Pearl Harbor in the Hawaiian Islands. The United States quickly became involved in World War II, throughout the Pacific and in Europe.

Internal problems of the 1930s no longer held center stage. Eyes turned across the seas where Americans were deeply involved in mortal conflict. Thousands of young men from churches of Christ left both the east and the west coasts to fight a war in countries they neither knew nor understood. In many ways, the war was an educational process for those involved and especially for those who recognized the immense opportunity for sharing the gospel at the war's conclusion.

Of special interest, then, was an article by G. C. Brewer in the February 18, 1943, issue of the *Gospel Advocate*. The war had been in progress only fifteen months, but Brewer believed it was time to begin preparation for evangelizing the world at the conclusion of hostilities. Brewer was, at the time, the pulpit preacher for the Broadway church in Lubbock, Texas. Throughout the 1930s, Brewer had warned of the perils of Nazism, fascism, and Communism. Now he urged his fellow Christians to begin preparation for preaching the gospel to people who would be disillusioned with these "isms" after the war.

> Some Christians see the prospect of the greatest opportunity for the gospel of Christ that has ever been offered to the church since the days of the apostles. People who have been distressed and oppressed will be looking for comfort and consolation from whatever source they can find.[53]

Brewer challenged churches of Christ to cooperate for mass evangelization of the world. In fact, the Lubbock church developed a plan for missionaries to be sponsored and supported as never before by churches of Christ. Again Brewer was an innovator, a role that would bring conflict with some of his more conservative antagonists, especially Foy E. Wallace, Jr.

In Abilene, the College church in 1943 announced a program to send missionaries to Africa. The church proposed sending ten workers over a several-year period. Four of the young prospective missionaries were already students at Abilene Christian College.[54]

Responding to Brewer's February article, George Benson, president of Harding College and former missionary to China, urged churches across the United States to accept the challenge.

> As one who has seen conditions in heathen lands at firsthand, I want to heartily commend Brother Brewer's message to the leadership of congregations throughout the United States. The

gospel message is the one message capable of giving peace, happiness, and prosperity in this world as well as being the one message that points the way to eternal life.[55]

Men and women were urged to begin selecting the countries where they would like to go after the war. By making an early decision, the worker could begin language study and become acquainted with the people of that country. Brewer found encouragement when churches in Lubbock, along with Union Avenue in Memphis, became interested in sending several workers to a number of countries following the conflict.

Cled E. Wallace, writing in the *Bible Banner,* scorned Brewer's ideas and plans. Whether he was opposed to the "plan" or had personal feelings toward Brewer cultivated over many years, Wallace attacked both the "plan" and Brewer with a vengeance. Included in his attack was Jimmie Lovell of Berkeley, California, who had suggested forming a committee to begin planning for mass evangelism following the war. Wallace wrote:

> It appears that the brother has little patience with anybody who questions the wisdom of his "plan" or offers any objections to it. My advice to him is to save some of his adjectives for future use for he is likely to need them. . . . "The Plan" is "plain and scriptural" for Dr. Brewer says it is. . . . Just what authority does it [Broadway church] have to "sponsor" a "Plan" for somebody else?[56]

The theme suggested by W. E. Brightwell in 1934—cooperation—became a point of major contention in 1943. It would continue to be for years to come.

Brewer responded: "As was expected, the agitation of this after-the-war-worldwide missionary effort called for the fallacious and threadbare cry of 'heathen at home.'" Instead of answering directly the criticisms of Cled Wallace, Brewer developed his ideas further. His plan called for sending well-educated workers to foreign countries. Although he did not name them, he already knew two men with Ph.D.s who were making plans to go.

> All the educated people have not gone to the devil, thank God, despite the efforts of the colleges to ruin them! Brethren, let us not let this enthusiasm flag, or our efforts in getting ready lag. Let us not disappoint these men and women who want to go for God![57]

Evangelistic outreach was also the theme of the *Christian Chronicle,* edited and published by Olan Hicks. First issued in June 1943, the paper reported from around the United States the efforts of numerous men and women, as Hicks established the rationale for the new weekly journal: "The reason for publishing this paper is to stir up missionary zeal and activity among members of the church everywhere, and to give to all a broad vision of the opportunities and responsibilities of the church today."[58]

Because the war continued across the seas, Hicks spent much of his time encouraging more work at home. He upbraided churches for just "keeping house for the Lord." "Congregations," he said,

> meet in the same old tumble-down buildings over behind the railroad tracks for forty years. . . . While the sills rotted out from under and the paint, if there happened to be any, washed off the walls, the memberships dwindled away until the four sad souls who remained could only excuse themselves by thanking God that where two or three of them were gathered together in His name there He was in their midst.

He concluded: "Let us pray God to forgive us for this and rise in all our might to the great and noble task before us."[59]

Hicks encouraged every good work. Reports came from the Pacific Northwest, from Otis Gatewood in Utah, from campaign efforts in Syracuse, New York, and from Harold Thomas in New England. On numerous occasions the paper featured the Old Hickory, Tennessee, church on the first page—for sending Clyde Findley to Wilmington, Delaware, for reaching a record 981 in Bible study during a meeting led by I. A. Douthitt, and for the evangelistic outreach of its preacher, Willard Collins.[60] On the Pacific Coast, Hicks headlined a radio network of twenty-four stations from California to Washington. Jean Valentine, of the Glendale, California, church, was the speaker on the "Back to the Bible" series.[61] Within a few weeks, editor Hicks was calling for a concerted effort to preach over a larger radio hookup in the areas where churches of Christ were the weakest.[62] He also shared G. C. Brewer's plan to train missionaries for the time when World War II would be over: "Let us develop plans to train—train intensively, thoroughly—many workers to shuttle into all parts of the world when the time is ripe."[63]

REACHING OUT TO THE WORLD

Almost four years passed while the world embroiled itself in a conflict that would cost millions of lives and cause uncountable destruction of property. But with the dropping of the atom bombs on Hiroshima and Nagasaki in August 1945, World War II came to an end. Now the world could regroup and rebuild. Most of this rebuilding would be the responsibility of the United States. Europe and Japan received millions of dollars to reconstruct their destroyed industrial complexes.

From the perspective of American churches, the reclaiming of the world for Christianity was even more important. On a smaller scale, it was equally important for churches of Christ. From Europe and the Pacific came letters to the *Gospel Advocate* and *Firm Foundation* from military personnel urging Christians to help the spiritually needy of the world. James Daniel of Lynchburg, Tennessee, reported regularly the work of the military church in Paris.[64] Sergeant Willis Page, in a lengthy article, asked the question, "What will the Churches of Christ do about Germany?" Indicating a rather mature understanding of the German people, he concluded: "Our purpose is to save men's souls, and to teach men the definite evilness of war. The sin of wars' murders is too great to forego the opportunity of eliminating it by a strong, positive Christian approach."[65] James E. Bates expressed a deep interest in England.[66]

Writing from the other side of the world, Harold Savely urged churches to send help to native Japanese Christians.[67] Charles E. Crouch reported from Seoul, Korea, that churches in that country were in desperate need. S. K. Dong, the best-known native preacher, could not carry on by himself.[68] Preaching from the pulpit he had occupied before entering the chaplaincy, Frank Traylor told the Pecos, Texas, church of the needs in the Philippines.[69] Whether from Europe or the Far East, Christians in the military recognized the responsibilities of American churches of Christ to meet the needs of both allied and defeated nations around the world.

Churches responded overwhelmingly and enthusiastically to the calls for assistance. The Broadway church in Lubbock, Texas, sent Paul Sherrod, an elder, and Otis Gatewood, a prospective missionary, to Germany to see personally the needs and to plan for their work in that country.[70] E. W. McMillan of the Union Avenue church in Memphis traveled to Japan to investigate and to recommend to his elders what should be undertaken.[71] Cline R. Paden of Brownfield, Texas, visited Italy to investigate the possibilities of mission work there.[72]

Not only did the defeated nations need the gospel, they also were in dire need of food. Woodrow Whitten of Los Angeles reminded churches of Christ of the crisis through the article, "The Church and the Starving Millions" in May 1946. Telling of the millions who were undernourished and dying, Whitten warned:

> Let the church be cold about this urgent need, and millions more will die; but the church will also die spiritually. Let the church not think to undertake any missionary work in Europe or Asia tomorrow if she does not wholeheartedly respond to today's demands. If the church is hesitant or preoccupied with other matters; if the churches go on building church buildings and planning feast days and entertainments while remaining cold or indifferent to the wails of human anguish, the church will be despised—and ought to be.[73]

Soon, articles were telling how CARE packages could be sent to Europe and Asia. Numerous articles by Gatewood and Norvel Young, the preacher at Broadway in Lubbock, urged churches of Christ to provide the necessary food and clothing for the German people.[74] Churches and individuals contributed thousands of dollars toward the effort. But already there were some who questioned the methods used, especially using government and private agencies not connected with churches of Christ. W. E. Brightwell, news editor of the *Gospel Advocate,* raised a warning flag about a suggestion that funds might be sent to a particular church—the Southwest church in Los Angeles—and that church, in turn, would purchase the packages.[75]

MILLIONS FOR COLLEGE AND CHURCH CONSTRUCTION

From 1945 through 1949, the schools—Abilene, Harding, Lipscomb, Freed-Hardeman, and Pepperdine—were making great plans for the future. The colleges asked for millions of dollars to construct campuses for the thousands of young people who would be seeking an education following World War II. With the United States government providing educational funds through the G. I. Bill, additional thousands returning from the war would need educational opportunities. Indeed, it would be a growth period for all the schools. Furthermore, the colleges began pushing for regional accreditation. Junior colleges, including Lipscomb, moved to senior college status. The senior colleges began upgrading their faculties by either hiring or training Ph.D.s. Within a few years, the senior colleges could point to faculties holding degrees equal to other, better-known colleges. Added to the five schools listed above was a new school, Florida Christian College, opened in Tampa in 1946 with L. R. Wilson as president.

The post-war years also marked an era of increased construction by churches of Christ across the United States. Throughout the 1930s, the *Firm Foundation* emphasized church growth. Often the articles included pictures of existing church meetinghouses. Some were relatively large and nice, but many were small and plain. Some churches, such as Union Avenue in Memphis, had earlier moved to large, commodious buildings. Another was the Broadway church in Lubbock. From 1946 to the end of the decade, both the *Advocate* and the *Firm Foundation* carried numerous feature articles about beautiful and functional new structures with fine educational facilities.

M. Norvel Young introduced a special feature among churches of Christ. He conducted, at the 1947 Abilene Christian College Lectures, a session on church buildings. The very fact that such a symposium was held shows a major change among churches of Christ. Young's ideas suggested an even greater change. He emphasized that low price should not be the major criterion for the selection of a building site. Conversely, the building should be located where it had the highest visibility. The new auditorium should be constructed with growth in mind, with good acoustics and a soundproof nursery for babies. The exterior of the building should "look like a church." Furthermore, "The exterior should be attractive, without unnecessary ornamentation, but with good lines of architecture."[76]

In the *Gospel Advocate* was an article from the *University Avenue Reminder,* out of Austin, Texas, on "Why a Large Church?" The economic advantages led the list, followed by the inspirational value of large churches, such as the Jerusalem church. Furthermore, the writer believed organizational strength could be gained by having a large congregation: "If the world-wide program of the church is to be carried on efficiently, then it follows that the local congregation must be a powerful and efficient organization." Even though large, such a church affords greater opportunities for Christian fellowship. Mentioned specifically was the greater opportunity for young people to marry in the church. Lastly, the article emphasized the influential value of a large church upon the total community.

> A large congregation can exert an influence in the community and command the attention of the masses as nothing else can. It is high time that this advantage be turned to the gospel instead of leaving it up to error to build the large congregations of the nation.[77]

The many articles emphasizing church growth show the direction of churches of Christ following World War II. This is not to suggest that no one voiced concern about the growth emphasis during the last years of the decade. From California, E. V. Pullias penned a lengthy warning for churches of Christ; the materialism of the times concerned him. On the other hand, he was fearful of "fads" and "isms" that might cause the church to lose its main thrust—preaching Christ. Among the many concerns was a fear of losing the young people. But above all, Pullias emphasized each generation's responsibility to God:

> The church of any generation that loves numbers and money in such a degree that it combs the community to persuade any and all to come and be members will certainly lose its power and spiritual leadership. Whenever church membership ceases to have real meaning in faith and manner of life, then one can be sure that the church has drifted from God's way.[78]

But the last years of the 1940s indicated growth in all directions. Mission work extended into every section of the United States. Young men and women crossed the seas in response to the missionary call of the gospel and the spiritual needs of millions of people. From every source there was continuation of the growth that had emerged throughout the 1940s. Solid evidence of this growth was produced when Norvel Young conducted the census reports among churches of Christ for 1946. As was true in 1936, churches did not respond as he thought they should. Growth, however, was clear. In the 3,365 churches reporting before the government canceled the census, 341,086 members were enumerated. Basing estimates on these figures and knowing that 10,089 churches of Christ existed in the United States, Young believed the total church membership was in the vicinity of 682,172.[79]

CONCLUSION

From 1930, when Foy E. Wallace, Jr., became editor of the *Gospel Advocate,* until 1950, when churches of Christ poised for tremendous growth in a new decade, many issues were suggested, debated, and even "fought" over. It was a time when churches of Christ became a people to be considered. It was certainly an era of determining directions churches would take in the 1950s. Issues facing churches of Christ in 1950 appeared minor compared to earlier decades. The 1950s would be a decade of reaching out to others around the world. It will not be a decade, however, without conflict.

CHAPTER 9

MEN WITH A
NEW VISION:
M. Norvel Young, Batsell Barrett Baxter,
Willard Collins, Don Morris, and Ira North

A new era dawned for churches of Christ in the 1950s. Two decades before, younger men had replaced those who had led for twenty-five years. Now those same men, including Foy E. Wallace, Jr., G. H. P. Showalter, and G. C. Brewer, were being replaced. The younger leadership possessed different qualities, including a wider worldview. They no longer saw churches of Christ as a regional religious movement. Therefore, these younger men—educated beyond the levels of scholarship provided by schools within the fellowship of churches of Christ—looked to newer methods for reaching into every section of the United States.

Battles fought in the 1930s by Wallace, Showalter, and Brewer did not concern the younger leadership. Even though the editor of the *Gospel Advocate,* B. C. Goodpasture, was somewhat older, he shared most of the new directions envisioned by younger men. This is not to suggest that the premillennial emphasis of the thirties died. It did not. In fact, internal difficulties in the 1950s found root in premillennialism and parallel issues, including institutionalism, raised during the depression decade.

Both the *Firm Foundation* and the *Gospel Advocate* caught the optimism of the new generation. Never had these journals been so positive and optimistic about the possibilities for growth and outreach. Led by editors Reuel Lemmons and B. C. Goodpasture,

181

they filled their respective papers with articles by younger men with unlimited optimism.

Representative of such a spirit was F. O. Howell of Memphis, Tennessee:

> The church has grown phenomenally, in the last decade. We have hundreds of young preachers well instructed, well prepared and full of zeal and courage, who are carrying and will carry the gospel message to the ends of the earth. We have more and better buildings and equipment to provide the programs and development of the present generation. More and better schools and colleges conducted by our brethren are available for the education of our young. We enjoy more and greater prosperity among the membership of the church than ever before in its history, and therefore more funds are available for the spreading of the good tidings than ever before, and more with which to care for the widows and orphans, and the poor and needy.[1]

Ira North, at the middle of the decade, wrote exultantly: "The church today is strong in its unity and fervent in its fellowship. The future is bright. Let us rejoice!"[2] Indeed, the decade of the 1950s was a time for great things.

Five emphases are a part of this chapter. Each area will be represented by an individual whose vision was evident throughout the fifteen years covered by this study. Beginning with his interest in foreign missions during the post-World War II years, M. Norvel Young—while serving as preacher for Lubbock's Broadway church—encouraged both visibility and new programs at the local level. Batsell Barrett Baxter, with a Ph.D. in speech from the University of Southern California, spoke to the nation by radio and television on the Herald of Truth. Willard Collins represents mass evangelism during the era. He was in great demand for areawide campaigns. During the 1950s, *growth* was the key word of the various colleges operated within the fellowship. Leading in the multi-million dollar developments was Don H. Morris, president of Abilene Christian College. At the local level, the Madison, Tennessee, church, where Ira North served as preacher, led other churches into congregational development and community outreach.

M. NORVEL YOUNG: ADVOCATE OF CHURCH GROWTH

The energies pent up by the global conflict of World War II exploded with the signing of the peace treaties of 1945. What waited in abeyance for sixteen years of depression and war burst forth with vigor within both the nation and churches of Christ. The strong negativism voiced in the *Bible Banner* and the *Vindicator* was no longer popular with preachers or churches. Among the new leadership of the 1950s, M. Norvel Young exhibited the spirit that dominated the late 1940s and the 1950s. Writing in the 1957 *Encyclopedia Britannica Yearbook,* Young emphasized building: "The keynote among Churches of Christ was well expressed in a new book about them entitled *THE CHURCH IS BUILDING.* More than 1,000 church buildings were begun or enlarged in 1956." [3] The authors of the new book were Young and J. M. Powell.

Nashville, Tennessee, was the birthplace of Norvel Young in 1915. His father served as an elder in the Belmont church and as a member of the Lipscomb Board of Directors. Young attended Lipscomb when it was a junior college, then moved on to Abilene Christian College for his undergraduate degree. Returning to Nashville, he earned his M.A. degree at Vanderbilt University. Following graduation, he moved to California, where he served two churches for three years. His home city always seemed to call, as it did in 1940 when he became the pulpit minister for the Belmont church. He received the Ph.D. degree from Nashville's George Peabody College in 1942, submitting a dissertation on the history of Christian colleges. Before moving to the Broadway church in 1944, he served the David Lipscomb College church from 1941 to 1944. He continued with Broadway until 1957.

In 1938, Young married Helen Elizabeth Mattox. In her own right she has had a tremendous influence as a writer in *20th Century Christian* and *Power for Today.* She remains in demand as a lecturer and speaker for women's meetings.

In 1957, George Pepperdine College called Norvel Young to be its president. He carried the same promotional talents he had exhibited at Broadway to Pepperdine. Within a short while the Pepperdine lectureships were drawing crowds of thousands.

Early in the 1950s, many articles began appearing in the *Firm Foundation* and the *Gospel Advocate* emphasizing the need for attractive meetinghouses in good communities. Norvel Young, recognizing the changed economic status of churches of Christ since the 1930s, called for churches to construct buildings on the best streets in the city. Furthermore, buildings should be designed so they are most conducive to worship.

This interest in buildings culminated in the publishing of *The Church is Building* in 1956. In the introduction, Burton Coffman estimated that, as of 1956, churches of Christ had invested $147,000,000 in new buildings. In line with the nationwide emphasis of the 1950s, he noted several reasons a congregation should have a fine building:

1. They save money. (It would be impossible to rent buildings of the caliber being constructed).
2. They advertise.
3. They preach the gospel.
4. They give stability to congregations.
5. They remind men of their faith in God.[4]

Willard Collins indicated the growth in 1954 by relating a conversation with L. S. White. Early in the twentieth century, White and Jesse P. Sewell were the only two full-time preachers among churches of Christ south of the Ohio River and from coast to coast. Collins then recalled James E. Laird, an elderly preacher in Georgia, who remembered when all members of churches of Christ in Memphis could get into one elevator. Furthermore, not many years earlier, only one congregation existed in either Dallas or Houston. Representative of the changes that had occurred by 1954, Collins pointed to the Union Avenue church in Memphis with a thousand members; moving westward to Little Rock, Collins told of the Sixth and Izard congregation, with a weekly contribution of $1,300 and a membership of nearly a thousand; and in Dallas, Collins chose as a representative congregation the Skillman Avenue church, with a new building and 252 baptisms in 1952.[5]

The 1957 records reported by Norvel Young were only a continuation of the enthusiasm engendered by the figures of the early 1950s. In *Britannica,* he told of 500 new congregations in one year, "Making a total of 15,500 with approximately 1,650,000 members in the United States." [6] Later reports suggest that Young's enthusiasm may have been excessive, but the ongoing activity suggested optimism. At the end of 1957, Reuel Lemmons believed that more new buildings had been constructed during the past two years than during any comparable period in modern times. He, too, expressed optimism for the future.

The Broadway church in Lubbock provided leadership in developing educational programs for the local church. For many years, Norvel Young had been encouraging churches to do more in Bible school work. Broadway led among churches of Christ in placing its Bible school program under a specialized director, Alan Bryan. He quickly became a leader in educational ministry among churches of Christ. Bryan urged churches to:

1. Enroll babies in a nursery roll. In this way parents can be encouraged to attend.
2. Reach out to the more than half the population not enrolled in Bible schools.
3. Encourage the one-third of the church membership not enrolled in the educational program to attend classes.
4. Create extension programs to reach out to shut-ins, the sick, and the elderly.
5. Concentrate on the 500,000 new homes established in 1954.
6. Plan comprehensive vacation Bible schools and Saturday preaching programs. [7]

The most active proponents of the new vacation Bible school movement among churches of Christ were Norvel Young, Alan Bryan, and Ira North. As early as 1951, Young encouraged churches to consider a special school during the summer months for the teaching of the Bible. Having just completed such a session at Broadway, Young urged: "May I appeal to the elders and teachers of churches who are missing this opportunity to teach the Bible to plan for at least one week, if not two, of vacation Bible school training this year!" [8]

As the 1950s progressed, churches explored other innovative ideas. Hulen L. Jackson in 1957 called for churches to try "night" vacation Bible schools. He believed they would increase attendance. Following the lead of Saner Avenue, sister Dallas churches Trinity Heights and Edgefield reported increases in attendance over the previous year. Would children attend? They came in increased numbers, as did senior high school students and adults. Trinity Heights recorded a membership increase of 40 percent.[9]

By 1959, Bible school enrollments soared in many congregations across the United States. Previously, Norvel Young had suggested the possibility of going to dual worship services to accommodate increased attendance.[10] Alan Bryan explored the possibility of two Bible school sessions each Sunday morning. The Vandelia Village church in Lubbock, Texas, a young congregation, did not have adequate facilities for growth. By adding services, they increased attendance by nearly 200 per Sunday. Experiences at Madison in the Nashville area were the same when an expanded program began in 1958.[11]

Not only did Bryan and Young encourage Sunday Bible study and vacation Bible schools, Bryan also suggested Saturday morning Bible classes for children. Outreach to children not attending churches of Christ could be enhanced.[12] Reuel Lemmons encouraged summer camps. Besides leadership training for young people, camping "develop[s] teachers, leaders, counselors, and interested helpers of the youth of the church among the adults."[13] Several fellowshipwide camps were in operation during the 1950s, including Yosemite and Blue Ridge Family Encampments.

In addition to the *The Church is Building,* several other widely-used books among churches of Christ appeared during the 1940s and 1950s. With the emphasis on growth and the involvement of every member in soul winning, Otis Gatewood published *You Can Do Personal Work* in 1945. Based in part on his experiences in Salt Lake City, the book provided a text for classes on personal evangelism. Ivan Stewart added a second volume on personal work with his *From House to House* (1956). John Paul Gibson's *The Church at Work* was a practical handbook for elders and preachers. In 1963, Ira North and Stafford North edited a small volume updating Gibson's book, titled *At Work for the Master.* Six years later, Ira North authored *You Can March for the Master,* a church-growth manual. The training school, especially for young men in the local congregation, was the target market for Batsell Barrett Baxter's *Speaking for the Master.* These volumes shared a common goal—the need to involve all members of the congregation in the work of the church.

Dr. M. Norvel Young continued his work at Broadway until 1957, when he accepted the presidency of George Pepperdine College in Los Angeles, California. Quickly, he rallied churches to support the lectureships sponsored by the college. Reuel Lemmons said of Young's appointment:

> This is a time of rejoicing on the part of brethren everywhere. The support that had been denied the college in the past should now make up for lost time in taking advantage of the opportunity afforded to now have a college on the Coast that follows the same pattern as our other Christian colleges.[14]

BATSELL BARRETT BAXTER: SPEAKER TO THE NATION

Before the 1950s, mass media were not used for evangelism among churches of Christ. Local radio broadcasts were evident in every region, but a national effort had never been tried. As mentioned previously, a call was made during the 1930s to investigate the possibilities of national radio, but for some, the costs were prohibitive.

The optimism of the 1950s encouraged a different view. James Walter Nichols shared his ideas about a national radio program with a number of friends at the 1950 Abilene lectures. Nichols, along with James D. Willeford, had developed a radio broadcast over several stations in Iowa and Wisconsin. For several months, the two men talked with various churches about sponsoring the program. Finally, two years after the initial discussions, James Nichols presented the first Herald of Truth program from the city auditorium in Abilene, Texas.[15] The dream had become a reality.

Enthusiasm for the national broadcast had already been whetted by Batsell Barrett Baxter, who on January 21, 1951, presented a sermon on Columbia Broadcasting System's "Church of the Air" series. His subject was "Tragedy of the Divided House."[16] Two years later, on February 15, 1953, J. P. Sanders, then dean of David Lipscomb College, spoke on the same network.[17]

The Herald of Truth became the radio outreach of the Highland Church of Christ in Abilene, Texas, during the fall of 1951. Within a matter of weeks, the church contacted sister churches and indi viduals by mail, telling of plans for the national radio program. In just three months, Highland raised $250,000 for the first year's efforts. This tremendous undertaking could only have happened through the cooperation of thousands of congregations and individuals throughout the United States.

In 1953, James Nichols traveled to Chicago to film thirteen television programs for the Herald of Truth, a feat accomplished in only two or three days. On May 2, 1954, the series began on the DuMont Network with some twenty stations carrying the telecasts. The Highland elders hoped that many stations would use the Herald of Truth to fulfill some of their public service broadcasting requirements. Also, prints were made available at a minimum cost to churches wishing to contract with a local station. Indeed, it was an ambitious plan.[18]

In 1954, the Herald of Truth began featuring guest speakers on the radio portion of the broadcast, a practice carried over into 1955. Guest speakers included: James D. Groves, Detroit; A. R. Holton, Washington, D.C.; George Bailey and Don Morris, Abilene; and Willard Collins of Nashville. The acceptance of the program by the American Broadcasting Company pleased the elders at Highland.[19] Because of costs, television was not as extensively developed as radio, until late in the 1950s. In 1958, Herald of Truth conceived a plan allowing individual congregations to purchase a program featuring their local preachers in an actual worship period. The churches, in turn, donated the program to Herald of Truth to be broadcast nationwide. Nashville's Hillsboro church filmed the first program with Batsell Barrett Baxter preaching. This was Baxter's initial relationship with Herald of Truth.

In August 1959, the Highland elders announced the appointment of Batsell Barrett Baxter to develop a new thrust for Herald of Truth. Baxter accepted the new challenge. He had experienced extremely close ties with churches of Christ since birth. Beginning in 1916, his father, Batsell Baxter, became associated with Christian education from Tennessee to California. Young Baxter, whose Christian education began at Lipscomb, graduated from Abilene Christian College in 1937. While at Lipscomb, Baxter preached his first sermon at the Chapel Avenue Church of Christ.

From Abilene, Baxter moved to Los Angeles when his father accepted the presidency of George Pepperdine College. While teaching at Pepperdine and preaching, he earned his Ph.D. in speech from the University of Southern California. In 1945, Baxter moved to Nashville, where he became the head of the Department of Speech at David Lipscomb College. His father was by then serving the school as chairman of the Department of Bible.

Baxter filled the pulpit of the Belmont church for one year before accepting the call of the Trinity Lane church in East Nashville. In 1951, he became the pulpit preacher for the Hillsboro church, succeeding B. C. Goodpasture, who had accepted an appointment as an elder of the congregation. The association with the Hillsboro church continued until Baxter's death.[20]

Preaching remained central to Baxter's life. An outstanding teacher, he excelled as a public speaker. In fact, an entire generation of young preachers among churches of Christ attempted to capture the qualities of Baxter's preaching. His dissertation, a study of preaching, helped mold his distinctive style.

At the death of Baxter's father, David Lipscomb College appointed young Baxter chairman of the Department of Bible. He continued in this capacity until his death from cancer on March 31, 1982. With the passing of Dr. Baxter, an era of leadership among churches of Christ began to slip away.

As lead speaker for the Herald of Truth, Baxter could easily wear the title "speaker to the nation." When chosen for the responsibility, Baxter drew this praise from his friend and coworker, Willard Collins: "I have known Batsell Barrett Baxter for 14 years, and I commend him to you as a man prepared in mind and heart for this great undertaking." Collins concluded his statement by urging: "With the speaker Batsell Barrett Baxter and with the plans in the minds of the elders of Highland in Abilene, let's go forward and help with this work.[21]

Quickly, Baxter moved into the new endeavor. Just as quickly, a wide audience recognized him to be the ideal person to present the gospel through the Herald of Truth to the American nation. Dan Harless, coworker with Baxter at Hillsboro and a scriptwriter for Herald of Truth, commented on Baxter's power: "Batsell Barrett Baxter has in his voice the quality of quiet urgency which I think is unsurpassed in the ministry today."[22]

While Baxter concentrated on television, Herald of Truth brought in the dynamic, young evangelist John Allen Chalk to do the radio broadcasts. In addition to these English broadcasts, Juan Monroy spoke to the Spanish-speaking people of Europe[23] and

Pedro Rivas to his people in Mexico. At the height of its outreach, Herald of Truth radio could be heard over four hundred commercial stations and three hundred stations of the Armed Forces Network. More than 150 stations carried the television programs.[24] By 1965, Herald of Truth and Batsell Barrett Baxter were well established on the national scene, giving greater visibility to churches of Christ.

Another brotherhood endeavor that gave additional national and international visibility to the church has been World Radio. When Alton Howard, Bill Smith, and Leon Telford of West Monroe, Louisiana, went fishing in 1963, they had no idea their conversation would lead to a world-spanning radio ministry. Since beginning that year with V.E. Howard (who has preached on the radio longer than any other individual in our fellowship) doing English broadcasts and Hal Frazier, French, World Radio has grown to five hundred programs on two hundred stations on five continents. Over one hundred of these stations are outside the boundaries of the United States. Other English speakers have included Tom Holland, Calvin Warpula, and Larry West. Native speakers are used in the international broadcasts. This radio outreach is under the direction of the White's Ferry Road Church of Christ in West Monroe, Louisiana.[25]

WILLARD COLLINS: EVANGELIST

"A gospel meeting," said Willard Collins, "is a harvest time for souls."[26] Of all those engaged in evangelistic work among churches of Christ since World War II, none has been as successful as Collins. From 1949 to 1956, Collins held some 100 meetings. During these efforts, there were 1,220 baptisms and 549 restorations. He produced these numbers while serving as vice president of David Lipscomb College.[27] When cities desired an areawide campaign, his name was often the first mentioned.

During the 1950s and the 1960s, all conservative religions used citywide evangelistic efforts. Billy Graham, beginning his campaigns during the 1950s, tapped the ready response of the American people to mass evangelism. Churches of Christ—seeing the techniques of the areawide efforts—used campaigns with great success between 1950 and 1965.

The citywide campaign, however, was not new to churches of Christ in the 1950s. As discussed previously, the Tabernacle Meetings of N. B. Hardeman in Nashville provided a pattern for the 1950s and the 1960s. In 1945, the churches in Houston, Texas, had sponsored Foy E. Wallace, Jr., in the much-discussed Music Hall Meetings.

Even before Batsell Barrett Baxter became the speaker for Herald of Truth, he conducted areawide meetings. The first effort, in 1956, was with the Broadway church in Lubbock, Texas, with support from other city churches. The crowds overflowed the 3,500-seat auditorium. One hundred and four responses were received—fifty-two for baptism and fifty-two for restoration. A book of sermons, *If I Be Lifted Up,* resulted from the campaign.[28]

In 1964, Batsell Barrett Baxter accepted an invitation to return to Lubbock for an eight-day campaign in the South Plains Coliseum. Possibly this was the single most outstanding preaching event of Baxter's life. During the eight days, some 70,000 people gathered to hear discussed "Make God's Way Your Way." In response to the preaching, five hundred people were either baptized or restored. On the final night, 125 responded, twenty-five for baptism. One hundred churches throughout the West Texas-Eastern New Mexico area supported the endeavor.[29]

The areawide meeting that sparked additional campaigns across America was the Collins-Craig meeting at the opening of Nashville's Municipal Auditorium, October 7-14, 1962. Under the oversight of the Charlotte Avenue church, the sessions drew more than 90,000 people. The event attracted attention to churches of Christ in Nashville and the middle Tennessee region.

Willard Collins, a native of Marshall County, Tennessee, was born in 1915. Emphasizing public speaking, he had an outstanding record in academic and co-curricular involvement during his high school years. He accepted Christ at Lewisburg's Church Street Church of Christ in 1927. Entering David Lipscomb College in 1934, he worked, as a student, with Athens Clay Pullias. As he had in high school, Collins excelled in debate and public speaking.

During the same year he entered college, Collins preached his initial sermon at Farmington, a community in Marshall County. From the first, he impressed his hearers with his booming voice. Continuing his preaching, Collins filled appointments with many churches during his two years at Lipscomb. Soon, he was in demand for special preaching efforts. His first meeting was with the Prairie Hill church near Duncan, Oklahoma, in August 1936, resulting in fifteen baptisms and two restorations.[30]

Even though spending much of his life preaching, Collins served only two churches on an extended basis. His only full-time work was with the Old Hickory, Tennessee, church. Beginning there in 1938, he continued until he became Associate Director of the Lipscomb Expansion Program in December 1943. The church prospered under his ministry, becoming one of the most mission-minded churches in the fellowship. In 1946, Collins accepted the pulpit position with the Charlotte Avenue church, succeeding Athens Clay Pullias, who had recently become president of David Lipscomb College. He continued this work until 1955.

While serving as vice president of Lipscomb, Collins conducted thirteen meetings each year. One special effort stands out among all his successes. Returning to Old Hickory in 1949, Collins preached twelve days, resulting in 111 baptisms and 55 restorations resulting. His nationwide efforts, however, were yet to come.

In October 1962, Nashville opened a new 10,500 seat Municipal Auditorium. As early as January of that year the Charlotte Avenue church had announced the selection of Willard Collins and Mack Wayne Craig to lead in an eight-day meeting in the new auditorium. It would be the first event in the multi-million dollar structure. At the time of the meeting, Craig was the regular preacher for Charlotte Avenue and dean of David Lipscomb College.[31]

And an event it was! On Sunday evening 15,500 attended— 2,500 stood and 5,000 to 8,000 were turned away for lack of space. On Wednesday night the smallest crowd attended—9,585. In all, 90,467 participated in the week-long event. It was the largest attended event ever held by churches of Christ. Chartered buses came from all over middle Tennessee, southern Kentucky, and northern Alabama. Both local newspapers and the television stations gave daily coverage to the meeting. A cooperative effort, ninety-eight congregations participated financially and otherwise in the Collins-Craig meetings.[32]

Building on the success of the Nashville Campaign, Collins preached, within one year, in areawide meetings in Shreveport, Louisiana; Gadsden, Alabama; Ardmore, Oklahoma; Corpus Christi, Texas; and Fort Worth, Texas. Following the last service at

Shreveport, twenty-eight accepted baptism. The Fort Worth meeting covered four nights, with 9,000, 6,000, 6,000 and 8,000 in attendance. Thomas Warren said of Collins:

> The preaching of Willard Collins left nothing to be desired. The preaching was both true to God's word and was powerfully delivered. It was the kind of preaching which both makes and leaves a deep impression on the hearts of those who heard.[33]

During July 1964, Willard Collins conducted a unique citywide meeting in St. Louis. Some thirty churches in the greater St. Louis area financially supported a televised meeting from the Chase Park Plaza Hotel. Using St. Louis' designation as the "Gateway to the West," the sponsors called the series "Gateway Campaign for Christ." Eleven thousand attended the five evenings at the hotel, but the estimates for total audiences was two and a half million from an area of 250 miles surrounding St. Louis.[34]

Among the younger evangelists, none was in greater demand than Jimmy Allen, a professor of Bible at Harding College in Searcy, Arkansas. With his dynamic style, especially suited for large gatherings, Allen preached in a large evangelistic campaign in Dallas, Texas, during July and August of 1964. Following the theme "15 Keys to Living," Allen spoke to a total attendance of 125,000, surpassing the 90,000 people who had attended the Collins-Craig meeting in Nashville in 1962. On the final night, more than 12,000 packed the Dallas Memorial Auditorium. Approximately 2,000 people were turned away for lack of space. A total of 727 responses were reported for the entire effort, of which 222 were baptisms and 505 were restorations. Responses increased in various Dallas-Fort Worth churches during the campaign.[35]

In April 1965, Allen moved east of the Mississippi River to Memphis, Tennessee, where he conducted an eight-day campaign. Charles Nelson, then chairman of the Department of Music at David Lipscomb College, led the singing. The average attendance in the 13,000-seat coliseum was 8,500. The final Sunday evening drew about 11,000 participants. Allen's style clearly appealed to the huge gatherings, as 270 responded for baptism and 383 were restored.[36]

Both the *Gospel Advocate* and the *Firm Foundation* editorially endorsed the campaign concept. B. C. Goodpasture encouraged the efforts in Nashville, Memphis, and Atlanta. Reuel Lemmons not only endorsed the concept, he also preached in at least two successful areawide meetings. During April 1963, he spoke in the special campaign in Ponca City, Oklahoma. Lemmons stated that such meetings attract the attention of the community as regular meetings in a local building cannot.[37] Later in the same year, Lemmons spoke in a different setting in Phoenix, Arizona—an outdoor arrangement in a city park. The editor wrote about the meeting: "Strangers came to look and stayed to listen. Neighbors who would not have gone to a church building came repeatedly. Many lingered after the services to ask questions." Furthermore, he added, cooperative campaigns speak loudly of church unity in a community. "The very demonstration of brotherly love and cooperation that knits together preachers, elders, singers, planners, workers, and Christians of every congregation in such an effort has its effect."[38]

IRA NORTH: BUILDER OF THE LOCAL CHURCH

Shortly before his death, Ira North wrote: "The golden key to church growth is found in Ephesians 4:4. It is imperative to keep the unity of the Spirit in the bond of peace." North wrote from experience. He had served as preacher for the Madison Church of Christ in Madison, Tennessee, since 1952—almost thirty-two years. When he accepted the preaching responsibilities at Madison, the church had fewer than five hundred in Bible school. In May 1982, the Madison church set a record among churches of Christ with an attendance of 8,410. When North accepted Madison's call, the congregation counted 400 members; in 1982, the membership was 4,100.[39] In all the years of this ministry, North said that Madison had never had a divisive spirit. The members were too busy.

West of the Mississippi, the Broadway church in Lubbock paralleled Madison's growth. In fact, Broadway was far and away the most dynamic church within the fellowship during the late 1940s and the early 1950s. When Ira North became the preacher at Madison, a friendly competition began between the two churches. In Ira North's concept of church growth, a growth that would surpass Broadway's, one thing stands out—the setting of goals.

A strong believer in the Bible school, he emphasized special drives to bring new faces to Bible classes. By 1954, the average in Sunday Bible school had grown to 900. For May 2, 1958, the goal was 2,000 in Bible classes.[40] In addition to Carroll Ellis, who began a meeting on that Sunday, the congregation brought in special teachers for a number of classes, including Sam Davis Tatum, former juvenile court judge, and Mack Craig, principal of David Lipscomb High School, who taught a class for young people. When the Madison leaders tallied the attendance, 2,317 students were in Bible school.[41] This was the largest Bible school attendance ever among churches of Christ. Broadway previously held the record with 1,600.

Ira North, the son of Mr. and Mrs. O. L. North of Lawrenceburg, Tennessee, was born on August 31, 1922. From that very moment, his parents began a fund to send Ira to a Christian college. When time came for their son to attend Lipscomb, he had already married Avon Stephens. The same year, 1939, young North preached his first sermon at Ethridge, Tennessee. The Norths sent both their son and his wife to school. Finishing two years at Lipscomb, the young family went west to Abilene Christian College where Ira received his B.A. degree. Graduating from Abilene, North moved to Urbana, Illinois, where he earned his M.A. degree in speech, while preaching for the South Lincoln church. Fulfilling a life-long ambition, he returned to Nashville to teach speech and Bible at Lipscomb. He also accepted the pulpit position of the Lindsley Avenue Church of Christ. North completed his education at Louisiana State University at Baton Rouge, earning a Ph.D. in speech. While there, he ministered to the North Boulevard church.

On returning to Lipscomb, he accepted the pulpit of the Madison church. This was in 1952. The story of the Madison church and Ira North must include Avon, Ira's wife. Throughout North's ministry, Avon was his constant companion. North made it a policy for Mrs. North to travel with him wherever he went: "Anywhere a preacher's wife is not welcome is no place for the preacher to be." She participated fully in the work of the Madison church.[42]

Madison and North did not rest on their laurels. They constructed a new auditorium over the basement meeting area in 1954. It had seating for 1,550, which soon proved to be too small.

Instead of launching a new building program, the elders initiated two identical morning worship periods. By 1956, they needed additional Bible school facilities. They added an annex of thirty-two rooms, but quickly these filled to overflowing, necessitating the use of conference rooms, broom closets, and offices.

To facilitate the work of the church, the elders—J. L. Hunter, W. H. Roark, Stanley Lillie, and A. C. Dunkleberger—set in motion several works that spurred the growth of the Madison church: they organized a program whereby every guest who attended Bible classes was visited; they established a personal work program involving a large percentage of the members; they initiated a vacation Bible school that attracted hundreds of youngsters; they began a Bible camp for the Madison youth; and they put the women to work teaching and helping in benevolence.[43]

Many of these programs were first conceived by Ira North, but he quickly gave credit to the elders for their farsightedness and willingness to accept challenging programs. Stan Lillie had a habit of calling North "Commissioner." On one occasion he said to North: "Now Commissioner, I want you to remember that to build a great church you must begin with the children. You can't do much with us old people. We are set in our ways and not prone to much get up and go. However, remember you can teach the children, and let us do everything we can to provide a teaching program and a Sunday school that will be absolutely excellent in every way."[44] This is where they began. In 1956, another attendance drive brought 3,002 to Bible classes.[45] To accommodate the crowd for worship, the church used six auditoriums. Said North: "Our purpose is to save more souls for Christ. We want to teach everyone we can the pure New Testament, undenominational way of life."

North believed that Madison's youth needed additional Bible instruction. Approached with the possibility of sending the young people to summer camp, the elders responded: "We have no money." North suggested the use of Short Mountain Camp near McMinnville. Soon a benefactor gave a camp to the church. Located only twenty minutes by interstate highway from Madison, Valley View Bible Camp has served as an invaluable tool of the Madison church.[46]

While still in the basement auditorium, the elders appointed eleven men to investigate what the church might do to help orphans. They suggested a cottage arrangement where "parents" would care for six homeless children. But the church did not have the finances or a location for such a program. A member of the congregation owned a subdivision close to the church property. North called on her to see if she might give the property for such a project. To his surprise she said: "You can have it. I have always wanted it used for the glory of God, the good of the church. Send old Brother Lillie up here and a lawyer, and we'll work out the details." The lack of money still loomed large. A plan evolved whereby every Bible class would give a contribution every Sunday for the support of the homeless children. The program has worked beautifully. Since the beginning, over $2,350,000 has gone to this endeavor.[47]

Growth continued at such a constant pace that the elders made a decision in November 1961 to construct a new 3,000-seat auditorium. Each year the elders of the Madison church organized a special two-day session called Operation Forward, which included the preachers, song leaders, zone leaders, and Sunday Bible teachers. The 1961 session emphasized the great changes in the community and church since 1950. The elders then unveiled a "Twenty-Year Development Program" for the Madison church, including the new facility. Even though the announcement of the new building came in 1961, construction did not begin until 1964.[48]

Fashioned after the storied Ryman Auditorium in downtown Nashville, the new building would be oval-shaped and have a balcony. No person in the 3,000-seat auditorium would be over seventy feet from the pulpit. The members oversubscribed the initial bond issue in ten minutes.[49] In 1965, when the project was well under way, the second bond issue sold in only eight minutes. In eighteen minutes, the church had subscribed almost a million dollars for new construction.[50]

An important ministry of the Madison church has been "The Amazing Grace Bible Class," taped each Sunday evening for national distribution. "Amazing Grace" has been shown in more than 265 markets, including some of America's great cities such as Chicago, Detroit, and Philadelphia. It also received approval for broadcast over the Armed Forces Television Network. The Madison church pays the entire cost of production, which began in 1971, through a collection made each Sunday night.

The Madison church has often contributed large amounts in response to pleas by the elders. When the elders, after twenty years of deliberation, decided to construct a Family Life Center, the congregation responded with the single largest contribution in the history of the church—$464,000. The elders decided to build only after increased drug traffic in the schools and in the community centers became evident. The elders also now believed the church should join with the home in providing wholesome places for the entire family. The contribution for a retirement center—$456,000—was the second largest contribution given by the church.[51] In 1993, the church sponsors the Golden Age Apartments and the Ira and Avon North Villa, both for seniors.

Ira North did not limit his activities strictly to the Madison church. He continued as professor of Bible and speech at Lipscomb until 1962, when the duties at Madison demanded more of his time. Within the Nashville community, he served for fifteen years on the Metropolitan Welfare Commission and for a number of years was active on the executive board of the Middle Tennessee Council of the Boy Scouts of America. The *Nashville Magazine* recognized him as the most powerful religious figure in the Nashville community. He served over four years, 1977-1982, as editor of the *Gospel Advocate*. On January 15, 1984, Ira North died, a victim of cancer.[52]

Ira North constantly said that Madison was more than "Firey" Ira North. After preaching in a meeting at Madison in 1961, Reuel Lemmons wrote:

> Never in our experience have we found a group of elders, a preacher of the gospel or a congregation any more sound in the faith, nor more zealous for the unadulterated gospel than the brethren at Madison. The support given sound gospel preaching would warm the heart of any lover of the Truth.

Knowing that Madison had been criticized for its work, especially for its slogan "The Church Is On The March," Lemmons suggested: "Most such remarks are made by those who are neither on the march nor willing for the Lord's people to be. The Madison church has literally marched off and left its critics." In closing his editorial, Lemmons pointed to "a good conservative eldership" and "a working membership" as keys to making Madison a growing church. Ira North would add an important ingredient: "Unity of the Spirit in the bond of peace."[53]

DON MORRIS: COLLEGE BUILDER

Formal, higher education was not new among churches of Christ in 1950, but the schools operated by members of churches of Christ grew and multiplied during the next fifteen years, far beyond the expectations of the founders. In 1950, there were five colleges within the American fellowship. By 1965, this number had grown to seventeen. Besides the colleges, seventeen elementary and secondary schools began operation. Indeed, many Christians recognized the importance of education in helping young people keep the faith and perpetuating the church through the training of preachers and Christian workers. In addition to the schools in the United States, two schools are located in Canada (Great Lakes Christian College and Western Christian College) and one in Japan (Ibaraki Christian College).

For the established colleges, the 1950s became a period of physical development. In preparation for the great influx of students and to compensate for the hiatus of construction during World War II, major construction became the norm on the campuses of Abilene Christian, David Lipscomb, Freed-Hardeman, Harding, and Pepperdine. With the exception of Pepperdine, none of the schools had attained accreditation as a senior college. To gain accreditation, the colleges had to improve. David Lipscomb College constructed an almost new campus by 1950, including an administration–classroom building, dormitory space, and the largest gymnasium in the Mid-South. The same feverish construction was taking place at Abilene and Harding.

More important than new buildings, the schools began building stronger faculties. Each school added Ph.D.s as soon as they became available from America's graduate schools. By 1954, all four senior colleges were accredited by the appropriate regional associations.

Abilene Christian College, on December 9, 1951, became the first of the three nonaccredited schools to apply for and gain acceptance by the regional association. This acceptance opened new vistas for the school. The accomplishments of Abilene Christian were led by Don H. Morris, a 1924 graduate of the college.

Sixteen years later, in 1940, Abilene Christian elected Morris president of his alma mater. The years of World War II had seen few students on the campus. But as soon as the war ceased and the influx of former military personnel crowded the school, a time of growth appeared.

The tremendous task suited Don Morris. As president, he surrounded himself with men who had been Abilene Christian faculty members and supporters for many years. As dean, Morris chose Dr. Walter H. Adams. Lawrence L. Smith became the business manager of the school. All had been classmates on the old campus on North First, across Abilene from the present campus. Friends of the school called the three administrators the "Abilene Triumvirate." During the twenty-nine years Morris served as president, the school constructed twelve buildings, including such important structures as the Bible Building in 1955, and Moody Coliseum, Gibson Physical Education Building, and McGlothlin Campus Center in 1968.

In the area of student and faculty personnel, the school made great leaps forward. Led by Adams, Abilene developed a strong faculty. In 1940, only six doctorates were among the forty teachers. At Morris' retirement in 1969, the dean could count 181 teachers, with sixty-eight holding the doctorate. The student body increased from 661 to 3,110. Departments offering degrees increased from fourteen to seventeen. To better serve the many students who desired a graduate degree from a Christian college, Abilene inaugurated a graduate program in 1953. With the expanded undergraduate offerings and the graduate program, many students who would have gone elsewhere for their college training chose Abilene Christian instead.[54]

On January 9, 1974, Don H. Morris suffered a heart attack and died on the campus of the school he loved so dearly. In October of the same year, Robert D. Hunter, vice president of Abilene, spoke to the National Development Council about Don Morris.

> Don H. Morris had the unique ability to unite and blend into a harmonious circle of service the many diverse points and personalities which have had so much to do with the development of our school. He showed us all how we could work together to build a great institution, and his influence will be felt for all time to come.

Hunter paid the highest tribute to Morris when he added: "He saw the best in everyone he came to know. He considered the ACC family as if it were his own. In fact, it was."[55]

While Morris was building Abilene, other men and women were constructing schools on a somewhat smaller scale. In Nashville, Athens Clay Pullias led Lipscomb as its president throughout the growth years of 1950-1965. In 1954, Lipscomb received accreditation by the Southern Association of Colleges and Secondary Schools. In order to accomplish that most important goal, the school had to build its faculty with men and women who held doctorates. A small endowment had to be gathered. But with the accreditation, the school began to grow at a much faster pace from 1955 to 1965. By 1966, when the school celebrated its seventy-fifth anniversary, the campus had expanded beyond the new construction begun shortly after World War II: two new residence halls had been constructed; during the celebration of 1966, the school dedicated a new $2,000,000 science building; and the following year a new high-rise residence hall rose from the ground, as did a much-needed dining facility in the center of the campus. By the middle of the 1960s, the school's reputation in pre-medicine, pre-law, and business had been firmly established. Yet every student studied Bible every day.[56]

In 1965, Dr. George S. Benson retired as president of Harding College. Benson had become the leader of Harding in 1936 after serving as a missionary in China. He found a school in debt, but left it in 1965 with assets of $25,000,000. This included an endowment of $13,000,000. With campuses in Searcy, Arkansas, and Memphis, the college had 1,518 students plus 745 in elementary and high school at the combined locations. Receiving accreditation in 1953, Harding quickly pursued a graduate program on the Searcy campus. Later, the Harding Graduate School of Religion became a reality in Memphis. Mirroring its founder, J. N. Armstrong, and its president, George Benson, the college has long been noted for its interest in missions.[57]

George Pepperdine College was the only accredited senior college within the fellowship of churches of Christ in 1950.[58] Financially, the college was better endowed than sister schools. Because of its accreditation and financial resources, Pepperdine entered graduate education many years before the other schools. In the 1944-45 school year, a graduate program in religion was begun with W. B. West, Jr. as coordinator of the program. Pepperdine conferred the first M.A. degrees in 1947.[59]

Because of a lack of enthusiasm among churches of Christ on the West Coast for the presidency of Hugh Tiner, Dr. M. Norvel Young became the president of the school in 1957.[60] He quickly began looking for opportunities to expand. During the early 1960s, the school grew to some 2,000 students. Young led in organizing specialty campuses throughout the Los Angeles area. Pepperdine began, in Heidelberg, Germany, the first European program among schools within the brotherhood of churches of Christ.

N. B. Hardeman resigned from the presidency of Freed-Hardeman College in 1950. The trustees chose H. A. Dixon as president, a position he filled until his death in 1969. Of the five major schools within the fellowship, Freed-Hardeman was the only one continuing as a junior college throughout the period under study. The school has always prided itself on its training of preachers. Along with the development of a much more satisfactory physical plant, the college added a third year of Bible. The senior colleges allowed students who had completed that third year to enroll as seniors. In 1974, Freed-Hardeman opted to become a senior college.

Alabama Christian began in 1942 as Montgomery Bible School with Rex Turner, Sr., and Leonard Johnson as administrators. By 1950, the school had 200 students and attempted to offer four-year programs in Bible and business, but then decided to remain a two-year school. In 1953, the school amended its charter to become Alabama Christian College. Outgrowing its facilities, the school relocated to a new campus in 1964, receiving accreditation as a junior college in 1971. In recent years the school has added the baccalaureate degree. The school is now called Faulkner University.

Florida Christian College began planning in 1944 for its campus in Tampa, Florida. But before the school formally opened, the developers wanted all debts on purchased property removed. The school opened in the fall of 1946 with L. R. Wilson serving as the first president, followed in 1948 by James R. Cope. Because of doctrinal differences, Florida Christian became associated with the noninstitutional group within churches of Christ during Cope's presidency.

Even though he had not planned it for his future, Central Christian College elected L. R. Wilson as its first president before it accepted its first students in September 1950. Located in Bartlesville, Oklahoma, the school began as a junior college. Serving reluctantly, Wilson did not choose to remain in office a long time. James O. Baird succeeded Wilson as president in 1954. During Baird's tenure, the board decided in 1958 to move the campus to a 200-acre site in Oklahoma City. To better identify the college, the school became Oklahoma Christian College in the following year. In line with other moves, the school expanded to a four-year college in 1962. Four years later, the school received accreditation by the North Central Association of Colleges and Schools.

From the Ohio Valley to Portland, Oregon, enthusiasm for schools and education continued to grow during the 1950s. In Parkersburg, West Virginia, Ohio Valley College, under the leadership of Don Gardner, began as a junior college in 1956. Lubbock Christian College accepted its first students in September 1957. F. W. Mattox was the first president. Fifteen years later the school received full accreditation as a senior college.

Halfway across the continent in York, Nebraska, a group of Christians contracted to assume control of the campus of a college established in 1890. Under the leadership of Harvey Childress, the school opened in the fall of 1956 as York College. At first, the governing board desired to establish a four-year school, but by 1959 they decided to continue as a junior college. Since 1956, four new buildings have been constructed on the campus to care for four hundred students. The two-year school received accreditation in 1970 from the North Central Association of Colleges and Schools. York began a limited number of four-year programs in 1992.

Although Columbia Christian had operated for several years as an elementary and secondary school in Portland, Oregon, not until 1956 did the board of directors decide to launch a new college in the Pacific Northwest. L. D. Webb served the school as its first president, followed by Dr. T. H. Ethridge, who remained at the school only one year, followed, in turn, by Robert Rowland. The administration of J. P. Sanders gave stability to the school during the 1970s. Today, Columbia Christian is a four-year senior college.

Northeastern Christian Junior College, located at Villanova, Pennsylvania, opened its doors to students in 1959 under the leadership of J. Harold Thomas. The school has never been large, having only 138 students in 1965. Thomas served until 1962 when Elza Huffard accepted the presidency of the school. He filled the office until 1980 when Larry Roberts became the president.

In 1954, a group began a work which would eventually become Michigan Christian College. In 1959, the school opened to its first students as North Central Christian College in Rochester, Michigan. Elected as first president of the college was Otis Gatewood, a missionary who had returned from Germany just a year earlier. In 1964, the school's name became Michigan Christian College. Since 1959, over 3,400 students have passed through the Michigan school.

Even with the increase in Christian colleges, the number of young preachers being trained was not sufficient to fill the pulpits already available. Batsell Barrett Baxter, in a survey made in 1963, concluded that the numbers of young men training to preach was actually down in 1963 compared with 1961-62. In casting about for the reason why fewer young men were choosing to preach, Baxter suggested the materialism of the early 1960s as a factor. Later in 1963, Norvel Young named secularism as the cause.[61]

The answer to the preacher shortage, many believed, could be found in establishing special preacher schools, usually two-year programs of intensive Bible study. Sunset School of Preaching was a pioneer in the field. Supported by the Sunset Church of Christ in Lubbock, Texas, the school's first goal was to train native preachers for Latin America. In 1964, the school had sixty-five students enrolled, many of whom were from Spanish-speaking countries.[62]

During 1965, three new preacher schools were announced, two west of the Mississippi and one to the east. In Nashville, Roy Hearn unfolded the plans for the Nashville School of Preaching.[63] In Hurst, Texas, the Brown Trail church began a school to deal with the preacher shortage. Under the direction of Roy Deaver, the church wanted to bring twenty-five men to Hurst for their education. They asked churches across the country to provide $50,000 in funding.[64] In Denver, the Bear Valley Church of Christ began a school under the leadership of Roy Lanier, Sr.[65] In the same decade, Preston Road Church of Christ in Dallas had a school in the planning stage. Representatives from Memphis visited Sunset with the possibility of establishing a training school in Memphis.[66] Prompted by increased awareness of the need for more preachers through their work with World Radio, the White's Ferry Road church began a school of preaching in 1970. By 1984, over fifty schools of various kinds were offering special instruction in Bible and related subjects.[67]

Why such a tremendous rush to establish special schools of preaching? Roy Hearn believed the movement to be one of the most significant steps taken in decades among churches of Christ. He, like others, named the dire shortage of preachers—three churches for every preacher—as the reason. Explaining the function of the schools, he emphasized: "Only the Bible and closely related subjects, such as Bible geography and church history, are taught." Possibly because of the growing interest in theology within the fellowship's graduate schools, Hearn added:

> Attention is not diverted by secular subjects. The emphasis is fully on the Bible and such related work as will well equip men for preaching sound doctrine, rather than what Barth, Brunner, "Kant and Kompany' think about it.[68]

Whatever the motive for such schools, they quickly spread throughout the United States.

CONCLUSION

The fifteen years ending with 1965 were indeed tremendous for the growth and development of churches of Christ. During the decade and a half, churches of Christ became more visible than ever before across the United States and around the world. By means of Herald of Truth and World Radio, the message preached by churches of Christ was being carried to the four corners of the world. Large and attractive meetinghouses opened to large crowds in many areas of the United States. Churches were catching the possibilities of growth manifested by the Madison and Broadway churches. The schools—from elementary through graduate school—were prospering as never before. In 1963, the schools enrolled over 18,000 students. Besides the church-related schools, Bible chairs began near thirty-five state and private universities and colleges. By the beginning of the 1960s, 200 families were serving as missionaries in foreign countries. Norvel Young estimated that 2,007,650 people were worshiping in 16,000 congregations around the world. There was every reason for the optimism exhibited during the 1950s and the early 1960s. There was no rea-

son, many felt, why the growth of fifteen years should not continue indefinitely. Most shared the view of Reuel Lemmons: "The
church is no longer smothered in insignificance. Brethren are
forced to cease their praying thus: 'Lord, comfort the faithful
few.'"[69]

CHAPTER 10

POINTS OF DISAGREEMENT—1950-1965: Issues Among Churches of Christ

Fanning Yater Tant, B.C. Goodpasture, and Reuel Lemmons

Churches of Christ became much more visible from 1950 to 1965 than in any comparable period in the twentieth century. In fact, some believed, the church was growing faster than at any other time since the Apostles. But this optimism did not characterize everyone within the wider fellowship of churches of Christ. Many preachers who had voiced their strong views about "innovation" during the 1930s openly opposed what they perceived as institutionalism among churches of Christ.

By the end of World War II, therefore, the cry against institutionalism renewed with vigor. Beginning in 1946, N. B. Hardeman, through the pages of the *Gospel Advocate*, encouraged churches to support Christian schools from their treasuries. G. C. Brewer and Batsell Baxter urged this same position during the 1930s. As Foy Wallace had opposed Brewer's arguments, so now he opposed Hardeman's positions. Both the *Gospel Advocate* and the *Bible Banner* led vicious attacks on opposing views of church support of schools. Any semblance of brotherly kindness disappeared.

Hardeman compounded the issue when he interjected orphan homes into the debate. The support of colleges and orphan homes by churches, said Hardeman, must stand or fall on the same arguments and on the same biblical principles: "Come on out and condemn the right of the church to give to an orphan's home or a home for the aged." Later in 1947, Hardeman continued: "If the church can do part of its work caring for orphans—through a human institution—why can it not do another part of its work—teaching the Bible—through a human institution?" Wallace agreed that both stood or fell together, but the orphan home, said Wallace, "does not offer the threat of power or danger of domination that exists in colleges."[1]

The bitterness did not disappear. Through the *Gospel Advocate*, Hardeman apologized for the harsh statements he had made against Wallace. Said Hardeman: "I offer to the brotherhood a genuine apology. Never again do I expect to descend to such low levels." Wallace, not pleased, responded: "No apology was made for what was said; he only apologized 'to the brotherhood' for saying it."[2] The battle lines were drawn; they would not go away.

Closely akin to the college–orphan home controversy, the sponsoring church issue surfaced full-blown in the early 1950s. When the war concluded, the Broadway church was interested in Germany; the Brownfield, Texas, church focused on Italy; and the Union Avenue church of Memphis saw opportunities in Japan.

Of the three areas of work, Italy was the most difficult. With the Catholic church so dominant, the young missionaries were constantly harassed. Mobs stoned the preachers and their meeting places; the government closed the Frascati Orphan Home. Feelings within churches of Christ became inflamed against the Catholic church and the Italian government; the conflict intensified. Showing denominational support for churches of Christ, members of America's churches asked their congressmen to intervene.

Therefore, it stunned churches of Christ when Cled Wallace, writing on the front page of the new *Gospel Guardian,* discussed "That Rock Fight in Italy." He penned: "When a few Americans camp in the pope's back yard and begin to take yanking liberties with the old gent's whiskers, they cannot expect to escape dodging a few rocks and it doesn't appear that resolutions and protests adopted in Dallas and Houston will correct matters to any great extent." Cousin Glen L. Wallace stated to Cled: "You have done an injury to these young men in Italy that cannot be repaired."[3]

The *Bible Banner's* replacement, the *Gospel Guardian,* began publication in 1949. Publisher Roy Cogdill appointed Fanning

Yater Tant as editor. Foy Wallace, although sharing the same views, was not associated with the new journal. Because of an article by Tant in the first issue, disagreement ensued between the two men. In turn, Wallace began *Torch* in July 1950. He pursued the same themes he had followed in the *Banner.* The *Guardian* gave the new paper a hearty welcome, but the tensions remained. Throughout the 1950s, Foy Wallace remained outside the mainstream of churches of Christ and the conflicts associated with the fellowship.

The Herald of Truth, as previously mentioned, began in 1952. Although welcomed by the vast majority of churches of Christ, the *Gospel Guardian*—and, later, other publications of the noninstitutional persuasion—argued that the Bible does not provide scriptural authority for a church to sponsor such a program. The sponsoring church concept developed into a major divisive issue during the 1950s and the 1960s.

Beginning on one side of the mainstream of churches of Christ and then moving to the other extreme, the Leroy Garrett–Carl Ketcherside movement was a secondary concern in the 1950s. But by the early 1960s, both Garrett and Ketcherside had moved from a "Sommerite" position to an ecumenical stance. Their goal was to unite all segments of the Restoration Movement. This effort exposed another fissure within churches of Christ.

YATER TANT: THE INSTITUTIONAL ISSUE

What had been brewing under the surface burst into the open with Cled Wallace's "That Rock Fight in Italy." Glen L. Wallace quickly posted a private letter to his cousin expressing concern. Cled Wallace reprinted the letter with comments on the front page of the *Guardian*. Cousin Glen then wrote in the *Firm Foundation:* "In Cled's rock throwing at his fellow Christians in difficult fields, the enemy has received a lot of comfort. I hope my 'beloved kinsman' sleeps well."[4]

Editor Tant deplored the front-page article. He attempted to explain its appearance. Tant suggested, however, that the foreign mission work among churches of Christ needed careful study. Because of "high hysteria," he called for a "cooling off" period before discussing the topic in earnest. No allowance for such a luxury was forthcoming. Tant, without cooling off, asked: "Does the

Gospel Guardian stand alone among the papers in the 'brother-hood' questioning the scripturalness of one church's [sic] becom-ing the equivalent of a 'missionary board?'" Cled Wallace and publisher Cogdill quickly joined Tant by calling for an in-depth study of the philosophy for support of foreign missions. Wallace pointed his finger at both the *Firm Foundation* and the *Gospel Advocate:* "The way the *Gospel Advocate* and *Firm Foundation* are going along with about every fad the brethren can think up, in-cluding church support of colleges, I think it a waste of time to court their favor."[5]

With Tant and Wallace focusing the attack, the conflict soon be-came heated and often less than brotherly. Yater Tant, as editor of the *Gospel Guardian,* was in the thick of the battle. The son of J. D. Tant, he was suited for conflict. This was exactly where his fa-ther would have been.

The elder Tant was a Texan by birth, but lived in several states, including Tennessee. While the family was living in Tennessee in 1908, Yater was born. When time came for him to attend college, the younger Tant enrolled in David Lipscomb College. In 1926, even as a student, he began preaching for the Joseph Avenue church in Nashville. Later, while serving Louisville's Bardstown Road church as preacher, he received his B.A. degree from the University of Louisville. Three years later he obtained an M.A. de-gree from Louisville Presbyterian Theological Seminary. Preaching carried him into Arkansas, Illinois, and Oklahoma for full-time work. During the 1930s, he often wrote articles for Wallace's *Bible Banner.* From the very first, he possessed an ex-cellent writing style. He was a natural candidate, therefore, for the editorship of the *Gospel Guardian.* This relationship with the *Guardian* continued until 1971. In 1975, he began *Vanguard.* It ceased publication in December 1984.

Whether the combatants wished it or not, the discussions quickly degenerated into personality conflicts and vicious name calling. G. C. Brewer referred to the *Guardian* writers as a "king-dom of crankdom," and more specifically, he called Tant, Cogdill, and their friends "quibblers," even using the word "demagogues" to describe the leaders of the noninstitutional movement.[6] Cled Wallace, referring tongue-in-cheek to the *Gospel Guardian* posi-tions he and others espoused as an illness the larger brotherhood was attempting to diagnose, chided: "The mystery should soon be cleared up. Dr. Grover Brewer, a well-known specialist on our sort of disorder, has been called in, or just came in—the *Gospel Advocate.*" In the same issue, Cogdill said of Brewer: "You would think that he regards himself as one of the original twelve seated on a throne judging Israel." [7]

What was the true issue? *Gospel Guardian* scribes believed that the sponsoring church method of doing mission work was parallel to the missionary society of the nineteenth century. A pattern is clear, they argued, within the New Testament; it does not include sponsoring churches. Churches can cooperate, but the funds should be sent directly to the church or individual needing help. From Paul's gathering of funds for the saints in Jerusalem, those favoring sponsoring churches used the first-century church as an example of an eldership disbursing funds contributed by a number of churches. Such cooperation is biblical, said the *Guardian,* if the funds are used only locally as was the money in Jerusalem. Thus, Broadway in Lubbock and the church in Brownfield, Texas, were unscripturally disbursing funds because they were accepting money to be used in distant fields, not in their local communities. They were nothing more than small missionary societies with one eldership controlling the money contributed by other churches. [8]

What did those supporting the sponsoring church method have in mind? What arguments did they use? Brewer led the defense: "This [sponsoring] church . . . agrees to see that the missionary is supported in his work; it agrees to underwrite him and, therefore, to relieve him of worry and relieve him of the necessity of laboring with his hands to feed his family while he preaches the gospel." Brewer reminded his *Guardian* friends that those who are so opposed to "sponsoring" have been known to sponsor citywide meetings. He was referring specifically to the 1945 Music Hall meeting in Houston, Texas, when the churches in that city, with the notable exception of Central, cooperated to support Foy Wallace, Jr., in a special effort. Brewer supported such an arrangement. In fact, small churches would not be able to support a missionary if they did not help through another church willing to oversee the mission effort in a foreign country. [9]

B. C. GOODPASTURE: STRONG VOICE AGAINST NONINSTITUTIONALISM

The *Advocate's* B. C. Goodpasture gave the most space in opposition to the noninstitutional positions. He himself wrote little,
but at times he would write short responses to something said by
Tant, Cogdill, or Cled Wallace. In reference to the "rock fight" article, he wrote:

> It will take more than a "kite tail" to make the "rock fight" arti-
> cle "fly." It would take a few balloons well-filled with gas or
> hot air! The former could be secured from any rubber com-
> pany, and the latter could be obtained, it is reported, in abun-
> dance, from the "Lufkin Diocese." Seriously, a "kite-tail" could
> be appended to the "rock-fight" article which could make it
> "fly," but not the kind the G. G. boys are accustomed to writ-
> ing.[10]

Cled Wallace, at the time preaching for the Lufkin, Texas,
church, said of Goodpasture: "He appears to entertain a dislike for
us. His bad humor must be stronger than his convictions, for he
has not said that much in favor of his side of this issue, since the
fracas started."[11]

In 1951, the Lufkin church divided over internal issues involving Roy Cogdill, his publishing company, and Cled Wallace.
Finally, Cogdill and a group from Lufkin's Fourth and Groesbeck
church withdrew to form a new congregation. The original church
withdrew their fellowship. Goodpasture responded to the happenings in Lufkin by asking Yater Tant to tell his readers "who is
sponsoring what" in East Texas. "Further, he might indicate where
the 'overflow editor' worships when in Lufkin—whether at the
meetinghouse or the *courthouse*." Goodpasture also wanted to
know "the details of 'the Lufkin plan' for starting new congregations."[12]

Benton Cordell Goodpasture was, according to many on all
sides of the issues, the most powerful person within churches of
Christ from the late 1940s until his death in 1977. David Edwin
Harrell penned a most interesting sketch of the editor for the
Florida College lectures in 1981. Harrell, a close friend of
Goodpasture's youngest son, Cliett, attended David Lipscomb
College, graduating in 1954. He was often a guest in the

Goodpasture home. Religiously, Harrell was and is within the non-institutional churches of Christ. What Harrell said about Goodpasture is not only interesting, but quite valuable in understanding the conflicts within the fellowship.[13]

Born in 1894 at Rocky Mound, Tennessee, Goodpasture attended the Nashville Bible School, where he studied under H. Leo Boles, posting an outstanding record as a student. In 1918, he married Emily Cleveland Cliett. From that year until 1939, he preached in Shelbyville, Tennessee; Florence, Alabama; and Atlanta, Georgia. In 1939, Leon McQuiddy, the publisher of the *Gospel Advocate,* selected Goodpasture as the *Advocate's* editor to replace John T. Hinds, who had died in 1938. The paper had gone west for its two previous editors. This time the selected editor lived east of the Mississippi River and was a graduate of the Nashville Bible School.

Goodpasture's reputation in 1939, suggested Harrell, was not as brotherhood-wide as the two previous editors. But he brought two very important recommendations with him—those of H. Leo Boles and Leon McQuiddy. Under his guidance the *Advocate* steered a steady course through a number of critical issues: the last stages of premillennialism, the Murch–Witty "unity" meetings, the war issues surrounding World War II, and the institutional conflicts of the 1950s. In the meantime, the *Advocate's* circulation continued to climb. By the early 1950s, the numbers grew to 20,000. During the centennial drive of 1955, the subscription list reached the 100,000 mark. It finally leveled off at about 30,000 near the time of Goodpasture's death. With such a medium, no man within churches of Christ had more influence from 1939 until 1977.

Goodpasture, as already noted, became immersed in the battle against the "antis," as the noninstitutional advocates were often called. Goodpasture sincerely believed they acted out of personal ambition: "It was started by disgruntled preachers who did not get the attention they thought they deserved." Harrell believed Goodpasture, as editor of the *Advocate,* often used intimidation toward those who would stray from the paper's stated positions. With Florida Christian College in mind, Goodpasture warned: The *Advocate* would "cast its influence only with men and colleges it deems worthy of its support." Noninstitutional enthusiasts believed this was the reason a number of men, including Earl West,

John D. Cox, Hugo McCord, Pat Hardeman, and C. M. Pullias, wrote articles in the *Advocate* during 1957 and 1958 repudiating their recently-held noninstitutional positions.

Why did Goodpasture follow his chosen path? Subtle changes were taking place within churches of Christ by the end of World War II. The fellowship was in the process of changing from a "bumpkin image" to a more sophisticated demeanor. Harrell continued: "[Goodpasture] was no common country preacher, and his contemporaries soon recognized that he was a man to be pushed to the front. Here was a man who would not shame the brotherhood in polite society." Secondly, Harrell believed Goodpasture's greatest talent was as a manager. "He managed his office well; he managed the *Gospel Advocate* well; and, in a very real sense, he managed the churches of Christ well." Thus, Rex Turner of Alabama Christian College, according to Harrell, could describe Goodpasture as a man of "intellectual capacity and scholarship," and "of enviable mental and physical endowments." He was "dignified," "spiritual," and blessed with "common sense."

Ed Harrell set the tone for the noninstitutional churches' more recent assessment of the institutional churches of Christ. He believed Goodpasture fit perfectly into the sociological pattern of leaders of maturing religious groups. He listed four changes: (1) From truth-oriented to group-oriented. "First generation religious leaders are committed to ideas, often being forced to abandon their parent group because of that commitment." The second generation needs a manager. (2) From open controversy to closed controversy. Means other than debate and open confrontation establish positions within the brotherhood. (3) From self-conscious rejection of society to self-conscious acceptance of society. There is a tendency to become more and more like the society surrounding Christians instead of attempting to influence society. (4) From builders to preservers. Harrell wrote: "In the 1950s the preserving of the churches of Christ empire became central in the thought of many people." Goodpasture was the unconscious leader of this change.

Is Harrell correct in his assessment? Or is he simply supporting a position he personally chose during the early 1950s? Whatever the conclusion, B. C. Goodpasture opened the pages of the *Advocate* to those who defended the "sponsoring church" method of missionary effort and supported those who debated the issues with the noninstitutional preachers and editors.

As early as June 15, 1950, the *Advocate* included an article by James D. Bales, professor of Bible at Harding College, titled "Sending Through Another Congregation." Bales quoted Acts 7:27-30, emphasizing the latter part of the selection: "Then the disciples, every man according to his ability, determined to *send relief unto the brethren* which dwelt in Judea: which they also did, and sent it *to the elders* by the *hands* of Barnabas and Saul." On the basis of this Scripture, Bales asked:

> What right has anyone—especially since he believes in congregational independency, and unless he can point out a Scripture which is being violated, or a principle of right which is being overthrown—to tell one congregation that it cannot send relief through some other Christian or Christians? The help supplied by Antioch was sent by Paul and Barnabas (messengers) to help the suffering at Jerusalem through the elders of the church.[14]

THE *FIRM FOUNDATION* JOINS THE FRAY

Bales also shared a lengthy discussion with Yater Tant in the *Firm Foundation,* using specifically the Broadway church's German involvement as an example. Germany was at the center of attention as Otis Gatewood traveled across the United States addressing large gatherings concerning the mission efforts in the country of the former enemy. Tant argued that working through Broadway—especially if individuals were sending contributions for the work—was circumventing the local congregation and its elders. Bales asked: What if the local elders were not doing mission work? Would it be wrong for the individual to support mission work? Bales also asked Tant: Is it wrong for an individual to feed the poor? Must he do everything through the local church? How can Tant teach through the pages of the *Gospel Guardian?* Is it a work of the local church? What if someone sends the subscription price to the *Guardian* to supply the paper to a student or anyone else, is this wrong because it was not done through the church treasury? Is the "Lubbock Plan" any different from the "*Gospel*

Guardian Plan?" Is not the *Guardian* asking churches and individuals to cooperate to destroy the "Lubbock Plan?"[15]

Cecil Wright of Denver, Colorado, took the lead through the *Advocate* to counter the *Gospel Guardian's* opposition to cooperative mission work.

> The present assault against sponsored cooperative mission work, instigated and conducted by the *Gospel Guardian,* has raged more than a year now, with little or no abatement. On various occasions the *Guardian* has sung paeans of victory, the last of which was an editorial in the issue of April 19, 1951, entitled "The Voice of the Turtle." This was somewhat to commemorate the anniversary of the *Guardian's* big push starting April 20, 1950 with its editor and its publisher as leaders in the affair. Previously there had been some preliminary encounters and border incidents, such as the "rock fight" articles. But war was not officially declared, battle lines were not definitely drawn, and an all-out offensive was not launched till then. Since that time, however, an almost constant barrage has been leveled against sponsored cooperation in mission work, its participants, and its defenders, in keeping with the *Guardian's* threat to wage battle "without restraint."[16]

Wright noted a change in Yater Tant's position from August 18, 1949, to April 20, 1950. On the earlier date Tant upheld the right of sending money to a missionary through a "sponsoring church." But by April 1950, the "sponsoring church" method had become the "apostasy"; it was now "digression." Wright quickly moved to the heart of the matter by suggesting that now editor Tant had placed "sponsoring church" in the same category as sprinkling for baptism.

Wright mentioned the Music Hall meeting of 1945 as a cooperative effort involving Roy Cogdill, *Guardian* publisher, and the Norhill church in Houston. Wright, like others, quoted from Cogdill's book, *The New Testament Church,* to point out that the very thing he was condemning in 1950 he had upheld in 1938. "Local churches cooperated in doing their work but such work was always under the supervision of a local church and its eldership (Rom. 15: 25,26; 2 Cor. 8:15; Acts 11:28-30)." Therefore, Wright closed his article with the following conclusion:

It seems irrefutable that this review has demonstrated the following: (1) That the sponsoring church method of cooperation in mission work, which the *Guardian* has been fighting "without restraint," is eminently scriptural. (2) That the *Guardian* itself also editorially endorsed it as scriptural as late as only eight months before it charged it with being a "new digression" and "apostasy" and began its fight "without restraint" against it on April 20, 1950. (3) That the *Guardian's* charge of its being "new" is absolutely false. (4) That the *Guardian's* charge of it being "digression" and "apostasy" is equally false. (5) That the *Guardian's* editor and publisher have themselves made concessions that allow the very thing they have been fighting against "without restraint." And (6) that the *Guardian's* fight "without restraint" has not only been palpably wrong, but consummate folly—utterly inconsistent, "purely arbitrary and grossly absurd"—having been directed against precisely the same kind of cooperation for work in one field that it endorses for another, and threatened to be waged "even to the point of division" on exactly the same basis that those who opposed the instrumental music "divided the church seventy-five years ago."[17]

Editorials appeared in both the *Firm Foundation* and the *Gospel Advocate* upholding the position of their staff writers. Goodpasture thought Cecil Wright's "devastating article on 'The Cooperation Controversy' knocked the ball out of the park." G. H. P. Showalter—responding to W. W. Otey who had condemned the Union Avenue church in Memphis for usurping the preaching of the gospel in Japan—concluded: "The churches of Christ from the days of the apostles, have had a common faith, and a common aim, purpose and ideal, and have co-operated together in the furtherance of the gospel." Critical of the *Guardian,* Showalter continued:

> This new idea just started a year or so ago and on which they are threatening to divide the church, had no counterpart in the work of the churches sixty or seventy years ago. We fail to find evidence that the motives that gave inspiration to it sprang from the spirit of Christ or the peace of the gospel.[18]

By 1955, the issue had become so well defined that some were defending the right of emergency cooperation. Reuel Lemmons, editor of *Firm Foundation*, responded:

> The very offering of the argument sets aside the Bible example in favor of something else, and the excuse is "that is an emergency." Since when did emergency make wrong right? If one can plead an emergency to set aside New Testament patterns of congregational cooperation, why can't we set aside God's law or God's example on baptism because "this is an emergency"?

He urged Christians not to allow a few men, whether elders or preachers, do their thinking for them. "This is the very thing that caused the first great apostasy."[19]

B. C. Goodpasture could not be compared to Showalter or Lemmons as an editorialist. Instead, he quoted copiously from others. Statements of the pioneers were often put forward to defend both sides of the issue. Goodpasture quoted H. Leo Boles and David Lipscomb. Referring to the formation of the Tennessee missionary society, Goodpasture turned to Lipscomb: "One extreme begets another. In running from this organization, others have run to the extreme of refusing all cooperation among churches in supporting missionaries." As to whether two or more churches might cooperate to help a special effort, he quoted Lipscomb:

> If one is not able to support one within itself let it or them confer with one or more neighboring churches, and let so many as are needed to support a man do it by regular contributions; but by all means avoid associations that ignore and take the work out of the hands of the churches.[20]

By the late 1950s, the damage had been done. Foy Wallace, Jr.'s, son, William Wallace, writing in *Vanguard,* said of those years: "Careless, reckless, inconsiderate, reactionary journalistic excesses, though not engaged in by all, nor by any at all times, appeared frequently enough to taint the images of writers and cloud the issues involved." He added:

> The *Gospel Guardian* fell more and more in disrepute because of the image created by unfortunate journalistic behavior, the Lufkin church split, and the strategy of opponents. In the estimation of this author, truth suffered and a good cause floundered because malevolent factors were much too prominent in journalistic and congregational affairs.

Wallace indicated why he thought the institutional churches won the battle:

The *Gospel Advocate* with its heritage and history, and with the backing of the institutional and sponsoring church interests, and with its large circulation, was accomplishing its goal, turning the sentiment of the bulk of the brotherhood against the *Guardian* and its cause. The dissent against brotherhood projects became a minority movement carrying the burden of unfortunate images, labels, and prejudice.[21]

THE HERALD OF TRUTH BECOMES AN ISSUE

In 1952, the Highland church in Abilene, Texas, asked sister congregations to help support a mammoth undertaking to preach over a radio network. The response, as discussed previously, was overwhelming. Soon the Herald of Truth was on the air. A year later, programming began on television.

Soon critics attacked the programs as unscriptural, contending that the Herald of Truth was in the same category as the missionary society and that the Highland elders were usurping the authority of local elders across the country. Roy Cogdill asked:

> In a giant undertaking like the $1,000,000.00 broadcast of the 'Herald of Truth' nation-wide program, whose right and authority is it to designate the elders of the Highland Church in Abilene to receive all of this huge sum of money and direct the program?

It was just one more promotional activity of the *Gospel Advocate* and its selected preachers whom it promoted, critics claimed.[22]

REUEL LEMMONS: AN ADVOCATE OF UNITY

By late 1954, a Lufkin, Texas, debate loomed between E. R. Harper, preacher for the Highland church in Abilene, and Yater Tant. Tant desired a repeat debate between Harper and Cogdill in Abilene. They agreed on the proposition: "The Herald of Truth as originated and now operated is in harmony with the scriptures."[23] Harper would affirm; Tant and Cogdill would deny. Tant and Harper exchanged their unpleasantries through the *Guardian* and the *Advocate*. Harper's major problem, suggested Tant, was illness.

Because of feelings already frayed, Reuel Lemmons, who had just become the editor of the *Firm Foundation,* feared the impending debate. Prior to the discussion, Lemmons prophetically wrote:

> I fear for the outcome of this debate. If I had it within my power I believe I would prevent its taking place. Not that I am against debates. I am not. They do good when conducted properly. But this one has all the earmarks of being able to do an awful lot of harm.

He added:

> Brother Harper and Brother Tant are both fighters. They have always been. There is something heroic about a fighter. Too often the sides taken are little determined by the truth presented.

Lemmons continued, indicating his grave concern:

> I believe we are seeing history made in the church right now. And I believe this debate and the later one at Abilene, will help mould church history. . . . It should make a man shudder to feel that he held the possible destiny of a great portion of the church in his hands.[24]

The debates changed few persons from their original positions. Those who supported the Herald of Truth continued to support it. Those who opposed it continued their opposition.

But on this and other issues, Reuel Lemmons emphasized the unity of the fellowship. Following the death of G. H. P. Showalter late in 1954, Lemmons became editor of the *Firm Foundation.* He had spent his life preaching, and accepted the editorship after serving the Central church in Cleburne, Texas, for twelve years.

Living in Tipton, Oklahoma, before entering college, Lemmons graduated from Abilene Christian in 1935. His family had moved to Oklahoma from Arkansas, where Lemmons was born at Pocahontas on July 8, 1912. Of all his work, Lemmons was most pleased with his mission emphasis, especially his involvement in the Spanish-speaking countries of the Americas. He spoke for many years over a powerful radio station in Mozambique (Portuguese East Africa) to English-speaking people in Africa. In 1950, he became a member of the board of Abilene Christian University.

The division among churches of Christ hurt him deeply. In 1963 he penned:

> We never cease to be amazed at the willingness of brethren to draw lines against each other. It seems some are determined to drive a wedge. Are they completely oblivious to the fact that they are tearing at the body of Christ—crucifying the Son of God afresh and putting him to open shame before a godless world? Continued cutting and rending operations keep the body of Jesus bleeding.[25]

OPPOSITION TO ORPHAN HOMES AND HOMES FOR THE ELDERLY

There was little or no opposition to homes for orphans and the elderly until the late 1940s. On the other hand, there had long been an underground doubt about schools within the Restoration Movement. Even Reuel Lemmons, a longtime member of the board of Abilene Christian University, voiced concern. Because they train most preachers, he believed schools have the power to lead the church astray.[26] Thus, the 1947 confrontation between N. B. Hardeman and Foy Wallace, Jr., was not simply about the right of churches to support schools. It indicated Wallace's fear of schools. When Hardeman suggested both homes and schools would stand or fall together as to their right to exist, the floodgate opened wide against church support of homes and schools.

G. C. Brewer had long championed the support of both homes and schools. In 1933, Brewer established the basis of his argument: What the individual can support, the church can support. Furthermore, churches can support and use organizations formed by individuals. From his perspective, no harm can come as long as the churches are free to give or not to give—as long as churches are not "under the control of a super government." Emphasizing 2 Corinthians 8:17-20, Brewer asserted that schools and homes are only messengers for the benevolent gifts of many churches. In fact, Brewer believed the best way for Christians to support all organizations is through church treasuries. In this way God receives the glory.[27]

Quickly, opposition to Brewer's positions arose. When Hardeman joined Brewer in 1947 in the call for churches to support educational institutions, the issue emerged full blown. The homes and the schools would stand or fall together. In 1951, Brewer responded to a letter suggesting compromise. Both homes and schools, stated Brewer, under a board or under the elders of a church are scriptural. He also agreed with his adversary that individuals can support homes and schools. He was asked:

> Since everyone agrees that it is scriptural to have a home under elders, why divide the church by suggesting that churches can support homes under a board of directors? Since Brewer agreed with his adversaries that individuals could support homes and schools, why divide the church by advocating church support?[28]

Brewer responded by suggesting that such decisions among churches was the first step in becoming sectarian. "The good brother does not see that this would be *to enact a law, to form a creed, to formulate and publish a party pronouncement* from which if anyone should dare to dissent he would be 'read out of the party!'" Using as a basis his conviction that a church can support what an individual can support, Brewer argued that it was inconsistent to allow representatives of the homes or schools to use the pulpit to publicly advertise the institutions and then to say that it is un-Christian to allow Christians collectively to support with their money what they have already supported through allowing speakers to fill the pulpit: *"For a Christian church to give Christian money to support a Christian school would be an un-Christian act, according to the creed of the quibblers."*

As to having homes under the elders, it would be unscriptural to have such a home "within the framework of a local congregation," suggested Brewer. In response to John T. Lewis' article in the *Gospel Guardian* advocating the care of orphans within the framework of the local congregation," Brewer listed what this work would entail:

> Note what we would have here now: an orphan home, chartered, licensed, State inspected and approved, with superintendent, matrons, nurses, kitchens, bathrooms, playgrounds, trucks and truck drivers, a farm with farm implements, farm superintendent and laborers—all of this in *"the framework of a local congregation"!*

He added:

> If having a home under an eldership makes it scriptural, why not place a school under a local eldership and make it scriptural? Why did the organizers of the missionary society not think of this method? Would it have stopped the opposition of Lipscomb and Fanning?[29]

The most outspoken defender of the orphan home and the home for the elderly was Guy N. Woods, both in debate and through the pages of the *Gospel Advocate*. In 1954, the whole issue, he stated, was not over five years old. Until that time, he averred, "there was virtually a universal endorsement of, and hearty support for, the benevolent activities among us." Instead of seeing it as scripturally-based opposition, he said: "There has been, and always will be, those in the church whose conception of Christianity is negative in nature, and who operate on the theory that the less they do the more orthodox they become!"[30]

Again both sides called upon the "pioneers." Both claimed David Lipscomb. B. C. Goodpasture constantly printed statements from Lipscomb concerning his association with the Fanning Orphan School and of church support of the Nashville Bible School. Both sides quoted H. Leo Boles as an authority. The *Advocate* and the *Firm Foundation* occasionally published an earlier article supporting cooperation in the Cuban work.[31]

On the other hand, the *Gospel Guardian* claimed to be in direct line with the journals which had stood firm against apostasy. In urging readers to subscribe to the paper, the following advertisement appeared in 1953:

JUST SUPPOSE——

Just suppose *The Gospel Advocate* had NOT made a fight against instrumental music and missionary societies . . .

Just suppose *The Firm Foundation* had NOT made a fight against sect baptism . . .

Just suppose *The Bible Banner* had NOT made a fight against the errors of premillennialism . . .

Just suppose *The Gospel Guardian* had NOT (1) exposed the modernism in "The Gospel Treasure Series" of Bible school literature three years ago . . . had NOT (2) pointed out the danger of a galloping trend toward centralization of control in foreign mission work . . . had NOT (3) shown the "deadly and undeniable parallel" between the institutional benevolence home and the missionary society . . . had NOT (4) exposed the insidious modernism in the Revised Standard Version of the scriptures at a time when the other journals among us were praising that false translation to the skies.

THE ISSUES ARE DEBATED

Inevitably the issues would be contested in debate. From Alexander Campbell onward, debating has been an integral part of the Restoration Movement. Early in the century, most debating within churches of Christ has been with denominational groups—especially Baptists. Since the late 1920s, however, several debates have occurred between various factions within the fellowship.[32] In the 1930s, premillennialism was the issue. By the late 1950s, debates became the norm on all issues. Carl Ketcherside questioned the scripturalness of full-time preachers and the right of Christian schools to exist. G. K. Wallace and Ketcherside put the topic to debate at Paragould, Arkansas, in 1952 and in St. Louis, Missouri, a year later.[33] In 1954, Bill Humble and Leroy Garrett discussed the same topics in Kansas City, Missouri.[34]

In 1954, the issues under discussion in the *Gospel Guardian* and the *Gospel Advocate* erupted into debate. Charles A. Holt, Jr., represented the *Guardian's* positions against W. L. Totty in Indianapolis, Indiana. Over the next several years, W. Curtis Porter and Guy N. Woods, along with Yater Tant and E. R. Harper, discussed the Herald of Truth issue. Roy Cogdill and Guy Woods debated both orphan homes and the Herald of Truth. Cecil Douthitt and Thomas Warren discussed orphan homes, and Totty and A. C. Grider met on two occasions, one in Mississippi and the other in Indianapolis, on the same issue.

During the 1950s, combatants believed debating was necessary to clarify the issues and establish the truth. Thomas Warren, then writing in the *Gospel Guardian,* upheld the right and even the need for debates:

> Members of the body of Christ are eager for the Bible to be discussed on the public platform. This is true because they know that truth will never suffer from sincere investigation.

Only those who do not want truth proclaimed and received by the masses of mankind need have any fear of such discussions. Ask the man who preaches where you go to church if he will engage in such discussions. If he will not, does that not arouse your suspicions that he may know that he is not preaching the whole truth of God's Word?[35]

According to William Wallace, however, "debates did more to consolidate and firm up brethren in their respective positions than they did to convert members from one side to the other." He added: "Churches continued to divide over the issues, and bitterness was intensified with broad coverage of problems in the journals, church bulletins, and sometimes on local radio programs."[36]

Among the most important debates was the 1957 Birmingham clash between Guy Woods and Roy Cogdill. They discussed whether or not the Bible allows churches to build and maintain benevolent institutions for the care of the needy and whether or not it is in harmony with the Scriptures for churches to support the Herald of Truth from their treasuries. Jack Meyer, the local preacher, believed the debate necessary because too many people and churches were complacent and opposed nothing. Meanwhile, the noninstitutional brethren were contemplating withdrawing fellowship from churches that supported homes and cooperative programs. Meyer noted what one local preacher had written in the *Gospel Guardian:* "There is very little question hereabouts regarding fellowship with the institutional crowd. The lines are already being drawn and we would not do right to ignore them. Bit by bit all contact with them is being broken."[37]

Cogdill opposed all homes because, he said, they were benevolent organizations in opposition to and in competition with the church. He also compared them to missionary societies. Woods denied the homes' competition with the church; instead he indicated how they aided the church in carrying out its responsibility in caring for widows and orphans. Woods followed the arguments of Brewer: A home for orphans is simply an attempt to replace the original home. Since the home came directly from God, along with government and the church, then the home should be replaced as closely as possible. Churches, therefore, could voluntarily support these God-ordained homes. They are not, argued Woods, parallel to the missionary society. Cogdill called for Woods to produce the passage that "authorizes the church to send its money to a human organization to take over and control its work for it." Woods countered: "It [Cogdill's position] is not a part of the New Testament teaching, it is contrary to the spirit of Christ, it is antiism, it is hobbyism, and it is dividing the churches of Christ all over the country." [38]

Although not a position widely enunciated, the most radical view offered by a noninstitutionalist was an issue in a debate between A. C. Grider and W. L. Totty in Indianapolis, Indiana. The two men had earlier met in Mississippi. On that occasion, Totty presented Grider the following proposition: "The Bible teaches that it is a sin for the church to take money from its treasury to buy food for hungry, destitute children, and those who do so will go to hell." Grider signed the proposition and agreed to meet Totty in Indianapolis on December 3 and 4, 1964. He shared a position with others of the noninstitutional persuasion: The church cannot scripturally contribute to the support of an orphan child since contributions are "for the saints." Since orphans are not "saints" the church cannot help them. Only individuals may do so. [39]

By 1964, the year of the Grider-Totty debate, the fellowship was no longer united. Furthermore, the possibility of the separate groups becoming one again was not a hope for the near future. Nevertheless, in 1968, a large group of men representing both sides met in Arlington, Texas, to discuss the issues then dividing churches of Christ. It was an extremely cordial gathering, but nothing of substance came from the meeting. Division remained. Not until 1988 in Nashville would another meeting be held. The issues of twenty-five years ago remained unresolved.

THE *FIRM FOUNDATION* AND THE *GOSPEL ADVOCATE* TAKE OPPOSING SIDES

Roy H. Lanier had served on the staff of the *Gospel Advocate* for fifteen years. Late in 1955, Lanier authored a series of articles on cooperation for the *Advocate*. Editor Goodpasture refused to publish two of the articles; they did not agree with the official policy of the paper. Because he could no longer write his convictions, Lanier resigned from the staff in 1957. Shortly thereafter, Reuel Lemmons of the *Firm Foundation* not only published a series of articles by Lanier titled "The Middle of the Road," but also gave them editorial endorsement. Lanier's position was between a liberal group that "believe[s] a group of men can form a corporation, build and maintain a home which is not under the oversight of elders of the church and that many churches can cooperate in the upkeep of the home," and a conservative group that "contend[s] that a church does not have the scriptural right to organize . . . its forces to operate a home to care for the aged people . . . or to care for orphans." The only scriptural orphan homes and homes for the elderly, stated Lanier, are the ones under the oversight of the elders of a local church.[40]

One year later, Reuel Lemmons became more involved when he penned an editorial under the title "Is The Home A Divine Institution?" No, said Lemmons, only marriage is divine. Human beings make homes. Therefore, to say that elders cannot have homes under their care is unscriptural. He remarked: "We find it impossible to believe the doctrine that 'the church is its own gospel preaching society but is not its own benevolent society.'"[41] From Nashville, Guy Woods responded with "unalloyed amazement and shocked surprise."[42] Already he had been critical of Lanier.[43] Woods had adopted the notion of the three divine institutions—the church, the home, and the state—in his debates. Others, including Thomas Warren, had done the same. There was a distinct possibility that even the mainstream churches of Christ might divide over the care of orphans.

By April 29, 1958, however, Lemmons clarified his position by saying that homes not under elders could not be supported by churches.[44] In response, Woods wrote: "We rejoice to learn this. We find tremendous satisfaction in the knowledge that the powerful pen of our Brother L is not dedicated to the destruction of these havens of the homeless among us." He quickly added: "We kindly urge the *Guardian* to take due notice of the following significant fact. . . . The *Gospel Advocate* and the *Firm Foundation* are fully agreed."[45] Lemmons acknowledged that churches could contribute to homes under a board of directors, but he would not change his views about the divinity of the home.

BATSELL BARRETT BAXTER AND REUEL LEMMONS: THE SCHOOL ISSUE

The school issue, so prevalent in the 1930s, remained alive in the 1960s. During November and December 1963, Batsell Barrett

Baxter preached three sermons for the Hillsboro Church of Christ in Nashville in which he upheld the right of churches to contribute to colleges. Basing his argument on the principle that the New Testament places responsibilities upon Christians and churches but does not give specifics, Baxter suggested three major responsibilities for the church: evangelism, benevolence, and edification. Using the example of the Antioch and Jerusalem churches of Acts 15, Baxter observed that edification was definitely practiced in the first century. Churches cooperated during the Hardeman Tabernacle Sermons for the purpose of teaching the Bible.[46]

But since the school is in many respects a secular institution, should not the support of such be limited to individuals? Baxter argued that *"the church is the people,"* and as a result, they are the church at all times. "Any 'good work' which the individual, as a Christian, is obligated to support financially, the church is equally obligated to support financially." Does this include the funds in the church treasury? Yes, concluded Baxter. Preaching the gospel is required by the Scriptures. Benevolence is emphasized in the Bible. Why not edification? Ephesians 6:4 places the responsibility for nurturing children upon the father. Still, the church has a responsibility to help the family in Bible classes and such other opportunities as are provided.

Therefore, a church can support a young preacher in an apprentice program. A local congregation can provide a "Bible Chair" at a state university. In the same manner, elders can choose to support a Christian school, especially for Bible instruction. Some might oppose such involvement because schools have ball teams, dramatics, and other things not specifically associated with Bible instruction. Baxter argued that an education must be broad—one that includes English, history, and speech. A Christian school is more than Bible classes.

Some are able to see without any difficulty the scripturalness of churches contributing to the support of benevolence organizations, said Baxter, but they cannot see the similarity in supporting schools. His conclusion was the same as Hardeman's: *"The Orphan's home and the Christian school must stand or fall together."*

Reuel Lemmons did not find the task before him a pleasant one. He and Baxter were very close friends, but he felt so strongly that Baxter had erred that he could not refrain from responding. Why was it so important to Lemmons? "There is grave danger that division may come to the church over this matter and victory in the field of opinion is not worth dividing the church of my Lord." He could not share Baxter's contention that the care of orphans and the support of schools must stand or fall together. Caring for widows and orphans is the responsibility of the church; the care of schools is nowhere indicated to be so in the New Testament.

Why was the orphan's home always emphasized before broaching the discussion of schools? Sharing the same feelings as the noninstitutional advocates, Lemmons had always believed the schools' supporters pushed the orphan issue in order to get the schools under the same banner. Baxter, he said, "argues the orphan home and then draws college conclusions." Lemmons further stated:

> And Bro. Baxter, and those associated with him in this movement, are violating the faith, perverting the gospel, and if division of the church throughout the nation results from this controversy, he and his associates must bear the shame and disgrace for bringing it about.

Furthermore, Lemmons did not share Baxter's reasoning which stated: "*If* Christian schools are needed and *can* be used by the church. . . . does this not establish a *strong implication* that the church *might* have *some* responsibility?" Baxter, said Lemmons, drew strong conclusions from "ifs," "mights," and "somes." Nowhere did Baxter have a Scripture to fortify his conclusions. Lemmons then turned to the "time honored" positions of the men of the past. What if Lipscomb College did accept contributions from churches? Would Baxter hold to David Lipscomb's "time honored" position on civil government?

The *Firm Foundation's* editor had grave misgivings concerning the entire thrust to place the colleges in the budgets of the churches. Having just gone through the issue of orphan homes and the resultant division, he believed the skirmish was just the beginning of a larger battle that could divide the church again. He concluded: "We do not believe the Bible teaches the position held by these college-in-the-budget brethren, and we gravely fear the consequences to the church if it is led down that path."[47]

Reuel Lemmons was reacting to all the difficulties that had plagued the fellowship for fifteen years. He had watched the debates over "sponsoring churches," the Herald of Truth, and the orphan and elderly homes. Being one who urged unity and peace upon the brotherhood, he feared that a new issue would bring another major division. Besides believing Baxter's position to be unscriptural, his fear for the future could be easily understood. Was the issue worth it?

LEROY GARRETT AND CARL KETCHERSIDE: FROM RIGHT TO LEFT

Restoration, by its very nature, spawns men and groups with diverse views. The American Restoration Movement has been no exception. Since 1906, when churches of Christ were officially recognized as a separate group, numerous factions have spun off from the main body of believers. In each case, the smaller group believed it held the truth revealed in the Bible. The larger group treated the faction as in error. On many occasions the groups debated, the smaller group calling the larger group digressive. The larger group most often referred to the smaller as a faction, as pursuing a hobby.

Leroy Garrett and Carl Ketcherside led such a faction. During the 1950s, they were even more to the right (conservative) than the noninstitutional churches. Late in the 1950s, the two men made a major shift—from a conservative to a very liberal position among churches of Christ. As conservatives, both men denied the right of individual congregations with established elders to employ full-time preachers. If a church did not have elders, then the evangelist, as an officer mentioned in the New Testament, has the responsibility for the church. Furthermore, the two men—following a longtime position inherited from Daniel Sommer—opposed Christian schools for the training of preachers.

Issues clashed through debate. Beginning with the G. K. Wallace-Carl Ketcherside debate in Paragould, Arkansas, in 1952, the issues were explored in depth. In 1953, they discussed the same questions in St. Louis, Missouri, the home of Ketcherside. Controversy had swirled around the Manchester Church of Christ, which practiced mutual edification, and the West End Church of Christ, where Steryl Watson ministered. Manchester called West End sinful because the members supported a full-time preacher. The work of an evangelist was only to preach to alien sinners,

Manchester maintained. Furthermore, they had made "minister" a title. Watson had warned the West End church about the "hobby-ism" of Manchester. Arriving in St. Louis prior to the debate, Wallace attended the worship at Manchester on Sunday morning before the discussion. He did not, however, partake of the Lord's Supper because he refused to fellowship a faction.[48]

Other debaters, including Guy Woods, challenged Leroy Garrett. Meeting in Stockton, California, they discussed evange-lists, schools, and orphan homes. Woods, unable to elicit a re-sponse to his arguments, characterized Garrett:

> We think we do him no injustice in saying that he fancies him-self another Alexander Campbell whose obligation is to lead the people back to Jerusalem from Rome, a Moses ordained of God to induce the people of the Lord to flee the fleshpots of Egypt.[49]

A second discussion involving Garrett took place one month fol-lowing the Stockton debate in Kansas City, Missouri. His oppo-nent was Bill Humble, then evangelist for the 39th and Flora Church of Christ in Kansas City. Again Garrett opposed a church having a full-time evangelist. He argued that an evangelist's re-sponsibility is to preach to those who have never heard the gospel. In a second portion of the debate, Humble affirmed the right of Christians to form schools; Garrett denied the scripturalness of such institutions. Pat Hardeman, writing in the *Advocate,* believed this would be Garrett's last debate. His brethren, he averred, would no longer support him.[50]

From the extreme right, Garrett and Ketcherside suddenly moved to the extreme left. Ketcherside looked at the fellowship of churches of Christ and decided that he was "sick and tired of the bitter wrangling and jarring of the party spirit." Reuel Lemmons, commenting on Ketcherside's change, stated: "He has swung from the extreme of the narrowest of sectarian spirits to the broadest cover-everything-stand-for-nothing-liberalism."[51] By 1963, Ketcherside was advocating a unity that would span major differ-ences between all groups within the Restoration Movement. Concerning the extent of God's grace, Ketcherside stated: "It is my opinion that some may be saved who have done all they know to do, but have never learned of Jesus or have been honestly mis-taken about some of His requirements."[52]

One position both Garrett and Ketcherside affirmed when on the extreme right did not change when they moved to the left. Both men distinguished between "the gospel" and "doctrine." The gospel, according to Ketcherside, is the preaching of the death, burial, and resurrection of Jesus Christ. Doctrine includes the teaching of the Bible to the church. In between, baptism is left in limbo. Such a position led Ketcherside to accept an idea foreign to the Restoration heritage. He stated: "Belief of the report made concerning Jesus is obeying the gospel, climaxed by manifestation of that faith by baptism. . . . [T]his is the only test of faith."[53] By placing baptism outside the framework of the gospel, Ketcherside could easily fellowship anyone without regard to his baptism. This point was central to Lemmons's response.

By 1965, the positions of both Garrett and Ketcherside were even more open. In his *Restoration Review,* Garrett stated, "Men like Dr. Criswell, Bishop Martin, and Billy Graham proclaim the glad tidings of heaven. They may err in their instructions as to how men are to respond to the gospel, just as we all err in many things, but they are as much preachers of the gospel as any of the rest of us." Lemmons, indicating the fallacy of Garrett's argument, responded: "No man preaches the gospel who does not tell men correctly how to become saved. . . . The gospel has facts to be believed, commands to be obeyed, and promises to be enjoyed."[54]

Flying in the face of the entire concept of the Restoration Movement, Ketcherside—in reference to those who encourage a return to the New Testament as the basis of unity—stated: "His [Lemmons] stock-in-trade remedy for disunity is the platitude, 'if everyone will just take the Bible for what it says, and do just what it teaches, we will all be one.' The old cliche has been proven unrealistic and unworkable." The emphasis of the reformers to return to the Bible as the only authority in religion was totally discarded, not to mention the thrust of the restorers of the nineteenth century who called for return to the New Testament.

FOY E. WALLACE, JR., REENTERS THE FRAY

From 1949 until the late 1950s, the voice of Foy E. Wallace, Jr., remained uncharacteristically silent. Beginning as a well-known preacher in the 1920s, Foy Wallace was at the center of most issues and events within churches of Christ until 1950. Expected to take the lead in the new *Gospel Guardian* and to support the issues that became prevalent in the paper, Wallace, for all practical purposes, retired from his journalistic endeavors. But according to his son, William Wallace, the father did not change his positions, ever continuing to preach against those things he considered to be error.

Because of a misunderstanding between the father and the son, the two remained alienated for twenty-two years. This misunderstanding probably occurred because of Foy Wallace's dislike for Yater Tant, a feeling reaching back to 1949, when the first issue of the *Gospel Guardian* appeared. Tant was responsible, Foy Wallace believed, for cultivating attitudes that caused William to rebuke his father. Whatever the cause, Foy Wallace was an unforgiving man. A reconciliation finally took place in March 1975, four years before the senior Wallace's death.[55] James Adams said of the man he greatly admired:

> He found it difficult to forgive and forget injuries real or imagined. To be guilty of a personal transgression against him was to him a mortal sin. Such a person became his enemy and, with him, his enemies could do no good and his friends could do no evil.[56]

Many among the noninstitutional churches continue to believe that Foy Wallace, Jr., was the person who defined for an entire generation the errors of institutionalism. One such person was James W. Adams, who claimed that Wallace warned him on numerous occasions of evils emerging within churches of Christ. When Cled Wallace indicated that the "sponsoring church" issue would be the next battle within the fellowship, Foy Wallace was in complete accord. As late as 1949, Foy Wallace spent several hours explaining to Adams why Boles Home was an unscriptural organization.[57]

In 1964, however, scathing articles appeared from Wallace's pen in both the *Firm Foundation* and the *Gospel Advocate* rebuking the noninstitutional position. Wallace now called the men of the minority party radical, not "merely because they are wrong, but because of the arrogance so manifest in proclaiming themselves so right above all of the other great and godly defenders of the faith before them."[58] In fact, he identified the differences dividing the fellowship as "pseudo-issues." He then classified the noninstitutional brethren as "antis," in the same category as the anti-Sunday school faction.[59]

Who were these people? Wallace said they were a revived ultra-reactionary Sommer-Ketcherside party of the 1930s and 1940s. In fact, they "out-Sommered Sommer and out-Ketchersided the Ketchersiders in hobbyism." [60] He stigmatized the preachers as church splitters, men who went into communities where a "loyal" church existed, preached their ideas, and then established a new congregation. Often connecting them with Daniel Sommer, Wallace wrote:

> Now comes a company of men of the same breed of crankyism, sprouted in Texas, and with the same disposition of dictatorship over the churches and of dictation to the preachers, vowing to revive the dissensions of Sommerism with all its resultant divisions.[61]

How can one define Foy E. Wallace, Jr., in later life? Earlier rebuked, Wallace in the 1960s received a warm welcome from the *Gospel Advocate* and the *Firm Foundation*. The man who rode premillennialism to leadership in churches of Christ, introduced another major issue into the fellowship—opposition to modern Bible translations. When he died in 1979, the *Gospel Advocate* published an entire issue on the life and work of Foy E. Wallace, Jr. Whatever impression one has of Foy Wallace, all must agree that he had a tremendous impact upon churches of Christ for over fifty years.

CONCLUSION

The era under discussion ended with what appeared to be peace within the mainstream churches of Christ. The noninstitutional churches were now a fellowship of their own, with little contact with the majority churches. But for some, other issues were on the horizon. The bitter fight against "antiism" caused a reaction. Instead of gravitating to the center and stopping, a rather large group moved to the left. In Texas, Reuel Lemmons urged his readers to remain in the middle of the road. Said Lemmons: "One of the reasons why we try to stay in the middle of the road while all the furor is going on between the extremists is because that's where the truth is." [62]

Such left-leaning ideas as expressed by Leroy Garrett and Carl Ketcherside caused concern. On the other hand, the reactionary attitudes then alive in America had a tremendous impact upon some within churches of Christ. Thomas Warren quoted Tom Anderson, the controversial reactionary editor of *Farm and Ranch,* as saying: "America is losing its sense of moral indignation. Coexistence is immoral. America is losing its guts. Pinks are people who are too nice to be red." From a later issue, Warren quoted: "The middle-of-the-road between good and evil is evil. When freedom is at stake, your silence is not golden, it is yellow." Using this theme as a basis of emphasis, Warren penned three articles titled: "Christianity Versus Relativism, Middle-of-the-roadism, Neutralism, and Compromise." [63] His point was: Any middle of the road position between truth and error is error. Did he have anyone in mind? Who was the enemy Warren saw? Was it a call to conflict within the fellowship?

The decade that included the assassinations of John F. Kennedy and Martin Luther King, the Vietnam War, and the revolts on college and university campuses would become a trying time for American religion. The influences that caused decline in religious fervor across America had an overwhelming impact upon churches of Christ. It is a story that cannot yet be told in full. The causes of the fear Reuel Lemmons had in 1955 were not yet dead. The next two decades would see renewed conflict among churches of Christ.

CHAPTER 11

CHURCHES OF CHRIST AND TWENTIETH-CENTURY POLITICS: A Testing of the Insider-Outsider Thesis

Do members of churches of Christ fit into a political mold? Has there been a changed political direction in this century? A simple answer might be: Yes, there has been a change from the Democratic party to the Republican party, traced especially to the election of 1960.

Simple answers, however—as might be heard from many pulpits or in casual conversation—do not provide a satisfactory answer. Conversely, students of the history and sociology of religion have attempted to locate answers by searching into the theological views of the members of churches of Christ and then comparing these ideas with the culture in which they live. Samuel J. Hill of the University of Florida stated in 1980: "Their [churches of Christ] place in southern culture is a curious one," characterized by "strangeness . . . ambivalence, and . . . awkwardness of . . . position on the southern regional scene." In *Mission Journal,* also in 1980, Hill remarked: "this religious tradition . . . [is] difficult to comprehend." The "southern Campbellite tradition defies all general, usual, and typical social scientific accountings for distinctive southern folk religion."[1] Charles Allen Scarboro, a sociologist, discovered that churches of Christ "support and exemplify the values and attitudes of the plain-folk of the . . . mid-South."[2]

David Edwin Harrell, Jr., searching for an answer, focused on sectional origins of churches of Christ. He stated:

> The sectional bifurcation of the Disciples of Christ—using the name to refer to the whole movement—is one of the most vivid American examples of the bending of the Christian ethos to fit the presuppositions of the community. All of the complex antagonisms in nineteenth-century American society—North and South, East and West, urban and rural, affluent and dispossessed—left their marks on the theology and institutional development of the group. Schism was a result of differences far more complex than doctrinal disagreement—far more than the simple statement that "The Christian Churches . . . took their instruments and their missionary society and walked a new course."[3]

Whether Professor Harrell is correct in his assessment of churches of Christ is not the purpose of this chapter to determine. He does, however, develop a very important point. All subgroups in a society, including churches of Christ, are influenced tremendously by the surrounding society. Furthermore, they react to that society in multiple ways. Therefore, this chapter emphasizes the political response by members of churches of Christ to their political society.

TWO MODELS TO HELP UNDERSTAND CHURCHES OF CHRIST

In order to get at an answer, two models will be used to explore this political response. C. Van Woodward in *The Burden of Southern History* suggests the first model. "Thirty years after Secession and Civil War," said Woodward,

> the South suffered a second alienation from the dominant national spirit. This received expression in the Populist upheaval of the nineties. . . . It did not win the allegiance of as large a proportion of Southerners as had the Lost Cause, nor did it involve those it did win quite so deeply. But the alienation was real enough, and the heritage it left was a lasting one.[4]

Ed Harrell used a much more descriptive statement to focus on populism within churches of Christ: "The twentieth-century Churches of Christ are the spirited offspring of the religious rednecks of the post bellum South."[5] Since churches of Christ were predominantly southern and rural, the impact of the Populist movement must be considered.

Who were the Populists? American farmers experienced dispossession during the rise of big business after the Civil War. They believed they were not getting their fair share of the nation's wealth. Indeed, they believed a vast conspiracy led by business, financiers, and the railroads kept prosperity from the farmers. Led first by the Grange (the Patrons of Husbandry), then the Farmers' Alliance, and finally the Populist party, the farmers were attempting to gain a voice in America's future and their own prosperity.[6] The Populists were especially strong in the regions where churches of Christ are most numerous.

The second model is closely akin to the alienation model suggested by Woodward. It is found in R. Laurence Moore's, *Religious Outsiders and the Making of Americans.* Churches of Christ emerged in the twentieth century as double outsiders. As a predominantly southern religious movement, they were outside the mainstream of American religion. The second outsider position happened when churches of Christ separated from the larger and more liberal Disciples of Christ. This outsider position is clear in the following statement from David Lipscomb.

> Nothing in life has given me more pain in heart than the separation from those I have heretofore worked with and loved. The majority seem to be going away and leaving those who stand firm for the old ways. I love to be with the majority, and would certainly go with them, if I were not afraid of offending God in doing so.[7]

Eight years later, Lipscomb responded to the director of the census who had surmised that at least two fellowships existed under the umbrella of the Disciples of Christ or the Christian church. Said Lipscomb: "There is a distinct people taking the word of God as their only sufficient rule of faith, calling their churches 'churches of Christ' or 'churches of God,' distinct and separate in name, work, or rule of faith, from all other bodies or people."[8] These two statements suggest an outsider position—a remnant faithful to God.

As alienated Populists and religious outsiders, how have churches of Christ responded to the political issues of the twentieth century? Is there a pattern discernible throughout the century?

Have churches of Christ cast off the outsider, alienation position of
the earlier years of the century? Has there been a true move of
these people toward the Republican party? These are some of the
questions dealt with in this chapter.

TWO ISSUES: PROHIBITION AND WOMEN'S SUFFRAGE

Two issues of prime importance on the American political
scene at the turn of the century were temperance/prohibition and
women's political rights. Both issues were championed by religious and political liberals. The issues ran in tandem. If women's
right to vote were secured by law, the argument went, then prohibition would more easily become the law of the land. Not only did
they both become law, they became amendments to the
Constitution—prohibition in 1919; women's rights in 1920.[9]

Editors of the *Gospel Advocate* and the *Firm Foundation* did
not share the normally accepted position of including prohibition
and women's suffrage in the same reform package. Both papers
supported prohibition, not as a political, but as a moral issue.
When critics accused the *Advocate* of becoming embroiled in a political matter by supporting prohibition, J. C. McQuiddy responded: "In the name of reason, cannot a man preach temperance
as taught in the Bible without entering politics? This is not a political question, but a moral one. It is the devil crying in you,
'Politics!'"[10]

With all the concern in the *Advocate,* the *Firm Foundation,* and
Daniel Sommer's *Apostolic Review* for prohibition, not one of the
papers mentioned the passage of the Volstead Act, making prohibition national law. Only indirectly did the *Apostolic Review* recognize its passage by a quotation from *The Presbyterian.*[11]
Nevertheless, the act was passed, and its passage was enthusiastically accepted by the religious community, especially in churches
of Christ.

Conversely, when Tennessee faced the precedent-setting vote
on the Susan B. Anthony Amendment in 1920, J. C. McQuiddy
led the opposition to the extension of women's voting rights. "I do
not believe that the good women of Tennessee want the ballot; but
even if they did, the question which man must determine is not affected by what women WANT, but by what they ought to have."[12]

On August 18, 1920, the Tennessee legislature ratified the Nineteenth Amendment, making it a part of the Constitution. The following day, President Wilson asked Governor Albert H. Roberts "to convey to the legislature of Tennessee my sincere congratulations on their concurrence in the Nineteenth Amendment." He added: "I believe that in sending this message I am, in fact, speaking the voice of the country at large."[13]

J. C. McQuiddy remained unconvinced. He said of the amendment's passage: "God pity the child [sic], when they have a motherless home, when they have a mother who is in politics, campaigning over the States and neglecting the purifying, refining, and ennobling influences which she should be exercising in her home!"[14] From McQuiddy's perspective, prohibition was a moral issue that would make the nation better. The women's voting rights amendment would weaken the fiber of the nation.

With these two issues, a pattern began to emerge that would remain true throughout the twentieth century. Churches of Christ, compared with mainline churches such as the Methodists, have a totally different way of looking at the world. Where liberal, mainline churches accepted a political agenda that included the "social gospel," churches of Christ have used selective involvement—favoring prohibition while opposing women's suffrage. Voting patterns within the churches of Christ show a changing of parties, especially on the national level, based on the degree to which the parties agree with the church's selective involvement in moral/political issues.

A populist stance among churches of Christ can be seen in the support accorded William Jennings Bryan, the Great Commoner, during the 1925 Scopes trial in Dayton, Tennessee. It had a definite relationship with the moral issue of prohibition. In 1922, A. B. Lipscomb extolled Bryan as a defender of the Bible. He concluded his article exultantly: "Thank God for Bryan!"[15] Bryan led successful fights for the passage of anti-evolution laws in Oklahoma and Florida. His influence was felt in Mississippi and Arkansas as those states accepted similar laws in 1926 and 1927, respectively. Tennessee passed the most visible anti-evolution law in 1925. All these states had a strong populist strain.

Bryan's death in 1925 signaled a significant shift in American politics. Beginning in 1896, Bryan had placed his stamp on the Democratic party. Never elected president of the United States, he helped to elect his choice only once—Woodrow Wilson in 1912. During the 1920 and 1924 campaigns, he was able to block those who would change the direction of the party. What was his goal for the Democrats? He wanted his party to morally reconstruct the nation.

Therefore, as long as Bryan lived, prohibition would remain an amendment to the Constitution of the United States. Neither party became the champion of repeal until 1928, when Alfred E. Smith, a Catholic, accepted the nomination of the Democratic party. Bryan had blocked his nomination in 1924. Alfred Smith, he believed, was the enemy of moral pietism.

Liquor and Catholicism were the issues in 1928. Senator William Borah of Idaho and Bishop James Cannon of the Methodist Church championed prohibition for the Republican party. Anti-Catholicism, especially as represented by an urban candidate from the Northeast, had a negative impact on southern voters. When the votes were counted, Herbert Hoover, riding the wave of prohibition and Catholicism and suspicion of an urban candidate, had overwhelmingly won the election. In the South—the region of greatest strength of churches of Christ—Hoover carried Tennessee, Texas, and Oklahoma.

Nevertheless, the political scene had changed in America. The Democratic party, as it had been in the 1880s, was again the advocate of a pluralistic society. Bryan's dream was dead. It was only a matter of time until a Democrat would win the election, giving new direction to the United States.[16]

In the midst of the Great Depression, in 1932, Franklin Delano Roosevelt, a Democrat, became president of the United States. When he accepted the nomination of the party, Roosevelt announced: "This convention wants repeal. Your candidate wants repeal. And I am confident that the United States of America wants repeal."[17] He added repeal to his planks of relief, recovery, and reform.

Even in the midst of the depression, the possible repeal of prohibition became the center of attention among churches of Christ, at least in their journals. G. C. Brewer led the opposition to repeal in the *Gospel Advocate*. Typically, he emphasized his nonpolitical involvement; it was a moral issue.

> It is not the political aspect of the question that we as Christians are concerned about, but it is the effect upon our youth that this political propaganda and the political controversies are having that gives us deep concern. . . . [W]e must expose the fallacies.[18]

In response to the advocates of repeal, C. R. Nichol wrote on the front page of the *Firm Foundation:*

> No; the 18th Amendment to the National Constitution of the United States did not make the bootlegger. He existed before the 18th Amendment. It is in conjunction with other lawless men that the bootlegger is enabled to ply his lawless business in open violation to the laws of our land. The good citizen will lend no such aid by buying their poison, or protecting them in their unlawful work.[19]

One week later, Nichol added: "Can Christians be indifferent to the program some propose to make for sale [4 percent beer] that which debauches the nation?"[20]

W. L. Oliphant, also in the *Firm Foundation,* summed up the feelings of many:

> We are passing through abnormal times. The minds of our people are disturbed. Many are ready to welcome any kind of change. Christian people should not be swept from their feet by vain and rash promises and be induced to give in to a sinful and nation destroying program; a program fostered by interests which are openly opposed to the church, or wholly indifferent to its welfare.

American society was quickly undergoing a major transformation.[21]

By the middle of 1933, the battle was over. Under the leadership of President Roosevelt, the Twenty-First Amendment replaced the Eighteenth. The state legislatures voted 73 percent in favor of the new amendment. Somewhat more disturbing to the prohibition advocates, the rural legislatures voted over 50 percent in favor of the amendment. Thus, the religious forces, including churches of Christ, could not stem the tide of the return of legalized liquor.[22]

Why was there such incongruity between the elections of 1928 and 1932 in the American South where churches of Christ were most numerous? As mentioned previously, Herbert Hoover, a Republican, won Tennessee, Texas, and Oklahoma in 1928. Churches of Christ have historically been strong in these states. Evidently anti-Catholicism was the major factor in the election. Prohibition was a secondary concern. In 1932, Roosevelt, a Democrat and pro repeal, carried all three states. In Tennessee, Roosevelt doubled the vote of Hoover. Texas polled 760,348 votes for Roosevelt to 97,959 for Hoover. Oklahoma's Roosevelt vote was two and one-half times that of Hoover.[23] The vote swung so dramatically because Populist Southerners were voting against the establishment, the Republicans, who were, in the populist mind, responsible for the depression. The repeal vote was a vote for Roosevelt and the hopes placed in him.

SOCIALISM AND COMMUNISM AS ISSUES OF CONCERN

Socialism and communism were important issues during the early years of the twentieth century. Even though Populists toyed with a mild brand of socialism in fighting big business, the idea of the government assuming the means of production did not agree with their views of free enterprise.[24] The origin of socialism, many claimed, was Marxism. Marxism, they knew, was anti-Christian. Therefore, conservative, biblically-based religious groups opposed both socialism and communism.

After the 1912 election, when Woodrow Wilson, a Democrat, became President, the *Firm Foundation* noted a Socialist movement centered in Oklahoma. In 1914, the Socialist candidate for governor polled 21 percent of the popular vote.[25] It had also invaded churches of Christ. W. F. Ledlow traveled to Comanche, Oklahoma, to hear Stanley Clark say: "Nearly every man who joins the Socialist party quits the church." Ledlow quoted a former preacher and now a Socialist office seeker as saying "All churches are wrong," and that the church is a "barefaced fraud." Calling the church a "hypocritical institution," he then named preachers "the worst cowards on earth."[26] G. H. P. Showalter, editor of the *Firm Foundation,* recognized the economic unrest then alive in the United States, but he did not believe socialism was the answer.[27]

Following the Bolshevik Revolution, a "red" scare spread across the United States. Many agreed with Billy Sunday, the revivalist, that ship space could be saved by standing "ornery wild-eyed Socialists and I.W.W.'s [International Workers of the World]" before a firing squad. Feelings were strong among churches of Christ. The *Apostolic Review* stated:

> There is no doubt that the followers of the "red flag" are haters of the religion of Christ. Of course some of their advocates will deny this, yet all one has to do is to examine the religious faith of Emma Goldman, and the other I.W.W.'s who stunned our country, and he will find them all atheists or "thereabouts". The extreme Socialists are practically all infidels too. Their politics is their religion.[28]

A. B. Lipscomb of the *Advocate* penned a series titled "The Menace of Bolshevism." Lipscomb concluded his articles:

> A system that proposes to substitute might for right, to incite class hatred and war, to burn and ravage at will, to break up and destroy the family, to abolish the Christian religion from the face of the earth is putrid, and it is time to dig the grave.[29]

The fear of communism waned after 1921. It would lie dormant for a decade. Early in the 1930s, G. C. Brewer began to question the direction of many institutions in American society, especially education. The issue that emerged was communism. In a series of six articles titled "Communism—Its Four Horsemen," Brewer penned the strongest indictment of communism to be found in journals among churches of Christ. Why should Christians concern themselves with such matters?

> They do not know that communists already have an alarming hold on the United States; that they are in our schools and universities and even in the churches; that communism is in many textbooks and that millions of high-school students are enrolled in the party.[30]

The same attitudes that destroyed William Jennings Bryan in 1925, believed Brewer, were again abroad in the United States.

Brewer described communism as "a Utopian dream embroiled with the witchery of a fairy tale." His conclusion: Every effort to practice communism has failed. Instead of being free, people become enslaved. In Russia "gangsters destroyed churches, killed priests, confiscated property, abolished marriage, made women common property, and turned loose all the hordes of hell." He estimated that twenty million people had lost their lives during the Russian Revolution.[31]

Brewer criticized George C. Counts and Charles A. Beard of Columbia University, who were involved in a national study of education. He called them "radical professors." They were "left-wingers." *Scholastic Magazine* was communistic.

> Let all patriotic and God-fearing teachers cease using Scholastic, and also let them ask and demand that the N.E.A. purge itself of communism; and let Christian parents awake and guard their children.[32]

Furthermore, communism had a fourfold plan to destroy American civilization. The four horsemen were: atheism, immorality, class hatred, and pacifism.[33] It was a conspiracy not unlike what the Populists saw in big business late in the nineteenth century.[34]

Brewer's concern for communism extended beyond World War II. It was America's greatest enemy.

> Communism now reigns over about ten million square miles of territory, dominates three hundred million people, and is estimated to have ten million men under arms. If this does not constitute a threat to civilization, then it would be hard to imagine such a threat.[35]

Indeed, his concern caused him to encourage his brethren to join hands with Catholicism—a concern in its own right—until they jointly defeated the menace. In 1953, Brewer began publishing the *Voice of Freedom,* a journal to oppose both communism and Catholicism.

CHURCHES OF CHRIST AND CHANGING POLITICAL ALLEGIANCES

The American South had supported Roosevelt during his first two terms as president. By the end of the second term, however, some of his southern support began slipping away. Yet, as long as World War II engulfed the world, Mr. Roosevelt would continue in the White House. The war made a profound economic difference in the South. Comparatively, Southerners remained far behind the rest of the nation, but they were enjoying some semblance of economic well-being. The economic change allowed Southerners to think differently toward many things, including the political direction of the United States.

The voting patterns of Southerners began changing during the early 1950s. Not until 1960, however, did the directions of Southerners—and members of churches of Christ—show a marked change. In that year, John F. Kennedy, a Catholic, narrowly defeated Richard Nixon. L. R. Wilson, editor of *Voice of Freedom,* opposed Kennedy's candidacy because of Catholicism: "We are concerned with our American system. . . . To make sure that we keep our present system, let us keep it out of Roman Catholic hands." [36] The October 1959 issue of *Voice of Freedom* had a record press run of 100,000 copies. Wilson warned the American non-Catholic community:

> When we lose our freedom, the Protestant denominations will lose their freedom. When they lose theirs, we will lose ours. In a nutshell: the freedom of all of us is bound up together. Here, we are waging an all-out fight to preserve the freedom of all non-Catholic bodies.[37]

As the election of 1960 approached, the attacks on John F. Kennedy became much more personal.

Reflecting a growing concern among many conservative religious groups, Wilson showed a populist and outsider position when he warned: "He [Kennedy] is not only a tool of the Vatican but also of the big labor bosses." In the Senate, "he has nearly always voted on the 'liberal' side. . . . He has been an appeaser of the Communists." [38] The "liberalism" of John F. Kennedy became a dominant theme during the election of 1960.

L. R. Wilson's views were likely stronger than those held by the average member of churches of Christ, especially as he described Kennedy's political positions. Nevertheless, a study by Royce Money in 1975 substantiates Wilson's views. Money sent questionnaires to churches of Christ in all regions of the United States. He found little variation between churches in the South and in churches far removed, likely suggesting the migration of members from the South. Seventy-five percent of the respondents considered themselves religiously conservative. Politically, the percentage was slightly higher—76 percent.[39]

The Money study indicated a shift from the Democratic party to the Republican party between 1952 and 1972. Yet the Grand Old party enjoyed only a slight majority among churches of Christ. The most significant shift was from Democrat to Independent. On the national level, the independent vote has most often gone to Republicans since 1960. Nationally, Richard Nixon polled 61 percent of the vote in 1972. He received 84 percent of the vote among churches of Christ.

These data suggest two things: (1) Members of churches of Christ, like other outsider religious groups, did not like the direction of the Democratic party; (2) equally important, the Republicans were not the total winners in the shift. Many Americans, including members of churches of Christ, no longer thought of themselves as party members. They had become alienated from the historic political process.

Why was there such a shift in the electorate during the late 1950s and the early 1960s? Sharing a common prejudice with most southern whites, members of churches of Christ had strong racial views. Southerners generally viewed civil rights as a political, not a moral, issue. Unquestionably, this caused an erosion of the Democratic ranks.[40]

The political trend among churches of Christ can be seen in a straw vote on the David Lipscomb College campus in 1956. Even though Dwight Eisenhower's losses were seven southern states, Lipscomb students gave him 228 votes to Adlai Stevenson's 189.[41] In 1960, the Republican vote increased. Catholicism was the catalyst that began the migration, even a flood, from the Democratic party, especially on the national level.

It was not the issue, however, that sustained the continued erosion of the Democratic party. Even before the election of 1960, L. R. Wilson penned a revealing article.

> Traditionally, we are Democrats. But we do not purpose to swallow any and everything that any party tries to shove down our throats. Even if both candidates on the Democratic tickets [sic] were Protestants, the platform is so liberal that we would have to oppose it. It is thoroughly socialistic. Thirty years ago the people of the United States rejected Norman Thomas and his socialistic program. But the program now put forth by the Democrats goes far beyond anything that even Mr. Thomas advocated in those days.[42]

This emphasis, according to Laurence Moore, showed churches of Christ as part of the large outsider movement then under way in America's conservative churches.[43]

Secularism quickly became the dominant theme among America's conservative churches. The Supreme Court decisions on Bible reading and prayer caused increased concern. A balanced reaction came from Batsell Barrett Baxter, chairman of the Bible department at David Lipscomb College and preacher for Nashville's Hillsboro Church of Christ. He deplored the move toward secularism, but saw the decisions as placing a greater responsibility on the home and the church.[44] More pointedly, M. Norvel Young asked in a title to an article, "Would George Washington Approve the Supreme Court Decision Prohibiting Prayer and Bible Reading?"[45] L. R. Wilson agreed with Baxter. Nevertheless, he bemoaned the fact that "majorities no longer have any rights in this country—only the minority seem to have any rights."[46]

The 1960s were among the most volatile in America's history. Vietnam, by the middle of the decade, was dividing the United States. Urban violence, involving blacks in such places as Watts (Los Angeles) and Detroit, separated America's people even more. In 1968, an assassin's bullet killed Martin Luther King, Jr. During the first months of 1970, the confrontation of students and national guard on the campus of Kent State University alienated much of America's youth from the "establishment."

Within the larger picture, some years, in retrospect, stand out as more important than others. One such year was 1963. It was the year of John F. Kennedy's assassination. Martin Luther King led the great Washington, D.C., rally for civil rights in August of that year. Betty Friedan published her book *Feminine Mystic*. In 1966 Friedan led in the formation of the National Organization of Women (NOW). For many Americans, 1963 marked the crumbling of their country's social mores. With the previous introduction of the birth control pill in 1960 and the Bible and prayer decisions of the Supreme Court, it is not surprising that challenges were hurled by both men and women in churches of Christ against the direction of the United States.

TOTTIE ELLIS AND LOTTIE BETH HOBBS:
LEADERSHIP FOR POLITICAL CHANGE

Response came from the usual sources. A change, however, was in the air. For the first time, women in churches of Christ overshadowed the men in leadership positions. The *Voice of Freedom* offered a forum for Rita Rhodes Ward and Mrs. David Howell. Their main thrust was "women's lib." Ward discussed marriage, social relationships, day-care centers, public schools, and religion. At the same time Mrs. Howell of Haleyville, Alabama, was condemning the Equal Rights Amendment as a fraud and anti-Bible.[47]

Influenced by Mrs. Howell, Tottie Ellis of Nashville became an outspoken leader of the anti-ERA forces in Tennessee, then across the United States. After her initial involvement, Ellis recognized Betty Tollitta Holbrook of Nashville, Arkansas, as the mother of the anti-ERA movement among churches of Christ. As a result of her newly-found interest, Ellis led 500 women in 1974 to the Tennessee state legislature to demand recision of the Equal Rights Amendment. They were victorious. Of herself, Mrs. Ellis said she went to the state legislature and never came home. A year later, she worked with Phyllis Schlafly to organize the Eagle Forum. At the initial meeting in St. Louis, the organization elected Mrs. Ellis as its vice president.

In 1978, Tottie Ellis led fifty-six bus loads of women from Tennessee to Houston, Texas, to participate in an anti-ERA rally. This show of strength was exhibited at the same time as the International Women's Year meeting in the Texas city. Returning to Nashville, Ellis organized an anti-ERA rally in her home city. A crowd of ten thousand gathered to show strength against the ERA and, in turn, to show a force in favor of pro-life and pro-family. Among the speakers were Senator Garn of Utah, Dr. Charles Stanley, who would become the 1985 president of the Southern Baptist Convention, and Phyllis Schlafly. Dr. Batsell Barrett Baxter led the invocation. Ellis believed the rally convinced people that the issue was not just politics, but sin. As a result, religious people became more involved in the conflict on the political level.[48]

Lottie Beth Hobbs of Fort Worth, Texas, organized the Pro-Family Forum to combat the Equal Rights Amendment. Why were she and thousands of others opposed to the amendment? Because it struck "at the very foundation of our entire social structure." Hobbs added: "It is actually an Extra Responsibility Amendment—a loss of rights for women—which will harm our entire society."[49]

If one year can be marked as important in defeating ERA, it must be 1977. Illinois was a pivotal state. To influence the legislature, hundreds, representing many religious beliefs, filled buses and converged on Springfield. The largest contingent came from churches of Christ. Failure to pass in Illinois spelled doom for the Equal Rights Amendment.

The designation of 1979 as the International Year of the Child had rather sinister implications for Lottie Beth Hobbs. She saw in the movement the destruction of the family. The IYC, believed Hobbs, was cut from the same cloth as the IWY (International Women's Year)—the same leaders and the same philosophies represented by the pro-Equal Rights Amendment forces. Therefore, Hobbs emphasized children in several of her publications. In 1984, an all-day, Pro-Family Forum seminar convened in Kansas City, Missouri. The focus was: "Who Controls Your Children?" The subjects ranged from rock music to gay rights to abortion.[50]

Political action by issue groups has been a weapon against perceived humanistic tendencies since 1960. These groups were important in electing Ronald Reagan in 1980 and in 1984. When the Democratic party selected Geraldine Ferraro as their vice-presidential candidate in 1984, the opposition of the anti-feminists rose to a higher pitch. Lottie Beth Hobbs published a nine-page pamphlet titled: *Do You Want Feminism in the White House?* Said Hobbs: "if elected [Ferraro] would be just one heart-beat away from the presidency and the leadership of the entire free world." Hobbs called November 6, 1984 "A Day of Opportunity and a Critical Decision." "For the first time in many years," she wrote, "voters have a clear-cut choice between two very diverse philosophies. . . . Seldom have we had a better opportunity to study the candidates' basic beliefs and DO SOMETHING ABOUT SUPPORTING OUR OWN BELIEFS AS WE HELP TO MAKE THIS CHOICE."[51] When the election was history and Reagan had been reelected, Hobbs titled her article: "Cause for Rejoicing."[52]

HAD THERE REALLY BEEN A CHANGE?

Values long held die hard. The editors of *UpReach,* a publication of Herald of Truth, had no idea that such negative response would be generated by Sandra Milholland's article, "I'm a Working Mother: Be Careful How You Say It." [53] Published in the November/December 1984 issue, the article produced letters from Michigan to California. A California letter writer asked: "*UpReach* as a feminist forum? I can't believe it. The article 'I'm a Working Mother. . . .' is obvious feminist rhetoric." From Texas, a writer called the article "smut." An Iowa writer stated: "If you want to save American families, how can you condone working mothers?" [54]

Answering the many letters, the editors quickly stated their belief about the Bible's views on home and family. Finally, they added: "We must deal with the world as it is, not as we would like for it to be. And the world today is a world where women work outside the home." Ministry to working mothers, they explained, must be more than saying "give up [your] jobs and go back home."

Response to the article speaks loudly to the last years of the twentieth century. A large segment of people in churches of Christ feels just as strongly about issues that have religious/political overtones as did the commentators early in the century. The difference at the end of the century is a call for greater political involvement to deal with the issues.

ASSESSING CHURCHES OF CHRIST WITHIN AMERICAN POLITICS

Now that more than eighty years of American history has been surveyed, what can be said about churches of Christ and the political issues? The first observation is that churches of Christ have not changed as much as some might think. Two constants remain from the first years of this study—women's rights and liquor. Add to these issues those of Roman Catholicism, communism, race, school prayer, ERA, and pornography, and it is possible to see churches of Christ as a part of a larger conservative religious force in the American social and political arena. As Moore suggested, this makes churches of Christ outsiders.

Even beyond this conclusion, one must respect the insights of Dr. Timothy Tucker, an astute historian. He believes that "the issues which turned the churches of Christ away from the Democratic party establishment have not made them reliably devoted to the Republican establishment." Thus churches of Christ cannot be depended upon to produce consistent political results over a long period of time. The reason is simple: Their concern is issues, not the larger political universals. They will support the party that supports their issue. This makes them Populists.

The issues of the 1960s, the 1970s, and the 1980s, believes Tucker, "do not show the churches of Christ as conservative, but instead, *radical,* i.e., *alienated*—a bit *unwashed, insecure,* and above all *unreconciled* to the dominant national trends." [55] Again, a populist mentality emerges. Equally, Moore's outsider model fits. Describing religious conservatives, Moore stated:

> Fundamentalist leaders and laypeople, whether separated from or joined to large Protestant denominations, have contributed money and labor to defeat legislation providing public support of abortions and sex counseling, equal rights for women and homosexuals, and day-care centers for mothers. They have rarely been in the forefront of the movement for racial equality; they have consistently been hostile to trade unionism; and they have adopted virtually the whole range of conservative rhetoric about welfare cheats, coddled criminals, and the threat of global communism.[56]

Of special interest is that fundamentalists, or as most wish to be called, "evangelicals," involve the majority of the American religious community. Because of their views, especially their perceived anti-intellectualism, they accept a self-imposed "lost generation" tag first applied after the Scopes trial in 1925.

What about members of churches of Christ as Populists and outsiders? Unquestionably, a person or a group of people should not choose to be outsiders simply because they desire to be different. On the other hand, neither should individuals or groups choose to conform simply because others expect them to do so. According to Laurence Moore, Will Herberg in his *Protestant, Catholic, Jew,* "seemed to be saying that American society was most dynamic when it encouraged people to preserve . . . their genuine religious peculiarities." [57]

Therefore, the distinctive characteristics, both religious and political, associated with churches of Christ should not be so quickly
dismissed. Instead, it should be acknowledged that the distinctive
qualities of the American Restoration Movement and churches of
Christ, through their dissent and outsider position, have contributed to make the United States what it is today.

CHAPTER 12

OUT OF BONDAGE:
Black Churches of
Christ in America
Marshall Keeble and G. P. Bowser

Almost unknown to their white counterparts, African-American churches of Christ have shown dramatic growth during the recent past. Except for churches with Boston connections, during 1983, the black church had the largest number of congregations with more than a hundred baptisms. In 1979, one estimate placed the membership of black churches at 50,000. James Maxwell, vice president of Southwestern Christian College in Terrell, Texas, suggested that there were about 90,000 members in 1985. The most definitive census of black churches of Christ was made by Dr. Mac Lynn in 1991. In what he classified as predominantly black churches, he counted 160,570 members.[1] Indeed, this is a much larger membership than the estimates of years past. Black churches in Ft. Lauderdale, Nashville, Houston, Los Angeles, and Baltimore have memberships exceeding 1,000. Nineteen African-American congregations now meet in the greater Chicago area.

Except for a few scattered churches meeting in the late nineteenth century, the growth of the black church has been the result of twentieth-century evangelism. Beginning in middle Tennessee with the activity of three or four families, the twentieth-century black church has emerged as a fellowship of strength. Not only are there some 1,222 congregations,[2] but these same people support

Southwestern Christian College, operated by black educators with special emphasis on evangelism. Already, the school is having a dramatic impact by educating leadership for African-American churches of Christ.

Present-day black churches of Christ did not emerge full blown in the twentieth century. Therefore, any understanding of the fellowship must focus on the nineteenth-century background, including the experience of black Christians under slavery. Furthermore, the emergence of the black church after emancipation established a foundation for the twentieth century. A name paramount in white churches of Christ, David Lipscomb, was important also to the black church.

Many factors played into the development of black churches of Christ. In the twentieth century, the place of Marshall Keeble and G. P. Bowser must be understood. Without these men it is impossible to tell the story. Moreover, an emphasis on both education and journalism is necessary. A look at the differences between black and white churches is helpful. These differences—especially the organization of the churches and the annual lectureships—have shaped African-American churches. The civil rights' issues also played a part. As these issues became volatile in the 1950s and the 1960s, many white and black Christians separated. The role of black preachers also shaped this movement. Often, he was the only educated person in a congregation, and so he also served in other capacities within the Negro community. Examples of these will be given.

This chapter does not pretend to tell the story of black churches of Christ in depth. Only in broad strokes can the history unfold in such a short space. The larger story awaits a telling by a historian from the ranks of African-American churches of Christ.

BLACKS WITHIN THE RESTORATION MOVEMENT

Even though in slavery, records show blacks as a part of the Restoration Movement from the earliest years. Slaves attended the preaching services of Barton W. Stone at Cane Ridge. As early as 1815, many slaves accepted the gospel and worshiped in the balconies constructed especially for them. By 1838, Cane Ridge had 122 members, with seventy-two Negroes in attendance. Alexander Campbell welcomed blacks into the churches where he preached in Pennsylvania, Ohio, and Virginia. Campbell even allowed slaves to worship with his family at Bethany.

A few separate African-American churches began meeting early in the nineteenth century. An example of a separate black congregation was the Celina, Tennessee, church, established in 1816. These new Christians thanked God they had found a church where they were "neither Jew nor Gentile." During the mid 1830s, a black church began meeting at Midway, Kentucky. The white brethren even constructed a building for the church. A slave, whose name appropriately was Alexander Campbell, served as preacher. He baptized 300 people and established a school for black children.[3]

The focus of work among the Negro race was in Nashville, Tennessee. The Restoration plea came to Nashville through the preaching of Philip Fall in 1825-1826. By the 1840s, the church was sponsoring two African-American Sunday schools with 125 pupils in 1849. According to Herman Norton, the schools were under the control of black members with white supervision. In 1859, Peter Lowery organized one of the Sunday schools with 200 members as a separate church. The Grapevine church met in West Nashville on the plantation of General William G. Harding. Two moves later, the church settled on Gay Street, where it became the Second Christian Church. Some twenty blacks, however, chose to remain with the white church.

Peter Lowery was the ideal leader for the church. An aggressive person, he purchased his freedom and the freedom of his mother, three brothers, and two sisters. As a businessman, Lowery accumulated real estate holdings worth $40,000. The city respected him as a leading Negro religious leader.

Shortly after the Civil War, problems arose within Nashville's black churches. Samuel Lowery, Peter Lowery's eldest son, had traveled to Ohio early in the war. To secure his return to Tennessee, he approached the American Christian Missionary Society about sponsoring him to preach among the freedmen. They agreed to do so, but Lowery was dishonest with both the society and the church in Nashville. He reported work he had not done. He even claimed credit for establishing the church begun by his father in 1859.

These incidents only inflamed already hostile feelings in Nashville toward the American Christian Missionary Society.

Tolbert Fanning exposed Lowery through the pages of the *Gospel Advocate*. He was "not respected by the Negro community" and the society had chosen the wrong man to share the light of the gospel. On the other hand, Samuel Lowery and Daniel Watkins' involvement with the very commendable Tennessee Manual Labor University added stature to the Negro cause in the city. The hostility aroused by Lowery's false reports to the American Christian Missionary Society harmed the cause of Christianity within the Nashville community.[4]

Even with these problems, black Disciples were increasing in numbers. In 1862, 7,000 blacks worshiped in five states; by 1876, 20,000 black Disciples met in fifteen states. The *Christian Standard*—desiring to give special emphasis to the work of black Disciples—began a special column, "Our Colored Brethren."

Although it led to some difficulties, the division into white and black churches seemed inevitable. David Lipscomb believed the white/black division was a mistake. In 1878, Lipscomb penned one of his most important articles on the race issue when he called it a sin for two churches to exist in one community—one black, the other white. Lipscomb would not include news of the black church in a separate column, insisting: "There should be no color line."[5]

The problems within the African-American church in Nashville demonstrated in a microcosm the issues that would divide the Restoration Movement on a national level. Patterned in part after the cooperative meetings held in Tennessee before the Civil War, black Disciples formed the American Christian Evangelizing and Education Association in 1867. Led by Rufus Conrad, the Association concerned itself with establishing both secular and Sunday schools. This was the first effort to organize black Christians beyond the local level. In 1873, a cooperative meeting convened in Nashville to emphasize mission work among Negroes. Six years later, Preston Taylor—preacher for the Colonial Christian Church of Mt. Sterling, Kentucky—spoke to the gathering. The following year (1880), he organized an annual Missionary Convention in Nashville. In 1883, Preston Taylor accepted an appointment as national evangelist to work among black Disciples. Taylor's was likely the only work among blacks supported by the larger American Christian Missionary Society during the 1880s.[6]

In 1886, Taylor moved to Nashville as minister of the Gay Street Christian Church. Much of the controversy that would lead to division centered on Taylor. Two years after beginning his ministry, the congregation charged Taylor with immoral conduct and even denied him the pulpit. The elders and the congregation divided, with the members siding with Taylor. A five-man committee, including David Lipscomb, arbitrated the controversy. The elders in their capacity, the committee concluded, had the authority to remove the preacher.

Taylor entered the funeral business, but decided to begin religious services in Keeble Hall on the Fisk University campus. After two years he purchased a lot on Lea Avenue in 1892. In 1894, he constructed a building for the Lea Avenue Christian Church. Lea Avenue, along with Gay Street, followed the direction of the Disciples of Christ early in the twentieth century. Gay Street—also known as Second Christian Church—was among the first Christian churches in Tennessee to introduce a musical instrument into their worship services. The two churches merged to become the Gay-Lea Christian Church, which continues to the present.

From within the context of these churches, two men led the way in establishing a congregation repudiating the use of instrumental music in worship. Alexander Cleveland Campbell left the Lea Avenue church when the leadership invited denominational preachers to fill the pulpit. When he publicly protested, the organ and the choir drowned out his remarks. S. W. Womack, in the meantime, withdrew from the Gay Street church. The two men, along with their families, formed a house church that eventually became the Jackson Street Church of Christ. Modern African-American churches of Christ must be dated from the time these men left the Lea Avenue and the Gay Street Christian churches.

David Lipscomb urged Womack to open his home as a place of worship. The little house church met for the first time away from Womack's home in an upstairs room at the corner of 8th Avenue, North, and Charlotte Avenue. In 1906, the church purchased the Fisk University Student Chapel on Jackson Street. The South College Street Church of Christ, where Lipscomb served as an elder, supported Womack in his preaching. The leaders of the work in Nashville were Campbell, Womack, Marshall Keeble—Womack's son-in-law—and George Phillip Bowser. As important as Alexander Campbell and S. W. Womack were to the black church, the two names most associated with black churches of Christ in America are Marshall Keeble and G. P. Bowser. Even though their work led in separate directions, both men deserve credit for the growth of churches of Christ among black Americans.

The most visible of the two was Keeble. As an evangelist, he preached throughout much of the United States and was responsible for thousands of baptisms and many new churches. On the other hand, Bowser—although an excellent preacher—worked through education and journalism to establish a strong base for the black church.

G. P. BOWSER: EDUCATOR OF BLACK CHRISTIANS

Born in Maury County, Tennessee, on February 17, 1874, G. P. Bowser brought a quality to preaching in Afro-American churches of Christ that was lacking in most preachers.[7] As a young man, he attended Roger Williams College in Nashville, a school operated by the African Methodist Church. Initially a Methodist, Bowser, along with his wife, was baptized by Sam Davis. They began meeting with the Jackson Street Church of Christ.

Although he preached, Bowser turned his attention to education. A school he established in 1907 met for a short time in the Jackson Street building. Somewhat earlier, in 1902, he began the *Christian Echo,* a paper that continues publication in 1993.

Bowser moved his school to Silver Point, Tennessee, in 1909, where he served as principal and teacher. His wife was matron, cook, and laundress. Miss Lillie Gipson was the second teacher for a school extending only through the ninth grade.

The Silver Point Christian Institute faced extreme difficulties throughout its existence. Annie Tuggle served as field agent for the school. Soliciting funds in Nashville, she decided to call on David Lipscomb. He, in turn, contacted A. M. Burton, who helped to construct a brick building for the Institute, completed in 1918 at a cost of $1,500.[8] Bowser added two new teachers, and the school reached its largest enrollment.

In the meantime, Burton purchased a building in Nashville for a new school, the Southern Practical Institute. The Christian Institute closed, and Bowser became principal of the new school. The school opened on January 5, 1920, with C. E. W. Dorris as superintendent. A substantial student body enrolled, but the school only remained open six weeks. Evidently, Superintendent Dorris required blacks to enter through a back door. Bowser would not accept such treatment of himself and his students. As a result, the school did not continue. The Bowsers then moved to Louisville, Kentucky, to work among black Americans.[9]

Later the Bowsers moved to Fort Smith, Arkansas, where he continued the *Christian Echo* and his preaching. In 1938 Bowser opened another school—this time for older men—in his home. The students earned their board by working in the print shop where they produced the *Christian Echo*. Associated with Bowser in the Christian Institute were four men who would become leaders in black churches of Christ—R. N. Hogan, J. S. Winston, Levi Kennedy, and G. E. Steward.

Considering the product, the school in Fort Smith was a success. As a result of his schools, Bowser was the father of Christian education among black churches of Christ. Even though he was not personally involved, he is represented as the founder of Southwestern Christian College. He enunciated a definite philosophy of education:

> Christianity is the only remedy that will completely solve the many problems of our age, therefore, Christian education is a dire necessity in this age. . . .
> The Bowser Christian Institute is preparing to play its part well in the great work of educating people in the divine principles of primitive Christianity. Our doors are open to all worthy boys and girls.[10]

Shortly after Southwestern Christian College opened in 1950, G. P. Bowser died.

MARSHALL KEEBLE: PREACHER TO BLACKS AND WHITES

Marshall Keeble followed a different road to leadership. Even though he served as president of Nashville Christian Institute, this was never the main emphasis of his life. He was primarily an evangelist. Born December 7, 1878, Keeble was the son of Robert and Minnie Keeble of Rutherford County, Tennessee. The elder Keeble was born in slavery. The family moved to Nashville when

Marshall was only four years of age, at which time they began worshiping with the Lea Avenue Christian Church. Preston Taylor, the local preacher, baptized young Marshall when he was fourteen. Keeble did not attend school beyond the seventh grade. He had to begin work in a bucket factory to help support his family while still in his middle teens.

One of the greatest influences on Marshall Keeble was S. W. Womack, whose family lived next door to the Keebles. The Womacks were also members of Lea Avenue. Marshall courted and married Womack's daughter, Minnie, who had graduated from the high school department of Fisk University. Keeble, on many occasions, stated that marrying into the Womack family was among his greatest blessings. Of Minnie, Keeble often repeated the truth that she was his best teacher.[11]

Marshall Keeble determined to be a preacher. The first notice of Keeble in the *Gospel Advocate* was in 1908. Soon his name became recognized throughout Middle Tennessee. Worshipers crowded the buildings wherever he went. What was his attraction? According to Arthur Lee Smith, Jr., the people "loved his sincerity and wit. His sermons were direct and frank; they were clothed in earnestness. The depth of his sincerity was impressive to those who heard him."[12]

Characteristic of Keeble's meetings was the attention given by whites. Two examples were the revivals held in Valdosta, Georgia, in 1930 and 1931. The white church arranged for the meetings. Not only did they support them with funds, they attended all the services in large numbers. On one Sunday, Keeble baptized fifty-nine. On the following Sunday, Luke Miller, a fellow preacher and song leader, baptized sixty—nine without coming out of the baptismal pool. In 1931, B. C. Goodpasture, then preaching in Atlanta, sat on the platform during every service. He, in turn, published the sermons under the title *Biography and Sermons of Marshall Keeble*. It was an all-time best seller for the Gospel Advocate Company.[13]

The Keeble family faced deep sorrow in 1932. Minnie Keeble became ill. Her husband returned from a meeting in the Midwest to remain close to her during the last two weeks of her life. She died on December 11, 1932, at the age of fifty-three. He was now without his greatest teacher and severest critic.

Marshall Keeble's preaching took him across the eastern half of the United States. Occasionally, he would even make his way to California. During the winter months, he would preach in Florida. When spring came to Tennessee, he headed north. He established so many churches on his way to Florida that by 1940, it took him an entire month to make the trip from Nashville.

In the midst of his travels while preaching the gospel, Keeble found time in 1934 to court and marry Laura Catherine Johnson. He would never talk to her in public—"It always disgusted me to see a preacher flirting around with a woman." Instead, he courted by mail. After Laura said "yes" to Keeble's proposal, B. C. Goodpasture conducted their ceremony on April 3, 1934, in Corinth, Mississippi.[14]

Another chapter in Keeble's life opened in 1942 when he became the first official president of Nashville Christian Institute. This added duty did not curtail his evangelistic efforts. His name, however, gave the school credibility among both blacks and whites. Being president of a school also raised Keeble's station among his own people. Without Keeble's name and his ability to raise funds for the school, the Nashville Christian Institute could not have survived as long as it did. The Institute is discussed later in this chapter.

Along with Mr. and Mrs. Houston Ezell of Nashville and Lucian Palmer, Keeble made a trip around the world in 1964. Their first stop was Nigeria. Noticing all the work done by other religious groups, Keeble stated to Houston Ezell:

> I tell you fellows—that's what wrong with the church of Christ. These churches get here fifty years ahead of us—get these children and train them, and line up the people and indoctrinate them. Then we send two missionaries over here and try to head them off.[15]

Leaving Nigeria, the party flew to Ethiopia where they visited churches. Next, they flew to Pakistan, and then on to India. Their around-the-world trip continued to Thailand, Singapore, and Hong Kong, finally bringing them to Korea. Here Ezell observed the mission work of the Vultee church. They then flew to the Hawaiian Islands and on to Los Angeles, finally arriving home in Nashville. Few men have had the experiences of Marshall Keeble—a world traveler at eighty-four years of age.

There is no way to measure adequately the success of Marshall Keeble. A. M. Burton, speaking at the announcement of the accreditation of the Nashville Christian Institute, stated:

> No one can appreciate Brother Keeble more than I can, I don't believe, since I have been working with him in a small way for the past thirty years. I have been wonderfully impressed with his humility, fearlessness, and sincerity. The small amount of money I have invested in him and his work, I suspect, has paid far bigger dividends than any other of the Lord's work in which I have had a part. . . .
>
> I feel most sure that there have been some 25,000 people baptized in these twenty-five years by Brother Keeble and those preachers whom he has converted and developed.[16]

Marshall Keeble died on April 20, 1968, at the age of ninety.

BOWSER AND KEEBLE COMPARED TO W. E. B. DuBOIS AND BOOKER T. WASHINGTON

It is obvious that both Marshall Keeble and G. P. Bowser were successful among African-American churches of Christ. According to Dr. Jack Evans, president of Southwestern Christian College, there were, however, philosophical differences:

> These men preached the same gospel message, but differed greatly in their methods of presentation, in their philosophies about formal education, in the approaches to strengthening the churches among black people, and in relationships and dealings with white members of churches of Christ.[17]

Evans noted the similarities of the two men to Booker T. Washington and W. E. B. DuBois, the two most important American black leaders of late nineteenth and early twentieth centuries.

Booker T. Washington emerged as the southern Negro leader after his Atlanta Exposition address in 1895. Hailed as one who understood the plight of the black people in the region, Washington stated: "In all things that are purely social we can be as separate as the fingers, yet as one as the hand in all things essential to mutual progress." Calling social agitation the "extremist folly," he remarked: "The opportunity to earn a dollar in a factory just now is worth infinitely more than the opportunity to spend a dollar in an opera house."[18]

Although he worked diligently—mostly behind the scene—for Negro rights, he would never openly confront southern whites. As a result, he received praise by the southern press. White philanthropists contributed to his work. All agreed that Tuskegee Institute was the right solution for southern blacks. His emphasis upon industrial education received wide acclaim throughout America.

Conversely, W. E. B. DuBois did not accept Washington's solutions. His background, especially his birth in Massachusetts, differed totally from Washington's. DuBois was not a Southerner with roots in slavery. Therefore, his solutions, first published in *The Souls of Black Folks,* were confrontational with the Tuskegee educator. In 1905 he remarked: "We will not be satisfied to take one jot or tittle less than our full manhood rights . . . and until we get those rights we will never cease to protest and assail the ears of America." As his ideas impacted blacks in churches of Christ, probably the most important influence was his ideas on education. He was a strong advocate of liberal arts education for the Talented Tenth of the Negro race. He believed America's black people needed leadership from that 10 percent who should gain the advantages of higher education.[19]

In many respects, Marshall Keeble and Booker T. Washington were similar. Both men accepted white paternalism because the immediate setting demanded it. On the other hand, DuBois and Bowser held such white involvement at arm's length. They both believed education was the primary need of the Negro. Keeble never professed to see racism in white men's words or events. Conversely, Bowser would have nothing to do with a school that required blacks to enter by the back door. Marshall Keeble's tolerance of racism even allowed him to praise "the white man for bringing us out of Africa." He told black Christians to wait until God "in His own good time" would change the racist climate in America. Bowser fought all such racist views.

The two men differed on the education of preachers. Keeble trained preachers by allowing them to travel with him—Luke Miller, John Vaughner, and youngsters often preached in Keeble meetings. Educating preachers at the Nashville Christian Institute was a late activity of Keeble's life. On the other hand, wherever

Bowser lived a school soon emerged. In all, Bowser involved himself with five schools, and some consider him to be the father of Southwestern Christian College. Jack Evans concluded:

> Thus, two schools of preachers emerged among the black ministers of churches of Christ, the "Bowser school," the more formally trained preachers and the "Keeble school," the less formally trained and more practical preachers. These "schools" are only now gradually merging in the work of Southwestern Christian College.[20]

In 1924, Bowser described his understanding of preacher education:

> The one thing needed, and I might say badly needed, is a stronger force of preachers—efficient preachers; intelligent preachers; earnest consecrated preachers. I am sure this cannot be accomplished without Christian schools, and I do not infer that schools can make preachers. I abhor the idea of a school as a preacher manufacturer. But I heartily endorse the idea of a school to train, prepare, and educate those who are inclined and desire to preach and teach the word.[21]

Bowser is sometimes called the black church's David Lipscomb.

Even though there were differences in approach, was one leader correct and the other wrong? What were their goals? What was necessary to attain those goals? Unquestionably, Marshall Keeble said and did those things necessary to keep his white brethren's support. He accepted financial help from A. M. Burton and was a close friend of white leaders such as B. C. Goodpasture. He believed accord had to be maintained between the races in order to reach black people with the gospel. Members of white churches of Christ did what they could within the context of southern culture to aid Keeble, even attending the Keeble revivals. Many whites responded to the gospel message under his preaching. Both blacks and whites recognized that before God an equality does exist. This was true even before these white Christians were willing to openly advocate social, political, and educational equality.

Marshall Keeble's name was a household word among all churches of Christ. Bowser, little known among white churches of Christ, worked among his own people, attempting—like DuBois to educate leadership for the Afro-American church.

A. M. BURTON AND THE NASHVILLE CHRISTIAN INSTITUTE

J. S. Winston, a close associate of G. P. Bowser, placed education among black Christians in the perspective of the Restoration Movement. Conservative Disciples—those later known as churches of Christ—did not provide education for blacks. Thus most Negro Disciples went with the Disciples of Christ/Christian Church after 1906.

> The white Christian church saw the need and advantage of having a Christian school for their young people, to develop ministers, teachers, etc., so they established Southern Christian Institute in Jackson, Mississippi, and Jarvis Christian College in Hawkins, Texas for the blacks. Therefore, through their educational programs they were able to gain many of the black churches to the digressive Christian Church Movement.[22]

Education was late, however, coming to black members of churches of Christ.

Two men stand tall in education among black churches of Christ. G. P. Bowser, without question, was the most outstanding black leader. A. M. Burton, although white, was another dynamic force behind education among black Christians. His money made possible better facilities at Silver Point Christian Institute. In 1920, he purchased the building for the Southern Practical Institute. He made a mistake, as later events would show, by selecting C. E. W. Dorris as superintendent. Nevertheless, Burton would continue his involvement in Negro education.

Not until the early 1940s did Burton become involved with the Nashville Christian Institute. With the demise of the Southern Practical Institute in 1920, many Afro-American Christians became interested in establishing a school. P. H. Black, J. R. Holmes, and Dr. J. D. Fowler purchased, in June 1920, seven acres of land near Fisk University. They scheduled the school to open in 1923. About the plans for the school, Black wrote:

> We are few in number, and we are having a hard pull, but by the help of God, we have shouldered the responsibility to erect and maintain an institution which means to us that men can be better educated along this line; we must admit that the colored people need it.[23]

The school, however, did not open. The depression seemed to kill the idea. Even with these problems, P. H. Black and his associates did not lose the dream.

The city of Nashville helped make the Nashville Christian Institute possible. Needing a location for the Ford Greene Elementary School, the city gave the Board of Trustees of NCI $11,500 and the Ashcroft school building on 24th Avenue, North. This 1934 transaction made it possible for the Nashville Christian Institute to plan for an opening in 1940.

Under the leadership of a board of directors, which included Marshall Keeble, the school began operating without accreditation. Meeting at night, it attempted to fulfill the needs of adults. The school did not receive accreditation until 1942. At that time, A. M. Burton became involved in the school. Marshall Keeble, although he had only a seventh grade education, became the first official president of NCI. From this point forward, whites were an integral part of the Institute's program.

Both blacks and whites served in the administration and on the faculty of Nashville Christian Institute. Following Keeble, Lucian Palmer and Willie T. Cato, both white, served as presidents. These men were personal choices of A. M. Burton and Athens Clay Pullias, president of David Lipscomb College. Except for C. B. Laws, all principals—Frank N. Thorpe, O. H. Boatright and James Dennis—were blacks. Among the best-known teachers were Mrs. Lambert Campbell (speech) and J. W. Brents (Bible), both white.

The Nashville Christian Institute closed its doors in 1967. Thousands of young people had attended some of its sessions, including hundreds who graduated from high school. Its greatest benefactors were too old to carry on the school; the costs of continuing seemed insurmountable. Another reason must be mentioned: Attitudes among whites had changed since the *Brown* decision of the United States Supreme Court in 1954. Since the Nashville Christian Institute was so much under the domination of white members of churches of Christ, the conclusion was that such schools were no longer necessary. Black young people could attend predominantly white schools. From this perspective, Nashville Christian Institute no longer had a mission. The proceeds from the sale of the property were invested to fund the Burton-Keeble scholarships at David Lipscomb University.

SOUTHWESTERN CHRISTIAN COLLEGE: BOWSER'S LEGACY

Southwestern Christian College, however, has existed in a different environment.[24] From the time of the Bowser Christian Institute in Fort Smith, Arkansas, a desire continued to grow for a school among black churches of Christ. Even though Bowser moved to Detroit after the closing of the Fort Smith school, many of the school's leaders continued to push for a full-fledged college. In 1945, J. S. Winston and G. E. Steward met with D. B. Rambo of Huntsville, Texas, and Don Morris and Walter Adams of Abilene Christian College to discuss Negro education. These men influenced others to consider the need for quality education for black Christians. John G. Young, a Dallas physician, headed a committee to explore the possibility of establishing a small school in Fort Worth, Texas.

During the fall of 1948, a school began operating on the grounds of the Lake Como Church of Christ. Because the first focus was on adult education, the classes met in the evenings. Named the Southern Bible Institute, the school had as its first president J. S. Winston. During its initial year, forty-one students enrolled.

The trial run was a success. As a result, the board began looking for larger quarters. While a search was under way in the Fort Worth area, the property of the Texas Military School at Terrell became available at a very reasonable price. Because of a lack of time, the school could not open in 1949. Therefore, the board of directors postponed operations until September 1950. By this time, the father of Christian education among black churches of Christ, G. P. Bowser, was ill with cancer. He visited the campus, but did not live to see the school open as Southwestern Christian College.

During the college's initial years, a decidedly white presence was evident: the chairman of the board was John G. Young, and the first president was E. W. McMillan. McMillan had served as chairman of the Bible department at Abilene Christian College from 1924 to 1934. After World War II, he filled the position of president of Ibaraki (Japan) Christian College from 1948 to 1950. A black man, Vanderbilt Lewis, served the school as its first dean, followed in 1952 by Grover Washington, who had been dean of Southern Bible Institute.

McMillan resigned in 1953. For the presidency, the board selected Dr. H. L. Barber, who served until 1956, when he resigned
because of ill health. By 1956, the school's indebtedness had sky-
rocketed to $122,550, but A. V. Isbell, the next president, success-
fully reduced the debt and pushed the school toward accreditation.

In 1963, Jack Evans became academic dean of Southwestern
Christian College. Four years later, in the midst of turmoil in the
African-American community at large, the board elected him as
the first black president of Southwestern Christian College.
President Evans and his wife are both graduates of Southwestern.
Because of the $90,000 debt, some suggested closing the school.
Black members of the board, however, opposed the closing. The
board, under the leadership of Jack W. Evans of Dallas, a white
businessman who would later become mayor of his city, agreed to
remain in place. If the black Jack Evans became president, many
thought, Southwestern would die.

The school did not die. Instead, under Evans's administration, it
has flourished as never before, receiving its accreditation as a junior college in 1973. The school paid its debts, and new buildings
rose on the campus. The board appointed Dr. James O. Maxwell, a
black, as vice president to help raise funds for the continued operation of the college. The school now offers a bachelor's degree in
Bible and Christian Education.

Southwestern Christian College is the fulfillment of a dream
stretching back to the early years of the twentieth century. From
that time, G. P. Bowser strongly believed that Negro people
needed education to compete in a white world. In 1985, the school
had a $2,000,000 operating budget. Developing more and more
along the lines of Bowser's ideas of education, the college is now
administered by black men and women.

ATTITUDES IN CHURCHES OF CHRIST TOWARD SEGREGATION

American blacks remained, for the most part, segregated until
the 1950s. Behind the scenes, however, the federal courts were
moving to abolish the distinctions. Through the insistence of the
National Association for the Advancement of Colored People, a
legal move was under way to declare the "separate but equal" pro-
nouncements of the Supreme Court unconstitutional. On May 14,

1954, the court handed down its landmark decision, *Brown v. the School Board of Topeka, Kansas.* The wall separating whites and blacks began to crumble.

Within churches of Christ, the outward expressions were little different from those in other predominantly southern groups. Although blacks had worshiped in a few white churches, separation was a fact. What was true in many fellowships was also true among churches of Christ. Nevertheless, there were those who believed separation should end. Writing at the end of 1951, W. L. Wilson of El Paso, Texas, asked some straightforward questions about "God and Jim Crow." In response, he stated several evils of segregation: lack of brotherhood, race hatred and riots, and limited opportunities of the Negro for education. On the other hand, whites are harmed because they deny themselves contact with people on the "fringe of life." [25]

How many shared Wilson's views no one can know. David Edwin Harrell suggested: "Churches of Christ appeared more genuinely interracial than any other major [southern] sect, though only by comparison." [26] In part, this was true because of white paternalism. On the other hand, some within churches of Christ were adamantly racist—including Foy E. Wallace, Jr. In 1941, Wallace showed concern over the increased attendance of whites at black meetings, obviously having in mind those of Marshall Keeble:

> The manner in which the brethren in some quarters are going in for the negro meetings leads one to wonder whether they are trying to make white folks out of the negroes or negroes out of the white folks. The trend of the general mix-up seems to be toward the latter. Reliable reports have come to me of white women, members of the church, becoming so animated over a certain colored preacher as to go up to him after a sermon and shake hands with him holding his hand in both of theirs. That kind of thing will turn the head of most white preachers, and sometimes affect their conduct, and anybody ought to know that it will make fools out of the negroes.

In the same article, Wallace condemned some blacks' desire for social equality. He specifically mentioned R. N. Hogan: "Hogan has been too much inclined to mix with the white people and to favor, in attitude[,] a social equality." Wallace added:

I am very much in favor of negro meetings for the negroes, but I am just as much opposed to negro meetings for white people, and I am against white brethren taking the meetings away from the negroes and the general mixing that has become entirely too much of a practice in the negro meetings.[27]

One month later, Wallace published a letter from Marshall Keeble:

Dear Sir and Brother in Christ:

For over thirty years I have tried to conduct my work just as your article in the *Bible Banner* of March suggested. Taking advice from such friends as you have been for years has been a blessing to my work. So I take the privilege to thank you for that instructive and encouraging article. I hope I can conduct myself in my last days so that you and none of my friends will have to take back nothing they have said complimentary about my work or regret it.

Please continue to encourage me in my work and *pray for me.*

Fraternally yours,
M. Keeble.

Responding to the letter, Wallace said: "This letter is characteristic of the humility of M. Keeble. It is the reason why he is the greatest colored preacher that has ever lived. . . .These men [Keeble and Luke Miller] know their place and stay in it."[28]

Most comments in the religious journals pointed to increased opportunities for evangelism among African-Americans. B. C. Goodpasture believed:

The colored people of this country need the gospel. . . . If the gospel is not preached to them in its purity, they will fall into the meshes of some of the present-day "isms." Both the Catholic and the Communists look upon the colored man as a promising prospect.[29]

Wallace believed that the gospel could control radicalism among the Negro race.

Norvel Young saw blacks "as a most wonderful challenge to Christians who burn with a desire to share the gospel with others." He added: "The religion of Jesus Christ will do more to help solve the race problem than anything else."[30]

The Supreme Court's *Brown* decision received little notice in journals among churches of Christ. Segregation was not a theme of the *Firm Foundation* until 1956. The Bible, Ross Dye stated, instructs men and women about how they should conduct themselves in "individual and congregational dealings with men of other races."[31] Churches should not become involved in political issues.

Dye's view was not unique. The noninvolvement of Christians in social and political issues was, in part, inherited from David Lipscomb. On the other hand, issues such as women's rights and prohibition early in the twentieth century were legitimate areas of Christian concern. Evidently, the nature of the issue determined the degree of involvement.

As described by Ed Harrell, churches of Christ were probably more open toward fellowship between races than other southern sects. Likely this openness led to a rather lengthy exchange of ideas during the 1960s. In the *Christian Chronicle,* then edited by James W. Nichols, both proponents and opponents of a closer relationship of races shared their views. In 1963, Nichols asked his readers to "Discuss the Negro Issue." Even Nichols had not realized what a floodgate he opened. Most of the letters favored integration. This does not mean that the majority in churches of Christ were integrationists, but it does represent an articulate minority. This interest in closer race relations culminated in a conference in Atlanta in 1968. The theme was: "Improving race relations in the churches of Christ." A Texan, in reference to the conclusions of the meeting, remarked: "Are you sure they were of the church of Christ? . . .I pray these were not of the Lord's Church."[32]

The most detailed study of attitudes—both black and white—toward race relations is the 1969 M.A. thesis by Carroll Pitts, Jr. He noticed only slight progress during the 1960s. In surveying the lectureships of the various Christian colleges, Pitts discovered little discussion of race relations.[33]

An exception was Carl Spain's lecture at Abilene Christian in the 1960s under the general title "Modern Challenges to Christian Morals." The Abilene professor "challenged the leaders of the brotherhood's schools to justify the theory of racial supremacy which held sway on their campuses." In an interview with the Associated Press, Spain bluntly remarked that there had been some instances when Negroes desired to enroll in Bible courses at Abilene Christian College's graduate school, but did not do so because of housing, eating, and other problems. He discussed the situation with other faculty members. Many shared his view that Negro preachers of the church of Christ who can qualify academically should be admitted to the graduate school.[34]

Noting that schools of other religious persuasions had enrolled blacks, Spain asked: "Are we moral cowards on this issue?"

The Atlanta meeting of June 1968, mentioned above, was the culmination of Spain's views. Some fifty men, both black and white, including Carl Spain, James W. Nichols, John Allen Chalk, Prentice A. Meador, Jr., R. N. Hogan, and Andrew J. Hairston attended the sessions.[35] Hogan was the same person Foy E. Wallace had accused of advocating social equality in 1941.

Important to a 1960s discussion of black/white relations was Marshall Keeble's death on April 20, 1968. Reuel Lemmons extolled Keeble and his influence in a lengthy editorial:

> We seriously doubt that any man, black or white, has ever been so universally accepted by the people of both races among the brethren. If he ever knew there were segregation lines he never indicated it. Indeed, because of his life and work there has been an infinitesimally small amount of racial prejudice in the Church of Christ.[36]

Most whites in churches of Christ shared his view.

African-Americans, however, did not share the same perspective. Said Roosevelt Wells, preacher for the Harlem church:

> Color is so entrenched in the church we have begun to wonder if the church is the one Jesus Christ built, where the "middle walls were broken down" and "made a unity of the conflicting elements," (Eph. 2:14, Phillips), making ONE NEW MAN, SO MAKING PEACE.[37]

He criticized Christian colleges for admitting non-Christians and non-Americans. Equally, he condemned white churches for selling their buildings to escape black infiltration. He angrily concluded: "For the most part the church of Christ is more racist than many in the kingdom of Satan."

Other black leaders, including R. N. Hogan—editor of the *Christian Echo*—and Andrew J. Hairston of Atlanta, were also critical of their white brethren. Hogan urged white colleges to drop their color barriers. Hairston suggested that churches of Christ have always emphasized "where the Bible speaks, we speak; and where the Bible is silent, we are silent."

> In matters pertaining to baptism, the one church, and a few other positive Bible tenets this has been true. Yet, for some, when it comes to the issue of race relations we are told to leave it alone and "God will fix it one day." [38]

The church, Hairston suggested, should let God "fix" baptism just like race relations.

Some years are pivotal. One such year was 1968. John Allen Chalk used the Herald of Truth to preach a series of sermons on race relations. The Atlanta conference protesting racial prejudice met. And the *20th Century Christian* produced a special issue on race problems, including several articles by black writers. [39]

Additionally, 1968 may have been the vital year of great change within black churches of Christ. The outstanding black leader, Martin Luther King, Jr., was assassinated in Memphis, Tennessee, on April 4. Violence erupted across the United States, costing forty lives. On April 20, Marshall Keeble died. With him died an era in churches of Christ. As Booker T. Washington's ideas were long dead in the larger black community, so were Keeble's views dead among black churches of Christ. G. P. Bowser's more militant emphasis triumphed.

A suggestion of the change prevalent in the 1960s was the activity of two prominent black leaders who, incidentally, were also preachers in churches of Christ. Both men were active in the civil rights movement. Franklin Florence led civil rights activities in Rochester, New York, while Fred Gray served the movement as an attorney in Alabama. Gray represented both Rosa Parks and Martin Luther King, Jr., during the Montgomery bus boycott of the mid-1950s. He helped Vivian Malone in her attempt to attend the University of Alabama. Fred Gray served as E. D. Nixon's attorney in the early 1970s, culminating in the "one-man, one-vote" decision, leading to single-member legislative districts in Alabama. In 1986, he served as president of the National Bar Association, a national association of black lawyers. [40]

NATIONAL MEETINGS AMONG BLACK CHURCHES OF CHRIST

Current indicators in the *Christian Echo* and the *Christian Chronicle* suggest that black churches of Christ are growing at a faster pace than white churches. Factual information is difficult to gather for white churches of Christ; it is even more difficult to glean from black churches. Nevertheless, there are several large black churches throughout the United States; several cities have multiple congregations. Because of the urban nature of strong black churches, much of the special efforts of black Christians has centered in larger American cities.

J. S. Winston wrote in 1973 that the primary weakness in black churches was the lack of qualified leadership, especially elders and deacons. He placed blame for the lack of educational opportunities among African-American Christians on white "Christian (?) colleges" for not admitting blacks.

In 1944, four men—G. E. Stewart, R. N. Hogan, Levi Kennedy, and J. S. Winston—met to discuss the need for an annual national lectureship. They agreed that it should be "designed to encourage the extensive study of doctrine, to unify our teaching, and encourage qualified congregational leadership." In 1945, Oklahoma City hosted the first Annual National Lectureship. The lectureship continues, meeting in many of the larger cities across the United States. Among host cities have been Dallas, Los Angeles, Memphis, and Chicago. Even though a national advisory committee exists, the lectureship is under the direction of a local church in the host city.

J. O. Williams, preacher for the Central Church of Christ in Milwaukee, Wisconsin, stated the purpose of the 1979 lectures:

> Our purpose is not to make laws, nor to change laws, neither infringe upon the autonomy of local congregations, but we are here as they were in the first century to get acquainted with each other, to teach and admonish with songs, sermons, lectures, and prayers. And if you will be like I have been in visiting Lectureships, you will return home a better person than you were when you came.[41]

As has been true in all cities, the Milwaukee Lectureship met in a downtown hotel, the Marc Plaza. Several thousand people, seeking to fulfill religious and social needs, attend the annual lectureships. The 1991 lectureship convened in Denver, Colorado.

Under the leadership of Orum Lee Trone, Sr., an annual youth conference is held every August. Each year the leadership selects a college campus where young people from all across the United States come for instruction, fellowship, and sight-seeing. Some 2,000 young people attended the 1982 conference in Chattanooga. Conferences have been held at Tulane University (New Orleans), University of California (Riverside), University of Maryland (College Park), and Washington University (St. Louis). The 1991 meeting convened at Loyola Merrymount in Los Angeles. Also, a Southeast regional conference meets each year.

Beginning in 1979, at the suggestion of Dr. Daniel Harrison, black Christians have pooled their efforts to evangelize a selected city. The first targeted was Chicago. The organizing committee selected G. P. Holt, then of Indianapolis, to do the preaching in McCormick Place. Chicago-area black churches funded the entire effort, with $170,000 spent on billboard, newspaper, radio, and television advertising. Area churches actively cooperated in personal work. The Chicago Crusade was the largest single campaign effort by African-American Christians up to that time. Attendance figures averaged 5,500 each evening, with the first night's crowd soaring to 9,000. At the end of the meeting, 237 responded, with 106 asking for baptism.

The first effort was so successful that the crusade became a biannual event. Again, the organizers chose Chicago. The 1981 crusade committee selected Jack Evans, president of Southwestern Christian College, as the keynote speaker. The 1983 edition, the most successful of the crusades, convened in Houston. Evans spoke on the theme "That we may all be one." When the crusade closed, 159 persons had been baptized and 366 had been restored or had requested prayers. The crowds ranged upward toward 10,000.[42] Detroit was the location of the 1991 crusade. Again, Jack Evans was the keynote speaker. Meeting in Cobo Hall, the meetings attracted 21,632, resulting in 107 baptisms and 99 restorations.[43]

Even though a national committee functions, all arrangements for the events are under the supervision of a local congregation of the host city. On the other hand, the organizational structure within the black church emphasizes the leadership of the preacher in the local church, and in turn, national leadership by some of the better-known preachers. For these reasons, most difficulties in black churches of Christ are within individual congregations. Over the years, churches have called four men to arbitrate differences. These men, closely associated with G. P. Bowser, were R. N. Hogan, Levi Kennedy, J. S. Winston, and G. E. Steward. Steward and Kennedy are now dead. Others have stepped into these vacated positions, including Dr. Jack Evans and Dr. James Maxwell, president and vice president of Southwestern Christian College, and G. P. Holt, the grandson of G. P. Bowser.[44]

LEADERSHIP IN BLACK CHURCHES OF CHRIST

Black churches, because of poor educational opportunities have never had strong elders and deacons. Therefore, J. S. Winston concluded, preachers—although not highly educated—assumed leadership roles by default. This attitude has carried through to the national level. For this reason the so called "Big Four" emerged.

Where Winston developed reasons for the lack of strong elders and deacons among black churches of Christ, Hogan—through the *Christian Echo*—attempted to establish from the Bible the dominant role of evangelists in black churches. Quoting 1 Timothy 1:3, Titus 2:15, Ephesians 4:11, and Hebrews 13:7, Hogan concluded that evangelists, since they set the elders apart to do their work, are not subject to the elders. The teachers or preachers are responsible for the instruction of the church.[45]

In line with the leadership position of preachers within local churches and on the national level, many black preachers hold responsible positions in business, education, and government. In 1986, men who held such dual positions included Andrew J. Hairston, judge of the Atlanta traffic court and preacher for the Simpson Street Church of Christ; Dr. David Jones, director of Secondary Programs for the Metro Nashville Public Schools and minister of Schrader Lane Church of Christ; and Dr. Daniel Harrison, professor of communications at Kennedy-King College in Chicago and preacher for the 79th Street Church of Christ in that city.[46]

Black churches of Christ are not widely involved in foreign mission work. Many of the efforts have been special campaigns to such places as Liberia and Jamaica. Nevertheless, some have accepted the call to missions, including F. F. Carson, to Nigeria, James M. Butler to Ethiopia, and Thomas Jackson to the Caribbean region.

On the other hand, one of the important contributions of Southwestern Christian College has been the training of native preachers to return to their countries. Former students are now in Ethiopia, Nigeria, West Africa, and the Caribbean. Jackson Sagoni is now working in Johannesburg, South Africa, while Carl Mitchell preaches in Kingston, Jamaica. William Miller returned to his native Bahamas.

INTEGRATION OF CHURCHES

With few exceptions, a gulf still exists between white and black churches of Christ. A substantial number of white churches have a few black members. Conversely, few whites place membership in predominantly black churches. As the recent past shows, white churches have most often moved to the suburbs when their inner-city community becomes more than 50 percent black. A few exceptions to this trend exist. In 1969, two congregations, the Butler Boulevard and Holmes Road churches, merged in Lansing, Michigan. Both preachers—W. D. Wiley, a black man, and Allen Killom, white—shared pulpit responsibilities for the combined church.[47] In 1968, the Strathmoor Church of Christ in Detroit began an integration process. By 1971, the eldership and deaconship became racially integrated. When the church added Robert L. Holt, a black man, to the preaching staff to work with Vernon Boyd, a white, the church was about 60 to 70 percent black. The church continues to grow.[48]

On the other hand, many African-American Christians desire to keep their racial identity. For so long, especially in the South, white churches began and sustained black churches. As a result, a paternalistic attitude developed. Therefore, there is fear that blacks will be engulfed if churches integrate.

THE DIRECTIONS OF BLACK CHURCHES OF CHRIST

G. P. Holt, in the legacy of his grandfather, continues to give direction to black churches to help them be successful in their communities. Writing in the *Christian Echo,* he urged preachers to speak to the needs of the community:

> The pulpit must have something relevant, serious and honest to say on perplexing problems and subjects. . . . To remain silent on difficult subjects is an embarrassed evasion of duty, rather than the solution to our problem.

He then added:

> If we are to make an inroad [sic] into the Black community, we must not be silent on the great issues of racism, war, poverty, and injustice. Simply to imitate white middle class churches, with dignified worship and an educated clergy, is not going far enough toward letting justice run down, as water and righteousness, as a mighty stream.

Sharing Jack Evans's view "that the gospel must be social in that it is designed for the betterment of society," Holt stated emphatically: "People are not only asking 'will there be life after death? They want to know will there be life after birth, and what kind of life will our children have after birth?'" The black minister, Holt stated, must be "concerned about pricking consciences." In all the church does, it must remain faithful "to the gospel of Jesus Christ."

Concluding his discussion of "Evangelizing the Black Community," Holt prayed:

> God of our weary years, God of our silent fears, thou who hast brought us thus far, on the way; thou who has by thy might, let [sic] us into the light keep us forever in the path, we pray; Shadowed beneath thy hand, may we forever stand true to our God, true to our native land.

CHAPTER 13

F ROM 1950 TOWARD THE TWENTY-FIRST CENTURY:
One Historian's Perspective

Historians have a tremendous responsibility. It is their task to research the facts of times past, put them in some understandable narrative form, and interpret the related ideas for the reading public.

Nearly forty years ago I read my first excerpts from the literature of the American Restoration Movement. In the 1960s, I began original research on David Lipscomb as a significant leader in the movement. This important person had a profound influence on his contemporaries and on me as well. Following the publication of my Lipscomb biography, *Crying in the Wilderness,* in 1979, I believed it was time for an interpretive history of churches of Christ. Churches of Christ, however, could not be understood without some emphasis on their roots—the American Restoration Movement. Thus, I began, without knowing it at the time, a fourteen-year study of the Stone-Campbell movement and churches of Christ. During those last days of 1979, I had no idea where my research would lead. My discoveries and conclusions have often surprised me. The men and women who became the focus of this study appeared without design.

The previous chapters, with a few exceptions, end more or less at 1965. It is impossible to understand the immediate past with the same balance as events of fifty or a hundred years ago. On the other hand, I would be shirking my responsibility if I did not share my conclusions and understandings as they impact present and future churches of Christ. Therefore, this chapter has the perspective of one who has spent over half his life studying the American Restoration Movement. The beginning point for this chapter, although there will be some emphasis on years previous, will be 1950.

THE 1950s: A TIME OF REVIVAL?

World War II was five years in the past. Now the United States was involved in a police action in Korea under the auspices of the United Nations. Again, America's young men left for war. This time, however, it was a battle against communism. In the minds of many, it was only one part of the most important conflict of the twentieth century. It was a defense of western democracy and Christianity.

The United States responded to the world challenge in a number of ways—including military action. On the home front, the 1950s witnessed the greatest response to religion ever experienced. Never before had Americans so associated their way of life with the Judeo-Christian ethic. As was true in other aspects of American life, the great enemy was communism. If given the opportunity, these Americans believed, communism would take away the freedoms Americans held dear—the democratic way of life and the right to worship God as dictated by each person's heart.

Religion affected all segments of American life during the 1950s—not just the poor and middle classes. The young, the middle, and the older generations responded as one to the religious revival some count as the most important in America's history. It was the decade when Billy Graham launched his crusades. Fulton J. Sheen, a Catholic, used with success the new medium—television. By 1957, Americans gave a record $3.4 billion to religious causes. In the same year, the investment in church buildings had doubled since 1950. Churches spent $868 million on fabulous buildings, often referred to as "plants."

Religion was alive at every level. *Time* magazine reported in 1954: "Today in the U. S. the Christian faith is back in the center of things." In 1940, fewer than half the population officially belonged to churches. By the late fifties, the figures soared to 63 per-cent. President Eisenhower opened a "Back to God" campaign by proclaiming what most Americans believed: "Recognition of the Supreme Being is the first, the most basic expression of Americanism. Without God, there could be no American form of government, nor an American way of life."[1]

Commercially, religion was big business. Bible sales escalated, reaching nearly ten million yearly by 1953. In the same year, one of every ten books sold was religious in nature. The most listened to records included "I Believe," "The Man Upstairs," and "It is No Secret What God Can Do." The movie industry produced such films as "The Robe," and "The Ten Commandments."

In Washington, religion was the "in thing." At Dwight Eisenhower's inauguration in January 1953, the float leading the parade emphasized a worshiping people with the slogans "In God We Trust" and "Freedom of Worship" in featured positions. The two words "under God" were added to the Pledge of Allegiance in 1954. Two years later, Congress adopted "In God We Trust" as a national motto. At the center of this accent on religion was President Eisenhower. He made "going to church" respectable for all Americans. Displaying the idea that permeated America, he re-marked during the campaign of 1952: "Our government makes no sense unless it is founded in a deeply felt religious faith, and I don't care what it is." In California, a billboard asked: "Faith in God and country; that's Eisenhower—how about you?"

Historians are constantly discussing the meaning of the reli-gious upsurge of the 1950s. Was it truly a return to the Judeo-Christian heritage? Or was it a civil religion where democracy and country became the objects of worship? Was it a genuine revival like the Great Awakening of the eighteenth century? These are not easy questions to answer.

Students of culture both challenge and defend the 1950s as an era of revival. A number of intellectuals—including John Dewey, Sidney Hook, and Irving Howe—described the rising interest in religion at the end of World War II as escapism and defeatism—a turn to otherworldliness resulting from despair in being unable to reform the world. This new interest in religion was a rejection of the liberalism of the New Deal.[2]

Conversely, by 1968 most historians and sociologists of reli-gion viewed the 1950s as a major revival. All contributors to an academic symposium—including William McLoughlin, Robert N. Bellah, Franklin H. Littell, Edwin S. Gaustad, Martin E. Marty, William A. Clebsch, and Michael Novak—believed that the religious upsurge would have an impact equal to other revivals in America history. McLoughlin suggested that the revival "constituted a general reorientation of the whole social and intellectual climate of Western society."[3]

In the midst of the era under study, the civil rights movement, campus unrest, and the Vietnam War destroyed much of the consensus of God and democracy that dominated the 1950s. By 1965, this lack of consensus began impacting religion. As quickly as the revival began in the 1950s, in the late 1960s it showed signs of weakening and dying. Nevertheless, one must agree that the 1950s offered an ideal time for growth and world outreach among churches of Christ. On the other hand, the late 1960s and the early 1970s gave signs that the same malady impacting American religion and culture was also influencing churches of Christ.

THE GROWTH OF CHURCHES OF CHRIST IN THE 1950S

By any definition, churches of Christ shared the unprecedented growth of American religion during the twenty years between 1950 and 1970. Even though accurate figures are not available, reports from individual congregations and reported baptisms in the papers suggest growth. Reuel Lemmons ecstatically wrote:

> According to newspaper releases and magazine reports of the past year [1953], and census figures from reliable resources in most of the nations of the world, the churches of Christ are growing faster than any other religious order. In the past five years churches of Christ have multiplied by the hundreds. In Germany, Italy, France, and Holland; in England and Australia; in Japan and India; in South America and Africa, the churches of Christ have grown phenomenally.

He continued: "I am happy to be a member of the church of Christ. I am glad to see it grow until the most powerful radio networks on earth regularly carry the plea of religious liberty and religious unity for which I stand."[4]

These statements could be multiplied many times over. Foy Smith, noting the religious population figures in *World Almanac,* determined that churches of Christ equalled the growth of any religious fellowship in America. B. C. Goodpasture warned that such figures seemed to be exaggerated—especially the percentage of growth. Yet he could state with pride that he believed churches of Christ had about 2,000,000 members in 1959.[5] J. Harold Thomas, who spent much of his adult life preaching in New England, could not bridle his enthusiasm in 1957: "Missionary activity in our own nation has resulted in the planting of hundreds of churches in areas where before . . . there was little or no strength."[6]

Early in 1950, Ralph Casey counted 20,647 baptisms that had been reported through the *Gospel Advocate* for 1949. In the same paper, he discovered thirty-seven new congregations.[7] Indeed, growth seemed unlimited. Figures compiled from the *Advocate* for 1954 through 1957 are almost as impressive:

Year	Baptisms	Restorations
1954	17,780	8,420
1955	19,765	4,265
1956	16,231	6,350
1957	16,940	7,339

Besides these figures, Mont Whitson recorded budgets for various churches for 1953. Three churches were at or above $100,000— Central of Houston, Hillsboro of Nashville, and Skillman Avenue of Dallas. The Broadway church of Lubbock proposed a budget of $200,000. Many of the churches budgeted 30 to 40 percent of their weekly contributions for mission work at home and across the seas.[8]

The same enthusiasm evident in the 1950s carried over into the first years of the 1960s. During this time, Willard Collins, Batsell Barrett Baxter, and Jimmy Allen held huge areawide campaigns. Thousands of people attended the week-long meetings. Hundreds responded to the invitation to accept Jesus.

The 1960s, however, introduced problems that would have devastating consequences for mainline churches. Churches of Christ were not exempt, Dean Kelley, author of *Why Conservative Churches are Growing,* not withstanding. According to Kelley, conservative churches of Christ fit the mold of the growing churches in America.[9] Leaders within churches of Christ knew better. By 1972, the crowds that had attended the revivals of Collins and Allen were no longer present. Baptisms, consequently, were few.

To make matters worse, Mac Lynn compiled figures suggesting that membership of churches of Christ was not as large as the exuberance of the 1950s suggested. In 1980, the total membership in churches of Christ numbered 1,239,612.[10] One must ask: Were the numbers larger in the 1950s? Did churches of Christ decline from 1960 to 1980? Or were the numbers inflated through the enthusiasm of the age?

Foreign missions have never been a strong emphasis of churches of Christ. When the separation from the Disciples of Christ occurred in 1906, there were only 12 missionaries supported by churches of Christ. Although the 1920s saw a larger contingent of missionaries—33 in 1926—the most sustained growth did not happen until after World War II. One year after the conflict there were 46 missionaries. Seven years later the numbers escalated to 229. By the end of the decade of the 1950s, there were 704 missionaries in foreign countries. The growth continued throughout the 1960s, culminating in 800 Americans engaged in missions in 1975. This was the largest number of missionaries ever among churches of Christ. The next reports showed decline. James O. Baird indicated 374 missionaries in 1982.[11] One year later the *Christian Chronicle,* using figures supplied by the World Mission Information Bank, listed 413 in 1982, increasing to 491 in 1984.[12]

Whatever the figures, the total number of missionaries declined dramatically after reaching a peak in 1975. At the same time stateside churches began to decline, the emphasis on missions also stumbled. It became a time of questioning.

CONCERN FOR CHURCHES OF CHRIST IN THE 1960S AND 1970S

By 1974, concern invaded mainstream churches of Christ. J. D. Thomas of Abilene Christian College invited men from all segments of the fellowship to state their views through answers to the question: "What lack we yet?"[13] Representatives of the brotherhood—including those perceived among avowed conservatives as liberals—dealt with the question in varying ways.

Reuel Lemmons, editor of the *Firm Foundation,* presented the lead article in the resulting book, *What Lack We Yet?* Lemmons emphasized leadership as the major problem among churches of Christ: "It is our sincere opinion that the church is suffering a leadership crisis, and that this is at least partially responsible for weakness in several areas." A result of this lack of leadership was the declining image and credibility of the church in the average community across the United States. Furthermore, stated Lemmons, "the distance between the church and denominationalism is less than it used to be."[14]

From Batsell Barrett Baxter's pen came an indictment based on the negativism emanating from every source. Both H. A. Dobbs and Glen Wallace feared the liberalism of the younger men who had become leaders in churches of Christ since 1950.

Juan Monroy of Madrid, Spain, looked at the church in the United States from a different vantage point—as a foreigner. He emphasized the following concerns he saw in American churches:

1. Too much professionalism in the pulpits.
2. Preaching in American churches is too superficial.
3. Churches of Christ have been slow to send missionaries.
4. Too much criticism among brothers in Christ.
5. Useless discussions of unimportant ideas.
6. A failure to be brother's keeper.
7. Too much fighting between liberals and conservatives.
8. Failure to use the printed word to reach the world.
9. Lack of social concern among American churches.
10. Churches lack vision.

In commenting on the lack of vision among American churches, Monroy stated:

> Vision and knowledge are gifts for which the Church should pray. Vision to see her own spiritual situation. Vision to see the needs of the world. Vision to understand the church possibilities at this critical hour. Vision to discover again God's power. And, knowledge to carry out her work with wisdom in a world overflowed by science and techniques.[15]

Batsell Barrett Baxter, appearing at Abilene Christian University in 1976, spoke on the present status of churches of Christ. Under the title "The Crisis," Baxter stated:

We must recognize that people and institutions grow old, get tired, become lazy and die. We see this happening in our own life-cycles and the life-cycles of those around us. The same pattern can also be seen in churches. There is a period of vigorous youth, then mature, more sedate middle-age, followed by a period of decline and ultimate death. Colleges and other institutions also grow old, become lethargic, and lose their usefulness. . . . Tragically, this same tendency is also seen in movements. There is great vigor in the early years, followed by decline and ultimately disappearance. This just must not happen to the Restoration Movement.[16]

His concerns sparked others to focus on the revitalization of churches of Christ.

In recent years, a few concerned individuals have suggested a rediscovery of the roots of restoration. Monroe Hawley, long-time preacher in Milwaukee, Wisconsin, published his concern in *Redigging the Wells* in 1976, the same year Baxter presented his lecture at Abilene. He dealt with such topics as "Are 'We' A Denomination?" "Traditionalism," "The Sectarian Spirit," and "Just Christians." He concluded:

Even though the quest for undenominational Christianity is admittedly difficult, it is obviously biblical and therefore not impossible to achieve. Those of us committed to it must first correct our own thinking and practice, and then, when we have grasped the non-sectarian plea, go and demonstrate to others that it is both possible and desirable to be JUST CHRISTIANS.

The heirs of the Restoration Movement must redig the wells of restoration just as Isaac "dug again the wells of water which had been dug in the days of Abraham his father" (Gen. 26:17).[17]

Sharing much of Hawley's theme, Rubel Shelly published a pamphlet, *Christians Only,* causing both positive and negative reactions within churches of Christ. Basically, his thesis was that churches of Christ have sanctioned a sectarian stance. There is more emphasis, he suggested, upon "Church of Christ" than upon being Christian. In 1984, he enlarged his study into a book-length work titled *I Just Want to be a Christian.* Shelly stated his theme in the title of the book. As Hawley had already discovered, Shelly explained that the thrust of the Restoration Movement has been blunted. The emphasis of the last fifty years has not been on New

Testament Christianity, but on a developing sectarian spirit, on both the right and the left. To emphasize his position, Shelly quoted from and included lengthy articles from M. C. Kurfees, G. C. Brewer, F. W. Smith, and other journalists of the 1920s.

Why did a "crisis" develop among churches of Christ in the late 1960s and the early 1970s? Juan Monroy, speaking at Nashville's West End church in 1984, suggested fear as a major cause of crisis. Because of conflict within the fellowship—among both liberals and conservatives—fear developed. Where churches of Christ were aggressive and innovative in the 1950s, the 1970s saw a turning inward. No longer was there major concern for reaching the unchurched in the United States or for sending missionaries into foreign countries. Much of this lack of an aggressive and innovative stance must be laid at the feet of mainstream churches of Christ. Many of the new breed, the leaders spawned by the 1950s, would by the 1970s do anything to avoid division within the fellowship. The emphasis was upon a united brotherhood.

Did the decline of missions parallel the difficulties experienced at home in the United States? The answer is yes, and both declined for many of the same reasons. The turning inward encountered by American churches during the volatile 1960s inevitably influenced missions. The worldwide problems centered in the Vietnam War certainly aroused an anti-American feeling. American churches were not as willing to make international commitments.

The 1960s were not good years for young people. They became alienated from the institutions of their parents. Therefore, college-age students were not as willing to commit to the missionary's life as had their parents' generation.

The economic downturn of the 1960s also had consequences for churches. Money was not as available for foreign missions. Churches, instead, began to spend more on home needs. Evangelism lost out. World vision, so prevalent in the 1950s, was gone by the late 1960s.

Just as tension gripped all of America during the 1960s, so it gained a stranglehold on churches of Christ. From both the liberal and the conservative positions, there was a pulling and tearing of the fabric of fellowship. The question is: Why?

TENSION WITHIN THE FELLOWSHIP

One thing, above all others, impresses readers of the multitude of in-house journals among churches of Christ. (According to the *Yearbook of American and Canadian Churches,* there were one hundred in 1985.) There seems to be constant tension within the fellowship. Always, talk abounds about liberalism—an all-inclusive term for ideas contrary to the perspective of the speaker or writer. From another direction, legalism is the issue. This tension, unknown to most critics outside the fellowship of the churches of Christ, has been present within the Restoration Movement and churches of Christ from early nineteenth century.

Even though extremes have always existed among the Disciples, the vast majority has endeavored to steer in the middle of the road. Within this broad expanse, ideas grow and flourish. Sometimes an idea or concept becomes so large, usually led by a strong individual, that the ensuing tension causes stretching of the fellowship. Sometimes this stretching leads to a tear, even to a break. How can these tensions be explained? Why are churches of Christ constantly stretched to the breaking point?

The very nature of churches of Christ invites tension and even the ultimate solution to these tensions—division. The call of the Restoration Movement and churches of Christ has always been to unity based on the restoration of the Christianity of the New Testament. But each church is autonomous. It is impossible to gain control of the hierarchy of the fellowship. Therefore, if any individual or a group of individuals feels strongly about a matter, they begin a paper to espouse these ideas. As a result, an insurgent movement begins either on the right or the left of the broad middle ground in churches of Christ. Everyone has this right. For two hundred years, literally hundreds of papers have been published to share conflicting views of the Restoration Movement.

The best word to describe those who—whether from the right or the left—attack the directions of the majority is "insurgent." It is a political term defined as: "1: a person who revolts against civil authority or an established government; esp: a rebel not recognized as a belligerent, 2: one who acts contrary to the policies and decisions of his political party." Applied to a religious movement, the definition suggests an established broad middle position where the majority of adherents feel comfortable and are able to act and react within the system.

Nevertheless, insurgents, whether on the right (conservative) or the left (liberal), do not accept totally the broad middle. Therefore, insurgency does not suggest an attack from outside the fellowship. Insurgents wish to remain identified with the larger brotherhood, although sometimes uncomfortably so. They believe change is necessary.

David Lipscomb was neither a radical (liberal) nor a reactionary (ultraconservative), although he held some positions that might be classified in one or both categories. He was radical when he accepted left-wing political positions. Yet he never forced these upon others. He was occasionally reactionary. Not until late in life did he accept multiple cups in the Lord's Supper.

If Lipscomb located himself on the liberal/conservative continuum, where would he be?

> Our position has been a peculiar one. We have been identified with a people that started out to return to unsectarian, Bible Christianity. They have divided into two parties, each turning in different directions. *We have stood between them.* It is part of human nature to form parties, become sectarian, and reject the oneness of the people and church of God. *We have tried to stand between the two parties on the foundation of truth.* (Emphasis supplied.)[20]

What Lipscomb said about the directions of the Restoration Movement was certainly true. On the one hand, liberal Disciples moved quickly away from positions enunciated by the early restorers. Conversely, some, running far beyond the Bible, began questioning everything not specifically mentioned in the Scriptures. Lipscomb located himself somewhere between the extremes.

The strength of the Restoration Movement, and more specifically churches of Christ, has been in the middle between the extremes. As was true of Lipscomb, those in the middle have attempted to be biblical without overreacting to the left or the right. Whenever there has been a move toward one extreme or both extremes, tension, and even division, follows.

Restoration ideas naturally produce tension because of problems inherent in the faith and opinion dialogue. How are these determined? Is it possible to disagree on minor differences and remain brothers and sisters in Christ? The nineteenth century provided both answers: Barton Stone's followers were willing to hold their opinions in abeyance; those who accepted Alexander Campbell's positions were less pliable, but sufficiently so to fellowship with Stone. On the other hand, the organization of the missionary society was a matter of expediency to some and a matter of faith to others. The same was true of the use of the instrument in worship. The latter two examples brought division; the first did not.

With the division of 1906, churches of Christ separated from Disciples of Christ. One would think that, having divided over a number of major issues, a small fellowship of 159,658 persons would be unable to find other tension-causing, even divisive, issues. Nevertheless, within a few years conflicts surfaced. In most cases, the stretching of the broad middle gravitated toward a reactionary position.

The early twentieth century witnessed the separation of a number of ultraconservative factions, including:

1. One-cup churches—These churches refused to accept the individual cups used by most churches in the 1920s. Led by Dr. G. A. Trott and H. C. Harper, they taught their ideas through the *Old Paths Advocate*. Most one-cup churches are located in California and Texas. Since the 1950s, the issue has not been widely debated.

2. Non-Sunday school churches—Even in the nineteenth century there was some concern about Sunday schools. The advocates argued that, since the Sunday school is not authorized in the New Testament, it should not be used. In 1936, G. B. Shelburne, Jr., established the *Gospel Tidings* to support the idea. Presently, 500 to 600 churches with 25,000 to 30,000 members practice this understanding of the Scriptures. The greatest concentration of the churches is in Texas, Oklahoma, Arkansas, Indiana, California, and Oregon.

3. Premillennial churches—The center of the movement remains in Louisville, Kentucky. As long as he lived, R. H. Boll gave leadership to the group, which continues to publish *Word and Work*. The fellowship counts some 12,000 adherents.

4. Noninstitutional churches—This fellowship is the largest of the nonmainstream churches of Christ. Within this fellowship of 2,004 churches, a number of papers are published, with *Guardian of Truth* being the largest and most important. The membership of

these churches equals about 15 percent of all churches of Christ.[21]

Mainstream churches of Christ, according to these perspectives, have been unfaithful to the Bible and to the plea of the Restoration Movement. As a result, these groups constantly kept pressure on the large middle element of churches of Christ. Tensions mounted until the discontented found it necessary to follow their own convictions into separate fellowships, yet continuing to use the designation "churches of Christ."

Whether non-Sunday school, one-cup, premillennial, or noninstitutional, the movements have had strong personal leadership. G. E. Shelburne gave direction to the non-Sunday school movement, centered in Amarillo, Texas. J. Ervin Waters was for many years the leading defender through debate of the one-cup position. However, he no longer holds these positions as an insurgent. R. H. Boll and premillennialism have been synonymous since early twentieth century. The noninstitutional leadership has long claimed Foy E. Wallace, Jr., as their instructor, although he did not follow the issues into open conflict with the broad mainstream churches. Unquestionably, Foy Wallace was a catalyst for ideas from 1930 through the 1960s. His views helped to produce insurgency within churches of Christ.

If insurgency attacks around the edges of the mainstream churches, how can one identify the large middle during the period shortly after World War II? Over all, agreement existed on the issues and even the methods for accomplishing the goals of the fellowship. Evangelism, at home and abroad, was needed. Concern increased for orphans and the elderly. Education at all levels, with a Christian perspective, became more widely recognized as a needed extension for the home. Therefore, the large middle supported the Christian school. Churches began planning for greater growth through larger and more comfortable buildings and through innovative methods of reaching their neighborhoods. G. C. Brewer represented the broad middle among churches of Christ.

This is not to suggest that all members, papers, and journals of the large middle fellowship were in accord. They were not. Since the early nineteenth century, differences of opinion have existed as to the operation of the Holy Spirit. Whether or not the Holy Spirit is indwelling or works only through the Bible remains an issue of contention. But the issue has not caused division. Neither have varying ideas about the Christian and war, even though Foy

Wallace introduced it as an issue during World War II. The *Firm Foundation* and the *Gospel Advocate* differed as to whether orphan homes and homes for the elderly should be under elders of a local church or whether churches could "buy" the services of homes under boards of directors. For the most part, the *Advocate* accepted church support for Christian schools. The *Firm Foundation* feared the end result of the practice. The papers, however, did not break fellowship. In some areas, especially in Tennessee, many churches allow an instrument's use in weddings. Not so in Texas. This difference has not become a point of friction within the larger fellowship.

Beginning early in the 1950s, the era of greatest growth, churches of Christ faced renewed insurgency. By the middle of the 1960s, the noninstitutional groups separated into recognizable churches. Nevertheless, new insurgent groups appeared on either side of the mainstream churches, attacking from both the right and the left. Both emphases developed from attitudes which evolved out of or in response to the noninstitutional controversies of the 1950s.

The most articulate spokesman for noninstitutional churches of Christ is one of the recognized scholars of Disciple history, David Edwin Harrell, Jr. Now serving as a professor of history at Auburn University, his references to mainstream churches of Christ have shown definite strains of insurgency. Harrell's rationale for much of his understanding of Disciple history came from the German Ernst Troeltsch, who defined the "religious sect." In turn, Americans have coined another term to explain this country's unique religious heritage—*denomination*. Using the formula many sociologists accept, Harrell followed churches of Christ in their evolution from a sect as defined by Troeltsch to a denominational status in the 1970s. Thus he attacked the large middle-of-the-road fellowship by suggesting:

> The time will come, no doubt, when the leaders of the denominational movement within the church will accept the responsibility and credit for their liberal leadership. The time may not be too far distant when considerable numbers of Churches of Christ will be proud of their denominational status. When that time comes a whole new set of religious values will become the intellectual justification for a denominational Church of Christ. The same intellectual assumptions that undergird the

Methodist or Christian church will be adequate props for the newly-oriented Church of Christ. A realistic balance in the present controversy will be reached only when the liberals make this adjustment toward honesty.[22]

Professor Harrell's statement places him safely within the classification of insurgent. As defined by sociologists, he remains in the "sect" category; as defined by himself, he is in the church. Without the larger mainstream churches of Christ, at which he can hurl accusing darts, there would be no opportunity for insurgency. His position has torn him away from the larger body of churches of Christ.

With the noninstitutional issues no longer a major concern in the late 1960s, insurgency emerged from both the conservative and liberal positions. The in-house conflicts over sponsoring churches, cooperation, support of orphan homes and homes for the elderly, and the Herald of Truth caused deep hurts not easily healed. Reacting to this internal bloodletting, a number of younger men and women moved toward more liberal positions—even to insurgency. The 1960s saw, for the first time, open criticism of churches of Christ by a left-leaning constituency.

In response, some of the leading advocates of cooperation and sponsoring churches became strong defenders of a conservative position, attacking both middle-of-the-roaders and theological liberals. Because of this stance, a number of these men must be classified as insurgents.

Thomas Warren identified the next concern within churches of Christ when he penned articles in 1962 on the theme "Christianity Versus Relativism, Middle-of-the-Roadism, Neutralism, and Compromise" for the *Gospel Advocate.* First asking: "Is our nation harmed by Middle of the Roaders?" Warren then quoted Tom Anderson, reactionary editor of *Farm and Ranch* magazine— "America is losing its sense of moral indignation." He then applied the same ideas to the church:

> Is the church losing its sense of moral indignation? Is the church losing its intestinal fortitude? Is the silence that pervades us in the face of error taught on every hand (both without and within the church) golden or yellow?[23]

This last statement reflected Anderson's use of the phrase: "Pinks are people who are too nice to be red." The *Farm and*

Ranch editor believed communism had infiltrated the United States government. He added: "When freedom is at stake, your silence is not golden, it is yellow." [23]

What threatened the church in the early 1960s? Reuel Lemmons had already emphasized and would continue to emphasize that truth, most often, is located between extremes. He even called himself a middle-of-the-roader. Such a position was questionable in Warren's eyes.

Warren looked beyond Lemmons to Carl Ketcherside. In reality, Lemmons and Warren shared similar positions on Ketcherside, who had moved from a noninstitutional position within churches of Christ to a position espousing "unity-in-spite-of-differences." Ketcherside had become "sick and tired of the bitter wrangling and jarring of the party spirit." He and his friend, Leroy Garrett, became leaders of insurgency from the left. The fellowship was now stretched from both directions.

Ketcherside, at one time a leader of conservative churches of Christ associated with Daniel Sommer, described churches of Christ as he had known them: "We have built walls around ourselves to protect what we believe is vital to keep others out. But we have forgotten that it is those inside the walls and not those who are outside them who are in prison." By 1975, Ketcherside had moved to a position on the left. He now referred to his brethren on the right as legalists: "A legalist is one who thinks that we are under a written code and relate to God because of our subservience to it. . . . As a legalistic institution the 'Church of Christ' currently resembles a police station more than the prophetic kingdom of heaven." [24]

Leroy Garrett called for a "separated but not divided" stance. He quickly rejected the separatism he viewed in churches of Christ—"Unless you see and do as I see and do I will not accept you as equal." He added: "Separatism is exclusivism." Instead of this view, Garrett suggested:

> Separated but not divided recognizes that because of tradition, race, social status, personal preference, or longstanding theological differences "they" are there and "we" are here, and that this is not likely to change in the foreseeable future. But still, because of our common loyalty to Christ (Can there really be any other test?), we can recognize and treat each other as equals in Christ and perhaps do some things together. [25]

In fighting legalism, Ketcherside and Garrett accepted an extreme position on the left among churches of Christ.

Ira Y. Rice, Jr.'s, *Axe at the Root,* a publication of 1966, had an immediate impact on churches of Christ. The quick selling of the first printing of 5,000 copies called for the second printing of 3,000 copies in 1967. In the same year, a second volume of *Axe at the Root* came from the press, followed in 1970 by the third volume. In the latter year, Rice began publishing *Contending for the Faith.*

Rice's first volume resulted from his contact with three young men—Derwood Smith, Robert Randolph, and Robert B. Howard—when he and his wife were studying Mandarin Chinese at Yale University. Howard was the new preacher for the Hamden, Connecticut, church while Randolph and Smith were graduate students at Yale. Because of what Rice perceived as liberal theology, these men held center stage in volume one of *Axe at the Root.*

The attacks, however, were against a target much broader than three young men. Graduate education, especially in theology, became the focus. Rice warned about the possibility of division even more far reaching than the noninstitutional conflict: "We are about to see a brotherhood-wide division among us which will make the 1946 Anti-Cooperation Movement seem insignificant by contrast." He continued:

> I refer, of course, to this "Educational Trojan Horse" which is being trundled into our midst from the denominational/secular, so-called "Divinity" Schools intentionally via our Christian colleges. No, I did NOT say that such is being intended BY our colleges; but those who are RESPONSIBLE for the *framing* and *shaping* of this Trojan Horse so intend—and if the presidents, vice-presidents, deans, boards of trustees and others responsible for *administering* our colleges do not guard carefully, such shall succeed in taking over, as they fully are determined to do.[26]

Rice claimed to have been the first person to warn churches of Christ about the "Anti-Cooperation Movement" in 1946.

By attacking the liberalism of men involved in graduate programs, Rice placed all Christian colleges under a cloud. He asked:

> Think straight, brethren, is our objective in those brethren getting those advanced degrees so they could foist *something*

NEW on the churches? Or is it *merely to satisfy the demands of accrediting bodies,* relative to our schools, while we continue earnestly to contend for THE FAITH which was once delivered unto the saints?[27]

Axe at the Root received an enthusiastic reception. Concern with liberal theology existed among churches of Christ. Many within the fellowship, having been educated in this attitude by Daniel Sommer and Foy E. Wallace, Jr., were already suspicious of Christian colleges. The second volume continued the invectives, but now they were broadened to include the new journal, *Mission,* and several young men, including Gary Freeman, Dwain Evans, Maurice Haynes, Bob Johnson, and Mack Langford. Because the *Christian Chronicle* published several Gary Freeman articles, Rice also attacked that paper. Volume three focused on Logan J. Fox, *Voices of Concern,* J. Harold Thomas, and Dwain Evans.

Ira Y. Rice's insurgent position became even more pronounced when he issued his *Contending for the Faith* in 1970. A large minority within churches of Christ shared his views. In his attack on liberalism, anyone in the broad expanse of churches of Christ who might even defend a person perceived as liberal became suspect. Such was the case of Ray A. Chester of Searcy, Arkansas, who indicated his disappointment when the *Christian Chronicle* ceased publication of Freeman's articles. Said Chester:

> I can think of nothing more dangerous to the quest for truth and its propagation than the climate where good men can be put down for nothing more than daring to express thoughts that seek to stir us out of our lethargic and complacent ways of thinking and acting. . . .
>
> I believe there was no more dangerous period in our nation's history than the McCarthy era when men were destroyed by slurs and innuendoes.

Rice responded:

> I gather that the *basic convictions* of RAY F. CHESTER will bear *further study.* When brethren start talking that way, they usually are headed as hard as they can tear—in the *wrong direction.*[28]

Insurgency from the left was new in churches of Christ. Until the 1960s, most who accepted liberal theological positions quietly left the fellowship. But in the 1960s, many chose to stay and attempted to change what they perceived as an emerging bitter legalistic spirit. This was Ketcherside's basic reason for moving from the right to left as an insurgent. Where his *Mission Messenger* had been the voice of Sommerism, it became the publisher of a book composed of series of essays, edited by Robert Meyers, titled *Voices of Concern.*

Meyers' book appeared in the same year Rice introduced his first volume of *Axe at the Root.* It suggested insurgency from the far left in churches of Christ. In the introduction, Meyers concerned himself with education, but from a totally different perspective than Rice:

> One fact seems too clear to overlook. As leaders in all churches are increasingly educated, the tension between party strictures and the free mind will increase dramatically. Men trained to study analytically and critically will not be content with unyielding orthodoxy. They will not submit to coercion. If they are driven out because they will not conform, the result will be intellectual suicide for the churches losing them.[29]

He remembered the tract racks filled with "Why I left" pamphlets written by former Methodists, Mormons, and Presbyterians. One missing, he suggested, was: "Why I Left the Church of Christ."

Included in Meyers' book was an essay by Logan Fox, whose family members were long-time missionaries to Japan. As a young man, he had been more conservative than his teachers. Not only did he condemn dancing, smoking, and drinking, he also condemned tea, coffee, and Coca-Cola. As he matured, he played the politics of the brotherhood. By 1962, he no longer played the games. As a result, he resigned his positions at Ibaraki Christian College and his professorship at Pepperdine University.

In assessing churches of Christ and the Restoration Movement, Fox stated: "It is my judgment . . . that the Disciples are the more rightful heirs of Campbell, while we in the Church of Christ are more the children of David Lipscomb, H. Leo Boles, and other post-Civil War leaders of the church in the South." One characteristic of churches of Christ, he said, has been "a negative attitude toward education and scholarship, as typified by our opposition to a critical study of the scriptures."

Concluding his article, Fox, from a position far to the left of David Edwin Harrell, agreed with his conservative brother: "All our protestations to the contrary not withstanding, *we are a denomination.*" He believed this should be openly recognized and accepted. He closed with the following sentence: "My prayer for myself and for all concerned Christians is that we may be given the wisdom and courage to focus our minds on the great central truths which Jesus taught and embodied, leaving partisan strife to die in the deserts where it was born."[30]

A number of the essayists in *Voices of Concern* left churches of Christ, including Ralph Graham for the Christian Church (Disciples of Christ); Pat Hardeman, Unitarian/Universalist (in recent years, Hardeman returned to churches of Christ); Roy Key, Christian Church (Disciples of Christ); and William P. Reedy, United Church of Christ. Categorically, Robert Meyers stated: "I have no intention of leaving them [churches of Christ] so long as one of their churches is free enough to hear such compassionate strictives as fill the pages of this book."[31] He did leave, identifying himself with the Congregationalists. The statement made by *Voices of Concern* intensified and focused the insurgency from more liberal elements within churches of Christ and from those who chose to leave.

As soon as the prospectus of *Mission Journal* appeared, Ira Rice questioned its soundness. He noticed those involved with the new journal, both on the editorial board and as trustees. Even though *Mission* used writers attacked by Rice during the early issues, the journal carried little that would cause disagreement among churches of Christ. Instead, Rice was critical of *Mission* because of its name: nowhere could he find an emphasis on foreign missions. In November 1967, an entire issue dealt with foreign missionary efforts.

But by the end of the decade, the journal adopted an insurgency position from the left. Under the editorship of Roy Bowen Ward, it became critical of churches of Christ. Although not as filled with diatribe as *Axe at the Root,* the criticisms were often as severe. The title, "Church of Christism," given to Don Haynes's article, included criticism of the fellowship.[32] In May 1972, Hubert Locke, recognizing that traditional ideas do grow and often dominate a group of people, concluded:

When our very human attitudes or values or customs are raised to the level of church dogma, or when they become normatively exclusive in the life of the church, or when they are made tests of fellowship, rather than matters of taste or opinion, then we commit the very error against which our whole Restoration heritage has historically striven, that of making human opinion into the will of God.[33]

Later in the same volume, David Walker asked: "Are We Really the Church of Christ?"[34] The emphasis on the "pattern" of the New Testament church for the twentieth century concerned him.

Joining *Mission* was *Integrity,* edited by Foy Ledbetter and based in Michigan. As both journals viewed the larger fellowship, they often attacked the entire brotherhood when only a small segment on the conservative right was of immediate concern. David Bobo suggested that those associated with both *Mission* and *Integrity* saw themselves as "free," not shackled by the denominational tendencies of churches of Christ. He also labeled both journals and their supporters as "liberals" or "modernists." At least, he said, this was the view from many within churches of Christ.[35]

Bobo was correct in his assessment. A reaction to the "liberal" element within churches of Christ led, in part, to the forming of the *Spiritual Sword* in 1969. Thomas B. Warren was the editor. The inevitable happened. With positions drawn on either side of the great middle-of-the-stream fellowship, those in the middle were often the ones harmed by the volleys. If anyone in the middle suggested solutions, he became branded—liberal or legalist.

In the early 1960s, a call went forth for more preacher training. Batsell Barrett Baxter, a spokesman for the large middle group of churches of Christ, urged Christian colleges to train more preachers. Ostensibly for the same reason, a number of preacher training schools emerged. The Memphis School of Preaching, said Roy Hearn, would not be concerned with Bultmann and Barth or other liberal theologians. Evidently Hearn's mention of liberal theologians was a veiled warning about the new graduate schools operated by colleges among churches of Christ. Too many of the teachers had gained their training from graduate schools where liberalism was the daily fare. Therefore, such warnings were directed at mainstream churches of Christ.

Moving farther to the right, the Discipling Ministry, originated by the Crossroads church in Gainesville, Florida, approached perceived problems through organized small groups and personal involvement. Led by Chuck Lucas, Crossroads Church of Christ emphasized structure and commitment to reach young people in college communities. Because of some "cultist" tendencies and disruption of congregational structure in a number of locations, Crossroads caused a reaction throughout mainstream churches of Christ. They, too, were held at arm's length.

Crossroads, however, chose in 1990 to rebuild bridges with middle-of-the-road churches of Christ. At the Orlando, Florida, workshop, the elders read a statement of their intentions to renew fellowship with churches of Christ.

The Boston Church of Christ, led by Kip McKean, developed a more ambitious program of evangelism. The church attracted large crowds of worshipers each Sunday in the Boston Gardens, the home of the Celtics. The Boston church quickly replaced Crossroads as the leader of the Discipling Ministry. From the right or conservative position, the Boston church represents insurgency. As of 1991, there were 103 churches in this sub-fellowship.

Contrary to the opinions of many, the Boston church represents a conservative movement, requiring more of converts than mainstream churches of Christ. In many respects, this movement has given up on churches of Christ. Their goal, through individual churches like Boston, is to evangelize the major cities of the world.

FLAVIL YEAKLEY ON CHURCHES OF CHRIST

Emphasizing growth patterns of churches of Christ in the 1960s and the 1970s, Flavil Yeakley, then of Abilene Christian University, published *Why Churches Grow* in 1977. Possibly to shock his readers, Yeakley predicted that churches of Christ would be only half the current size by the year 2000 if the 1977 growth trends continued. The next generation would see the demise of churches of Christ as a distinguishable group. Yeakley gave as the major reason for the declining growth rate the changing conditions of the world over the previous fifteen years and the failure of churches of Christ to adapt to these changes. What is the world's greatest problem? Yeakley believed it to be alienation. More and more people are having less and less identification with a primary reference group. For instance, the family has deteriorated since

1965. Divorce is presently approaching 50 percent. Within churches of Christ, the divorce pattern closely parallels the outside world, although the rate is not as severe. Yeakley noticed that the declining growth rate of churches of Christ is "almost a perfect mirror-image of the increasing divorce rate among members of churches of Christ."

Of special importance are the two directions churches of Christ are moving. One will stunt growth; the other will leave churches with little substance or life. Said Yeakley: "The declining growth rate in the church of Christ over the past 15 years has been caused, at least in part, by a trend in the opposite direction—a trend to become conservative in matters of opinion and liberal in matters of faith." Both extremes will eventually destroy the church. The conservatives "make their customs into a law in which they bind all others in the church." On the other hand, the liberals "treat the word of God as though it had no more authority than the word of man." Even the large mainstream of churches of Christ is turning to a more devotional literature. This is the type of literature currently popular with the publishing houses among churches of Christ.

Yeakley called for a third alternative. His plea was basically a restoration position. There must be biblically-based preaching from the pulpit and an outreach to the community and to the world. The key to revitalization is evangelism. Concluded Yeakley:

> Dynamic Christ-centered Bible-based gospel preaching is the main thing that we need to reach the lost, involve the members, and help Christians grow spiritually. If the churches of Christ can have that kind of preaching and start doing the work that is needed, we can reverse the declining growth trend of the past 15 years.[36]

RESPONDING TO THE NEEDS OF THE TIMES

The most recent attempt to deal with many of the same issues— from both the right and the left—is a small book by Leonard Allen, Richard Hughes, and Michael Weed titled *The Worldly Church*. Questioning the methodology of Alexander Campbell, they indicted members of churches of Christ for swallowing the methods of the Sage of Bethany to the spiritual destruction of the fellowship. The Baconian inductive method of interpreting the Bible, followed so closely in the nineteenth century, has not allowed Christians to enjoy transcendence—a close fellowship with God. Conversely, too many members of churches of Christ have opted to use the methodology of the world—business, psychology, especially of the "pop" variety, and other of the social sciences. The authors call churches of Christ to search for transcendence—a deeper relationship with God. The restoration should fit the late twentieth century. Leonard Allen's *Cruciform Church* is another attempt to give direction to churches of Christ.[37] His subtitle suggests his theme: *Becoming a Cross-Shaped People in a Secular World.*

Often criticized, the Tulsa Soul-Saving Workshop has given a different focus to churches of Christ than many of the special lectureships conducted by schools and churches. Begun in 1976 after only three months preparation by the Garnett and Memorial Drive churches, the workshop has drawn increasingly large crowds. The first workshop drew 9,000 persons! The emphasis has been a positive look at Christianity.

Sharing much of the same theme, Nashville Jubilee began in 1989. Sponsored on alternating years by the Madison, Antioch, and Woodmont Hills churches, the July annual gatherings have been immediate successes. The 1991 sessions drew over 12,000 participants from all over the United States and from several foreign countries. The larger plenary sessions are designed for celebration. Hundreds of classes cover a wide range of topics to interest children, young people, mature adults, and senior Christians. As a result of the format changes inherent in Jubilee and the Tulsa Workshop, criticism has been directed toward them by more traditional spokesmen within churches of Christ.

The most difficult problem facing any organization, including churches, is change. The means and the methods of dealing with different eras must change to fit the needs of new generations. George Barna and William McKay, in *Vital Signs,* suggested: "Congregations that choose to ignore the currents of societal change will render themselves defenseless against deterioration. . . . Churches that remain aloof and designed for observation more than participation will wither."[38]

In years past, the Restoration Movement and churches of Christ have responded to the needs of the times. The Campbells and Stone caught the spirit of the early nineteenth century. America was a new nation, a democracy that easily accepted a movement in religion that called for a return to the New Testament—the constitution of the church. It was a revolt against both creedalism in religion and secular rationalism in the thought patterns of the western world. It had a strong emphasis upon the individual's responsibility to search the Scriptures for oneself. Thus it appealed to new Americans, especially those who had made their way westward to the frontier of Tennessee, Kentucky, and Ohio.

During the depression decade of the 1930s, a different need emerged. Herbert A. Marlowe, Jr., of the University of Florida, suggested that humans have a number of legitimate needs, including physical, intellectual, psychological, and spiritual. Basic, of course, are the physical—food, clothing, housing. When the world is breaking apart, people have psychological needs, especially the need for structure.[39] For most within churches of Christ, the 1930s represented a crumbling of such structure. Therefore, the "hellfire-and-brimstone" style of preaching, the drawing of strict doctrinal lines within the fellowship, the rise of dogmatic leadership, and conversely, the feeling of strength through exclusiveness, set churches of Christ apart. Likely these things gave foundation to lives without underpinning. In part, this explains the dominance of Foy E. Wallace, Jr., during the 1930s. He supplied security through intolerant conviction of right. Yet by the end of World War II, his paper—the *Bible Banner*—no longer held sway. It became an embarrassment to many. The cultural needs of the depression decade had passed; churches of Christ were changing as the people became economically and socially more secure.

Post-World War II America was an era when communism was viewed as a threat to the American democratic system. Partly in response to the atheism of Marx's heirs, the United States became more religious than it had been in many years. Church-going became the norm. Many Americans responded to a much stricter biblical religion. In part, this must be considered as a cause of the growth of churches of Christ during the 1950s and the early 1960s.

But the world of the 1990s is different from the world of the 1950s. The changes in America and the world are best explained in John Naisbitt's *Megatrends*. According to Naisbitt, America is involved in the change from an industrial to an information society. Key to this change is high technology—television, satellites, computers, and medical technology unknown just a few years ago. These changes portend tremendous movement in all of American society, including religion. With the advent of high technology in the 1950s, a new phenomenon took place. Americans—beginning in California—became involved in group therapy. Transcendental meditation, Zen, and Yoga became important outlets for needs spawned by high technology. Naisbitt called it "high touch."[40]

In this high-tech society, individuals often become lost. When mainline churches became less and less involved with people, they began to decline. This trend continues. On the other hand, during this transitional period, people need some structure in their lives. Those churches which have structure plus high touch are the ones presently growing. For churches of Christ to supply the needs of the 1990s, two things are necessary: a strict adherence to the Bible and a "reaching out" to people in the neighborhoods. Those congregations which leave the Bible for a socially-involved ministry will die. Conversely, those which emphasize a strict doctrinal approach without people concerns will disappear.

CONCLUSION

What is the future of churches of Christ? No one knows; the future cannot be adequately predicted. Several things are certain, however. Never again will churches of Christ witness a time comparable to the 1950s. It is not likely that the 1930s will be repeated. Whatever the future holds, it will be, as in all eras past, an adaptation of the teachings of the Bible to the culture of the age.[41]

EPILOGUE

T HE FUTURE
BECKONS

On January 25, 1989, Reuel Lemmons died. No one within the broad fellowship of churches of Christ had the interests of the church at heart more than this man. From the time he became editor of the *Firm Foundation* in 1955 until his death, Lemmons attempted to be a peacemaker and a prophet. Stepping down as editor of the *Firm Foundation,* he accepted the editorship of *Image* in 1985, a new journal published from West Monroe, Louisiana. The spirit discovered while editor of the *Firm Foundation* emanated from his pen as long as he lived, whether as editor of *Image* or as guest columnist each month in the *Christian Chronicle.*

A key factor in understanding Reuel Lemmons was his eternal optimism that God's people, the church, can win the world if they will submit themselves to Jesus as Lord. In 1984, he spoke at Joplin, Missouri, in the discussions between representatives of Independent Christian Churches and churches of Christ. His was a spirit of love and concern for the body of Christ. One of his last speaking engagements was at the 1988 Nashville meeting where he gave the closing plea in a dialogue between mainline churches of Christ and noninstitutional churches. His emphasis did not change. He pleaded: "Let's remove the fences and increase the fellowship to where fellowship and brotherhood mean the same thing. . . . Apostasy can happen in any direction, to the right or to the left. . . . We can fall off on either side and hell is on either side of the road."[1]

In the midst of conflict among churches of Christ, Lemmons was a constant beacon light. He could search the past to find guidance for the present. Equally as well, he could give directions for the future. In August 1985, he wrote:

> The fortunes of the church ebb and flow. Sometimes we are on the pinnacle. Sometimes we are in the valley. Since the first century there have been numerous periods when men thought the church would die out. And it almost did. But it has sprung back. In fact, the proof of the divine nature of the church is its ability to come back from the grave.[2]

There are indications that such a resurrection is currently happening within churches of Christ.

Both Flavil Yeakley and Mac Lynn have reported a slight increase in membership among churches of Christ after twenty years of stagnation between 1965 and 1985.[3] What has happened during the past ten years to cause a shift, however slight, in the membership demographics of churches of Christ? Much of the increase, according to Lynn, can be found in the Boston churches.

Another recent Mac Lynn publication may suggest an additional reason. Completing what many felt was an impossible task, Lynn compiled a directory of churches of Christ outside the borders of the United States. He found 747,568 members in 13,908 churches. Instead of a declining number of Americans serving in these countries, he listed 660 American adults in approximately 121 countries where churches of Christ exist.[4]

The 1980s witnessed renewed outreach among churches of Christ. Following World War II, churches of Christ sent vast amounts of food and clothing to Germany. Those shipments, however, were small compared with the relief funds gathered and distributed during the 1980s and early 1990s. Led by Bill McDonough, missionary in West Germany, and the White's Ferry Road church in West Monroe, Louisiana, churches of Christ sent $2.5 million of relief to Poland in 1981 and 1982.[5] In 1983 White's Ferry Road and Richland Hills church in Fort Worth distributed upwards of $4,000,000 for Ghana, Botswana, and Zululand.[6] In 1985, and for several years thereafter, churches have given over $10,000,000 for relief to drought-stricken Ethiopia.

The relief coordinator for much of this caring ministry was Don Yelton of the White's Ferry Road church. In the Western Hemisphere, several million dollars were distributed to victims of hurricanes, earthquakes, and other natural disasters. Don Yelton states that from 1981-1992 churches of Christ have given over $25,000,000 in cash and $25,000,000 of goods to help relieve suffering around the world. This money and goods were distributed by various churches in the brotherhood and church-related organizations, such as Manna and Bread for the Hungry World.

Herald of Truth and World Radio began their ministries during the 1950s and the 1960s, respectively; they were joined in 1983 by World Christian Broadcasting Corporation. Constructing a transmitter in Anchor Point, Alaska, World Christian Broadcasting began beaming religious programing into China and the Soviet Union over KNLS. Radio was the best, the only way, to reach into these communist countries.

At the beginning of the decade, no one would have predicted the events that would transpire in Eastern Europe and the Soviet Union. Never have the opportunities been as great as they were when the Iron Curtain came down. If the 1950s spurred growth in the American Christian community because of the godless enemy represented by the Soviet Union, now the decline and fall of communism and the Soviet state in the early 1990s can again initiate growth through outreach.

When Mikhail Gorbachev allowed the eastern European countries the freedom to walk away from their subservience to the Soviet Union, an American flood engulfed those newly-independent countries. Among those who quickly entered these countries were representatives of churches of Christ. Eastern European Missions, headquartered in Vienna, Austria, and sponsored by the Bammel Road church in Houston, began sending Bibles into the countries in increased numbers. They had already sent 50,000 Bibles into the Soviet Union in April 1989, their first legal delivery.[7] Heretofore, 400,000 Bibles had been smuggled into the once closed society.

Under the leadership of the Prestoncrest Church of Christ in Dallas, $3.5 million dollars were raised for various ministries in Eastern Europe.[8] The Madison, Tennessee, church responded to the needs of Romanians by taking 80,000 pounds of cargo— $35,000 worth of food and 5,000 Bibles—in its Adopt-an-

Orphanage program.[9] Bill McDonough, director of Partners in Progress, a medical missions program of the Sixth and Izard church in Little Rock, Arkansas, responded to the plea of the Albanian government for assistance in 1992. It was a joint effort with Eastern European Missions.[10]

From the David Lipscomb University's business department, a very unique program of outreach began during the fall of 1991. Under the direction of Dr. Randy Steger, his marketing classes accepted the challenge of "marketing" the needs of Eastern Europe and the former Soviet Union. Specifically, they focused on medical care. Throughout the 1991-1992 school year, the classes raised over one million dollars of donated medical supplies by presenting their plea through marketing techniques learned in class. As a result, people with medical needs will now have access to better health care because of students whose business skills were used to benefit others.

The former Soviet Union became the focus of media outreach—both by radio and television. The Herald of Truth and World Christian Broadcasting quickly beamed their programs throughout the vast expanse of the former communist state. World Christian Broadcasting received permission to broadcast over the All-Union Radio Network. From WCBC studios in Franklin, Tennessee, Galina Koval, a native of St. Petersburg, records programs to be broadcast to her people.[11] From this beginning, World Christian Broadcasting established a base in St. Petersburg.

Herald of Truth, celebrating forty years of broadcasting in 1992, penetrated the former Soviet Union with television programming. Two groups of personal representatives of churches of Christ under the auspices of Herald of Truth and the Highland church in Abilene, Texas, have preached in Moscow and Kiev.[12] What does the future hold for these former communist countries? Only God knows. As the future unfolds, one thing is certain. Churches of Christ have focused on outreach during the 1980s and early 1990s in a way unlike any time since the 1950s. If such a focus continues, the future beckons with open arms.

A CONCLUDING STATEMENT

I believe the Restoration plea remains viable, although there is tremendous questioning from all sectors in the last years of the twentieth century. Churches of Christ cannot make the same mistake made by the American Puritans in the early 1670s. They ceased their quest for the pure Christianity of the first century. Instead, they sought only to restore the religion of their spiritual fathers who came to America in 1630. They were sure their fathers had fully restored the church of the New Testament.[13]

If churches of Christ accept the conclusions of their spiritual fathers, whether in the early nineteenth century or in the 1930s, their quest for the religion of Jesus will be lost. I believe an idea evinced by early restorers can be the key to rejuvenating the Restoration plea in our age and for the next generation. Freedom caught the fancy of early nineteenth century Americans—freedom from tyranny. As a result, the restorers offered freedom from the tyranny of creeds, confessions, clergy, and denominations. They were urged to become Christians only. Thousands responded to the restorers.

Freedom remains the clarion call of restoration. We may not face the same issues faced by nineteenth-century restorers. What they did was important—they focused the world on the church and its ordinances. The freedom call for this generation will deal with different concerns. First, it must be recognized that the methodologies of rural America will not work in an urban setting.

Second, if Flavil Yeakley is correct, and I believe he is, then it must be a freedom that responds to the widespread alienation in our society. The family is losing its central place. There is an increase of singles. Americans are more mobile. As a result, current society needs security. This must be offered through the church.

Third, Barna and McKay are correct when they call for less observation in religion and more participation. In this way, freedom can be found in nurturing someone to spiritual health. Such participation frees a person from a slavery to self.

Fourth, John Naisbett is right when he calls for high touch. Christians must free themselves from the shackles of religion that bind the spirit so tightly that it is impossible to really know Jesus. They must be free to feel the touch of the Master's hand.

Fifth, until the church knows Jesus as Lord there can be no complete Restoration Movement. Such an emphasis does not lessen the importance of the church. The Gospels—Matthew, Mark, Luke, and John—must become more central in preaching and private study. This new emphasis refocuses the church as the body of Jesus. If the late twentieth century has something significant to add to the Restoration Movement, it will be a stronger emphasis on freedom in Jesus.

APPENDIX 1

TIMELINE—
THE AMERICAN
RESTORATION MOVEMENT
AND CHURCHES OF CHRIST

The following timeline is offered to enable the reader to better visualize how some of the events and people of the Restoration Movement are parallel to events in the history of the United States.

It would be impossible to list all missionaries on such a timeline. Those listed are representative of all who have served since 1892.

TIMELINE—THE AMERICAN RESTORATION

Events in U.S. History				
1763, Treaty of Paris; End of French and Indian War		1770, The Boston Massacre	1774, The First Continental Congress meets	1776, Declaration of Independence issued

1763, Thomas Campbell born

1772, Barton W. Stone born

1768, James Haldane born

1769, Elias Smith born

| 1760 | 1765 | 1770 | 1775 | 178 |

MOVEMENT AND CHURCHES OF CHRIST

1783, Peace of Paris ending the American Revolution	1787 Constitution of the United States written 1788, George Washington elected president	1791, Bill of Rights now in force	1796, John Adams elected president
			1796, Walter Scott born
	1788, Alexander Campbell born		
1784, "Raccoon" John Smith born			

TIMELINE—THE AMERICAN RESTORATION

Events in U.S. History	1801, Thomas Jefferson begins presidency	1808, James Madison elected president	1811, earthquake in Mississippi Valley 1812, War of 1812	1816, James Monroe elected president
			1810, Tolbert Fanning born	
		1806, Robert Richardson born		
				1816, Alexander Campbell preaches his "Sermon on the Law"
		1807, David S. Burnet born		
	1801, Cane Ridge Revival		1812, The Campbells are immersed	
		1807, Thomas Campbell arrives in the United States		
			1812, Benjamin Franklin born	
		1808, Elias Smith begins *Herald of Gospel Liberty*		
				1818, Moses E. Lard born
		1809, Alexander Campbell arrives in United States		
	1804, "Last Will and Testament of the Springfield Presbytery"			
		1809, Thomas Campbell issues "Declaration and Address"		

| 1800 | 1805 | 1810 | 1815 | 182 |

MOVEMENT AND CHURCHES OF CHRIST

1820, Missouri Compromise passes Congress	1825, Erie Canal opens	1829, Andrew Jackson begins presidency	1831, Nat Turner Insurrection	1837, Panic of 1837
			1833, American Anti-Slavery Society forms	1838, Cherokees move to Indian Territory on Trail of Tears

1830, Campbells separate from Baptists; Mahoning Association ceases to exist

1820, Isaac Errett born

1830, *Christian-Baptist* ceases publication. Campbell begins *Millennial Harbinger*.

1820, Campbell-Walker debate baptism

1826, Barton Stone begins *Christian Messenger*

1831, David Lipscomb born

1823, Campbell-McCalla debate baptism

1832, Unity is theme among Campbell-Stone followers at Lexington, KY

1823, *Christian-Baptist* begins publication

1827-1829, Revival in Western Reserve among Mahoning Association churches

1829, John McGarvey born

| 1820 | 1825 | 1830 | 1835 | 1840 |

TIMELINE—THE AMERICAN RESTORATION

Events in U.S. History				
1840, Benjamin Harrison elected president		1850, Compromise of 1850; California admitted as free state		
	1844, James K. Polk elected president	1849, California gold rush	1856, James Buchannan elected president	

		1850, Daniel Sommer born		
1840, Alexander Campbell establishes Bethany College			1855, Tolbert Fanning begins the *Gospel Advocate*	
	1846, Elias Smith dies			1856, Benjamin Franklin begins *American Christian Review*
1841, Abner Jones dies				
		1851, James Haldane dies		
1842, James Garrison born				1857, Fanning-Richardson pivotal discussion on interpretation of the Bible
1843, Franklin College opens as Elm Crag School	1846, Austin McGary born			
1843, T. B. Larimore born				1859, N. B. Hardeman born
1844, Barton Stone dies			1854, Thomas Campbell dies	
1844, Tolbert Fanning begins *Christian Review*	1849, American Christian Missionary Society formed; Alexander Campbell first president			1859, Musical instrument introduced at Midway, KY

| 1840 | 1845 | 1850 | 1855 | 186 |

MOVEMENT AND CHURCHES OF CHRIST

1860, Abraham Lincoln elected president

1865, Civil War ends

1861, Civil War begins

1868, U. S. Grant elected president

1874, Women's Christian Temperance Union forms

1876, Custer dies at Little Creek Bighorn

1875, R. H. Boll born

1870, G. H. P. Showalter born

1875, Foreign Christian Missionary Society organized in Louisville, KY

1866, Alexander Campbell dies

1871, J. N. Armstrong born

1861, Walter Scott dies

1866, *Gospel Advocate* reissued under David Lipscomb's editorship

1872, James Garrison purchases *The Christain*

1878, Benjamin Franklin dies

1872, An organ placed in the new building of Cincinnati's Central Christian Church

1866, *Christian Standard* begins publication under editorship of Isaac Errett

1861, Missionary convention favors Federal Union

1878, Marshall Keeble born

1867, David Burnet dies

1874, N. B. Hardeman born

1868, "Raccoon" John Smith dies

1874, G. P. Bowser born

1861, *Gospel Advocate* suspends publication

1874, H. Leo Boles born

1869, *Apostolic Times* begins publication at Lexington, KY. Proposed as a moderate voice among Disciples

1878, David Lipscomb takes firm stand against instrument in worship

1869, Disciples begin the Louisville Plan to replace American Christian-Missionary Society

1874, Christian Woman's Board of Missions organized

860   1865   1870   1875   1880

TIMELINE—THE AMERICAN RESTORATION

Events in U.S. History			
1880, James A. Garfield elected president	1888, Benjamin Harrison elected president	1884, Grover Cleveland elected president	1896, William McKinley elected president

		1891, Sarah Andrews born	
	1886, Batsell Baxter born		1896, Foy E. Wallace, Jr. born
1882, James Garrison merges *The Christian* and *The Evangelist*		1891, Nashville Bible School opens with nine students	1896, John Sheriff moves from New Zealand to Africa as a missionary
	1886, Daniel Sommer purchases the *American Christian Review*	1892, J. M. McCaleb to Japan as a missionary	
		1892, The mission conventions of the Christian church meet in Nashville; Lipscomb and his accociates alarmed at the use of women in mixed sessions	1898, George Benson born
1884, G. C. Brewer born			
	1888, Isaac Errett dies		
		1893, Formation of the Disciples Divinity House at University of Chicago	
1884, Austin McGary begins *The Firm Foundation.* Rebaptism becomes the major issue			1899, David Lipscomb refuses to celebrate the fiftieth anniversary of the founding of the American Christian Missionary Society
	1889, Focus on liberalism in the St. Louis church where James Garrison serves as an elder	1893, John McGarvey begins his "Biblical Criticism" articles in the *Christian Standard*	
	1889, Daniel Sommer's "Address and Declaration" given at Sand Creek, IL	1894, B. C. Goodpasture born	

| 1880 | 1885 | 1890 | 1895 | 1 |

MOVEMENT AND CHURCHES OF CHRIST

1904, "Teddy" Roosevelt elected president	1908, William H. Taft elected president	1912, Woodrow Wilson elected president	1916, Woodrow Wilson reelected 1917, United States joins Allies in war against the Central Powers 1918, World War II ends

1906, A. B. Barrett establishes Childers Institute in Abilene, TX. Beginning of Abilene Christian College

1915, M. Norvel Young born

1915, Willard Collins born

1916, Batsell Barrett Baxter born

1906, Religious census recognizes church of Christ as separate from Disciples of Christ

1902, Don Morris born

1916, Sarah Andrews goes to Japan as a missionary

1911, John McGarvey dies

1902, R. N. Hogan born

1907, Roy Cogdill born

1916, R. H. Boll moves *Christian Word and Work* to Louisville; Changes title to *Word and Work*

1908, Fanning Yater Tant born

1902, G. P. Bowser begins the *Christian Echo*

1912, Reuel Lemmons born

1917, David Lipscomb dies

1908, Premillennial advocate Stanford Chambers begins *Christian Word and Work* in New Orleans

1917, Controversy over liberal direction of McGarvey's College of the Bible

1908, N. B. Hardeman and A. G. Freed establish National Teachers' Normal and Business College (now Freed-Hardeman University) in Henderson, TN

1918, Nashville Bible School becomes David Lipscomb College

1918, O.D. Bixler enters Japan as a missionary

1902, James Garrison urges Disciples to cooperate with the National Federation of Churches and Christian Workers

1909, Tennessee Orphans' Home organizes in Columbia, TN

1918, Abilene Christian College begins its annual lectureship

1909, Pittsburgh, PA, centennial celebration of the "Declaration and Address" causes division among Disciples of Christ; Charge of liberalism from *Christian Standard*

1919, Harry R. Fox, Sr. joins the missionary team in Japan

| 900 | 1905 | 1910 | 1915 | 1920 |

TIMELINE—THE AMERICAN RESTORATION

Events in U.S. History

- 1924, Calvin Coolidge elected president
- 1925, Scope's Trial on evolution in Dayton, TN
- 1928, Herbert Hoover elected president
- 1929, Beginning of the Great Depression
- 1933, Franklin Roosevelt begins his first term as president
- 1937, Amelia Earhart disappears on her flight around the world.

- 1920, *Gospel Advocate* opposes women's suffrage amendment

- 1925, Formation of the Central Church of Christ in Nashville

- 1925, George Benson goes to China as a missionary

- 1930, Foy E. Wallace, Jr. becomes the editor of the *Gospel Advocate*

- 1936, G. B. Shelburne, Jr., establishes the *Gospel Tidings* to support the non-Sunday school position among churches of Christ

- 1937, Founding of Pepperdine College

- 1937, *20th Century Christian* originates on Lipscomb's campus in Nashville

- 1933, Neal-Wallace debate on premillennialism

- 1922, Ira North born

- 1926, Evangelical elements of the Disciples of Christ establish a committee on Future Action

- 1938, Foy Wallace, Jr., begins the *Bible Banner*

- 1939, Yosemite Encampment holds first session

- 1922, James A. Harding dies

- 1927, The first session of the North American Christian Convention meet in Indianapolis

- 1934, Wallace-Norris debate on premillennialism

- 1939, B. C. Goodpasture becomes editor of the *Gospel Advocate*

- 1922, First of the Hardeman Tabernacle meetings at the Ryman Auditorium in Nashville

- 1927, Boll-Boles written discussion on premillennialism

- 1928, Austin McGary dies

- 1934, Wallace leaves the editorship of the *Gospel Advocate*; John Hines new editor

- 1939, Wallace's triumphal return to Nashville; Central church pronounced soft on premillennialism

- 1923, Hardeman-Boswell debate on instrumental music in Nashville

- 1929, T. B. Larimore dies

- 1938-1939, Unity meetings with the Christian church in Detroit and Indianapolis led by Claud Witty (churches of Christ) and James D. Murch (Christian church); H. Leo Boles' non-compromising speech delivered in Indianapolis

- 1924, Harding College begins in Morrilton, AR

- 1929, Homer King begins *Old Paths Advocate* representing the one-cup persuasion of churches of Christ

1920   1925   1930   1935   19[4]

MOVEMENT AND CHURCHES OF CHRIST

1941, United States enters World War II

1945, End of World War II

1948, Harry Truman elected president

1949, Beginning of Korean Conflict

1952, Dwight Eisenhower elected president

1954, *Brown v. Board of Education* decision of Supreme Court

1957, Congress passes Civil Rights Act

1957, Eisenhower sends troops to force integration of Central High School in Little Rock, AR

1940, Daniel Sommer dies

1942, Rex Turner, Sr., and Leonard Johnson establish Montgomery Bible School (presently Faulkner University)

1943, Turmoil at David Lipscomb College; premillennialism alleged cause

1944, J. N. Armstrong dies

1944, M. Norvel Young accepts the pulpit at Lubbock, TX, Broadway church

1945, First Annual National Lectureship among black churches of Christ meets in Oklahoma City

1946, World War II triggers outreach by churches of Christ

1946, Jacob C. Vandervis returns to the Netherlands, his native country, as a missionary

1947, Otis Gatewood and Roy Palmer enter Germany as missionaries

1948, Ralph Brashears organizes a Bible college in the Philippines

1948, Florida Christian College opens with L. R. Wilson as president

1949, Maurice Hall goes to France as a missionary

1949, Cline Paden leads in mission effort to Italy

1949, Demise of the *Bible Banner;* beginning of the *Gospel Guardian* with Yater Tant as editor

1949, Tension in Italy over opposition to missionaries; Cled Wallace writes about "That Rock Fight in Italy" in the *Guardian;* Initiates "sponsoring church" conflict

1950, Central Christian College begins operation with L. R. Wilson as president (now Olkahoma Christian College)

1950, G. P. Bowser dies

1950, Southwestern Christian College opens

1950, J. W. Brents and A. R. Holton organize the first Blue Ridge Encampment at Black Mountain, NC

1950, Abilene Christian College gains accreditation; Joins Pepperdine in accreditation ranks

1951, Henry Ewing to Rhodesia as a missionary

1952, Herald of Truth begins under the direction of the Highland Church of Christ, Abilene, TX

1952, Ira North becomes minister of the Madison Church of Christ in Tennessee

1952, Howard Horton and Jimmy Johnson respond to the call of Nigerians for American teachers

1953, David Lavender family goes to Italy to share the gospel

1953, G. C. Brewer begins the *Voice of Freedom*

1954, Harper-Tant debate over support of Herald of Truth

1954, G. H. P. Showalter dies

1954, Bill Richardson and Haskill Chessir respond to call from Korea for missionaries

1955, Reuel Lemmons becomes editor of the *Firm Foundation*

1955, Ira Rice, Jr. moves to Singapore as a missionary

1956, Ohio Valley College opens

1956, G. C. Brewer dies

1956, York College comes under control of members of churches of Christ

1956, Columbia Christian begins college classes

1956, R. J. Smith, Jr., first person in churches of Christ to cross the Iron Curtain into Poland; interpreters Josef Naumik and Henry Ciszik become nucleus of churches of Christ in Poland

1956, Batsell Baxter dies

1957, Lake Geneva Encampment opens in Wisconsin

1957, Woods-Cogdill debate in Birmingham concerning support of orphan homes

1957, *Restoration Quarterly,* with J. W. Roberts as editor, begins publication

1957, Lubbock Christian College begins classes

1958, Parker Henderson to Thailand as a missionary

1958, LeRoy Garrett begins publishing *Restoration Review*

1959, Roy Mullinax and Enoch Thweatt, Jr., enter Taiwan as missionaries

1959, Batsell Barrett Baxter becomes lead speaker for Herald of Truth

1959, Northeastern Christian Junior College begins in Villanova, PA

1959, B. C. Goodpasture estimates 2,000,000 members in churches of Christ

1959, North Central Christian College (now Michigan Christian) opens

---

TIMELINE—THE AMERICAN RESTORATION

Events in U.S. History			
1960, John F. Kennedy elected president	1968, Assassination of Martin Luther King and Bobby Kennedy	1970, eighteen-year olds receive the vote	1976, Jimmy Carter elected president
1963, Assassination of John F. Kennedy	1969, Richard Nixon begins his term as president		

1960, Ralph Henley & Ernest Stewart go to Jerusalem as missionaries		1970, Ira Rice, Jr. begins *Contending for the Faith*	1975, International Soul-Winning Workshop (Tulsa, OK) holds its first session	
	1965, Nigerian Christian hospital opens	1970s, Campus Ministry movement dominated by Crossroads Church of Christ, Gainsville, FL	1975, Tottie Ellis of Nashville elected vice-president of Eagle Forum	
1961, Thirteen missionary families settle in Sao Paulo, Brazil				
1961, Sunset School of Preaching (Lubbock, TX) begins	1966, Memphis School of Preaching accepts first students		1975, Carl Ketcherside abandons Daniel Sommer's position for progressive stance	1976, K. C. Moser dies
1961, Eastern European Missions formed to publish Bibles for countries behind the Iron Curtain	1966, Robert Meyers publishes his *Voices of Concern*		1976, Monroe Hawley's book *Redigging the Wells* appears	
1962, Marvin Phillips enters Australia as a missionary			1976, Batsell Barrett Baxter's "Crisis" speech at Abilene Christian College	
1962, Thomas Warren publishes articles condemning "middle-of-the-roadism"		1970, White's Ferry Road School of Preaching begins	1977, Flavil Yeakley's book *Why Churches Grow* is published	
1962, J.C. Choate family begins missionary work in Pakistan	1967, *Mission Journal* begins; Thomas Olbricht, editor		1977, J. Roy Vaughn becomes editor of the *Gospel Advocate*	
1962, Willard Collins leads Nashville's Municipal Auditorium meeting	1967, Jack Evans becomes the first black president of Southwestern Christian College	1974, Don Morris dies	1977, B. C. Goodpasture dies	
1962, Noninstitutional churches no longer fellowship mainstream churches of Christ	1967, Edward Short enters Taiwan as a missionary		1978, Ira North new editor of the *Gospel Advocate*	
1963, World Radio begins	1968, Marshall Keeble dies	1974, J. D. Thomas publishes *What Lack We Yet?*	1979, Foy E. Wallace, Jr. dies	
1963, Brown Trail School of Preaching in Fort Worth begins classes	1969, Jack Zorn begins Lads to Leaders		1979, Formation of the Boston Church of Christ by Kip McKean	
1963, J.C. Bailey goes to India as a missionary	1969, Thomas Warren issues the *Spiritual Sword*		1979, First Crusade sponsored by black churches of Christ; targeted city is Chicago	

| 1960 | 1965 | 1970 | 1975 | 198 |

MOVEMENT AND CHURCHES OF CHRIST

1981, Ronald Reagan begins first of two terms as president

1988, George Bush elected president

1992, Bill Clinton elected president

1981, Oklahoma Christian College begins publishing *Christian Chronicle*

1985, Roy Cogdill dies

1990, Prestoncrest Church of Christ spearheads drive to raise $3.5 million dollars for Eastern Europe

1985, A church begins meeting in Budapest, Hungary

1981, *Truth* and *Gospel Guardian* merge to form *Guardian of Truth;* Mike Willis, editor

1985, *IMAGE Magazine* begins; Reuel Lemmons editor

1990, Crossroads church in Gainsville, FL, askes to be restored to fellowship of larger body of churches of Christ

1982, Batsell Barrett Baxter dies

1986, Hettie Ewing, missionary to Japan for 40 years, dies

1982, Guy N. Woods succeeds Ira North as editor of the *Gospel Advocate*

1985, $10 million in relief for Ethiopia from U. S. church of Christ

1991, George Benson dies

1985, Furman Kearley replaces Guy Woods as editor of the *Gospel Advocate*

1983, Formation of World Christian Broadcasting Corporation

1991, David Lipscomb University celebrates its centennial

1988, Conference between institutional and noninstitutional churches of Christ in Nashville

1983, Reuel Lemmons resigns editorship of *Firm Foundation;* succeeded by William Cline

1991, John Dow Merritt, missionary to Zambia, Africa, for fifty years, dies at age 96

1988, Wil Goodheer becomes second president of European Christian College (now International Christian University)

1983, $2.5 million to Poland for relief from churches of Christ directed by White's Ferry Road church in West Monroe, LA; Churches of Christ gain legal recognition in Poland

1992, *Wineskins Magazine* begins publication

1989, Nashville Jubilee begins

1985, Fred D. Gray— elder of Tuskegee, AL, church—elected president of National Bar Association

1984, Ira North dies

1989, Reuel Lemmons dies

1984, Rubel Shelly publishes *I Just Want to be a Christian*

1989, Denny Boultinghouse appointed editor of *IMAGE Magazine*

1992, $1 million in medical supplies sent to Eastern Europe and the old Soviet Union by Dr. Randy Steger's marketing classes at David Lipscomb University

1984, First "Restoration Summit" meeting in Joplin, MO

80   1985   1990   1995   2000

APPENDIX 2

TIMELINE—
JOURNALS AND
PAPERS MENTIONED
IN THIS BOOK

This is not an exhaustive list of publications within the American Restoration Movement and churches of Christ. Most of the following publications are either quoted or mentioned in *A Distinct People*. Much of the information has been gleaned from R. L. Roberts, *Union List of Restoration Periodicals in Participating Christian College Libraries* (Abilene, TX: Abilene Christian University, 1982), Robert Shouse, *A History of Publications Among Brethren in the Periodicals of The Disciples of Christ* (Greenwood, IN: Private publication, 1991), and Claude Spencer, *Periodicals of The Disciples of Christ* (Canton, MO: Disciples of Christ Historical Society, 1943).

TIMELINE—JOURNALS AND PAPERS

NAME	DATE	ORIGINAL EDITOR	CURRENT EDITOR	NOTES
Herald of Gospel Liberty	1808-1817	Elias Smith		First journal among Disciples
Christian Baptist	1823-1830	Alexander Campbell		Named to appeal to Baptists
Christian Messenger	1826-1845	Barton W. Stone		
Millennial Harbinger	1830-1870	Alexander Campbell		W.K. Pendleton, Editor
Evangelist	1832-1842	Walter Scott		Superseded by Protestant Unionist
Christian Review	1844-1847	Tolbert Fanning, etc.		
Christian Magazine	1848-1853	J. B. Ferguson		Superseded by Christian Review
Western Evangelist became Christian Evanglist, 1852	1850-1858	Daniel Bates, Aaron Chatterton		Superseded by Evangelist (Iowa & Chicago) New Series, 1865-1882. Edited B. W. Johnson
Gospel Advocate	1855-	Tolbert Fanning	Furman Kearley	David Lipscomb became editor in 1866
American Christian Review	1856-1887	Benjamin Franklin		Purchased by Daniel Sommer
Gospel Echo	1863-1882	Alexander Proctor		Became Gospel Christian in 1872; merged with Evangelist, 1882
Lard's Quarterly	1863-1868	Moses E. Lard		
Christian Standard	1866-	Isaac Errett	Sam E. Stone	First published in Cleveland, OH, then in Cincinnati
Apostolic Times	1869-1885	John W. McGarvey, etc.		Continued under various titles until 1907
Christian Quarterly	1869-1876	W. T. Moore		Superseded by New Christian Quarterly, 1892-1896, J. H. Garrison editor; superseded by Christian Quarterly, 1897-1899, edited by W. T. Moore
Christian-Evangelist	1882-1959	James H. Garrison, B. W. Johnson		Other titles: Christian, 1960-1973; World Call . . . Disciple, 1974
Octograph	1883-1887	Daniel Sommer		Merged with American Christian Review
Missionary Tidings	1883-1918	Mrs. M. M. B. Goodwin		Published by Christian Woman's Board of Missions
Firm Foundation	1884-	Austin McGary	H. A. Dobbs	G. H. P. Showalter editor, 1908-1954; Reuel Lemmons, editor, 1955-1983
Christian Oracle	1884-1899	D. R. Lucas, C. C. Morrison		Superseded by Christian Century, continues to be published as an interdenominational journal
Christian Leader	1886-1960	John Rowe		Known as Christian Leader and Way, 1904-1913
Octographic Review	1887-1914	Daniel Sommer		Superseded American Christian Review
Christian Echo	1902-	G .P. Bowser	R. N. Hogan	Oldest journal among black churches of Christ
Christian Word and Work	1908-1916	Stanford Chambers		Superseded by Word and Work, published in Louisville, KY
Word and Work	1916-	R. H. Boll	Alex V. Wilson	Premillennial journal
Apostolic Review	1915-1940	Daniel Sommer		

Mentioned in This Book

Name	Date	Original Editor	Current Editor	Notes
Old Paths Advocate	1929-	Homer King	Don King	Journal for one-cup fellowship
Vindicator	1933-1964	E. C. Fuqua		
Gospel Guardian (1)	1936-1936	Foy E. Wallace, Jr.		Merged with Firm Foundation
Gospel Tidings	1936-1988	G. B. Shelburne, Jr.		Journal for non-Sunday school fellowship
20th Century Christian	1937-	J. P. Sanders	Prentice Meador, Jr.	Now called 21st Century
Mission Messenger	1938-1975	Carl Ketcherside		
Bible Banner	1938-1949	Foy E. Wallace, Jr.		
Discipliana	1941-	Claude Spencer	James A. Seale	Now published in Nashville
Christian Chronicle	1943-	Olan Hicks	Howard Norton	Not published Aug. 1979-Aug. 1981; now published by Oklahoma Christian University
Gospel Guardian	1949-1981	Fanning Yater Tant		Merged with Truth
Torch	1950-1954	Foy E. Wallace, Jr.		
Preceptor	1951-	Clinton Hamilton	Denny Brown	Noninstitutional journal
Bible Talk	1952-1958	Leroy Garrett		
Voice of Freedom	1953-1985	G. C. Brewer		Emphasized opposition to communism and Catholicism; in recent years, feminism
Truth Magazine	1956-1980	Bryan Vinson, Jr.		Merged with Gospel Guardian to become Guardian of Truth
Restoration Quarterly	1957-	J. W. Roberts	Everett Ferguson	First attempt at scholarly journal among churches of Christ
Restoration Review	1959-1992	Leroy Garrett		
Mission Journal	1967-1988	Thomas Olbricht		Represented more progressive ideas in churches of Christ
Integrity	1969-	Foy Ledbetter	J. Bruce and Dianne Kilmer	Represents more progressive views in church of Christ
Contending for the Faith	1969-	Ira Rice, Jr.	Ira Rice, Jr.	Represents more traditional views in churches of Christ
Spiritual Sword	1970-	Thomas Warren	Alan E. Highers	Represents more traditional views in churches of Christ
Faith and Facts	1973-	Robert Welch	Robert Welch	Represents noninstitutional churches of Christ
Vanguard	1976-1984	Fanning Yater Tant		A more moderate noninstitutional journal
UpReach	1979-	Batsell B. Baxter	Randy Becton	Published by Herald of Truth
Guardian of Truth	1981-	Mike Willis	Mike Willis	Merger of Truth Magazine and Gospel Guardian
Image	1985-	Reuel Lemmons	Denny Boultinghouse	Moderate to progressive journal
Wineskins	1992-	Mike Cope, Rubel Shelly, Phillip Morrison	Mike Cope, Rubel Shelly, Phillip Morrison	Moderate to progressive journal

3

TIMELINE—
CHRISTIAN COLLEGE
PRESIDENTS AND
THEIR TERMS

The following timeline of the Christian college presidents is designed to make it easier for the reader to see which presidents served concurrently at their respective schools.

Current Name and Date Founded	TIMELINE OF CHRISTIAN COLLEGE						
Magnolia Christian College 1976							
Southern Christian University[1] 1967							
Michigan Christian College 1959							
Ohio Valley College[2] 1959							
Northeastern Christian Junior College[3] 1957							
York College[4] 1956							
Lubbock Christian University[5] 1956							
Oklahoma Christian[6] (OCUSA) 1950							
Southwestern Christian College 1950							
Columbia Christian College[7] 1947							
Faulkner University[8] 1942							
Pepperdine University[9] 1937							
Harding University[10] 1924							
Freed-Hardeman University[11] 1919							W. Claude Hall 1923-1925
Abilene Christian University[12] 1906	A. B. Barret 1906-1908	H. C. Darden 1908-1909	R. L. Whiteside 1909-1911	James F. Cox 1911-1912	Jesse P. Sewell 1912-1924		
David Lipscomb University[13] 1891	James A. Harding 1891-1901 William Anderson 1901-1905 J. S. Ward 1905-1906 E. A. Elam 1906-1913			J. S. Ward 1913	H. Leo Boles 1913-1920	A. B. Lipscomb 1920-1921	Horace S. Lipscomb 1921-1923
	1905		1910		1915	1920	192

PRESIDENTS AND THEIR TERMS

L. D. Webb,
1947-1958

Rex A. Turner, Sr. and
Leonard Johnson, Co-Presidents
1942-1948

Batsell
Baxter
1937-1939

Hugh Marvin Tiner
1939-1957

J. N. Armstrong
1924-1936

George S. Benson
1936-1965

Hall L.
Calhoun
1925-
1926

N. B. Hardeman
1925-1950

Batsell Baxter
1924-1932

James F. Cox
1932-1940

Don H. Morris
1940-1969

H. Leo Boles
1923-1932

Batsell
Baxter
1932-1934

E. H. Ijams
1934-1943

Batsell
Baxter
1943-1946

| 1925 | 1930 | 1935 | 1940 | 1945 | 1950 |

TIMELINE OF CHRISTIAN COLLEGE

Current Name and Date Founded	1950	1955	1960	1965	1970
Magnolia Christian College 1976					
Southern Christian University[1] 1967					
Michigan Christian College 1959			Otis Gatewood 1959-1964	E. Lucien Palmer 1964-1971	
Ohio Valley College[2] 1959			Don Gardner 1959-1964	Lewis Case 1964-1966 / J. M. Powell 1966-1970	
Northeastern Christian Junior College[3] 1957		Rex Johnston 1957-1959	J. Harold Thomas 1959-1962 / Elza N. Huffard 1962-1980		
York College[4] 1956		Harvey A. Childress 1956-1957 / Gene Hancock, Jr. 1957-1960	Dale R. Larsen 1960-1978		
Lubbock Christian University[5] 1956		F. W. Mattox 1956-1974			
Oklahoma Christian[6] (OCUSA) 1950	L. R. Wilson 1950-1954	James O. Baird 1954-1974			
Southwestern Christian College 1950	E. W. McMillan 1950-1952 / H. L. Barber 1952-1956	A. V. Isbell 1956-1967			
Columbia Christian College[7] 1947	L. D. Webb 1947-1958		Truman H. Ethridge 1958-1959 / Robert H. Rowland 1959-1968		
Faulkner University[8] 1942	Rex A. Turner, Sr. 1948-1973				
Pepperdine University[9] 1937	Hugh Marvin Tiner 1939-1957		M. Norvel Young 1957-1971		
Harding University[10] 1924	George S. Benson 1936-1965			Clifton L Ganus Jr. 1965-1987	
Freed-Hardeman College[11] 1919	Hubert Allen Dixon 1950-1969				
Abilene Christian College[12] 1906	Don H. Morris 1940-1969				
David Lipscomb University[13] 1891	Athens Clay Pullias 1946-1977				

PRESIDENTS AND THEIR TERMS

Rod Tate 1976-1979	William Lambert 1979-1980	Cecil May, Jr. 1980-			
Rex A. Turner, Sr. 1967-1986			Rex A. Turner, Jr. 1986-		
Don Gardner 1971-1978	Walter Gilfilen 1978-1980	Milton B. Fletcher 1980-1991		Kenneth Johnson 1991-	
Justin B. Roberts 1970-1977	E. Keith Stotts 1977-1993				
Elza N. Huffard 1962-1980	Larry Roberts 1980-1986	Hyde S. Harper, Jr. 1986-1987	John R. Hall 1987-1991	Bill D. Bowen 1991-1993	
Dale R. Larsen 1960-1978	Gary R. Bartholomew 1978-1987	Don E. Gardner 1987-1991	Larry Roberts 1991-		
W. Joe Hacker 1974-1976	Harvie W. Pruitt 1976-1982	Steven S. Lemley 1982-1993	L. Ken Jones 1993-		
J. Terry Johnson 1974-					
Jack Evans 1967-					
Rex F. Johnston 1969-1974	J. P. Sanders 1974-1981	Kenneth Whorton 1981-1983	Michael C. Armour 1983-1986	Gary D. Elliott 1986-1991	William A. Free 1991-1992 / Don Gardner 1992-1993
E. R. Brannan 1973-1981	J. Walker Whittle 1981-82	Ernest Clevenger, Jr. 1982-1986	Billy D. Hilyer 1986-		
William Slater Banowsky 1971-1978	Howard Ashley White 1978-1985	David Davenport 1985-			
Clifton L Ganus Jr. 1965-1987		David B. Burks 1987-			
E. Claude Gardner 1969-1990			Milton R. Sewell 1990-		
John C. Stevens 1969-1981	William J. Teague 1981-1991	Royce Money 1991-			
Willard Collins 1977-1986	Harold Hazelip 1986-				

| 1970 | 1975 | 1980 | 1985 | 1990 | 1995 |

ENDNOTES

CHAPTER 1. NINETEENTH-CENTURY BACKGROUND

1. Sydney E. Ahlstrom, *A Religious History of the American People,* (Garden City, NY: Image Books, 1975), vol. I, pp. 442-443.

2. Mission, 1979, p. 11.

3. RQ, 1958, pp. 132-134.

4. An excellent discussion of Baconian inductive reasoning and Common Sense Philosophy is found in C. Leonard Allen's *The Cruciform Church* (Abilene, TX: Abilene Christian University Press), pp. 28-31.

5. Bill J. Humble, "The Missionary Society Controversy in the Restoration Movement, 1823-1875," (Unpublished Ph.D. Dissertation, State University of Iowa, 1946), pp. 33-42.

6. Ibid., p. 34.

7. Ibid., p. 40.

8. Quoted in Oliver Read Whitley, *Trumpet Call of Reformation* (St. Louis: Bethany Press, 1959), p. 80.

9. MH, 1832, pp. 501-502.

10. W. T. Moore, *A Comprehensive History of the Disciples of Christ* (New York: Fleming H. Revell Company, 1909), p. 343.

11. Humble, "The Missionary Society Controversy," pp. 83-88.

12. Noel L. Keith, *The Story of D. S. Burnet: Undeserved Obscurity* (St. Louis: Bethany Press, 1954), p. 191.

13. Humble, "The Missionary Society Controversy," pp. 105-112.

14. Cloyd Goodnight and Dwight E. Stevenson, *Home to Bethphage: A Biography of Robert Richardson* (St. Louis: Christian Board of Education, 1949), p. 118.

15. Ibid., pp. 118-119.

16. Ibid., p. 139.

17. Ibid., pp. 140-141.

18. James E. Scobey, ed., *Franklin College and Its Influences* (Nashville: Gospel Advocate Company, 1954, reprint), p. 14.

19. *GA*, 1955, p. 33.

20. *GA*, 1857, p. 5.

21. *RQ*, 1978, pp. 135-149.

22. *MH*, June 1957, pp. 399-401.

23. *GA*, 1857, pp. 35, 141-142. Alexander Campbell branded Russell's ideas "Calvinism in a new dress." *MH*, October 1857, p. 594.

24. An excellent discussion of positions leading to ultimate division and how Fanning's position has influenced churches of Christ is found in Gregory Tidwell, "Autosoterism Within Churches of Christ" (Unpublished M.A. Thesis, Vanderbilt University, 1986).

25. Joseph Franklin and J. A. Headington, *The Life and Times of Benjamin Franklin* (St. Louis: J. Burns, 1879), pp. 256-266.

26. J. S. Lamar, *Memoirs of Isaac Errett*, 2 vols. (Cincinnati: The Standard Publishing Company, 1893), vol. 1, pp. 162, 169.

27. Ibid., vol. 1, pp. 191-195.

28. R. L. Roberts, retired librarian at Abilene Christian University, stated in July 1983 at a conference on Abilene's campus that the first two divisions of Disciple churches were north of the Ohio River—Detroit and St. Louis. Therefore, causes other than the North/South division must be discovered.

29. Lamar, vol. 1, pp. 282-300.

30. Ibid., pp. 301-306.

31. *LQ,* 1866, pp. 330-336.

32. Lester E. McAllister and William E. Tucker, *Journey of Faith: A History of the Christian Church* (Disciples of Christ), (St. Louis: Bethany Press, 1975), pp. 256-268.

33. See Franklin and Headington, pp. 348-351, for Franklin's total view of organizations.

34. McAllister and Tucker, pp. 244-248; Earl West, *Search for the Ancient Order,* (Indianapolis: Religious Book Service, 1950), vol. 2, pp. 80-92.

35. West, *Search,* vol. 2, pp. 87-88.

36. Ibid., p. 86.

37. Ibid., p. 83.

38. Ibid., pp. 90-91.

39. *GA,* 1878, p. 215.

40. James Stephen Wolfgang, "A Life of Humble Fear: The Biography of Daniel Sommer, 1850-1940," (Unpublished M.A. thesis, Butler University, 1965), p. 18.

41. Ibid., p. 63.

42. Matthew C. Morrison, *Like a Lion: Daniel Sommer's Seventy Years of Preaching* (Murfreesboro TN: Dehoff Publications, 1975), p. 95.

43. *GA,* 1901, p. 312.

44. *GA,* 1892, p. 408.

45. Quoted in Leroy Garrett, *Stone-Campbell Movement* (Joplin, MO: College Press, 1981), p. 492.

46. Wolfgang, p. 108.

47. *FF,* 1884, p. 1.

48. *GA,* 1914, pp. 276-277.

49. For a discussion of David Lipscomb as a moderate, see Robert E. Hooper, *Crying in the Wilderness: A Biography of David Lipscomb* (Nashville: David Lipscomb College, 1979).

50. *GA,* 1909, p. 454.

51. Tidwell, pp. 1-11.

52. Ibid., p. 45.

CHAPTER 2. DIVISION IN 1906

1. This chapter is based in large part on a chapter in Hooper, *Crying in the Wilderness*, pp. 279-302.

2. *GA*, 1897, p. 789; 1887, p. 281.

3. *GA*, 1894, pp. 237, 814.

4. William R. Hutchison, *The Modernist Impulse in American Protestantism* (Cambridge and London: Harvard University Press, 1976), pp. 113-115.

5. George Marsden, *Understanding Fundamentalism and Evangelism* (Grand Rapids, MI: William B. Eerdman's Publishing Co.), pp. 146-147.

6. *Christian,* September 20, 1877, pp. 4-5.

7. *Christian,* May 12, 1881, p. 4.

8. *Christian,* May 26, 1881, p. 4.

9. *Christian,* June 16, 1881, p. 1.

10. *CE,* 1887, pp. 100-101.

11. Hooper, *Crying in the Wilderness,* pp. 254-255.

12. Richard Halbrook, "John W. McGarvey: How He was Viewed by His Correspondents," *Discipliana* 37 (Fall 1977), p. 36.

13. Ibid.

14. *CS,* 1894, p. 949.

15. *CS,* 1896, p. 687.

16. William Tucker, "Higher Criticism and the Disciples," *Discipliana* 22 (September 1962) p. 52.

17. Fred A. Bailey, "The Status of Women in the Disciples Movement," (Unpublished Ph.D. Dissertation, University of Tennessee, 1979), pp. 55-56.

18. Ibid., pp. 34-41.

19. Ibid., pp. 77-78.

20. Ibid., pp. 113-114.

21. Ibid., pp. 114-115.

22. Ibid., pp. 116-117.

23. *GA*, 1902, p. 503.

24. *GA*, 1890, p. 647.

25. *GA*, 1896, p. 679.

26. *GA*, 1907, p. 681.

27. *GA*, 1907, p. 633; 1899, p. 520

28. *GA*, 1899, p. 424.

29. Ibid., pp. 32-33.

30. *GA,* 1902, pp. 24, 41.

31. *GA,* 1897, p. 145.

32. *GA,* 1897, pp. 145, 241, 322.

33. *GA,* 1908, pp. 56-57.

34. *GA,* 1902, p. 728.

35. *GA,* 1907, p. 457.

36. Ibid., p. 713.

37. J. A. Lord to David Lipscomb, July 8, 1904; David Lipscomb to J. A. Lord, no date.

38. *GA,* 1906, p. 201.

39. Alfred Thomas DeGroot, *The Grounds of Division Among the Disciples of Christ* (Chicago: Privately printed, 1940), p. 132.

40. Ibid., p. 133.

CHAPTER 3. THE OUTSIDERS

1. The best study of fundamentalism is George Marsden, *Fundamentalism and American Culture* (New York: Oxford University Press, 1980). Marsden's development of the theme is followed in this chapter. He emphasizes the importance of Baconian inductive reasoning on American religion.

2. Alexander Campbell, *The Christian System* (Cincinnati: Standard Publishing Company, n.d.), pp. 125-152, 265-292.

3. Allison N. Trice and Charles Roberson, *Bible vs. Modernism* (Nashville: McQuiddy Press, 1935).

4. *FF,* March 4, 1919, p. 2.

5. *FF,* July 18, 1922, p. 4.

6. Marsden, p. 217.

7. *GA,* 1922, p. 386.

8. *GA,* 1925, p. 348.

9. Marsden, pp. 184-187.

10. *GA,* 1923, p. 608.

11. *GA,* 1925, p. 751.

12. *GA,* 1925, pp. 757-758.

13. E. A. Elam ed., *The Bible Versus Theories of Evolution* (Nashville: Gospel Advocate Company, 1925), p. 11.

14. Ibid., p. 100.

15. Ibid., p. 112.

16. William Banowsky, *The Mirror of a Movement* (Dallas: Christian Publishing Company, 1965), p. 121.

17. Ibid., pp. 125-126.

18. Alexander Campbell discussed the question in detail in the *Millennial Harbinger* during 1841, 1842, and 1843 under the title "The Coming of the Lord."

19. This topic is discussed in more detail in chapters five and seven.

20. Herman Norton, *Tennessee Christians* (Nashville: Tennessee Book Company, 1971), p. 160.

21. *GA,* 1906, p. 243.

22. *GA,* 1939, pp. 1146-1167.

23. Stephen Eckstein, *History of the Churches of Christ in Texas* (Austin: Firm Foundation Publishing House, 1963), p. 292.

24. *FF,* September 7, 1920, p. 2.

25. *FF,* February 18, 1940, p. 4; February 25, p. 4.

26. *FF,* September 16, 1919, p. 2.

27. Ibid.

28. *FF,* April, 20, 1926, p. 4

29. *FF,* January 28, 1919, p. 2.

30. *GA,* 1904, p. 72.

31. Based on a paper presented at the International Convention of Phi Alpha Theta, Robert E. Hooper, "The Cry of the City: Two Urban Southern Churches and the Needy," 1981.

32. *GA,* 1914, p. 1301.

33. *GA,* 1918, p. 1021.

34. *GA,* 1926, p. 938.

35. *GA,* 1926, p. 569.

36. *GA,* 1926, p. 161.

37. *GA,* 1927, p. 1237.

38. *GA,* 1928, P. 1035.

CHAPTER 4. A SEARCH FOR DIRECTION—1906-1930

1. *GA,* 1908, p. 760.

2. *GA,* 1909, p. 1356.

3. *GA,* 1909, pp. 1486-1487.

4. *GA,* 1917, pp. 648, 766-767.

5. *GA,* 1927, pp. 1091-1092.

6. The biographical sketch of Hardeman is from James Marvin Powell and Mary Nell Hardeman Powers, N.B.H.: *A Biography of*

Nicholas Brodie Hardeman (Nashville: Gospel Advocate Company, 1964).

7. Summaries of the schools can be found in M. Norvel Young, *A History of Colleges Established and Controlled by Members of Churches of Christ* (Kansas City, MO: Old Paths Book Club, 1949).

8. Banowsky, *The Mirror of a Movement* represents a study of the Abilene lectures since their inception.

9. *FF,* July 22, 1919, p. 3; GA, 1928, p. 447.

10. *FF,* September 4, 1923, p. 2.

11. *FF,* August 22, 1922, p. 4.

12. *FF,* March 18, 1919, p. 3.

13. N. B. Hardeman, *Hardeman's Tabernacle Sermons,* (Nashville: Gospel Advocate Company, 1953 reprint), vol. 1, p. 12.

14. William Woodson, *Standing for Their Faith* (Henderson, TN: J and W Publications, 1979), pp. 74-75.

15. Ibid., pp. 88-93.

16. Ibid., pp. 93-94.

17. Ibid., p. 96.

18. *CS,* 1920, p. 1017.

19. *FF,* June 26, 1923, pp. 2-3.

20. *GA,* 1923, p. 678.

21. *GA,* 1923, p. 714.

22. See *FF,* March 25, 1919, p. 2; September 14, 1920, p. 2; October 19, 1920, p. 2; October 10, 1922, p. 4; December 14, 1926, p. 2.

23. *GA,* 1965, p. 762.

24. Charles R. Brewer, ed., *Missionary Pictorial* (Nashville: World Vision Publishing Company, 1966), no pagination, missionaries listed alphabetically. Miss Andrews' biographical sketch is based on her entry.

25. *GA,* 1923, p. 498.

26. *GA,* 1927, p. 799.

27. *GA,* 1945, p. 662; 1946, pp. 1076-1077.

28. *GA,* 1949, pp. 476-477.

29. *GA,* 1961, pp. 640, 662, 701.

30. *GA,* 1949, p. 476.

31. *GA,* 1925, pp. 604, 628.

32. *GA,* 1928, p. 1092.

33. *GA,* 1927, pp. 1060-1061.

34. *GA,* 1925, p. 604; 1927, pp. 783, 1085; *FF,* July 17, 1928, pp. 2-3; October 9, p. 3.

35. *GA,* 1925, p. 604; *FF,* October 2, 1928, p. 4.

36. *GA,* 1928, pp. 7, 14, 87; 1929, p. 775; *FF,* May 1, 1928, pp. 10-11.

37. *GA,* 1925, p. 438.

38. *GA,* 1927, pp. 542, 700, 967, 1085, 1118; 1928, p. 1180; 1929, pp. 7-8. *FF,* May 1, 1928, pp. 10-11.

39. *GA,* 1928, p. 1159; 1929, p. 63.

40. *GA,* 1928, p. 818.

41. *GA,* 1928, p. 1158. Robert S. King, a postman in Nashville and an elder of the College church, was among the strongest advocates of mission work among churches of Christ. In 1925, he urged churches to recognize their mission; *GA,* 1925, p. 438. Writing in the *Firm Foundation,* November 11, 1924, King stated: "The Church of Christ is five hundred thousand strong in the United States and we have sent out fifteen missionaries to tell eight million people that 'God so loved the world. . . .' How can we boast of preaching the whole truth when our practice is so far short?"

42. *FF,* July 20, 1926, p. 2.

43. *GA,* 1926, p. 366.

CHAPTER 5. INTERNAL ISSUES—1906-1930

1. *GA,* 1925, p. 1.

2. R. H. Boll, *Truth and Grace* (Cincinnati: F. L. Rowe, Publisher, 1917), pp. 6-12. The volume includes a biographical sketch by E. L. Jorgenson.

3. Robert Welch, "R. H. Boll: Premillennial Visionary," in *They Being Dead Yet Speak,* ed. Melvin D. Curry (Temple Terrace, FL: Florida College Bookstore, 1981), p. 52. Boll's early life is sketched by Welch.

4. *GA,* 1915, p. 444.

5. *GA,* 1915, p. 482.

6. *GA,* 1915, p. 1110.

7. *GA,* 1920, pp. 202-203.

8. *GA,* 1925, p. 195.

9. *GA,* 1918, pp. 969-974.

10. *FF,* July 7, 1925, p. 3.

11. *FF,* January 25, 1927, p. 2.

12. The biographical sketch follows Leo Boles and J. E. Choate, *I'll Stand on the Rock* (Nashville: Gospel Advocate Company, 1965).

13. *GA,* 1927, pages in each issue beginning with p. 458 and ending on p. 1048.

14. *GA,* 1898, p. 21.

15. The series is located in the *GA,* 1920, pp. 811, 862, 908, 958-959, 1004-2005, 1098-1099; 1921, pp. 14-16, 67-68, 114-115, 162-163.

16. *GA,* 1920, p. 1098; 1921, p. 58.

17. *FF,* December 12, 1922, p. 2.

18. *FF,* January 9, 1923, p. 3.

19. *GA,* 1921, pp. 67-68.

20. N. B. Hardeman, *Hardeman Tabernacle Sermons,* (Nashville: Gospel Advocate Company, 1928), vol. III, p. 122.

21. Ibid., p. 125.

22. Ibid., pp. 156-157.

23. *GA,* 1929, p. 62.

24. *GA,* 1929, pp. 100-101.

25. *GA,* 1929, p. 245.

26. *GA,* 1929, p. 277.

27. *GA,* 1929, p. 424.

28. *GA,* 1907, p. 409.

29. The biographical sketch of Larimore is based on F. D. Srygley, *Larimore and His Boys* (Nashville: Gospel Advocate Company, 1955).

30. Ibid., p. 70.

31. Scobey, ed., *Franklin College and Its Influences,* p. 411.

32. *GA,* 1929, p. 498.

33. Srygley, *Larimore,* p. 262.

34. Ibid., p. 230.

35. Ibid., p. 260.

36. See Earl Kimbrough, "T. B. Larimore: Evangelist to the World," in *They Being Dead Yet Speak,* ed. Curry. This is an excellent short summary of Larimore's life and influence.

37. *GA,* 1929, p. 485.

CHAPTER 6. FROM OUTSIDERS TO TENTATIVE INSIDERS

1. Charlotte Fanning, "Tolbert Fanning," Mimeographed manuscript. Available in the David Lipscomb University Library.

2. See Hooper, *Crying in the Wilderness,* chap. 8. For an in-depth account of Lipscomb's views on politics and government, see also Hooper, "The Political and Educational Ideas of David Lipscomb," (Unpublished Ph.D. Dissertation, George Peabody College for Teachers, 1965).

3. *FF,* May 8, 1917, p. 2.

4. Morrison, *Like a Lion,* p. 121.

5. Ibid., pp. 124-128.

6. *GA,* 1917. p. 275.

7. *GA,* 1917, p. 401.

8. *GA,* 1917, p. 790.

9. *FF,* October 31, 1916, p. 3.

10. *FF,* April 24, 1917, p. 1.

11. *FF,* May 29, 1917, p. 3.

12. *FF,* June 11, 1918, p. 2; June 18, 1918, p. 2.

13. Edward Needles Wright, *Conscientious Objectors in the Civil War* (New York: A. S. Barnes and Company, Inc., 1961), pp. 222-223.

14. *GA,* 1918, p. 125.

15. *GA,* 1918, p. 1209.

16. *GA,* 1918, p. 587.

17. *FF,* February 26, 1918, p. 3.

18. *GA,* 1918, p. 953.

19. *FF,* February 4, 1919, p. 1.

20. *FF,* November 25, 1919, p. 3.

21. *GA,* 1919, p. 10.

22. *GA,* 1919, p. 297.

23. *GA,* 1919, p. 1260.

24. *GA,* 1920, p. 30.

25. Ibid., p. 31.

26. *GA,* 1919, pp. 126, 299.

27. *GA,* 1920, p. 11.

28. *GA,* 1921, p. 730.

29. *GA,* 1921, p. 331.

30. *GA,* 1922, p. 1188.

31. *GA,* 1919, pp. 1036-1037.

32. *GA,* 1920, p. 204; For a general discussion of the idea in American history, see J. Leonard Bates, *The United States 1898-1928: Progressivism and a Society in Transition* (New York: McGraw-Hill Book Company, 1976), p. 211.

33. Russell F. Weigley, *History of the United States Army* (New York: The McMillan Company, 1967), pp. 399-400.

34. *GA,* 1923, pp. 10, 34-35, 57-58, 85, 108-109, 132-133, 155, 179-180, 202-203, 258, 259, 281.

35. *GA,* 1931, p. 667.

36. *GA,* 1936, p. 951. For a study of the secular peace movements in the 1930s, see Charles Chatfield, *Pacifism in America 1914-1941* (Knoxville: University of Tennessee Press, 1971).

37. *GA,* 1939, p. 934.

38. Ibid.

39. *GA,* 1940, p. 581.

40. *GA,* 1939, p. 893.

41. *FF,* July 30, 1940, p. 8; October 22, 1940, p. 1.

42. *GA,* 1945, p. 60.

43. *FF,* September 21, 1941, p. 4.

44. *FF,* August 1, 1944, p. 3.

45. *FF,* December 23, 1941, p. 4.

46. *FF,* March 17, 1942, pp. 1-2.

47. *FF,* June 13, 1944, pp. 3-5.

48. *GA,* 1942, p. 124.

49. *GA,* 1942, p. 245.

50. *GA,* 1943, p. 220.

51. Ibid.

52. Mulfand Q. Sibley and Philip E. Jacob, *Consumption of Conscience* (Ithaca, NY: Cornell University Press, 1952), p. 168.

53. *FF,* December 14, 1943, p. 3.

54. *BB,* October 1943, pp. 3-6.

55. *BB,* September 1942, p. 4.

56. *GA,* 1943, p. 440.

57. *GA,* 1945, p. 393.

CHAPTER 7. A PEOPLE TO BE CONSIDERED—1906-1939

1. Joel Carpenter, "Fundamentalist Institutions and the Rise of Evangelical Protestantism, 1929-1942," *Church History* 49 (No. 1, 1960), pp. 62-75.

2. Woodson, (see chap. 4, n. 14) pp. 132-134; *FF,* November 1, 1932, p. 1.

3. *FF,* December 20, 1932, p. 5; December 19, 1933, p. 4.

4. *GA,* 1936, p. 713.

5. Ibid.

6. *GA,* 1938, p. 1229.

7. *GA,* 1940, p. 1880.

8. *GA,* 1931, p. 18.

9. *FF,* April 20, 1937, p. 4; June 20, 1939, pp. 4-5.

10. *GA,* 1931, p. 18.

11. *GA,* 1932, p. 431; *FF,* September 8, 1931, p. 4; March 9, 1937, p. 4.

12. Based on the count of missionaries mentioned in the *Gospel Advocate* during the late 1920s.

13. *FF,* January 6, 1931, pp. 8-9.

14. Buford W. Hooper, the author's father, was transferred, along with a host of Old Hickory men, to Richland, Washington, by the Dupont Company. By 1944 the Old Hickory church had lost 150 members by transfer to other Dupont facilities. *CC,* January 19, 1944, p. 1.

15. *GA,* 1926, p. 271.

16. *GA,* 1927, p. 1240.

17. *FF,* January 5, 1926, p. 6; March 30, 1926, p. 2.

18. *FF,* January 25, 1927, p. 8.

19. *FF,* March 3, 1936, p. 2; *GA,* 1936, p. 292.

20. *GA,* 1939, p. 732.

21. Carpenter, pp. 66-67.

22. *FF,* October 4, 1938, p. 4; *GA,* 1939, pp. 541, 974, 995.

23. *FF,* June 12, 1934, p. 4.

24. *FF,* October 8, 1935, p. 5.

25. *FF,* January 6, 1931, p. 4.

26. *FF,* March 21, 1933, p. 2.

27. *FF,* September 9, 1930, p. 3.

28. *FF,* August 23, 1933, p. 2.

29. James W. Adams, "Foy E. Wallace: Militant Warrior," in *They Being Dead Yet Speak,* ed. Curry, pp. 171-186.

30. The biographical sketch of Brewer follows his autobiographical study, *Forty Years on the Firing Line* (Kansas City, MO: Old Paths Book Club, 1948). An excellent overview of Brewer is

given by Ron Halbrook, "G. C. Brewer: Perennial Protagonist," in *They Being Dead Yet Speak,* ed. Curry.

31. *GA,* 1932, p. 824.

32. *GA,* 1932, p. 920.

33. *GA,* 1932.

34. Charles M. Neal and Foy E. Wallace, Jr., *Neal-Wallace Discussion on the Thousand Years Reign of Christ* (Nashville: Gospel Advocate Company, 1933), pp. 194-195.

35. *GA,* 1933, p. 613.

36. *FF,* March 6, 1934, p. 4; March 26, 1934, p. 4; *GA,* 1934, pp. 284-285; G. C. Brewer, "A Plea for Unity," *Abilene Christian College Bible Lectures, 1934* (Austin, TX: Firm Foundation Publishing House, 1934), pp. 182-184.

37. *GA,* 1934, pp. 284-285. An excellent discussion of the events and the impact of the millennial discussions can be found in a series of articles by William Wallace in *Vanguard.* See especially July-November, 1982.

38. *GA,* 1934, p. 658.

39. *GA,* 1934, p. 765.

40. *GA,* 1934, pp. 814, 899.

41. *GA,* 1934, p. 980.

42. *GA,* 1935, pp. 60-61.

43. *GA,* 1935, p. 77.

44. *FF,* November 29, 1934, p. 1; *GA,* 1934, pp. 1104-1105, 1109.

45. J. Frank Norris and Foy E. Wallace, Jr., *Norris-Wallace Debate* (Fort Worth: Fundamentalist Publishing Co., 1935), pp. 1-6.

46. *BB,* July-August, 1944.

47. *GA,* 1934, p. 1105.

48. *FF,* February 5, 1935, p. 1.

49. *FF,* April 16, 1935, p. 2.

50. *FF,* March 12, 1935, p. 5.

51. *GGI,* October 1935, p. 2.

52. Ibid.; See *Vanguard,* December 1982, pp. 326-328.

53. Ibid.

54. Quoted in *Vanguard,* December 1982, p. 327.

55. Ibid.

56. *FF,* September 29, 1936, p. 1.

57. *Vanguard,* December 1982, p. 328.

58. *BB,* July 1938, p. 3.

59. *GA,* 1938, p. 1028.

60. *GA,* 1939, p. 224.

61. G. C. Brewer, *Contending for the Faith* (Nashville: Gospel Advocate Co., 1941), pp. 191-198.

62. *BB,* April 1939, p. 4.

63. *GA,* 1939, p. 429.

64. *GA,* 1939, p. 453.

65. *BB,* June 1939, p. 2.

66. *BB,* January-February 1939, p. 2.

67. Ibid.

68. *FF,* September 8, 1939, p. 5.

69. *GA,* 1939, p. 196; see also pp. 500, 716.

70. An open letter from Price Billingsley to Horace Busby. Copy in the library of Abilene Christian University.

71. An open letter from Price Billingsley to Leon McQuiddy. Copy in the library of Abilene Christian University.

72. *Vanguard,* 1982, p. 328.

73. F. L. Rowe to J. Edward Meixner. Letter in the library of Abilene Christian University.

74. Wilbur J. Cash, *Mind of the South* (New York: A. A. Knopf, 1941), pp. 134-135.

CHAPTER 8. ISSUES OF CONSEQUENCE—1930-1950

1. Wolfgang, "A Life of Humble Fear," (see chap. 1, n. 39) pp. 131-138.

2. *CS,* 1938, p. 22.

3. *CS,* 1938, pp. 417, 418, 428.

4. *CS,* 1938, pp. 470, 1007.

5. *GA,* 1937, pp. 821, 964.

6. *GA,* 1937, p. 1142.

7. *GA,* 1938, p. 4.

8. *GA,* 1938, p. 172.

9. *GA,* 1938, p. 198.

10. *GA,* 1938, p. 384.

11. *FF,* May 10, 1938, p. 4.

12. *GA,* 1938, p. 742.

13. *GA,* 1938, p. 524.

14. *CS,* 1938, p. 1007.

15. *GA,* 1939, p. 476.

16. Ibid.

17. *CS,* 1939, p. 551.

18. *CS,* 1939, p. 773.

19. *CS,* 1939, p. 869.

20. Wolfgang, p. 138.

21. *GA,* 1956, pp. 434-435.

22. *GA,* 1956, pp. 292-293.

23. *GA,* 1956, pp. 394-395.

24. *GA,* 1956, pp. 614-615.

25. *FF,* February 7, 1933, p. 5; *GA* 1933, p. 228.

26. *GA,* 1931, p. 964.

27. *GA,* 1932, p. 366.

28. *GA,* 1933, p. 228.

29. *GA,* 1930, pp. 4-5, 317.

30. *GA,* 1930, p. 472.

31. *FF,* March 31, 1931, p. 4; December 1, 1931.

32. *GA,* 1931, p. 411.

33. L. C. Sears, *For Freedom: The Biography of John Nelson Armstrong* (Austin, TX: Sweet Publishing Company, 1969) pp. 240-246.

34. *GA,* 1932, p. 818.

35. *FF,* January 26, 1937, p. 4.

36. *GG,* January 4, 1937, p. 1.

37. *GA,* 1932, p. 496.

38. *GA,* 1932, p. 818.

39. *GA,* 1937, p. 170.

40. *FF,* September 1, 1936, p. 1.

41. Brightwell pinpointed institutionalism as the next major battle among churches of Christ. *GA,* 1934, p. 1151.

42. *GA,* 1936, p. 587.

43. *GA,* 1938, p. 703.

44. *GA,* 1936, pp. 611, 659.

45. *GA,* 1936, p. 611.

46. Ibid.

47. *GA,* 1936, p. 659.

48. *GA,* 1934, p. 1151.

49. *BB,* July 1938, p. 3.

50. *BB,* April 1947, p. 7.

51. *FF,* May 1, 1934, p. 4.

52. *GA*, 1956, pp. 434-435.
53. *GA*, 1943, pp. 154-155.
54. *GA*, 1943, p. 362.
55. *GA*, 1943, p. 491.
56. *BB*, August 1943, p. 6.
57. *GA* 1943, p. 592.
58. *CC*, June 30, 1943, p. 2.
59. *CC*, October, 13, 1943, p. 2.
60. Ibid., p. 1; January 19, 1944, p. 1.
61. *CC*, June 30, 1943, p. 1.
62. *CC*, July 28, 1943, p. 2.
63. *CC*, July 7, 1943, p. 2.
64. As an example, *GA*, 1945, p. 165.
65. *GA*, 1945, pp. 619-620.
66. *GA*, 1945, p. 701.
67. *GA*, 1945, pp. 608-609.
68. *GA*, 1945, pp. 735-736.
69. *GA*, 1946, p. 94.
70. *GA*, 1946, p. 621.
71. *GA*, 1948, p. 414.
72. *GA*, 1947, p. 882.
73. *GA*, 1946, p. 517.
74. *GA*, 1946, p. 452; 1947, p. 194.
75. *GA*, 1946, pp. 610, 620.
76. *GA*, 1948, p. 107.
77. *GA*, 1948, p. 707.
78. *GA*, 1948, pp. 50-52, 54-55.
79. *GA*, 1946, p. 1109; 1947, pp. 18, 60, 813.

CHAPTER 9. MEN WITH A NEW VISION

1. *FF*, January 23, 1951, pp. 4-5.
2. *GA*, 1955, p. 348.
3. *FF*, 1957, p. 264.
4. M. Norvel Young and J. Marvin Powell, *The Church is Building* (Nashville: Gospel Advocate Company, 1956), Introduction.
5. *FF*, March 30, 1954, p. 7.
6. *FF*, 1957, p. 264.
7. *FF*, May 18, 1954, p. 5.

8. *FF,* September 18, 1951, p. 4; *GA,* VBS special, March 8, 1956.

9. *FF,* June 23, 1953, p. 13; 1957, p. 59.

10. *FF,* January 20, 1953, p. 7.

11. *FF,* 1959, p. 441.

12. Ibid.

13. *FF,* 1958, p. 402.

14. *FF,* 1957, p. 434.

15. Batsell Barrett Baxter, *Every Life a Plan of God* (Abilene, TX: Zachry Associates, 1983), pp. 86-87.

16. *GA,* 1951, p. 45.

17. *GA,* 1953, p. 77.

18. *FF,* May 25, 1954, p. 5.

19. *FF,* November 2, 1954, p. 4.

20. Baxter, *Every Life*, pp. 15-27, 41-46, 51-69.

21. *FF,* 1959, p. 790.

22. *The Tennessean,* "Sunday Showcase," January 27, 1967, p. 10.

23. *Herald of Truth Magazine,* Spring, 1968.

24. Ibid., Winter, 1967.

25. *CC,* November 1988, p. 11.

26. *GA,* 1956, p. 350.

27. *GA,* 1964, pp. 81, 88.

28. Baxter, Every Life, pp. 139-140.

29. *GA,* 1964, pp. 694-695.

30. *GA,* 1964, p. 88. For an extensive look at Collins, see Robert E. Hooper and Jim Turner, *Willard Collins: The People Person* (Nashville: 20th Century Christian, 1986).

31. *GA,* 1962, p. 75.

32. *GA,* 1962, pp. 659, 696-699.

33. *GA,* 1963, pp. 500-501.

34. *GA,* 1964, p. 573.

35. *GA,* 1964, pp. 553-555.

36. *GA,* 1965, p. 277.

37. *FF,* 1963, p. 258.

38. *FF,* 1963, p. 642.

39. Ira North, *Balance* (Nashville: Gospel Advocate Company, 1983), Introduction.

40. *FF,* May 18, 1954.

41. *GA,* 1954, p. 606.

42. North, *Balance,* Backcover.

43. *GA,* 1957, pp. 99-100.

44. North, *Balance,* p. 82.

45. *GA,* 1957, p. 99.

46. North, *Balance,* pp. 110-112.

47. Ibid., pp. 124-126.

48. *GA,* 1961, p. 776.

49. *GA,* 1964, pp. 420-421.

50. *GA,* 1965, pp. 376, 377.

51. North, *Balance,* pp. 112-116.

52. *The Tennessean,* January 16, 1984.

53. *FF,* 1961, p. 658.

54. The Abilene *Reporter-News,* February 21, 1970; *Celebrating an Uncommon Commitment,* Abilene Christian University Publication, 1980.

55. *Uncommon Commitment,* p. 41.

56. The *Nashville Tennessean,* October 9, 1966.

57. *GA,* 1965, pp. 302-303.

58. Publications of various schools provided source material.

59. *GA,* 1965, pp. 316-317.

60. *FF,* 1957, p. 434.

61. *GA,* 1963, pp. 338, 344, 373, 420, 425.

62. *FF,* 1964, p. 387; *GA,* 1965, pp. 471, 474.

63. *GA,* 1965, pp. 712-713.

64. *GA,* 1965, pp. 523, 534.

65. *FF,* 1965, p. 418.

66. *GA,* 1965, p. 474.

67. Lynn, *Where the Saints Meet,* 1984, pp. 387-389.

68. *GA,* 1965, p. 471.

69. *FF,* 1963, p. 2.

CHAPTER 10. POINTS OF DISAGREEMENT—1950-1965

1. The best interpretation of the events surrounding the issues of post-World War II from the noninstitutional position is that of William Wallace in a long series of articles in *Vanguard,* edited and published by Fanning Yater Tant. The author of the articles is the son of Foy E. Wallace, Jr. These articles appeared under the general heading of "Roots and Heritage: A Series Renewing

Historical Backgrounds." The articles appeared between July 1981 and August 1984.

2. *Vanguard,* 1983, pp. 92-94.

3. Ibid., pp. 179-180.

4. *FF,* February 14, 1950, p. 5.

5. *Vanguard,* 1983, pp. 179-180.

6. *GA,* 1950, pp. 228-229; 1951, p. 677.

7. *GG,* May 11, 1950, p. 1.

8. Ibid., p. 9.

9. *FF,* April 25, 1950, p. 2.

10. *GA,* 1950, pp. 378-379.

11. *GG,* August 3, 1950, p. 10.

12. *GA,* July 12, 1951, pp. 290, 434.

13. Ed Harrell, "B. C. Goodpasture: Leader of Institutional Thought," in *They Being Dead Yet Speak,* ed. Curry, pp. 242-252.

14. *GA,* 1950, pp. 379-380. For Roy Cogdill's reaction, see *GG,* June 15, 1950, pp. 9-10.

15. *FF,* January 16, 1951, pp. 1-2; January 23, 1951, pp. 1-4.

16. *GA,* 1951, p. 359.

17. *GA,* 1951, p. 519.

18. *FF,* April 3, 1951, pp. 6-7; July 17, 1951, pp. 8-9.

19. *FF,* 1955, p. 486.

20. *GA,* 1954, p. 922.

21. *Vanguard,* 1984, p. 104.

22. *GG,* 1954, p. 248.

23. *GG,* 1954, p. 372.

24. *FF,* 1955, p. 214.

25. *FF,* 1963, p. 66.

26. See Lemmons's review of Batsell Barrett Baxter's sermons upholding the support of schools by the local congregation later in this chapter.

27. *GA,* 1951, pp. 677-678.

28. Ibid.

29. Ibid.

30. *GA,* 1954, p. 808.

31. *GA,* 1950, pp. 282, 361; 1951, p. 146; 1954, p. 922; *GG,* May 18, 1950, p. 2.

32. See Morrison, *Like a Lion,* pp. 105-117.

33. *GA,* 1953, p. 162.

34. *GA,* 1954, p. 540.

35. *GG,* March 12, 1953, pp. 8-9.

36. *Vanguard,* 1984, p. 161.

37. *GA,* 1958, pp. 51-52.

38. Roy E. Cogdill and Guy N. Woods, *Woods-Cogdill Debate* (Nashville: Gospel Advocate Company, 1958), p. 185.

39. *GA,* 1965, pp. 21-22.

40. *FF,* 1957, p. 103.

41. *FF,* 1958, p. 66.

42. *GA,* 1958, pp. 194-197.

43. *GA,* 1957, pp. 226-229.

44. *FF,* 1958, pp. 258, 274.

45. *GA,* 1958, p. 289.

46. Baxter's ideas were published in a pamphlet titled *Questions and Issues of the Day* (Nashville: Hillsboro Church of Christ, 1963). The school question is discussed on pp. 23-32.

47. *FF,* 1964, pp. 98, 107-108, 114, 123.

48. G. K. Wallace and W. Carl Ketcherside, *Wallace-Ketcherside St. Louis Debate* (Longview, WA: Telegram Book Company, 1954).

49. *GA,* 1954, pp. 1265, 273.

50. *GA,* 1954, p. 540.

51. *FF,* 1962, p. 210.

52. *FF,* 1963, p. 562.

53. *FF,* 1963, p. 594. For Lemmons' response, see *FF,* 1963, p. 562.

54. *FF,* 1965, p. 564.

55. *Vanguard,* 1984, p. 132.

56. Adams, in *They Being Dead Yet Speak,* ed. Curry, pp. 183-185.

57. Ibid.

58. *GA,* 1964, p. 324.

59. *GA,* 1964, p. 375.

60. *GA,* 1964, p. 356.

61. *GA,* 1964, p. 390.

62. *FF,* 1960, p. 418; 1962, p. 322.

63. *GA,* 1962, pp. 342-343.

CHAPTER 11. CHURCHES OF CHRIST AND 20TH CENTURY POLITICS

1. Quoted in Timothy Tucker, "'Unspotted from the World': Churches of Christ and American Religion," (Unpublished seminar paper, Cornell University, 1981), p. 34.

2. Ibid., p. 36.

3. David Edwin Harrell, Jr., "The Sectional Origins of the Churches of Christ," *Journal of Southern History* 30 (August 1964), p. 264.

4. C. Van Woodward, *The Burden of Southern History* (New York: Vintage Books, 1961), p. 141.

5. Harrell, "Churches of Christ," p. 277.

6. See Eric Goldman, *Rendezvous with Destiny* (New York: Vintage Books, 1961) for an excellent short discussion of the Populists.

7. *GA,* 1899, p. 104.

8. *GA,* 1907, p. 457.

9. Since both issues were so important in Tennessee, where churches of Christ had a large population early in the twentieth century, two studies are especially important. For women's rights, see Elizabeth Taylor, *The Woman Suffrage Movement in Tennessee* (New York: Bookman Associates, 1957). For prohibition, see Paul C. Isaac, *Prohibition and Politics* (Knoxville: The University of Tennessee Press, 1965).

10. *GA,* 1918, p. 272.

11. *AR,* June 8, 1920, p. 16.

12. *GA,* 1920, p. 715.

13. Taylor, p. 124.

14. *GA,* 1919, p. 1073.

15. *GA,* 1922, p. 217.

16. Norman H. Clark, *Deliver Us From Evil* (New York: W. W. Norton and Company, Inc., 1976), pp. 182-183. This is not a typical interpretation of prohibition or of the 1920s. Representative of the more widely accepted view is Herbert Asbury, *The Great Illusion* (Garden City, NY: Doubleday and Company, Inc., 1950).

17. Clark, pp. 190-191.

18. *GA,* 1931, p. 442.

19. *FF,* June 14, 1932, p. 1.

20. *FF,* June 21, 1932. p. 1.

21. *FF,* August 16, 1932, p. 1.

22. Clark, pp. 201-206.

23. *The World Almanac and Book of Facts for 1935* (New York: New York World-Telegram, 1935), p. 909.

24. Goldman, p. 48.

25. Garvin Burbank, "Agrarian Radicals and Their Opponents: Political Conflict in Southern Oklahoma, 1910-1924," *Journal of American History* 58 (June 1971), pp. 5-23.

26. *FF,* October 28, 1913, p. 1.

27. *FF,* November 18, 1913.

28. *AR,* April 6, 1920, p. 3.

29. *GA,* 1920, p. 241.

30. *GA,* 1936, p. 686.

31. *GA,* 1936, pp. 734-735.

32. *GA,* pp. 926-927.

33. *GA,* pp. 950-951, 959.

34. Goldman, p. 37.

35. *GA,* pp. 178-179.

36. *VF,* 1959, p. 146.

37. *VF,* 1959, p. 146.

38. *VF,* 1960, p. 618.

39. Royce L. Money, "Church-State Relations in the Churches of Christ since 1945: A Study in Religion and Politics," (Unpublished Ph.D. Dissertation, Baylor University, 1975), pp. 116-134.

40. See Carroll Pitts, Jr., "A Critical Study of Civil Rights, Practices, Attitudes and Responsibilities in Churches of Christ," (Unpublished M.A. Thesis, Pepperdine College, 1969).

41. *The Babbler,* November 9, 1956.

42. *VF,* 1960, p. 130.

43. R. Laurence Moore, *Religious Outsiders and the Making of Americans* (New York: Oxford University Press, 1986), pp. 156-158.

44. *GA,* 1962, pp. 963-694.

45. *GA,* 1963, p. 132.

46. *VF,* 1963, p. 132.

47. *VF,* 1974, pp. 6-7, 29-30, 61-62, 88-89, 100-101, 125-126, 167-168.

48. Based on a lengthy interview with Mrs. Tottie Ellis, 1985.

49. Lottie Beth Hobbs, "Ladies! Have You Heard?," *Pro Family Forum,* 1975.

50. Lottie Beth Hobbs, "Parents, Have You Heard About IYC and Kiddie Lib?" *Pro Family Forum,* 1978; *Pro Family Forum Alert,* March, 1984, p. 1.

51. *Pro Family Forum Alert,* October, 1984, p. 1.

52. *Pro Family Forum Alert,* November, 1984, p. 1.

53. *UpReach,* November/December, 1984, pp. 15-16.

54. *UpReach,* March/April, 1985, p. 31.

55. Lengthy discussions with Dr. Timothy Tucker and his responses to a rough draft of this paper. Professor Tucker is one of the most insightful men I know in American politics and religion. It was he who first introduced me to Laurence Moore's insider-outsider model of American religion.

56. Moore, p. 157.

57. Ibid., p. 19.

CHAPTER 12. OUT OF BONDAGE

1. From a special printout of all predominantly black churches compiled by Mac Lynn, David Lipscomb University. This material appeared in Mac Lynn, *Churches of Christ in the United States,* (Nashville: Gospel Advocate Company, 1991).

2. Ibid.

3. James Maxwell quotes James Rogers, *The Cane Ridge Meetinghouse* and Louis Cochran, *The Fool of God* in a mimeographed outline "Black Roots in the Restoration Movement," (n.d.).

4. Norton, *Tennessee Christians,* pp. 129-134.

5. *GA,* 1878, p. 311.

6. The early history of the black church in Nashville follows the paper of Jim Mankin, "Continuity and Diversity: Black Members of Post-Bellum Churches of Christ in Nashville, Tennessee," (Independent Study in Church History, Fuller Theological Seminary, n.d.). Mankin made extensive use of Hap Hyda's dissertation "A History of Black Christian Churches in the United States through 1899," completed at Vanderbilt University in 1972.

7. The biographical sketch of G. P. Bowser follows Jack Evans, "The History of Southwestern Christian College, Terrell, Texas," (Unpublished M.A. Thesis, Texas Western College, 1963), pp. 3-

14. A more detailed study of Bowser is R. Vernon Boyd, *Undying Dedication: The Story of G. P. Bowser* (Nashville: Gospel Advocate Company, 1985).

8. Annie C. Tuggle, *Another World Wonder* (Privately published, 1973), p. 47.

9. Ibid., pp. 65-66.

10. Evans, "Southwestern Christian College," pp. 10-11.

11. J. E. Choate, *Roll Jordan Roll: A Biography of Marshall Keeble* (Nashville: Gospel Advocate Company, 1968), pp. 1-22.

12. Arthur Lee Smith, Jr., "A Rhetorical Analysis of the Speaking of Marshall Keeble," (Unpublished M.A. Thesis, Pepperdine College, 1965), p. 26.

13. Choate, *Roll Jordan Roll,* pp. 64-65.

14. Ibid., p. 72.

15. Ibid., p. 136.

16. Ibid., pp. 114-115.

17. Response by Dr. Jack Evans to a questionnaire sent by Robert Hooper.

18. Harvey Wish, ed., *The Negro Since Emancipation* (Englewood Cliffs, NJ: Prentice-Hall, Inc., 1964), pp. 40-41.

19. Ibid., pp. 48-49.

20. Evans' response to Hooper questionnaire.

21. Choate, *Roll Jordan Roll,* p. 112.

22. *ChE,* May 1973, p. 2.

23. Choate, *Roll Jordan Roll,* p. 110. The development of the Nashville Christian Institute follows Choate.

24. Evans, "Southwestern Christian College," p. 12ff.

25. *FF,* December 18, 1951, pp. 3-4.

26. David Edwin Harrell, Jr., *White Sects and Black Men in the Recent South* (Nashville: Vanderbilt University Press, 1971), pp. 45-48.

27. *BB,* March 1941, p. 7.

28. *BB,* April 1941, p. 5.

29. *GA,* 1946.

30. *FF,* November 3, 1953, p. 7.

31. *FF,* 1956, p. 213.

32. *FF,* 1956, pp. 82-83.

33. Carroll Pitts, Jr., "A Critical Study of Civil Rights Practices, Attitudes and Responsibilities in Churches of Christ," (Unpublished M.A. Thesis, Pepperdine College, 1969).

34. Ibid., p. 52.

35. Ibid., pp. 73-74.

36. Ibid., pp. 78-79.

37. Ibid., p. 79.

38. Ibid., p. 88.

39. Ibid., p. 104.

40. Press release from Southwestern Christian College, (n. d.).

41. Program, 35th Annual Lectureship, April 17-20, 1979, Marc Plaza Hotel, Milwaukee, Wisconsin.

42. Gleaned from the *Christian Echo.*

43. *ChE,* February 1992, p. 10.

44. Interviews with Dr. Jack Evans and Dr. James Maxwell, February 1985.

45. Vernon Boyd, "Organizational Differences Between the Black and White Churches of Christ," (Mimeographed copy of a speech given at the Lake Geneva Encampment, August 15, 1973, Williams Bay, Wisconsin).

46. *Southwestern Communique,* February, May, and September, 1984.

47. *ChE,* January 1969, p. 10.

48. *ChE,* July 1981, p. 9.

49. *ChE,* November-December 1979, pp. 4, 7.

CHAPTER 13. FROM 1950 TOWARD THE 21ST CENTURY

1. Douglas T. Miller and Marion Nowals, *The Fifties: The Way We Really Were* (Garden City: Doubleday and Company, Inc., 1977), p. 85. The religious overview of the 1950s is based on this study.

2. William G. McLoughlin, "Introduction: How is America Religious," in *Religion in America,* ed. William G. McLoughlin and Robert N. Bellah (Boston: Houghton Mifflin Company, 1968), p. ix.

3. Ibid., p. x.

4. *FF,* June 8, 1954, pp. 1-2.

5. *FF,* 1958, p. 612; *GA,* 1959, p. 34.

6. *FF,* 1957, p. 806.

7. *GA,* 1950, p. 30.

8. *GA,* 1953, p. 221.

9. Dean M. Kelley, *Why Conservative Churches Are Growing* (Macon, GA: Mercer University Press, 1986, reprint). Kelley's descriptions of conservative churches fit churches of Christ.

10. Bernard Quinn and others, eds., *Churches and Church Membership:* 980 (Atlanta: Glenmary Research Center, 1980), p. 2.

11. *CC,* August 1983, p. 14.

12. *CC,* September 1984, p. 1.

13. J. D. Thomas, ed., *What Lack We Yet?* (Abilene, TX: Biblical Research Press, 1974).

14. Ibid., p. 12.

15. Ibid., pp. 132-137.

16. Quoted in *Personal Evangelism,* July, August, September 1979.

17. Monroe Hawley, *Redigging the Wells* (Abilene, TX: Quality Printers, 1976), pp. 15, 216.

18. *CC,* August 1983, p. 14.

19. *Webster's New Collegiate Dictionary* (Springfield, MA: G. C. Merriam Company, 1974).

20. *GA,* 1908, pp. 8-9.

21. Lynn, *United States,* pp. IX-X.

22. David Edwin Harrell, Jr., *Emergence of the "Church of Christ" Denomination* (Athens, AL: CEI Publishing Co., 1972), p. 27.

23. *GA,* 1962, pp. 342-343.

24. *Mission Messenger,* February 1975, p. 27.

25. *Restoration Review,* May 1985, p. 90.

26. Ira Y. Rice, Jr., *Axe at the Root* (Dallas: Privately published, 1966), p. 2.

27. Ibid., p. 71.

28. *Axe at the Root,* vol. II, p. 131 (Three volumes bound in one cover).

29. Robert Meyers, *Voices of Concern* (St. Louis: Mission Messenger, 1966), p. 2.

30. Ibid., pp. 28-32.

31. Ibid., p. 262.

32. *Mission,* April 1972, pp. 300-306.

33. *Mission,* May 1972, pp. 355-357.

34. *Mission,* June 1972, pp. 355-357.

35. David Bobo, "The Churches of Christ: Where from Here?" *Lexington Theological Quarterly* 16 (January 1981), 33-34.

36. Flavil R. Yeakley, Jr., *Why Churches Grow* (Broken Arrow, OK: Christian Communications, Inc., 1979), pp. 85-101.

37. Leonard Allen, Richard Hughes, Michael Weed, *The Worldly Church* (Abilene: Abilene Christian University Press, 1988); Leonard Allen, *Cruciform Church* (Abilene: Abilene Christian University, 1990).

38. George Barna and William Paul McKay, *Vital Signs: Energizing Social Trends and the Future of American Christianity* (Westchester, IL: Crossways Books, 1984), pp. 39-40.

39. *Mission,* July 1984, pp. 16-19.

40. John Naisbett, *Megatrends* (New York: Warner Books, 1984), pp. 35-52.

41. A book that attempts to deal with change and churches of Christ is Rubel Shelly and Randall Harris, *The Second Incarnation* (West Monroe, LA: Howard Publishing Company, 1992).

EPILOGUE.

1. From notes taken by Dr. David Lawrence of the David Lipscomb University history faculty, December 1988.

2. *CC,* August 1985, p. 19.

3. See Mac Lynn, *Churches of Christ in the United States* (Nashville: Gospel Advocate Company, 1991), unnumbered pages under the heading Statistical Analysis; See Yeakley in *CC,* September 1990, p. 1.

4. Mac Lynn, *Churches of Christ Around the World* (Nashville: Gospel Advocate Company, 1990), p. XX.

5. *CC,* October 1981, p. 1; December 1989, pp. 12-13.

6. *CC,* February 1984, p. 1.

7. *CC,* Ibid., pp. 12-13.

8. *CC,* May 1991, pp. 12-13.

9. *CC,* April 1991, pp. 1, 4.

10. *CC,* March 1992, p. 1.

11. *CC,* March 1992, p. 2.

12. *CC,* November-December, pp. 1, 4.

13. For an interesting interpretation of the Puritans that has relevance for churches of Christ, see Theodore Dwight Bozeman, *To Live Ancient Lives* (Chapel Hill: University of North Carolina Press, 1988).

APPENDIX 3. TIMELINE—COLLEGE PRESIDENTS

1. Attained university status 1991.

2. Consolidated with Northeastern Christian Junior College fall 1993.

3. Consolidated with Ohio Valley College fall 1993.

4. Founded in 1890; members of the churches of Christ assumed administration in 1956.

5. Attained university status 1987.

6. Attained university status and became Oklahoma Christian University of Science and Arts 1990.

7. Originally opened as Columbia Christian Bible School; became Columbia Christian College in 1956; closed May 1993; plans to reopen fall 1994 with Oklahoma Christian University of Science and Arts, establishing a branch campus on Columbia Christian College property.

8. Previous names—Montgomery Bible School, Alabama Christian College; attained university status as Faulkner University 1985.

9. Attained university status 1971.

10. Previous names—Arkansas Christian Junior College, Harper Junior College; became Harding College 1924; attained university status 1979.

11. Origin 1869; previous names—Henderson Male and Female Institute, West Tennessee Christian College, Georgie Robertson Christian College, National Teachers Normal and Business College; became Freed-Hardeman College 1919; attained university status 1990.

12. Previously named Childress Classical Institute; became Abilene Christian College 1912; attained university status 1976.

13. Previously named Nashville Bible School; became David Lipscomb College 1918; attained university status 1988.

PEOPLE INDEX

GENERAL INDEX

Abilene Christian College (ACC), 72, 73, 74, 114, 135, 137, 144, 145, 146, 150, 152, 153, 159, 166, 167, 168, 171, 173, 177, 178, 182, 183, 187, 188, 195, 199, 200, 201, 269, 273, 286
Abilene Christian University, 220, 221, 287, 288, 302
Abilene Christian University Lectureships, 55
"Address and Declaration," 19
Advocate, see *Gospel Advocate*
Alabama Christian College, 202, 214
All-Union Radio Network, 310
A.M. Burton's Life and Casualty Insurance Company, *see* Burton's Life and Casualty Insurance Company
American Broadcasting Company, 188
American Christian Bible Society, 8
American Christian Evangelizing and Education Association, 258
American Christian Missionary Society, 9, 13, 14, 15, 37, 81, 257, 258
American Christian Review, 12, 14, 17, 19, 63, 158
American Red Cross, 113
American Revolution, 2
Amish, 107
Anabaptists, 109
An Appeal for Unity (Sommer), 158
Anti-Burgher Seceder Presbyterian brethren, 3, 4
Antioch Church (Franklin, KY), 113
Antioch Church of Christ (Nashville, TN), 304
"Ancient Order of Things, The," 4, 49
Apostolic Review, 110, 163, 240, 245
Apostolic Times, 17
Armed Forces Network, 190
Armed Forces Television Network, 197
Articles of Confederation, 6
Association, *see* Mahoning Association of Baptist churches
At Work for the Master (North), 186
Auburn University, 294
Axe at the Root (Rice), 297, 298, 299, 300
Baconian inductive reasoning (or method), 4, 49, 53, 304
Bammel Road Church of Christ (Houston, TX), 309
Banner, see *Bible Banner*
Baptism, 4, 5, 10, 20, 50, 107, 232
    immersion, 4, 50
    rebaptism, 20, 21, 22, 87
Baptists, 4, 5, 13, 14, 15, 26, 40, 46, 50, 60, 102, 109, 127, 156, 238, 239, 257, 299